REGIME THEORY AND INTERNATIONAL RELATIONS

Regime Theory
and
International Relations

Edited by

VOLKER RITTBERGER

with the assistance of
PETER MAYER

CLARENDON PRESS · OXFORD

Oxford University Press, Great Clarendon Street, Oxford OX2 6DP

Oxford New York
Athens Auckland Bangkok Bogota Bombay
Buenos Aires Calcutta Cape Town Dar es Salaam
Delhi Florence Hong Kong Istanbul Karachi
Kuala Lumpur Madras Madrid Melbourne
Mexico City Nairobi Paris Singapore
Taipei Tokyo Toronto
and associated companies in
Berlin Ibadan

Oxford is a trade mark of Oxford University Press

Published in the United States by
Oxford University Press Inc., New York

First published 1993
First issued in paperback 1995
Reprinted 1997

British Library Cataloguing in Publication Data
Data available

Library of Congress Cataloging in Publication Data
Regime theory and international relations / edited by Volker
Rittberger with the assistance of Peter Mayer.
Includes bibliographical references and index.
1. International relations. 2. International relations—Social
aspects. 3. Social norms. I. Rittberger, Volker, 1941-
II. Mayer, Peter, 1961- .
JX1395.R36 1993 327—dc20 93-8313
ISBN 0-19-827783-0
ISBN 0-19-828029-7 (Pbk)

Printed in Great Britain
on acid-free paper by
Bookcraft (Bath) Ltd
Midsomer Norton, Avon

CONTENTS

FIGURES

TABLES

ABBREVIATIONS

ABM	anti-ballistic missile
Art.	Article
ATBM	anti-tactical ballistic missile defences
CDU/CSU	Christlich-demokratische Union/Christlich-soziale Union (Christian Democratic Union/Christian Social Union)
CFCs	chlorofluorocarbons
CFE	conventional forces in Europe
Ch(s).	chapter(s)
CIA	Central Intelligence Agency
CoCom	Co-Ordination Committee for Multilateral Export Controls
CSBM	confidence- and security-building measures
CSCE	Conference on Security and Co-Operation in Europe
DC	developed country
DDT	dichloro-diphenyl-trichloroethane
EC	European Community
ECE	Economic Commission for Europe (of the UN)
EPC	European Political Co-Operation
EURATOM	European Atomic Energy Community
FAO	Food and Agriculture Organization (of the UN)
Fig.	figure
FPT	foreign policy type
FRG	Federal Republic of Germany
G-7	Group of Seven
GATT	General Agreement on Tariffs and Trade
GB	Great Britain
GDR	German Democratic Republic
GNP	gross national product
GRIT	graduated reciprocation in tension reduction
IAEA	International Atomic Energy Agency
IAS	issue-area specific power structure
ICJ	International Court of Justice
IGO	international governmental organization

ILO	International Labour Organization
IMF	International Monetary Fund
INF	intermediate-range nuclear forces
INFCIRC	Information Circular (of the IAEA)
LCD	least common denominator
LDC	less developed country
LPAR	large-phased array radar
LRTAP	long-range transboundary air pollution
Med Plan	Mediterranean Action Plan
MNC	multinational corporation
N	number of cases
NATO	North Atlantic Treaty Organization
NGO	(international) non-governmental organization
NPT	Non-Proliferation Treaty
OECD	Organization for Economic Co-Operation and Development
OPEC	Organization of Petroleum Exporting Countries
OPS	overall power structure
PCBs	polychlorinated biphenyls
PCIJ	Permanent Court of International Justice
PD	prisoners' dilemma
PVO	private voluntary organization (Ch. 5); Voyska Protivovozdushnoy Oborony (Soviet Air Defence Command) (Ch. 15)
SALT	Strategic Arms Limitation Talks/Treaty
SCC	Standing Consultative Commission
SDI	Strategic Defense Initiative
sect(s).	section(s)
SIPRI	Stockholm International Peace Research Institute
SO$_2$	sulphur dioxide
SPD	Sozialdemokratische Partei Deutschlands (Social Democratic Party of Germany)
START	Strategic Arms Reduction Talks/Treaty
UNCHE	United Nations Conference on the Human Environment
UNCLOS	United Nations Conference on the Law of the Sea
UNCTAD	United Nations Conference on Trade and Development
UNEP	United Nations Environment Programme
UNESCO	United Nations Education and Science Organization

UN(O)	United Nations Organization
US(A)	United States of America
USEPA	United States Environmental Policy Act
USSR	Union of Soviet Socialist Republics

EDITOR'S INTRODUCTION

1

SINCE the mid-1970s the analysis of international regimes has become a major research programme within the discipline of International Relations. International regimes, according to the most widely accepted definition of the term, are sets of 'principles, norms, rules, and decision-making procedures around which actor expectations converge in a given issue-area' of international relations (Krasner 1983*a*: 1). Put differently, regimes are rules of the game agreed upon by actors in the international arena (usually nation states) and delimiting, for these actors, the range of legitimate or admissible behaviour in a specified context of activity. Examples of such contexts or issue areas are states' policies regarding trade in manufactured goods, proliferation of nuclear weapons, international whaling, or controlling transboundary air pollution in Europe. Suspicions that the study of international regimes would soon turn out to be a passing fad have not been confirmed. On the contrary, international regimes, in both their theoretical and empirical aspects, continue to arouse strong interest within the community of International Relations scholars, suggesting that regime analysis may have been an innovation in International Relations in the same fashion in which policy research has enlivened the development of political science in general.

Regime analysis, which cannot be separated from the broader study of international 'governance without government', has broken new ground in international relations theory because it has tackled—more successfully than other approaches—the puzzles of international co-operation and of international institution-building in a world of sovereign states, a world which is anarchical in the sense that there is no central government capable of making and enforcing international rules of conduct. Regime analysis has thus filled analytical gaps which other theoretical approaches either did not address at all (such as Waltzian neo-realism) or proved ill-equipped for (such as integration theory).

Conducted within a 'dividing discipline' (K. J. Holsti), the study of international regimes has shown remarkable integrative capacity in more than one respect. The 'regime perspective' has been applied successfully to a wide variety of issue areas in international politics, bridging the gap between experts in international security and specialists in international political economy by providing them with a common core concept as well as a set of related theoretical propositions to guide analysis. Scholars with different intellectual backgrounds have been attracted by this approach and have entered into a fruitful dialogue representing neo-liberal, critical, and even realist basic orientations. Finally, regime analysis has rather quickly spread beyond the confines of the North American International Relations community, whose offshoot it is, and found considerable resonance among European, in particular Scandinavian and German, political scientists, who have adapted this approach to their own research needs and aspirations. Up to now, the reception accorded by the European and American scholarly communities to each other's work has been very asymmetric, however (and perhaps more so than is justified by the differences in quantity and quality of the work that is being done on both sides of the Atlantic).

The present volume reflects this integrative capacity of regime analysis and, at the same time, seeks to enhance integration and communication among students of international regimes, where it is as yet underdeveloped. Thus, it assembles scholars from four different nations (United States, Germany, United Kingdom, and Sweden), and American and European authors have an equal share in the contributions. The main purpose of this volume, however, is to take stock of more than ten years of collective research on the origins and forms as well as the functions and consequences of international regimes, to point to achievements and shortcomings of these efforts, and to suggest and explore paths on which progress in the study of regimes may be attained.

2

The volume breaks down into five parts. In Part I (composed of Chapters 1 and 2) research on international regimes in Germany and the United States is reviewed. The second part of the volume (Chs. 3–6) focuses on fundamental conceptual and theoretical problems of regime analysis. Part III (Chs. 7–12) is devoted to the explanation of regime formation and change. Part IV (Chs. 13–15) addresses regime consequences. Part V (Ch. 16), finally, attempts to draw together the various lines of analysis pursued in the preceding chapters and, in this way, provides both a summary of the volume and an assessment of the state of regime theory.

In *Chapter 1*, opening the first part of the volume, Volker Rittberger traces the development of regime analysis in Germany and its (asymmetric) relationship with its Anglo-American counterpart and source of inspiration. Differences between German and US scholars regarding the (geo-)political context of research and the basic philosophical orientations and value premises are pinpointed in order to account for different thematical foci in practical research. The efforts of German regime analysts to clarify the concept of international regime and to make it more amenable to their particular research interests are described. The theoretical approaches towards explaining the formation of international regimes which have been favoured by German students of international regimes (and for some of which there is no equivalent in American regime analysis) are outlined. Finally, the chapter reports conceptual work and empirical findings of German scholars in a widely neglected field of regime analysis, the study of regime consequences.

In *Chapter 2* Robert O. Keohane looks back at more than a decade of research on international regimes in the United States, the insights it has provided as well as the lacunae it has not yet been able to close. The chapter is meant as an attempt to facilitate a transnational continuation of this research programme. Keohane addresses the fundamental methodological commitments underlying this research programme and discusses different definitions of its key concept, international regime. He considers possibilities of resolving empirically the questions whether and how regimes make a difference in international politics and reviews some of the work already done in this field. Finally, Keohane turns to the issue of explaining various property dimensions of regimes (institutional membership, strength, scope, and property rights), discussing approaches to be found in the regime literature and adding arguments from a 'contractualist' perspective.

In the first chapter of Part II, *Chapter 3*, Andrew Hurrell places regime theory within the Grotian tradition of thought on international relations, which centres on the concept of international society and attributes a key role to international law as both expression and foundation of this society. In the light of this tradition of thought Hurrell examines the strengths and the weaknesses of ('rationalistic') regime theory. His central claim is that the analytical rigour that regime theory has introduced into the study of international co-operation has produced not only gains, but significant costs as well by obscuring some of the most important insights of the international society tradition into the workings of international rules and norms.

In *Chapter 4* Friedrich Kratochwil examines two interrelated aspects of the regime concept that have not received due attention in the scholarly debate so far. In the first part of his contribution he develops a typology of contracts in order to provide a conceptual justification for the issue-specificity of international regimes, which, he argues, is widely acknowledged, but insufficiently understood among regime analysts. The second part of Kratochwil's chapter is devoted to a discussion of the formal–informal, explicit–implicit, and public–secret dimensions of international agreements and their repercussions on the strength of regime norms and rules.

In *Chapter 5* Virginia Haufler challenges the state-centrism characteristic of the bulk of regime analysis by exploring the logical possibility of, and supplying evidence for, the existence of (both corporate and non-corporate) private regimes. In doing so, she argues that the conventional definition of 'international regime' does not presuppose states as members of regimes and that the claim that transnational co-operation among corporations must necessarily take the form of either a cartel or an oligopoly leaving no room for an application of the regime concept is untenable. Moreover, she questions the view that non-corporate private regimes, even if they exist, cannot be assumed to have a noteworthy impact on international politics, and addresses more generally the relationship between international regimes and non-state actors.

In *Chapter 6* Andrew Kydd and Duncan Snidal examine advantages and pitfalls of game-theoretically informed analyses of international regimes by critically reviewing recent work in this field. They discuss the extent to which the application of new game-theoretical solution concepts (such as 'trigger', 'correlated equilibrium', and 'cheap talk') to problems of international co-operation may enhance our understanding of the role of international regimes by incorporating factors such as beliefs, communication, and information into the analysis. They deal with an attempt to reconcile the central argument of the bureaucratic politics literature that states cannot be considered unitary actors with the assumption that states are rational actors. Finally, they consider the (informal) use of game theory as an 'interpretative device' in order to shed light on the interaction between domestic and international politics in processes of regime-building (the two-level game approach).

In the opening chapter of Part III, *Chapter 7*, Stephen D. Krasner looks into the determinants of the formation, content, and implementation of human rights regimes, arguing that such regimes, which essentially deal with the relationship between rulers and ruled, can be better accounted for from a realist perspective with its emphasis on power and interest than on the basis of liberal co-operation theory focusing on problems of market failure. Four cases of human rights regimes—regarding religious practices in the seventeenth century, the slave trade in the nineteenth century, minority rights in Central Europe in the late nineteenth and early twentieth centuries, and liberal individual rights in the twentieth century—are analysed in order to substantiate this claim.

In *Chapter 8* Peter M. Haas uses neo-realist, institutionalist, and cognitivist assumptions to derive four environmental regime patterns, i.e. distinct styles of collective management and lesson-drawing associated with regime formation, persistence, and change. Subsequently, he evaluates the empirical validity and explanatory force of these patterns in the light of the international regime controlling the pollution of the Mediterranean Sea (Med Plan), emphasizing the way that the original regime pattern was transformed by the emergence of an epistemic community in the issue area.

In *Chapter 9* Christer Jönsson examines the potential value of cognitive theory for the study of international regimes. Cognitive theory explores the limits of rationality and points to judgemental heuristics and biases that operate when human beings have to cope with a complex, ambiguous reality. Drawing from insights gained in various branches of cognitive science he develops and illustrates a number of pertinent hypotheses accounting for regime formation, persistence, and change. Moreover, Jönsson addresses the relationship between the cognitive and the more established structuralist approach in regime analysis.

In *Chapters 10* and *11* Oran R. Young and Gail Osherenko, and Manfred Efinger, Peter Mayer, and Gudrun Schwarzer, respectively, report results from two large-scale projects which were devoted to the study of the determinants of regime formation. Young and Osherenko tested power-based, interest-based, and knowledge-based hypotheses against the evidence of several Arctic cases, most of which relate to environmental and natural resources issues, whereas Efinger, Mayer, and Schwarzer evaluated systemic, problem-structural, and situation-structural hypotheses in the light of a variety of issue areas, in most of which western democracies confronted eastern socialist states. Both chapters conclude with considerations on how the present stage of single-variable accounts might be overcome in favour of more complex, multivariate theories of regime formation.

In *Chapter 12* Michael Zürn explores the domestic sources of regime formation. For this purpose he addresses, in a first step, the characteristics of a regime-conducive foreign policy, i.e. a constellation of foreign policy strategy and instruments that, when implemented by an actor in the issue area, makes regime formation likely. In a second step, he then goes on to generate hypotheses about the relationship between domestic politics variables and other unit properties, on the one hand, and the pursuit of a regime-conducive foreign policy, on the other.

In *Chapter 13*, commencing the third part of the volume, Thomas Biersteker analyses fundamental methodological problems associated with the study of regime consequences. Biersteker argues that the student of regime effects has virtually no choice but resort to counterfactuals (statements of what would have happened if history had, at some point, deviated from its actual course) in order to substantiate his or her (causal) claims. Subsequently, Biersteker suggests several guidelines to be heeded when constructing historical counterfactuals. Finally, he illustrates the counterfactual method with reference to the case of the global debt regime and its consequences for the course of the debt crisis of the 1980s.

In *Chapter 14* Helmut Breitmeier and Klaus Dieter Wolf address conceptual issues of the study of regime consequences. They propose a categorization of the dependent variable based on the value premisses of the peace research tradition. In addition, they discuss, and provide examples for, different types of hypotheses purporting to explain regime consequences. In the second part of their contribution they examine the consequences of environmental regimes in order to probe the analytical value and explanatory force of the concepts and types of hypotheses introduced in the first part.

In *Chapter 15* Harald Müller looks into three security cases in order to evaluate different approaches to account for regime compliance in situations in which defection seems to be in the interest of the actor concerned: the Strategic Defense Initiative of the US Government, the construction of an early-warning radar at Krasnoyarsk in Siberia (both measures threatening, or violating, the superpowers' strategic nuclear weapons control regime), and Germany's nuclear export control policy (which for a long time was incompatible with central norms of the non-proliferation regime). By tracing the domestic controversies over compliance or defection Müller seeks to shed light on the nature of the impact that international regimes can have on states' foreign policy decisions.

The concluding Part V (*Chapter 16*) of the volume, co-authored by Peter Mayer, Volker Rittberger, and Michael Zürn, is composed of two parts: in the first part of the chapter, regime analysis is located in the wider context of thinking about social order. (For readers unfamiliar with the subject, this chapter may therefore prove helpful as an introduction to regime analysis.) In this connection, the basic underlying concern of regime analysis, i.e. its normative interest in the conditions of international 'governance without government', is discussed, a comparative perspective on regimes and governance across different levels of political organization is offered, and an attempt to define the heterogeneous nature of contemporary international order is made. In the second part of the chapter the state of regime theory is assessed with respect to its three main tasks: (1) explaining the formation, persistence, and demise of regimes, (2) accounting for regime properties and their change, and (3) determining regime consequences and explaining their variation. Focusing on the contributions made in the preceding chapters, this part of the concluding chapter may serve at the same time as a summary of the volume.

3

First drafts of most of the chapters in this volume have been presented and discussed at a conference on 'The Study of Regimes in International Relations—State of the Art and Perspectives', Tübingen, 14–18 July 1991. I would like to take this opportunity to thank the participants of this conference, whose critical questions and advice have helped to improve many of the original papers. I am also grateful to the Deutsche Forschungsgemeinschaft (German Science Association) and the University of Tübingen, without whose generous funding and support the conference could not have taken place. Once the authors had finalized their chapters, much of the work that goes into a book such as this still remained to be done. Special thanks are due to Peter Mayer for his valuable assistance in the various stages of this project. I gratefully acknowledge the excellent help I received from my research assistants Harald Beck, Doris Fuchs, and Christoph Weller in producing the manuscript of this volume, including the index. Thanks are also due to Mary Pattenger, who checked some of the chapters written by authors for whom English is not the first language, as well as to Claudia Dedeke, Hans Peter Schmitz, Marion Urban, and Bernhard Zangl, who read the proofs of the book. I also wish to take this opportunity to thank an anonymous reviewer arranged by the publisher for his or her most insightful and valuable comments and suggestions. Finally, I would like to express my gratitude to Oxford University Press for publishing this volume and in particular to its political and social science editor, Tim Barton, for his support, advice, and patience (of which we needed quite a bit).

V. R.
Tübingen
November 1992

PART I

Research on International Regimes

Research on International Regimes in Germany

The Adaptive Internalization of an American Social Science Concept

VOLKER RITTBERGER

IN this chapter, an attempt will be made to trace the path of research on international regimes in Germany with special emphasis on its (asymmetric) interaction with Anglo-American work in this field (sect. 1), to pinpoint the differences of context and of the state of the discipline of International Relations between the Anglo-American world (e.g. Holsti 1985) and Germany (e.g. Rittberger 1990c) which may have provided different perspectives on the focus of regime analysis (sect. 2), and to elaborate the extent to which research on international regimes has been modified or altered by German scholars in the process of internalizing this research programme (sects. 3–5).

1. RECEPTION AND DIFFUSION OF REGIME ANALYSIS IN GERMANY

While, on several occasions during the 1980s, members of the German International Relations community made at best a loose and rather *ad hoc* use of the term 'international regime' (e.g. Müller and Rode 1984), a more systematic reception of this concept set in very slowly and with a lag of several years. Faupel (1984) was the first to respond to the publication of the Krasner (1983c) volume and to sketch his own thoughts on the subject. He conceptualized international regimes as a form of institutionalized international collaboration distinct from governments, treaties, or international organizations. Faupel, however, de-emphasized the

normative contents of the concept of regime, and related it
strongly to routinized and institutionalized transactions between
and among states. Thus, his definition of the concept remained
rather broad and lacked the issue area orientation which accounts
for part of its success. The lack of a sharp conceptualization
showed up, for example, in his claim that the Concert of Europe
practising balance-of-power policies could be perceived as an
international regime, and that the *détente* of the 1970s could have
evolved into an international regime if only the Soviet Union had
understood, or alternatively had wished to play by, the rules of
the game.

The concepts of international regime and of regime analysis
were given their first thorough, critical treatment in German in
an often-quoted article by Wolf and Zürn (1986). Ever since,
research on international regimes has aroused a growing interest
(and, in parallel, a controversy about its merits) within the
German International Relations community. German International
Relations scholars sought to master the new subject and to add to
this international research programme by following two tracks. On
the one hand, the International Politics Section of the German
Political Science Association (Deutsche Vereinigung für Politische
Wissenschaft) devoted several of its meetings to the discussion of
regime analysis and solicited contributions to this area of research
from its members. By the end of the decade, the results of these
joint efforts—quantitatively impressive, yet of mixed quality—
were published in several volumes, one exclusively dealing with
international regimes (Kohler-Koch 1989*b*), and two others containing several relevant chapters (Albrecht 1989, Hartwich 1989).[1]
On the other hand, 'centres' of regime analysis evolved in Frankfurt
(Müller 1989*b*, 1993) and in Tübingen. The research team located
in Tübingen followed a more systematic approach to making use
of, and adapting, the regime analysis of American vintage to
urgently felt needs of theoretically informed empirical research on
crucial problems of contemporary international relations. In view
of the emphasis in American regime analysis on West–West and
global issue areas, it was recognized that East–West relations

---

[1] The 1988 annual meeting of the German Peace Research Association
(Arbeitsgemeinschaft für Friedens- und Konfliktforschung) provided another
forum for exchanging views about the merits of international regime analysis
(Moltmann and Senghaas-Knobloch 1989: 183–242).

would be a critical testing-ground for both the theoretical and the political robustness of regime analysis. Thus, a long-term project of comparative case studies about 'East–West regimes' was launched in 1986 which has aimed at improving the conceptualization of international regimes, at refining the explanation of regime formation, and at breaking new ground in analysing the impact of international regimes on the quality of international relations (peace, justice, sustainability). Besides several articles, a research monograph (Efinger, Rittberger, and Zürn 1988) and an edited volume (Rittberger 1990*d*) with several case studies and a more general chapter generalizing the evidence on the formation and the consequences of East–West regimes have resulted so far from this research project. Moreover, as spin-off products of the work of the Tübingen team, several of its original members have pursued research projects of their own: comparative studies of arms control verification arrangements (Efinger 1991*a*), of marine environmental protection regimes (List 1991), and of global common resources regimes (K. D. Wolf 1991), as well as a study primarily oriented towards breaking new ground in regime theory (Zürn 1992).

Not surprisingly, the reception in Germany of the concept of international regime and its associated research perspectives was mixed. The advocates of regime analysis hoped to have discovered a key to building a robust theory of international co-operation (including co-operation among states having different socio-economic systems). Thus they perceived themselves as responding creatively to a political challenge, i.e. identifying possibilities and conditions of stabilizing *détente*, on the one hand, and at the same time, to the negative (self-)assessment of German International Relations as lacking an adequate theoretical grounding (Czempiel 1986*b*). Their critics, some of whom did not conceal their mistrust of this latest 'imperialistic' import from across the Atlantic, were happy to cite the alleged flaws of regime analysis which authors familiar with Anglo-American regime analysis had already pointed out. Some German scholars sought to dismiss regime analysis as a contribution to theory-building in International Relations because of its alleged status-quo orientation, its fixation on the state-as-actor model, its inherent tendency to underrate the significance of subsystemic factors, etc. In short, regime analysis was said to be just another fashion borrowed from American social science and bound to pass away as so many others had done before (Hüttig 1989, 1990).

Today, the critique of some of the former adversaries, while still being sceptical, has somewhat mellowed. In view of the intensive efforts to internalize regime analysis and to adapt it to specific needs and aspirations of the German International Relations community they are ready to admit that theoretical discourse among students of international relations has been revived, that interdisciplinary exchange has been encouraged, bringing together political scientists, international law experts, economists, and historians, and that the increasingly stale study of international organizations has been supplemented and enriched (Junne 1990, 1992).

2. POLITICAL CONTEXT AND THEMATIC FOCI: THE UNITED STATES AND GERMANY COMPARED

Although scholars in the United States and in Germany use the same core terms while working on problems within the framework of regime analysis, they differ in their thematic foci as well as in their explication of the concept of international regime, and in their theoretical orientations. These differences—some of them smaller, others larger—deserve to be explored since an understanding of them may strengthen the basis for further mutual enrichment.

A major difference lies in the political context in which regime analysis was embraced by International Relations scholars as an appealing intellectual endeavour. In the United States, scholarly interest in international regimes represented one distinct reaction to a seemingly dramatic decline of American hegemony in the 1970s and expressed worries about the stability of international order once its backbone was no longer capable of maintaining it (Keohane 1984). Later, however, regime analysts such as Krasner (1985) and Young (1989a) addressed other international problematics, such as North–South and global resources issues, as well. In contrast, the German reception of regime analysis occurred at a time when the crisis of *détente* (or the 'Second Cold War' as authors such as Halliday (1983) called it) was causing great anxiety in large parts of the populace in Germany, and in Europe in general. In addition, the distaste for multilateralism shown by the Reagan Administration aroused concern about the directions of US foreign policy, especially its confrontational style, among various élite strata and political activists in Germany (and other parts of Europe), whose criticisms were often mistaken for an expression of 'Anti-Americanism'.

In any case, these different political settings seem to account for different choices of objects for study: American regime analysis has concentrated (though not exclusively) on issue areas in West–West relations mostly within the economic realm. German research on international regimes has instead centred on East–West (Efinger, Rittberger, and Zürn 1988; Kohler-Koch 1989*b*, chs. by Efinger, Müller, Ropers and Schlotter, and Zürn; Rittberger 1990*a*, 1990*d*; Rittberger and Zürn 1991*a*, 1991*b*) as well as on North–South and global issues (Zürn 1987; Kohler-Koch 1989*b*, chs. by Betz, Brock, and Wolf; K. D. Wolf 1991). Whereas, in the American debate, the examination of international security regimes has not played a major role (at first largely confined to Jervis's work and later somewhat enhanced through the volume edited by George, Farley, and Dallin (1988)), the German research effort in the field of regime analysis, almost right from the beginning, has paid a great deal of attention to the formation and consequences of international regimes in the issue area of international security, and it has been eager to demonstrate the usefulness of the concept of regime for studying international co-operation in this issue area as well. (In addition to previously cited publications see Brzoska (1991), Efinger (1990), (1991*a*), Efinger and Rittberger (1992), Rittberger, Efinger, and Mendler (1990), Schrogl (1990)).

This was, to be sure, an offshoot of the emphasis on East–West relations which has characterized a vast segment of German international relations research. Another early thematic focus of German regime analysis lay in the area of international co-operation for environmental protection, again with a regional emphasis on transboundary air and river pollution, and on the marine environment of the Baltic and the North Sea (List 1990*a*, 1991, List and Rittberger 1992, Prittwitz 1989, Strübel 1989, Schwarzer 1990*a*). This regional and sectoral specialization may be seen as a quite useful division of labour between American and European students of international regimes, resulting in the coverage of all major sectors of international politics and thus providing a rich source to be mined for theory-building about international regimes.

However, with the end of the Cold War, and the transformation of conflicts in what used to be called East–West relations (Rittberger and Zürn 1991*b*), this transatlantic division of labour also may be changing. Whereas a regional emphasis on regime formation in Europe on the part of the German research community is likely to continue, the sectoral specialization with its strong emphasis on security issues is giving way to a preoccupation with a much broader range of issue areas. In addition to the already mentioned and increasing work on international environmental regimes the various efforts at bringing human rights and minority rights protection under the purview of international regime analysis (Mendler 1990, List 1992) represent a significant departure from past trends.

3. CONCEPTUAL AND PHILOSOPHICAL DIFFERENCES AND *RAPPROCHEMENTS*

More fundamental differences between American and German regime analysis concern the conceptual and philosophical underpinnings of the research programme.

3.1. Defining 'International Regimes'

In response to Stein's (1983: 115) criticism that 'scholars have fallen into using the term "regime" so disparately and with such little precision that it ranges from an umbrella for all international relations to little more than a synonym for international organizations', efforts were renewed to define the concept of international regime more adequately and more precisely. By and large, the conceptualization of international regime as merely 'patterned behaviour' (e.g. Puchala and Hopkins 1983: 63) did not gain much support in German writings about regimes since the heuristic value of the concept of international regime was held to depend on its power to select from among the variety of interactions and even

co-operation between and among states (Kohler-Koch 1989*a*: 18–
20). Behaviour occurring with some regularity is not necessarily
co-operative; and even patterns of co-operation may be caused by
structural constraints rather than originate in normative considerations and the recognition of 'inconvenient obligations' (Keohane).
Therefore, a definition of international regime so broad as to
encompass mere regularities of co-operative behaviour would fail
to capture the phenomenon which lies at the heart of regime
analysis: the institutionalized co-operation of states for managing
conflicts and interdependence problems, instead of relying on self-
help strategies, either individually or collectively (alliance), even
though self-help action may seem to produce greater individual
benefits or less individual costs in the short term.[2]

This basic thrust of international regime analysis is, at first sight,
adequately reflected in the widely accepted definition of Krasner
(1983*a*: 2) which states that regimes are 'sets of implicit or explicit
principles, norms, rules, and decision-making procedures around
which actors' expectations converge in a given area of international
relations'. While Haggard and Simmons (1987) rightly questioned
whether the notion of 'implicitness' would not defy any effort to
operationalize the concept's definition, Wolf and Zürn (1986)
argued that an observable behavioural element should be added
to Krasner's definition in order to distinguish regimes from mere
promises or contracts to which the parties may or may not live up.
Thus, they added the criterion of effectiveness to the four principal
components of Krasner's definition. As a result, a regime is said
not to have come into existence if the pertinent norms and rules
are disregarded by states at their discretion. Instead of distinguishing between strong and weak regimes, or between declaratory,
action-guiding, and implemented regimes (Ropers and Schlotter
1990: 4), it was suggested that norms and rules which do not shape
the behaviour of states cannot be considered reliable predictors of
states' behaviour capable of producing convergent expectations.
In this view, even explicit norms and rules if they remain largely
inoperative fail to indicate the existence of an institution, and
therefore do not form part of an international regime.

To give an example (Mendler 1990): looking at the issue area

---

[2] This interpretation of regime analysis is further developed in Ch. 16, sect. 2,
below.

of 'working conditions of foreign journalists', which was the object of Basket Three agreements within the CSCE, the question arose whether, from a perspective focusing on different degrees of institutionalized co-operation, these agreements had already evolved into an international regime. No doubt it was possible to discover in the aftermath of Helsinki I (1975) a weak principle, some norms, and even a few rules circumscribing the range of permissible action on the part of both public authorities and foreign journalists. Yet norm observance and rule compliance varied so greatly over time and across countries, especially in Eastern Europe and the Soviet Union, that—using effectiveness as a criterion—it did not seem warranted to acknowledge the existence of an international regime.

By stressing the behavioural (or compliance) component of regimes these German regime analysts thought to provide a useful delimitation of cases. On the one hand, the political science concept of international regime is not identical with the concept of a legal regime since its existence does not presuppose a binding legal instrument; however, it is predicated on normatively recognized social practices as is any other institution. On the other hand, the political science concept of international regime transcends the notion of established patterns of conference diplomacy (e.g. the CSCE process) and their outcomes (e.g. treaties). Since these may turn out to be mere 'paper regimes', it was held that a more restrictive use of the term would be analytically advantageous.

In the meantime, a debate between those favouring a contract-oriented procedure (requiring only agreements about rules and procedures) and those favouring a more behaviour-oriented procedure (requiring rule-consistent behaviour in addition) of identifying international regimes has developed.[3] This has led to a new consensus, at least about the operational definition of international regime, among researchers from both sides of the Atlantic. The solution, which is likened to 'the use of a sliding scale', has been summarized as follows:

We agreed to begin with a universe of cases including all arrangements that meet the explicit rules test. This would be followed by an effort to identify that subset of the initial universe meeting the explicit rules test and also achieving prescriptive status in the sense that actors refer

---

[3] See also Ch. 2, sect. 3, below.

regularly to the rules both in characterizing their own behavior and in commenting on the behavior of others. Beyond this, analysts should seek to pinpoint a smaller subset of arrangements that meet the first two tests and that give rise to a measure of rule-consistent behavior as well.[4]

According to the new consensus, no arrangement should be called an international regime unless it passes the first two tests, i.e. the mere existence of explicit rules pertaining to an issue area in international relations will not do. On the other hand, sets of explicit rules with prescriptive status in the above sense do not need to be honoured under all circumstances to qualify as a regime (although it can be assumed that most of the cases which pass the second test will be arrangements that also 'give rise to a measure of rule-consistent behavior').

3.2. Scholarly Background and Analytical Perspectives

Another major difference between American and German approaches to regime analysis derives from premises and pre-occupations which set German regime analysts apart from their American colleagues. In Germany regime analysis was introduced above all by scholars who had been active in peace and conflict studies. Therefore, regimes were conceptualized as part of a conflict process model of international relations. The basic under-lying assumption of this model is that conflict tends to be pervasive in international relations (as in social relations, in general), and that international regimes could be conceived of as social institutions which regulate conflicts between states by constraining their behaviour through the observation of norms and rules in their dealing with disputed objects (Efinger, Rittberger, and Zürn 1988: 69). In this analytical perspective, the formation of international regimes represents a collective response to a variety of conflict situations. Instead of turning to self-help strategies, including the threat or use of force, states may manage their conflicts in a

---

[4] See Oran Young's (1991c: 3) report on the 'Regimes Summit' held at Dartmouth College, Nov. 1991. Participants in this conference included scholars from the United States (*inter alia* Robert Keohane, Edward Miles, and Oran Young), Norway (Arild Underdal and researchers from the Nansen Institute), and Germany (members of the Tübingen group).

regulated, more peaceful manner.[5] The value premiss which shows up in this analytical perspective points towards the quest for stable peace (Boulding 1978), or for international security communities (Deutsch *et al.* 1957), supported by international regimes as institutions of conflict management which help prevent the recourse to self-help strategies. (On the implications of an even broader concept of peace for regime analysis, see sect. 5 below.)

According to this line of reasoning, the existence or formation of international regimes as such is desirable. While it is recognized that regimes can be formed to serve evil purposes, it is maintained that regimes are a means of peaceful conflict regulation *among* the participants. Thus, it follows that one major analytical task consists in systematically gathering historical evidence about this kind of international institution and in identifying the conditions which are likely to facilitate and promote, or constrain, their coming into existence. This relatively strong interest of German regime analysts in the topic of regime formation, as compared to the American preoccupation with regime change (and regime decay), appears to be another consequence of the differing contexts within which regime analysis originally emerged.

In an American perspective, the world may have appeared to be already one of international regimes (Young 1980), particularly when focusing on the relations among developed western countries (or the western world including the western-oriented developing countries). However, in Europe, directly confronted with the often troublesome relations between capitalist and socialist countries, the lack of international regimes for the management of conflicts stood out in the perception of international political life. Yet, regime-analytic work soon indicated that norm- and rule-guided (or, in the words of the new consensus, normatively recognized and rule-consistent) collective conflict management in various issue areas was also possible here (Rittberger 1990*d*). Still, East–West regimes had not grown, at least until the late 1980s, into a layer of institutionalized co-operation for conflict management

---

[5] Even though German research on international regimes was clearly influenced by an interest in stabilizing and promoting East–West *détente*, the disappearance of the Cold War and the transformation of conflicts in Europe (or, more broadly speaking, in the CSCE region) does not invalidate the basic idea that international regimes represent a collective response to the challenge of managing international conflicts peacefully (Rittberger and Zürn 1991*b*).

comparable to the one extending across West–West issue areas (Rittberger 1990*a*). However, in the wake of the (Eastern) European revolutions of 1989/90, and the ensuing transformation of the conflict mix in the international relations of the CSCE region, new demands as well as opportunities for regime formation are likely to arise (Rittberger and Zürn 1991*b*).

4. PREFERRED APPROACHES TOWARDS EXPLAINING REGIME FORMATION

In so far as the question of (initial) regime formation had been addressed in the American literature on international regimes, power-structural approaches—the theory of hegemonic stability being the most intensively discussed example—and game-theoretic explanations have occupied a prominent place. Of course, the power-structural approach has been picked up in Germany as well. However, since the focus here has been on East–West relations in which not hegemony but rather a bipolar balance of power (nuclear deterrence) has prevailed, the hegemonic stability theory from the beginning seemed somewhat inappropriate. Therefore, in the German literature, to the extent to which it aspired to theory-building, other theoretical emphases crystallized (Kohler-Koch 1989*a*). The creative energy did not so much flow into the reception and possible further development of power-structural approaches, but was dedicated to other theoretically interesting explanations.

4.1. The Problem-Structural Approach

There is one special strand of explanation in regime analysis that has been introduced exclusively in the German literature on international regimes. This approach was in fact developed as a reaction to the American preoccupation with the theory of hegemonic stability. This theory obviously failed to explain the phenomenon that, among the same state actors, co-operation occurred in one issue area, whereas in other issue areas unregulated conflict management persisted. The 'problem-structural approach' draws on older efforts to explain foreign policies of states by issue or issue area characteristics (Rosenau 1966). It holds that certain inherent characteristics of issues or conflicts predetermine the way in which these issues or conflicts will be dealt with. In the Tübingen research project on East–West regimes, a conflict typology has been developed which is based on the distinction between 'consensual' and 'dissensual conflicts' (Aubert 1963, Kriesberg 1982: 30–42) and consists of four types of conflict which vary in their degree of regime-conduciveness. In dissensual conflicts the actors disagree about what is desirable, not just for each of them individually but for all of them collectively. In consensual conflicts the actors are confronted with a situation of scarcity in which every actor desires the same valued object but cannot be satisfied fully because there is not enough for everybody. Subdividing dissensual conflicts into conflicts about values and conflicts about means, it is hypothesized that conflicts about values (which, by their very nature, leave very little room for compromise) usually defy co-operative conflict management, whereas conflicts about means are more easily dealt with in a co-operative way. Turning to consensual conflicts, we distinguish further between conflicts of interest about relatively assessed goods, i.e. objects whose valuation by an actor is not independent of the size of other actors' shares in these objects (e.g. power, prestige, weapons), and conflicts of interest about absolutely assessed goods which obtain their value independently of what other actors have (e.g. food). Here, it is hypothesized that the former type of conflict of interest, which often prompts intense competition, is far less conducive to regulated conflict management than the latter type, which, in general, displays the highest propensity for regime formation (Efinger, Rittberger, and Zürn 1988: 92–7; Rittberger and Zürn 1990: 29–32). Table 1.1 summarizes the problem-structural hypotheses.

TABLE 1.1. *Type of Conflict and Regime-Conduciveness*

Type of conflict	Regime-conduciveness
conflict of interest about absolutely assessed goods	high
conflict about means	medium
conflict of interest about relatively assessed goods	low
conflict about values	very low

These hypotheses have been tested in two ways. One consisted of examining several case studies of East–West and West–West regime formation and of determining whether or not these cases deviated from what we would expect on the basis of our problem-structural hypotheses. In general, this typology achieved considerable empirical support, yet alternative, especially situation-structural (game-theoretic) explanations (see sect. 4.2. below) seem to be more promising if we deal with issue areas dominated by conflicts of interest.[6] Considering, for example, the issue area of long-range transboundary air pollution, it took more than a decade until an international regime was established in 1984/5. Since the conflicts in the issue area were identified as conflicts of interest about absolutely assessed goods (money to be spent on abatement technology) regime formation should not have encountered so many difficulties and should not have taken so long. However, modelling the situation structure according to states' preferences prevailing in the issue area from 1970 to the beginning of the 1980s, the case represents a 'Rambo' game in which some actors reach their optimum by refusing to co-operate at all; thus regime formation is not to be expected. In this case, the situation-structural explanation proved stronger than the problem-structural one. As far as issue areas dominated by conflicts about values are concerned, however, the problem-structural approach suffices to explain the failure of international regime formation (Rittberger and Zürn 1991a: 172f.).

The other test of the problem-structural hypotheses involved a statistical analysis of data on East–West conflicts (coded on the basis of the above-mentioned conflict typology) and conflict-managing interactions (coded on the basis of a four-point ordinal scale ranging from 'no co-operation' to 'existing agreement'). The results of this quantitative test of our problem-structural hypotheses were quite encouraging: the contingency coefficient which was used to examine the correlation between the conflict typology and the mode of conflict management reached values of higher than 0.5. However, it would be premature to take these findings for established facts before independent replications of these tests have been carried out and, more importantly, before

---

[6] Efinger, Mayer, and Schwarzer, in Ch. 11, sect. 2.3, below, report results of an empirical test of the problem-structural and the situation-structural as well as other hypotheses purporting to explain regime formation.

similar data on West–West interactions have been analysed, separately as well as together with the East–West data set, in the same fashion (Efinger and Zürn 1990).

Despite its weaknesses (e.g. problems of operationalization; neglect of context variables), the problem-structural approach and the hypotheses which it allows one to generate seem to account for a considerable amount of variation in the outcome of inter-state interactions. Therefore, it should be acknowledged as a theoretical perspective which deserves to be looked at more closely by other researchers as well as in other research programmes. Especially in combination with other explanations of international behaviour, it might advance the process of international relations theory-building.

4.2. The Situation-Structural Approach

From the beginning game-theoretic approaches to the analysis of international regimes have been present in the American discussion of international 'co-operation under anarchy' (Oye 1986). However, they remained in the shadow of 'structural' and 'functional' explanations of regime formation.[7] In Germany, game theory in general, and its application to international relations in particular, faced serious reservations or prejudices, even more than regime analysis had encountered. The dislike refers to what Junne (1972) once called the 'limited rationality of strategic thinking'. Only slowly are these reservations being overcome. A German difference from the American scene, then, is the low level of attention and the scarcity of resources that have been devoted to game-theoretic regime analysis.

Following the examples set by a number of American scholars Zürn (1992) in particular has developed the 'situation-structural approach', which builds upon, but also differs from, current game-theoretic approaches in International Relations. Instead of focusing on a small or a large number of selected games, he has constructed a typology of 2×2 games representing 'problematic social situations' (Raub and Voss 1986), i.e. situations in which the

---

[7] For the functionalist (or contractualist) perspective on various issues in regime analysis see Ch. 2, sects. 4 and 5, below.

individual interpretation of rationality diverges from its collective interpretation. Problematic social situations are social traps in which the rational pursuit of self-interest can lead to a collectively suboptimal outcome.[8] It is in such situations, and in the absence of a central governing authority, that the quest for finding a co-operative solution to avoid, or at least to minimize, the suboptimal collective outcome arises.

However, the existence of a problematic social situation is only a necessary condition for the emergence of a lasting co-operative solution, e.g. an international regime. To find out whether indeed, and how easily, an international regime will be formed the already mentioned typology of problematic social situations demonstrates its usefulness. Four types of problematic social situations are distinguished:

Co-ordination games with distributional conflict, such as 'battle of sexes', and *co-ordination games without distributional conflict*, such as 'assurance'. In either type of situation the formation of an international regime can be expected within a relatively short period of time once the situation has been recognized by the actors. Situations of the former type are somewhat more complicated to handle and therefore involve a greater risk of the actors ending up with a collectively suboptimal outcome. Overall, however, co-ordination games come close to being sufficient conditions of regime formation.

Dilemma games, such as the 'prisoners' dilemma'. Here, the situation as such does not augur well for the formation of a regime since it contains powerful incentives for non-cooperation by every actor. Regime formation thus depends on exogenous factors exerting a favourable influence, as e.g. the 'shadow of the future', i.e. the expected diachronic iteration of the game, and the (small) number of actors. In a dilemma-type situation an international regime is likely to be established only after a lengthy process of interaction during which exogenous factors must contribute to confidence-building between the parties involved.

'Rambo' games. Since in such a situation one actor reaches his/her optimum by refusing to co-operate while the collective outcome might be (and often is) suboptimal, regime formation is next

---

[8] An outcome is collectively suboptimal if either it is not Pareto optimal or there is another Pareto optimum in which benefits are more equally distributed.

to impossible. Again, an exogenous factor such as cross-issue linkage may help the aggrieved actor induce the other party to be more co-operative (Rittberger and Zürn 1990: 38–42; 1991a: 173–5).

Empirical research using a variety of historical cases clearly supports the usefulness of the fourfold typology of problematic social situations and its application to international regime formation. This is not to claim that more systematic efforts are unwarranted. Such efforts might not only build upon an already existing base of tested hypotheses but also use a methodology for the comparative analysis of real cases instead of making inferences from deductively constructed games. The methodological step forward consists, in particular, in the modelling of historical conflict situations by ascertaining empirically the preferences of actors (and their ordering) independently of their actual behaviour (Zürn 1992: 238–48).

5. FINDINGS ABOUT REGIME CONSEQUENCES

It was mentioned earlier that the preoccupation with the analysis of regime formation among German International Relations scholars was due to their standing in the tradition of peace and conflict studies. This background was also felt when in German research on international regimes questions about the impact or consequences of international regimes were dealt with (Efinger *et al.* 1990: 273–9; Rittberger and Zürn 1990, 1991a).

In accordance with their specific scholarly background German students of international regimes paid special attention to the potential relationship between regimes and different forms (or levels) of peace. The question 'Do regimes matter?' has been specified and reformulated as 'Do regimes matter for peace?' In this line of reasoning, the idea of 'peace in parts' (J. S. Nye) re-emerges in a somewhat different form. Here this idea carries two assumptions. One is that conflicts, once they have become regulated, will stay regulated ('robustness' or 'resilience'). The other is that international regimes affect the overall relations between states which have been interconnected through international regimes: these diffuse consequences are called the 'civilizing' effect of international regimes, i.e. regimes reduce the overall probability of their members' falling back on (potentially violent) self-help strategies in their dealing with one another.

The assumption that international regimes foster peace by reliably reducing the disposition of states to employ, or threaten the use of, force towards one another seems empirically supported if we accept the robustness of a regime as an indicator. Taking as a point of departure the domain of conflicts in East–West relations and the worsening overall relations between the two superpowers from the late 1970s until the mid-1980s, it is striking that norm- and rule-consistent behaviour in issue areas in which regime formation had already taken place (Austria, Baltic Sea, Berlin, intra-German trade) continued more or less undisturbed, whereas in issue areas which had defied effective regime formation (confidence- and security-building measures, conventional arms control, working conditions of foreign journalists) a non-cooperative, or even confrontational, policy style prevailed. The accomplishment of international regimes as to the promotion of peace seems to lie in the effect of insulating certain issue areas against a negative 'spill-over' from tensions which have arisen between and among the same actors elsewhere.

Regarding the 'civilizing' effect of international regimes, research on East–West regimes has shown that decision-makers perceive the formation of regimes in general, and in security-related issue areas in particular, as a kind of confidence-building measure which is likely to add to the improvement of overall relations (Efinger and Rittberger 1992). Furthermore, it may be said that international regimes, once firmly established and operative, are likely to have a model-like impact, their principles, norms, and rules pointing to possibilities for regulated conflict management in other issue areas (or regions of the world) (List and Rittberger 1992). Finally, conflict management by an international regime can pave the way towards conflict resolution since, in the long run, commonly agreed-upon and jointly observed principles, norms, and rules may become internalized into the laws and practices of states, so that the original differences of position about a given object of contention vanish over time. International regimes may thus cause a reshaping of interests among the participating actors (states).[9]

---

[9] Müller, in Ch. 15, sect. 5, below, describes such an effect for the case of West Germany's nuclear export control policy.

So far, the rooting of research on international regimes by German International Relations scholars in peace and conflict studies seems to permit the conclusion that international regimes are a good thing *per se*. However, these same roots put this conclusion into doubt if we move towards a more broadly conceived notion of peace. Peace researchers in Germany and, above all, in Scandinavia have pointed to the difference between 'negative' and 'positive' peace.[10] Following this distinction, international regimes—mainly those in the economic realm and of a global reach—may be assessed as adding to 'structural violence' while, perhaps, contributing to 'negative' peace, i.e. the absence of 'direct violence'. For instance, a great deal of controversy exists in scholarly writings about the activities of the International Monetary Fund towards Third World countries, especially in the field of external debt management. The international regime of external debt management entails a distribution of costs among banks, host countries of lenders, and borrowing Third World countries which puts the burden of adjustment very strongly on the shoulders of the borrowing countries, not necessarily enhancing their prospects of prosperity and, very often at least, provoking domestic instability, unrest, and violence (Haggard 1985).[11]

The possible interrelationships between international regimes and 'positive' peace have been given close attention in some of the work by Zürn (1987) and K. D. Wolf (1991). Both address the question under what conditions international regimes entail a just distribution of benefits and costs among the regime-participating states (justice being defined with reference to Rawls's 'difference principle'). Following an earlier suggestion by Krasner (1985), they argue that 'market-oriented', 'state-oriented', and 'internationalist regimes' differ significantly in the degree to which they provide a just distribution of benefits and costs within the issue area covered by the regime. Internationalist regimes are expected to entail the most nearly just distributive outcomes because they are characterized by decision-making procedures which can be used

---

[10] The classical statement has been Galtung's (1969); its early reception in Germany is well documented in Senghaas (1971). In a somewhat similar vein Czempiel (1986a: 47) defines peace as a process of change in international relations which consists of the simultaneous decrease in collective (direct) violence and increase in distributive justice.

[11] For an assessment of the effects of the global debt regime see Ch. 13, sect. 4, below.

for the authoritative (re-)distribution of resources. Conversely, market-oriented and state-oriented international regimes are likely to produce more efficient, but less just outcomes.

Whereas the criterion of justice seems to apply *primarily* to relations between actors the structure of which is highly asymmetrical usually on more than one dimension, as, for instance, in North–South relations, no such restriction has to be added when introducing the distinction between 'internal' and 'external international regimes' and discussing its relevance as regards the impact of regimes. In general, it is suggested that external regimes, which primarily serve to make sure that their member states co-operate to manage conflicts among themselves about their dealing with *other* countries (as, for instance, in the case of CoCom), are less likely to foster international peace. Conversely, internal regimes, which institutionalize co-operation for conflict management only among their members, will be more conducive to peaceful international relations. Anecdotal evidence seems to support this argument.

Another central issue in the study of regime consequences refers to the extent to which the publicly stated goals of regimes are actually achieved. The question of *goal attainment* can only be studied on a case-by-case basis. Yet, pursued at some length, the results of these investigations may lend themselves to formulating hypotheses about the interactive effects of various regime consequences. Furthermore, it may turn out that only certain types of regimes exhibit a high propensity towards goal attainment. As to empirical evidence, there is hardly a single case of an effective international regime which could be said to fail the test of goal attainment *in toto*. However, taking regimes in issue areas of environmental protection as examples, the degree of goal attainment can be very limited, sometimes only permitting the conclusion that, without the regime, the environmental conditions would be worse (List 1990a, 1991). In fact, this assessment alone could justify the energies spent on studying international regimes. However, as our knowledge about international regimes as building-blocks of international governance increases, this minimalist conception of regime impact may turn out to be overly cautious.[12]

---

[12] Most of the issues of this section are further discussed, both theoretically and in the light of empirical cases, in Ch. 14 below.

6. CONCLUSION

Looking back at this brief overview of how German International Relations scholars first embraced the research programme on international regimes, initiated by their North American colleagues, and then struggled to adapt it to prevailing 'interests of cognition' (Habermas) in the German International Relations community, I think the claim is not overstated that this research programme, rather than further dividing the discipline, has offered a meeting-ground for transnational scholarly dialogue and cross-fertilization. Although it is still true that the communication gap between International Relations scholars in North America, on the one hand, and in Europe, and in Germany in particular, on the other, has not yet significantly narrowed (exceptions demonstrating the rule), joint state-of-the-art assessments of research on international regimes contribute to reducing the asymmetries in scholarly communication across Europe and across the Atlantic. It seems to me that the different scholarly interests and political, even moral, concerns which lie behind the collective efforts on both sides of the Atlantic to advance theory-building and empirical research on international co-operation and institutions complement each other well. The variations of emphasis reflecting different intellectual traditions and exposures to historical contexts should be seen as a source of mutual enrichment rather than of estrangement. Regime analysis is certainly not the golden egg of international relations theory development; yet, aside from Morgenthauean realism, no other research programme in International Relations has spawned such a transnational, cohesive scholarly community. Before it will have outlived its usefulness, there still are a good many lacunae of both a theoretical and an empirical nature needing to be filled.

The Analysis of International Regimes

Towards a European–American Research Programme

ROBERT O. KEOHANE

1. INTRODUCTION

The concept of international regimes originated not from social scientists' urge to invent new terms for their own sake, but as a way to understand international co-operation, defined as co-ordinated mutual adjustment of states' policies yielding benefits to participants. Systematically organized co-operation is extensive in world politics; yet very few rules are hierarchically enforced. Rather, most co-operation appears to be organized horizontally rather than vertically, through the practice of reciprocity. Specific agreements are embedded in a multi-layered system in which agreements are 'nested' within a more comprehensive set of agreed-upon rules. Understanding the formation and impact of these systems of rules is therefore essential for an appreciation of the conditions under which international co-operation could occur (Keohane 1983: 150).

This chapter could not have been written without the extensive and valuable discussions with participants at a meeting in Tübingen, Federal Republic of Germany, in July 1991, and a smaller working group meeting at Dartmouth College, New Hampshire, USA, in November 1991. I am grateful to Volker Rittberger and Oran R. Young, respectively, for organizing those meetings. My thinking on definitions of international regimes has benefited from these discussions, particularly from contributions by Volker Rittberger and Michael Zürn. My observations on the impact of international regimes reflect insightful contributions at the Tübingen meeting by Thomas Bernauer, Friedrich Kratochwil, Harald Müller, Volker Rittberger, Oran Young, and Andrei Zagorski. I am particularly grateful to Jeffry Frieden for comments on an earlier version of this chapter and for suggesting the term, 'contractual environment'. Parts of sections 4 and 5 draw verbatim, with permission of the publisher, on Keohane (1990).

Over the past decade, much thought and effort has gone into the study of international regimes. The definition of the concept has been debated and sharpened. A number of good descriptive studies of specific regimes have been completed, and theories purporting to explain regime formation and impact have been devised. As the papers for this volume indicate, the concept of international regimes can no longer be considered a passing fad (Strange 1983). However, until recently, research on international regimes was conducted almost entirely by North Americans, and therefore limited by the political and cultural assumptions that North American social scientists bring to the study of international relations, as well as by our lack of linguistic versatility. Furthermore, progress in integrating conceptual, theoretical, and empirical work has been disappointing: we still do not have a well-tested theory of international regimes. These papers, however, reveal extensive areas of agreement: indeed, they reveal that social scientists on both sides of the Atlantic who are interested in systematic empirical and theoretical analysis are thinking in quite similar terms.

This chapter represents an attempt to facilitate a transnational investigation of the formation, nature, and effectiveness of international regimes. Its discussion proceeds in four parts. The next section (sect. 2) raises issues of methodology, arguing for a Weberian conception of 'objective' social science. Section 3 briefly examines concepts and definitions: what do we mean by 'international regimes'? Section 4 addresses the theoretical issue on which all study of regimes depends: do regimes matter, and if so, how and under what conditions? Section 5, finally, considers some other questions that theories of regimes should seek to explain, such as increases over time in the number of regimes; variations in their membership, strength, and scope; and variations in property rights and rules.

2. A WEBERIAN APPROACH TO 'OBJECTIVITY' IN SOCIAL SCIENCE

In the humanities, increasingly in history, and on the margins of the social sciences, it has become popular to deny the possibility of objective knowledge. As Gordon S. Wood (1991: 12) writes, 'the blurring of fact and fiction is part of the intellectual climate of our postmodern time—dominated as it is by winds of epistemological skepticism and Nietzschean denials of the possibility of objectivity'. The debunkers of objectivity have criticized a caricature of positivistic social science, according to which social change occurs deterministically; social scientists observe behaviour unmediated by their own perceptions and beliefs, permitting them clearly to distinguish fact from value; and causal propositions can be verified. It should not be necessary to emphasize that sophisticated contemporary social scientists make none of those assumptions. They see social reality as subject to random variation, effects of conjunctures between unrelated events, and historical 'path-dependence', in which earlier events probabilistically affect later ones. Thus it would be naïve to believe that one could predict the future from the present, as if human affairs were like a highly complicated clock. Furthermore, the evidence we have of human affairs must be interpreted by observers before it is intelligible, partly because much of it derives from arguments, justifications, and other forms of discourse rather than strictly from behaviour. Human fallibility guarantees measurement error and bias (some deriving from observers' values), and causal inferences can never be finally verified.

Nevertheless, methods of historical and social scientific research, requiring evidence that other observers can also gather and evaluate, permit us to have some confidence in professional accounts of events. Descriptive inference permits us to generalize, and to understand the likely range of error of our generalizations. Methods of causal inference, qualitative as well as quantitative, permit us to test and evaluate—sometimes to falsify, never finally to verify—causal hypotheses. We expect social scientists to be self-conscious about their own biases, and to try to guard against them; more important, we expect criticism from scholars with different values to expose the effects of bias on supposedly objective findings. What Max Weber referred to as 'objectivity' does not require that we accept what he called 'fantastic' claims about determinism in human affairs, much less that social reality can be observed directly. It does, however, necessitate detailed historical research, the careful use of abstract concepts, or 'ideal types', and the disciplined comparison of observation with concept.

Winston Churchill is reputed to have said that democracy is the worst possible system of government—except for the alternatives. Objective social science in Weber's sense is similar: it is highly flawed, and could perhaps be readily discarded if better alternatives were available. To 'deconstruct' reality, however, is hardly a response to the human need for what Weber (1949*a*: 88, 92, 111) called 'knowledge of the cultural significance of concrete historical events and patterns'. For those of us who seek to understand international co-operation, and the significance of arrangements to ensure it, the disciplined use of historical and social scientific methods is the surest path to that knowledge. Students of international relations who disagree may seek other paths; but only convincing findings, reached through a process that meets criteria of intersubjective validity, are likely to persuade the rest of us that their efforts are not in vain. Until that happens, belief in objectivity in Weber's sense, albeit not in the naïve sense that 'true reality' can be known, is a precondition for participation in a sophisticated positivistic, empirical and theoretical, research programme on international regimes.

3. CONCEPTS AND DEFINITIONS

An extraordinary amount of attention is paid in contemporary writings on international institutions to definitions. Of course we need a clear understanding of the meaning of terms when they are used, and the novelty in political science (although not in international law) of the term 'international regime' has necessitated explicit discussions of how this term should be defined. Yet it is counterproductive to dwell excessively on definitional issues when important theoretical and empirical questions are unresolved. Hence I will be brief, and I will seek to be clear.

The most widely used definition of international regimes is the one devised in the fall of 1980 by contributors to the 1982 special issue of *International Organization* on the subject. Participants in that enterprise recognized that unless they could agree on a single definition, their attempt to reorient a field was likely to fail. They defined international regimes as 'implicit or explicit principles, norms, rules, and decision-making procedures around which actors' expectations converge in a given area of international relations' (Krasner 1983*a*: 2). This definition has been enormously important and valuable, but its complexity makes it subject to confusing differences of interpretation. Indeed, its ambiguities have proved quite contentious and confusing.

The most fundamental issue is whether regimes are to be identified on the basis of *explicit rules and procedures*, or on the basis of *observed behaviour*, from which rules, norms, principles, and procedures can be inferred. Defining regimes simply in terms of explicit rules and procedures risks slipping into the formalism characteristic of some traditions of international law: that is, purely nominal agreements could be considered to be regimes, even though they had no behavioural implications. The futile and empty Kellogg–Briand Pact of 1927, to 'outlaw war', could on a formalistic definition be considered an international regime.

Yet there are compelling theoretical and methodological reasons to reject a 'thick' substantive definition of regimes, based on observed behaviour. Theoretically, as Stephan Haggard and Beth Simmons (1987: 494) have pointed out, the result of focusing on implicit regimes 'begs the question of the extent to which state behaviour is, in fact, rule-governed'. It would be circular reasoning to identify regimes on the basis of observed behaviour, and then to use them to 'explain' observed behaviour. Methodologically, a substantive definition of regimes provides that regimes only exist if actors' expectations actually converge; and some measure of convergence must therefore be found. Friedrich Kratochwil and John Ruggie (1986: 764) argue 'that we *know* regimes by their principled and shared understandings of desirable and acceptable forms of social behavior'. Yet it is enormously difficult, indeed ultimately impossible, to determine 'principled and shared understandings'. To what extent principled, to what extent shared? How are we to enter into the minds of human beings to determine this? And which human beings will count? Even if we could devise a way to assess convergent expectations intersubjectively, what standard of convergence would we require to determine that a regime existed?

Volker Rittberger (1990*b*: 3) and his colleagues at Tübingen have proposed requiring that international arrangements be above certain levels of indicators of effectiveness before they would qualify as international regimes. If the levels of effectiveness required were to be more than minimal, however, this approach would require investigators to solve very difficult problems of causal inference as a precondition to identifying the regimes that they study. Such a methodology would seem virtually to assure that investigators would be for ever stuck at the first level: identifying the phenomenon to be studied. Furthermore, as noted above, the key theoretical issue—the relationship, if any, between regimes and state behaviour—would become a definitional question. Such an approach would invert the usual order of scientific investigation, in which description, and descriptive inference, precede explanation. It is odd to have to explain behaviour (in terms of regime rules) before identifying the practices to be analysed.

Yet the drawbacks of a purely formal conceptualization remain substantial. It therefore seems sensible to define *agreements* in purely formal terms (explicit rules agreed by more than one state) and to consider *regimes* as arising when states recognize these agreements as having continuing validity. This definition has 'thin' substantive content: a set of rules need not be 'effective' to qualify as a regime, but it must be recognized as continuing to exist. Using this definition, regimes can be identified by the existence of explicit rules that are referred to in an affirmative manner by governments, even if they are not necessarily scrupulously observed. Thus, establishing that a regime exists is an issue for descriptive inference, based on publicly available texts, rather than psychological insight or causal inference.[1]

Such a definition meshes well with the sociological concept of *institutions*, defined as persistent and connected sets of rules (formal and informal) that prescribe behavioural roles, constrain activity, and shape expectations. Since an institution's rules must be 'persistent', they must continue to be taken into account by participants, but no minimum standards of effectiveness are implied. International institutions include formal intergovernmental or transnational organizations, international regimes, and conventions. International organizations are purposive entities, with bureaucratic structures and leadership, permitting them to respond to events. International regimes are institutions with explicit rules,

---

[1] On the issue of how best to conceptualize international regimes see also Ch. 1, sect. 3.1, above.

agreed upon by governments, that pertain to particular sets of issues in international relations. Conventions are informal institutions, with implicit rules and understandings, that shape the expectations of actors (Keohane 1989*a*: 3 f.).

4. DO REGIMES MATTER? IF SO, HOW?

Work on international regimes has been theory-driven. Indeed, the American literature on international regimes has been shaped —one might say distorted—by its advocates' theoretical struggles with neo-realists, as represented by Kenneth Waltz. Waltz's (1979) articulation of a systemic theory of international relations, self-consciously deductive and rigorous yet consistent with the core propositions of realism, challenged institutionalists by downplaying the role of international institutions within 'self-help systems', just as it annoyed students of foreign policy by stressing the primacy of international structure, without by any means denying the need for a theory of foreign policy (Keohane 1986*b*).

Regime theorists have proposed a number of reasons why regimes should matter. Within a modified neo-realist framework, international regimes can affect both the *capabilities* and the *interests* of states. International regimes can affect capabilities by serving as a source of influence for states whose policies are consistent with regime rules, or which are advantaged by the regime's decision-making procedures. In *Power and Interdependence* (1977) Joseph S. Nye and I referred to these influence resources as 'organizationally dependent capabilities'. Regimes may also alter the underlying power capabilities of states, whether by reinforcing the dominance of rich, powerful states, as dependency theory argues, or by dissipating the hegemon's resources, as claimed by some versions of hegemonic stability theory (Krasner 1983*b*). International regimes may also, as claimed by functional theories, alter calculations of interest by assigning property rights, providing information, and altering patterns of transaction costs. Outside of a neo-realist framework, regimes can have other effects on state action: by altering bureaucratic practices and rules (or 'habits'); by promoting learning about cause–effect relationships; by altering ideas about the legitimacy and value of practices; by becoming embedded in higher-level normative networks;[2] by increasing the political salience of certain issues; by changing the balance of political influence within domestic politics; or by enhancing the political or administrative capacity of governmental or non-governmental organizations within countries. To some extent neo-realist and institutionalist theories are complementary. Students of international regimes need not discount the roles of interests and power in world politics. Nor do sophisticated neo-realists have to deny that ideas can be important or ignore the impact of regimes on domestic politics. Regimes could conceivably have any or all of the effects attributed to them, under different conditions. Thus the theoretical debate is not nearly as divisive as the intellectual chasm that separates scholars seeking 'objective' knowledge in Weber's sense and those who deny its possibility. Disputes about the effects of international regimes, or about the conditions under which they come into existence, are *not irresolvable* because of deep epistemological or methodological conflicts. They are simply *unresolved* because we have not done the work necessary to formulate theories in testable ways or to test them empirically.

With respect to theoretical presumptions, therefore, a programme of research on international regimes can 'let a hundred flowers bloom'. Indeed, diversity of theoretical viewpoints is desirable, since it will help to generate more interesting hypotheses. The only requirement is that theories need to be formulated in such a way that hypotheses are derived from them, and that these hypotheses are in principle subject to falsification through empirical work. Proponents and sceptics of each theory should seek imaginatively to think of *observable consequences* of the theory, and of ways to test whether these hypothetical consequences in fact obtain.

These consequences need not be at the level of the international system. Of course, the most obvious implications of theories of regimes will be at this level: the unit of analysis will be the regime itself, and inquiry will focus on its characteristics. However, many theories of international regimes will have implications at the level of the state. For instance, if regimes transmit information, governments' procedures for handling and disseminating information

---

[2] See Ch. 15, sect. 6, below.

should change as they join regimes, or as the rules of the regimes are modified. If regimes operate through reciprocity, we should observe foreign policy actions designed to monitor other states' actions and respond in a tit-for-tat fashion. In general, social scientists should encourage stringent tests by giving more credence to hypotheses that pass such tests than to those whose propositions are banal and obvious. The more stringent the test proposed, the more impressive a hypothesis that passes it.

What we essentially seek to ascertain is how much explanatory leverage we will gain by including international regimes, among other undoubtedly important factors, in our explanations of state policies and their outcomes. In so far as we can show that regimes are often effective, students of international relations will have to take them systematically into account in explaining state policy. Having established the significance of regimes, we can then treat effectiveness as a variable, to be assessed comparatively across regimes: *under what conditions*, we will ask, do regimes matter, and in what ways? Effectiveness, and its preconditions, will become central subjects for theoretical and empirical investigation rather than defining characteristics of regimes.

Oran Young (1989*a*: 206 f.) is right to observe that the proposition that international regimes are significant has often been 'relegated to the realm of assumptions rather than brought to the forefront as a focus for analytical and empirical investigation'. Nevertheless, some good recent work has sought to examine whether the existence of international regimes has been associated with changes in patterns of state behaviour (Young 1979, Nye 1987, P. M. Haas 1989). Yet there remains a fundamental difficulty in assessing the impact of international regimes: causal inference is difficult where experimental or statistical research designs are infeasible. We do not have a hypothetical institution-free baseline from which to measure the impact of actual institutions on state capabilities. Likewise, we might be tempted to attribute co-operation among states, in accordance with international rules, to constraints on short-range self-interest, or changes in long-range self-interest, resulting from those rules. But both the co-operation and the regimes could in principle be reflections of some third set of forces, such as patterns of complementary interests and underlying distributions of power, without regimes having any effect at all. If it were possible to use an experimental design, we would control for other explanatory factors, such as distributions of power and interest, and vary institutional characteristics. Unfortunately, we cannot actually perform such an experiment. As Rittberger and Michael Zürn (1990: 47) argue:

Investigating the consequences of international regimes requires a counterfactual argument. In case the conflicts in the issue area are not managed by a regime, then one has to speculate about what a regime *could* do. And if a regime does exist, one has to cope with the question of what *would be* without it.[3]

One could try to deal with this problem, in part, by using a research design that compared behaviour before and after the institution of a regime. Clearly, one would have to control for other factors that might also have changed; but with a careful design and a sufficient number of cases, a researcher could hope to isolate the impact of changes in explicit rules. I believe that such research would be worth while. To do so, however, requires a strict definition of 'international regime', such as the one I proposed above, that links the concept to specific, observable behaviour.

One way of assessing the significance of international regimes is to see whether governments routinely follow their rules. We know from theory that co-operation does not take place automatically, even in a co-ordination game lacking fundamental conflicts of interest. We also know that in world politics, distributional conflicts are endemic, even when incentives exist for co-operation: taking this fact into account, Rittberger and Zürn (1990: 16) refer to regimes as one form of 'regulated conflict management'. Routine rule-following in situations requiring co-ordination, where various actions would be possible, is evidence for the impact of regimes.

More far-reaching effects of regimes can occur when actors alter their conceptions of self-interest through mutual persuasion and the accumulation of scientific knowledge. This phenomenon has been observed in the European Community, the International Monetary Fund and World Bank, on environmental issues such as ozone depletion (E. B. Haas 1990, P. M. Haas 1990, Keohane and Hoffmann 1991, Benedick 1991, Haas, Keohane, and Levy 1990), and in the East–West regimes studied by Rittberger (1990*d*) and

---

[3] For an extended argument along the same lines see Ch. 13 below.

his colleagues. Another test, ingeniously proposed by Rittberger and Zürn, is to examine the 'resilience' of regimes when faced with a deterioration of overall relations among the participants. By this standard, the Baltic environmental regime, the regime for access to West Berlin, and the intra-German trade regime all qualify as resilient, and therefore as having had an impact. Another related test of the significance of regimes would be whether their rules continue to apply even when the conditions under which one would expect states to follow such practices, in the absence of such rules, have disappeared. On this standard, the GATT regime for international trade in manufactured goods seems quite significant, since it is difficult to imagine such a liberal regime being reconstructed in the present environment.

To understand more precisely the conditions under which regimes matter, it is probably essential to undertake research at the subsystemic, or unit, level of analysis. For such analysis, degree of compliance with regime rules is the appropriate dependent variable. The key methodological problem here is to sort out, and discard, situations in which the state would have behaved in ways that were consistent with the regime rules even had those rules not existed: that is, situations in which compliance was 'convenient'. Only where compliance is inconvenient—that is, where regime rules conflict with governments' perceptions of what their self-interests would be if there were no such institutions—is the impact of the regime tested. In these instances of inconvenient commitments we should expect that if regimes were unimportant, the rules would be violated; but that in so far as the rules are obeyed, we can infer that regimes had an impact.[4] In my own empirical research I am seeking to understand better the conditions for institutional impact by examining major cases of inconvenient commitments in the history of American foreign policy since 1789. My purpose is to determine under what conditions institutional commitments are more or less likely to be kept. At the current stage in my work, only a few points seem clear: there is substantial variation in the extent to which commitments seem to matter, both across issues and over time; enforcement of commitments against the United States has been quite rare;

---

[4] Under this premiss Müller, in Ch. 15 below, examines 'the politics of compliance' in three security cases.

and unenforceable commitments are nevertheless sometimes honoured, although no single motivation, whether based in reciprocity, concern about reputation, or moral principle, seems reliably to ensure compliance.

5. EXPLAINING VARIATION AMONG REGIMES

Students of international regimes need to understand not only the impact of regimes, but variations in their number, membership, strength, and scope; and differences among them in the property rights and rules that they prescribe.

5.1. *What Accounts for the Rise of International Regimes?*

The increase in the number of international regimes since 1945 is reflected in the growth in multilateral international organizations, which typically have regimes associated with them, from fewer than 100 in 1945 to about 200 by 1960 and over 600 by 1980 (Jacobson 1984). How should we account for this trend?

The institutionalist literature written in the 1980s took its cue from microeconomics, seeking to explain institutionalized cooperation by using the metaphor of supply and demand. In this view, regimes are supplied by states acting as 'political entrepreneurs who see a potential profit in organizing collaboration' (Keohane 1983: 155). Hegemonic states may have incentives to serve as entrepreneurs, but relatively small groups of states can also overcome collective action problems to do so (Snidal 1985). The key variable here is concentration of capability, as in Waltz's theory. Since capabilities became somewhat less concentrated among the advanced industrialized democracies after the 1950s, supply-explanations that emphasize the greater ease of collective action when a single hegemon predominates do not account for the proliferation of international regimes.[5]

At any rate, favourable conditions on the supply side—not

---

[5] Game-theoretical formulations such as Duncan Snidal's (1985), with their emphasis on strategic interaction and the role of k-groups, help to explain why expectations of discord drawn from naïve hegemonic stability theory were incorrect.

necessarily hegemony—could only be necessary conditions for the formation of international regimes. To obtain a fuller account, it is necessary to look at demand as well as supply. The most obvious source of variation in demands is changing interests, or preferences, of states. Preferences can be altered by changes in domestic political institutions or coalitions. For instance, Nazi Germany was less willing to enter into international arrangements in the 1930s than was its Weimar predecessor; and after Second World War, the Federal Republic of the 1950s was positively anxious to be included in arrangements that would have been anathema to the Nazis. As this example suggests, domestic political changes can either improve or worsen prospects for the formation of international regimes.

Preferences are also affected by variations in levels of interdependence. First, even if states were unitary decision-makers, their ability to attain their objectives would be affected by the actions of others. At higher levels of interdependence, the opportunity costs of not co-ordinating policy are greater, compared to the costs of sacrificing autonomy as a result of making binding agreements. The result can be expected to be higher demand for international agreements. Secondly, high levels of interdependence are likely to affect domestic political institutions and coalitions, and therefore the preferences of governments (Katzenstein 1985, Gourevitch 1986, Rogowski 1989, Karns and Mingst 1990).

Another source of change in the demand for regimes, in addition to rising levels of interdependence and changes in domestic politics, lies in the 'contractual environment' within which states operate. In the absence of appropriate institutions, the abilities of states to make agreements may be thwarted by externalities, uncertainty, informational asymmetries, and fears that partners will behave opportunistically. They may be unable to make credible commitments even to establish mutually beneficial arrangements. International regimes arise to resolve these problems, although if the barriers to information exchange are sufficiently high, such institutions may never be formed in the first place. If no contractual problems existed, no institutions would be needed, and if contractual problems were utterly severe, no institutions would be possible. For international regimes to be devised, contractual problems must be significant but not overwhelming.

To account for the increase in the number of international regimes, contractualists make two principal arguments:[6]

1. Regimes perform the functions of reducing uncertainty and the costs of carrying out transactions for their members; but institutions are themselves costly to create and maintain. As the number and importance of related issues within a given policy domain increase, the costs of creating new institutions will fall relative to the costs of inventing new rules and procedures for each issue that arises. In other words, increases in issue density will lead to a *demand for the creation of international regimes*.

2. International regimes that succeed in establishing relatively clear rules, which provide standards for judgement of behaviour, and stabilizing expectations, thus reducing uncertainty, will become valued and will therefore tend to create a *demand for the maintenance of international regimes* (Keohane 1984).

According to this line of argument, we should expect that a combination of increasing interdependence (leading to high levels of issue density) and success of existing institutions will tend to lead both to an expansion of institutional tasks and to an increase in the number of functioning international regimes.[7] If collective action dilemmas are serious, increases in the number of players and especially in the diffusion of capabilities among them will raise the costs of co-operation. However, international regimes may not suffer as a result; indeed, rules such as those in the GATT, limiting unconditional most-favoured-nation treatment to members, can be interpreted as institutional responses to collective action problems.

Although increasing interdependence and previous institutional success will tend to expand the tasks assumed by international regimes, this increase in activity will not be uniform across issue areas, since specific features of the environment will vary. In some

---

[6] In *After Hegemony* I referred to a 'functional theory' of international regimes. However, since that phrase carries connotations of sociological functionalism, with which I do not identify, I now use the language of 'contractualism' rather than 'functionalism'.

[7] In contrast to Volker Rittberger and Michael Zürn (1990: 29), who have stated that 'the functional theory of international regimes does not contribute to explaining regime formation', I believe that explaining regime formation is one of the most important contributions of this theory. The theory helps us to understand why increasing international interdependence has been associated with increasing numbers of international regimes.

cases rules may be self-enforcing; in others they may be enforceable with appropriate regimes; in still others no conceivable international arrangements will ensure compliance with inconvenient rules.

The contractual line of argument has many ramifications for different aspects of internationalism, as sketched in the sections below. However, it has only begun to be tested, and the results from case studies are mixed. International regimes often seem to reduce uncertainty and transaction costs, in response to rising interdependence (Keohane 1984, Oye 1986, Zacher 1987, Kapstein 1989). However, several case studies of regime change find contractual arguments insufficient to account for observed behaviour, arguing that the effects of regimes to which they point were insignificant (Moravcsik 1989), that ideological hegemony was important (Donnelly 1986), or that changes in states' conceptions of their preferences, as affected by transnational networks, were more important than contractual theories assume (Smith 1987, P. M. Haas 1990). It is difficult at this point to generalize about the relative importance of these contractual factors, as compared to the effects of shifts in the distribution of capabilities and changes in the interests or preferences of states, as shaped by changes in interdependence, interacting with domestic politics. There seems to be some merit in the contractual arguments, but effects predicted by these arguments are neither uniform nor overwhelmingly strong.

It is important to emphasize that sensible adherents of the contractual approach would propose it not as a *substitute* for the analysis of power, interests, or interdependence, but rather as a useful *supplement* to those traditional modes of political analysis.[8] I discuss it here not as a theoretical panacea but as a relatively novel way of throwing light on some puzzles of internationalism. It is particularly important that my discussion of contractualism should not be interpreted as implying that international institutional arrangements are 'optimal'.

In seeking to account for the increase in the number of international regimes, the contractual theorist will not ignore the structure of world power or domestic politics. But she should also

---

[8] As Ernst B. Haas (1964: 26–50) has emphasized, any clear separation between functional and power arguments is misleading.

expect to find an incremental pattern of change, promoted by officials of international organizations as well as by those of central governments: we should observe responses of regimes to problems involving externalities, uncertainty, and high costs of transactions. Increased interdependence should lead to intergovernmental attempts to promote co-operation, as in Europe during the 1980s.

5.2. What Explains Variations in Institutional Membership, Strength, and Scope?

In the world political economy, issues of trade have been more institutionalized than those of money, and much more so, at least on a global basis, than those involving oil. Some commodities, such as coffee, have been subject to elaborate international regimes; others have not. With respect to the physical environment, international regimes governing tanker discharges, fisheries in many areas of the open sea, and Antarctica have preceded comparable attempts to regulate deep-sea mining, transboundary flows of pollutants, including nuclear fallout, or actions that adversely affect the atmospheric ozone layer. Even among those areas in which international regulation takes place, differences exist in patterns of representation, secretariat autonomy, the status of experts, revenue base, voting, budgeting, the monitoring of compliance, and a variety of other organizational characteristics (E. B. Haas 1990: 65).

Different explanations of variation across issue areas could be devised. Analysts could focus on the distribution of power; on the preferences of states as affected by interdependence or domestic politics; on the contractual environment; or on some combination of these factors. Even for the same states, domestic politics differs across issue areas; and the states that are involved in different issue areas are not the same. Thus complementary interests in one area may contrast with conflicting interests in another as a result of differences in domestic politics. The distribution of capabilities and the intensity of interdependence differ across issue areas. Contractual environments also vary: externalities, uncertainty, and transaction costs differ from one issue area to another. I emphasize contractual theories here in the hope of making some useful points that might otherwise be overlooked.

Institutional Membership

Different international institutions apply different criteria for membership. Two questions differentiate the major situations. (1) Is membership in principle open to all states within a certain geographical area that accept certain general principles and rules, or is it explicitly limited on the basis of domestic political arrangements or as a function of selection by present members? (2) If the former, how rigorously do members employ the criteria embedded in the rules?

Restricted institutions (e.g. NATO, OPEC, OECD, EC) deliberately limit membership to a relatively small number of states that have some set of interests in common, or that have specified domestic political arrangements. The rationale for these institutions, as traditionally constituted, would disappear were their memberships to become universal. *Conditionally open institutions* (e.g. the IMF, GATT, the GATT codes) are open in principle to states that are willing to accept a set of prescribed commitments, which not all states may be able (much less willing) to make. Conditionally open institutions adopt measures to exclude nonproviders from benefits secured by co-operation. For instance, major GATT members, during the Tokyo Round of the 1970s, perceived that they could benefit from agreements on a number of specific issues, such as government procurement and subsidies, but that many GATT members would not make commitments to provide benefits (e.g. open markets for foreign suppliers and transparency and limitation of export-promoting subsidies) on these issues. They therefore agreed to codes open to all GATT members, but they sought to limit their benefits to those countries that adhered to the obligations of the codes. *Open institutions* such as the United Nations can be joined by all sovereign states, with the exception perhaps of pariah states, with minimal further requirements for membership. Some institutions that were originally conceived of as conditionally open, requiring commitments and a certain form of government, such as the United Nations (which initially excluded defeated enemies and certain states considered fascist, such as Franco's Spain), have become open institutions; others that began as open, such as certain fisheries regimes, have become only conditionally open (Young 1989a: 51).

International institutions of all three types are doubtless

constructed to help states achieve their interests. I would suggest, consistent with a contractual perspective, that the differences in form among them are closely connected with differences in function. Restricted institutions either seek to achieve gains *vis-à-vis* outsiders (a function for which there must be outsiders to exploit) or to build strong bonds of community (requiring similar political systems). They arise for the former reason when states perceive unexploited opportunities in their relationships with potential adversaries, whether in security or economic affairs. The heart of the original peace and security provisions of the United Nations Charter, Chapter VII on 'action with respect to threats to the peace, breaches of the peace, and acts of aggression', not only places responsibility for enforcement on the Security Council (a restricted institution), but proposes the establishment of a Military Staff Committee and the earmarking of national contingents for 'combined international enforcement action'. At this time, the United Nations was partly designed as a way to co-ordinate against a revival of the fascist challenge. In 1948 the future NATO states discerned unexploited opportunities in their relationship with the Soviet Union. OPEC perceived comparable opportunities at its formation in 1960 and especially during the 1970s: greater cohesion, it was thought, could produce higher oil prices or maintain the high prices already attained. The European Community uses its enhanced bargaining power to exploit opportunities with its trading partners, and also seeks to build community among its own membership. Whatever else they do, restricted institutions engage in *cartelization*.

Conditionally open institutions are designed largely to cope with the problems of insufficient contributions, or 'free-riding', associated with problems of collective action. In a word, they are designed to foster *collaboration*. If no price were imposed for membership in such institutions, co-operation would be highly suboptimal, since contributors would not receive reciprocal benefits from the free-riders, and would therefore reduce their own contributions. To achieve either specific (tit-for-tat) reciprocity, or diffuse reciprocity in which benefits do not depend on specific quid pro quo, some conditions for membership are essential. The original conception of the United Nations, in which opposition to fascism was a condition for membership, reflects this conception of conditional openness. To understand the value of charging a 'price for admission', consider what would happen to GATT if states were asked to abide by rules of non-discrimination without the assurance that their trading partners would do so!

Open institutions serve as fora for the exchange of opinions, but the benefits that members are willing to confer on each other are limited owing to the difficulty of enforcing rules, or ensuring reciprocity in concessions. Open institutions arise when none of the three principal reasons for limitation—the desire to exploit unexploited opportunities *vis-à-vis* adversaries, the search for community, and the need to control free-rider problems—is compelling. Open institutions may be useful in pure co-ordination games, but are unlikely to be very effective in situations requiring collaboration or suasion.[9] In general, the activities of open institutions are likely to be limited principally to symbolic issues and to operations involving relatively small quantities of resources. In so far as significant resources are allocated by open institutions, informal means of controlling those institutions will be used to circumvent the organization's nominal decision-making practices. Open institutions controlled by the entire membership are normally limited to the function of *consultation*.

The Strength of International Regulation

In a pioneering paper, Brent Sutton and Mark Zacher (1988) ask a question that has not been given sufficient attention: what is regulated internationally and what is not regulated internationally in the world, and why? They use theories of market failure, uncertainty, and transaction costs to account for variations in the degree of regulation of specific issues within the general domain of international shipping. Across areas such as international shipping services, financial transactions, market access, liability for damages, and crime, there is substantial variation in the extent to which regulation occurs (Zacher 1990).

Vinod Aggarwal (1985: 20) focuses on a similar variable, which

---

[9] Players in co-ordination games may prefer different outcomes but have no incentives to diverge from existing equilibria, and enforcement institutions are therefore unnecessary. Such institutions are essential, however, to ensure continued co-operation in collaboration games. Suasion games often involve attempts by dissatisfied players to link other issues to the issue in question, through promises or threats (Martin 1992).

he calls the 'strength' of an international regime, referring to 'the stringency with which rules regulate the behavior of countries'. Extreme 'weakness' of a regime denotes lack of regulation in the Sutton–Zacher sense. Aggarwal seeks to specify changes in the strength of international textile regimes between 1950 and the early 1980s, and to account, chiefly on the basis of international and domestic structure, for variations in the strength of these regimes, particularly what he sees as the precipitous decline of the Multifibre Arrangement after 1977.

The most extensive and sophisticated efforts to explain which issues are regulated through international institutions were undertaken by students of regional political integration in the 1960s and early 1970s. They developed a highly differentiated and sophisticated conception of integration, which is related to the 'strength' of regimes but which is explicitly multidimensional. These scholars not only sought to assess the descriptive argument that European politics was becoming more centralized and less subject to veto by individual states, but tried to account for inter-regional variation in the success of integrative efforts (Nye 1971, Lindberg and Scheingold 1970).

The reinvigoration of the European Community with the Single European Act and current discussions of a loosely defined 'political union' have begun to prompt renewed attention to processes of political integration. The European Community is becoming an example of the 'pooling and sharing of sovereignty', described well neither by the metaphor of 'co-operation under anarchy'—since the elaborate networks of rules, obligations, and organizations are far from anarchic—nor by the image of centralization implicit in the concept of political integration (Keohane and Hoffmann 1991). Yet as an international institution it is *sui generis*, characterized by more diffuse reciprocity, and greater mutual influence on members' policies, than the typical international regime. More research is needed to understand the political dynamics that made European regimes, centred on the European Community, so much stronger than other international regimes, even to the extent of eroding the sovereignty of politically and administratively capable member states.

The Scope of International Regimes

The political integration literature also directs our attention to variations in the policy scope of international regimes. We observe substantial variation in the scope of international regimes, ranging from narrowly regional to global. Such variation is apparent on such diverse issues as trade, currency areas, shipping, and regulation of the physical environment. Consider, for example, the natural resource regimes studied by Oran R. Young. International regimes are often quite narrowly regional: Young mentions the North Pacific halibut regime, the Fraser River salmon regime, and the North Pacific fur seal regime. Yet global regimes have also been instituted, as is the case for whaling.

Young (1989*a*: 121 ff.) suggests from a normative standpoint that the optimal size of a regional authority for natural resources should reflect costs and benefits. Relatively small regional organizations avoid serious collective action problems and can tailor their rules to the specific conditions of the area; at some point in their expansion, transaction costs will tend to rise more rapidly than is justified by the gains of increased size, such as economies of scale and the internalization of externalities within a regime. Young is using what I have called a contractual approach to make a normative point, but the point is also relevant to explanation: if we assume calculating rationality by actors, we can expect that actual arrangements will *roughly* correspond to this cost-benefit logic. One worthwhile way to evaluate the validity of contractual arguments would be to see whether they could explain variations in the scope of institutionalized internationalism across issue areas.

5.3. What Accounts for Variations in Property Rights and Rules?

Ernst Haas (1990: 2) has observed that 'all international organizations are deliberately designed by their founders to 'solve problems' that require collaborative action for a solution'. Problems are solved by international regimes largely by creating rights and rules: as Young (1989*a*: 15) has argued, 'the core of every international regime is a cluster of rights and rules, [whose] exact content is a matter of intense interest to these actors'. People who construct regimes have purposes in doing so, and the rights and rules of regimes reflect visions of what sorts of behaviour should be encouraged or proscribed. International regimes vary in their purposes even within issue areas, as is illustrated by the contrast between GATT's espousal of non-discriminatory trade and UNCTAD's emphasis on special privileges for developing countries. The content of the rights and rules of international regimes changes over time. Even if we understood why certain areas of activity are regulated while others are not, and the strength and scope of international regimes, we would not fully comprehend international regimes unless we had some insights into the purposes that they are meant to serve (Ruggie 1983*b*, 1991*a*, Nau 1990).

The purposes of international regimes have not only changed over time; they vary across issue areas in the extent to which they are designed to support, supplement, or supplant a world market economy. International arrangements to maintain currency convertibility, the GATT regime limiting the rights of states to impose restrictions on trade, and international legal regimes providing for enforcement of contracts, support the market. Lending by the World Bank or the IMF to developing countries and arrangements such as the Multifibre Arrangement in textile trade modify market arrangements. Proposals for a New International Economic Order or for an authoritative regime to control extraction of seabed minerals would have supplanted market mechanisms with authoritative allocation, involving either political allocation of resources or limitations on the rights of non-state actors.

Purposes matter, but so do power and history. Stephen D. Krasner (1985) has shown that variations in access to rule-making, and the leverage provided by state sovereignty, help to account for differences in the rules of international economic regimes. In what could be called an 'archaeological' approach to international regimes, Judith Goldstein (1986) has emphasized the extent to which contemporary international regimes reflect the views of dominant states at the time of their founding. Social scientists need to look not only at the purposes of contemporary leaders of states, but also at the power of access, and the weight of the past, to understand the content of contemporary international regimes.

6. CONCLUSIONS

International regimes have been the subject, during the last decade, of substantial research in the United States, and increasingly in

Europe. Yet there are still huge gaps in our knowledge. We do not have very much solid scientific knowledge about the sources of change in international institutions over time, or the causes of variation across issue areas. We need to keep inquiring, first of all, about the impact of regimes on states' capabilities and preferences, and therefore on their policies. It is also intriguing to ask why international regimes have become so much more numerous; why their institutional arrangements—including membership, strength, and scope—vary so much; and what accounts for variations in the rights and rules that they establish.

A good deal of thinking has already been done about international regimes, although we hardly have well-specified theories. Approaches that could be useful for explaining variations among issue areas and international institutions include neo-realist arguments stressing relative state capabilities; arguments about interdependence and domestic politics, separately or together; contractual theories emphasizing responses to externalities, uncertainty, and transaction costs; and models of organizational adaptation and learning. None of these perspectives has established itself as superior, but all contain promising elements. To evaluate these theories systematically, investigators require a common definition of the concept 'international regime' and a consistent empirical methodology. Such a definition, and methodology, are now shared across the Atlantic. The next step will be to elaborate comparable categories for analysis so that generalizations about international regimes can be tested with evidence from many cases, gathered by investigators from a variety of countries, with different geographical and normative perspectives. Then we will be *en route* to a genuinely transnational, and social scientific, research programme to help us understand international regimes, and broader patterns of co-operation and discord, in a world characterized by astonishing change.

PART II

Conceptual and Theoretical Problems of Regime Analysis

3

International Society and the Study of Regimes

A Reflective Approach

ANDREW HURRELL

1. INTRODUCTION

This chapter seeks to place the growth of the undoubtedly US-dominated literature on regime theory within the broader tradition of thought on the existence of international society. This tradition was in many ways a distinctively European one whose central expression lay in the emergence of ideas about the role and function of international law. More recently it has come to be associated with the work of such writers as Martin Wight and Hedley Bull. This chapter addresses three questions: First, what does regime theory tell us about co-operation in international life that theories of international society do not? Second, to what extent can ideas about international law and society illuminate some of the weaknesses of regime theory? And third, to what extent, if at all, does this analysis suggest areas for further research?

2. THE CORE PROBLEM

Regime theory cannot be described as a fad, as is sometimes alleged by its critics, because its central question is one which has

I would like to thank Volker Rittberger, William Wallace, Iver Neumann, and Lars-Erik Cederman for their comments on an earlier version of this chapter.

been fundamental to the evolution of western thought about international relations: how is co-operation possible between states claiming sovereignty but competing for power and influence in a situation of anarchy? Equally the search for origins is not about finding earlier uses of the term 'regimes', but rather about tracing similarities and differences between the multiple answers that have been given to this basic question. The idea that co-operation between states was indeed possible and that some form of international society could indeed exist has been a persistent theme of European thought and is extremely deep-rooted. The academic study of international relations is often presented as being founded on the fundamental difference between domestic 'society' and international 'anarchy'. Yet one of the most striking features of European thought before 1914 was just how few theorists actually accepted such a dichotomy. Indeed the distortions produced by such a rigid dichotomy and by the parallel bifurcation of theorists into realist or idealist camps have become a theme of much recent writing (Walker 1987, Ashley 1988). It was perhaps only the extreme nature of post-war US realism that produced a situation in which co-operation came to be seen as an 'anomaly' in need of explanation.

But confusion has also arisen in the writings of those who have attempted to derive and explore an international society tradition. Thus, for example, Bull's use of the term 'Grotian' was applied in two quite distinct senses and (except in an early paper first written in the 1950s and published in 1966) he never systematically explored the differences between various conceptions of international society.[1] His central purpose was to contrast the Grotian tradition with a Hobbesian, or realist, tradition on one side, and with a Kantian, or cosmopolitan, tradition on the other. Yet the positions with which the Grotian tradition is contrasted turn out on closer inspection to be concerned with many of the same

---

[1] Bull (1977: 322) used the term 'Grotian' in two senses: first, to describe the doctrine that there is such a thing as international society; and, second, to contrast the solidarist conception of international society from the more pluralist Vattelian conception. The distinction between the solidarist and pluralist conceptions is laid out in his 'The Grotian Conception of International Society' (Bull 1966). One important feature of Bull's later work is the move away from the pluralist/realist positions dominant in *The Anarchical Society* and towards a more genuinely 'Grotian' position (Bull 1983). For a thorough discussion of the Grotian tradition and the problems raised by it see Bull, Kingsbury, and Roberts (1990).

themes and, at times, to be making many similar arguments. Thus the past decade has seen the recasting of Hobbes, picking up the argument made nearly thirty years ago by Stanley Hoffmann (1965: 61) that Hobbes should be viewed as 'the founder of utilitarian theories of international law and relations'. Increasingly Hobbes has been viewed as a precursor of precisely those theorists who seek to construct models of co-operation, and indeed of justice, based on rational prudence (Bull 1981, Hanson 1984, Gauthier 1986). Indeed, for both Bull himself, just as for earlier theorists such as Pufendorf, Wolff, and Vattel, the first stage in the argument in favour of international society consists in the application of Hobbes's own arguments about the differences between domestic and international life: that states are less vulnerable than individuals and have less fear of sudden death; that they are unequal in power and resources; and that, if they are rational, they will be less tempted to destroy each other than will individuals in a state of nature and will be able to develop at least minimal rules of coexistence based on self-interest and rational prudence (Bull 1977: 46–51). On the other side, there is a good deal to justify the view of Kant not as a cosmopolitan intent on fostering a global society of mankind, but as a 'statist', deeply committed to the creation of a law-governed international society between sovereign states (Hurrell 1990).

It is also the case that modern discussions of regime theory and older ideas about international society have to come to terms with the same essential problematic: what is the relationship between law and norms on the one hand and power and interests on the other? The difficulties here are twofold. On one side, there have always been those who claim that the rules and norms of international life are purely reflective of the power and interests of states: they are just power politics translated into a different idiom, 'a record of the methods and results of power politics' (Donelan 1990: 36). Classical international law was always susceptible to this line of attack because of the role of custom and practice in the creation of legal rules and because of the extent to which it accepted almost all of what states actually did: thus treaties under duress were valid; there was no restraint on the right to wage war; successful conquest was accepted as legitimate; and the definition of state sovereignty gave no place to self-determination or the rights of citizens.

This line of criticism has been very common and unites liberals, realists, and Marxists. Thus, liberals from Kant onwards have bemoaned the role of the 'sorry comforters' such as Grotius, Pufendorf, and Vattel in legitimizing the immoral and aggressive actions of states. For realists such as E. H. Carr, the fine language of law and morality was merely a rationalization and a cloak for the particular interests of a particular group of states who happened to have a vested interest in protecting the status quo. For Carr (1981: 87, 88), supposedly abstract and universal legal and moral norms were merely 'the unconscious reflexions of national policy based on a particular interpretation of national interests at a particular time', or the 'transparent disguises of selfish vested interests'. Such a position follows very closely the traditional Marxist view of law, including international law, as reflecting the class interests of a particular group or group of states.[2] These kinds of arguments are reflected in many of the most common criticisms of regime theory. On the one hand, the perspective of critical theory that it is inherently conservative, statist, and technocratic (Cox 1986, Ashley 1981, M. Hoffman 1989). On the other, the general structuralist position that rules and norms are a direct reflection of power and interest. Crudely put, one is better off studying underlying power structures than wasting time on surface phenomena (Strange 1983).

Yet, if one danger arose from the possibility that norms and rules might be purely reflective of state interests and might therefore have no independent compliance pull in themselves, then there has always been an equal and opposite danger: that the norms and rules of international life are so far away from the power political 'realities' that their study becomes an empty and formalistic exercise, well captured by the derogatory force of the term 'legalistic'. There was certainly a clear need to get away from two of the central preoccupations of progressivist international lawyers: first, the idea that constitution-making would in itself enable states to live together in a more harmonious and peaceful manner—Clark and Sohn's (1958) *World Peace through World Law* being a clear exemplar; and second, the preoccupation with enforcement or with finding some functional equivalent for

[2] Nevertheless, it is important to stress the extent to which Soviet policy came to accept the positive role of international law as providing an essential framework for coexistence and the 'co-ordination of wills'.

enforcement (hence the idealist obsession with collective security). It was of course precisely against this tendency that the regime theorists were reacting. On the one hand, there was the need to achieve maximum distance from such perceived formalism and from anything tainted by the sins of idealism. On the other, to be academically credible, ideas of co-operation had to take into account the harsher and more Hobbesian world of the early 1980s, the structuralist turn in the overall direction of international relations theory, and the need to achieve as much theoretical rigour as the other social sciences had purportedly been able to do. Whilst the nature of this reaction is understandable within the context of the evolution of the discipline, it is hard to avoid the conclusion that the rejection of international law was too absolute and all-encompassing.

The central problem, then, for regime theorists and international lawyers is to establish that laws and norms exercise a compliance pull of their own, at least partially independent of the power and interests which underpinned them and which were often responsible for their creation (Koskenniemi 1989: ch. 1). To avoid empty tautology it is necessary to show not only that rules exist and that they are created and obeyed primarily out of self-interest or expediency, but also that they are followed even in cases when a state's self-interest seems to suggest otherwise. Whilst arguments about regime creation are important, it is this fundamental question that lies at the heart of the matter: do regimes make a difference? If so, how, why, and to what degree? On the one hand, the rules of a system that depends on self-enforcement must be sufficiently close to the power and interests of states if they are to have any meaningful political impact. Thus Oscar Schachter (1982: 26, 25) argues that international law is 'a product of political and social forces, that it is dependent on behaviour and that it is an instrument to meet changing needs and values'. But on the other side, it 'is in essence a system based on a set of rules and obligations. They must in some degree be binding, that is, the rules must be accepted as a means of independent control that effectively limits the conduct of the entities subject to law.' If their political impact is to be significant, international norms cannot be the automatic and immediate reflection of self-interest. There has to be some notion of being bound by a particular rule despite countervailing self-interest.

Despite their lack of interaction, this central question is one which unites regime theorists and international lawyers.[3] Indeed their mutual concerns have in many ways grown closer. On the one hand, many lawyers have come to view international treaties and conventions over such matters as the environment, not as a definitive and unchanging set of rules, but rather as a means of creating law-making frameworks. Their purpose is to provide a framework for negotiation in which the techniques and general principles of international law can be employed, first to negotiate and formalize accepted but very general principles, and second to create a means of facilitating ongoing negotiations from which more specific, 'harder' rules may subsequently emerge (Birnie 1992). On the other, regime theorists such as Robert Keohane appear to have become less interested in the rather generalized definitions of regimes and more concerned with the need to focus on specific sets of rules.[4] Take, for instance, the definition of regimes given by Stephen Krasner in 1983: 'implicit or explicit principles, norms, rules, and decision-making procedures around which actors' expectations converge in a given area of international relations' (Krasner 1983*a*: 2). And compare this with Keohane's 1989 definition: 'institutions with explicit rules, agreed upon by governments, which pertain to particular sets of issues in international relations' (Keohane 1989*a*: 4). The apparently growing stress on explicit, persistent, and connected sets of rules brings regime theory and international law much closer together.[5]

3. THE DIFFERENCES BETWEEN REGIME THEORY AND INTERNATIONAL LAW

Perhaps the most important difference that marks regime theory from international law and older notions of international society concerns the reasons why states obey rules that are usually

---

[3] For exceptions to the lack of interaction between regime theorists and international lawyers see Kratochwil (1989) and Onuf (1989).

[4] It is worth recalling, however, that one of the claims to originality and innovation of regime theory was precisely that it included patterns of co-operation that were embodied neither in formal international organizations nor in specific sets of legal rules.

[5] The definitional issue is also addressed by Keohane in Ch. 2, sect. 3, above.

unenforced and mostly unenforceable. There have been many answers to this question: power and coercion, self-interest and reciprocal benefits, institutionalized habit or inertia, the existence of a sense of community, procedural legitimacy of the process of rule creation, or the moral suasion that derives from a shared sense of justice. Previous explanations of co-operation have often tended to produce an aggregate list of these kinds of factors without providing any precise guide as to their interrelationship. This was one of the most common criticisms of Bull's work.

Regime theory seeks above all to be far more discriminating and to try and derive testable hypotheses about which factors explain co-operation under which conditions and in what circumstances. Regime theory has certainly examined the role of power and there has, of course, been a heated debate over the role of power and, in particular, hegemonic power in the creation and maintenance of regimes. Leaning towards realism, regime theorists stress the close connections that exist between the emergence of institutions and the distribution of power. But it is a cardinal feature of rationalist regime theory that power alone cannot explain the emergence or impact of institutions. Whilst the steam may be running out of the hegemonic stability debate, the role of power and coercion in the *implementation* of rules remains fundamental. For international lawyers the idea of decentralized sanctions, whether in the form of direct retaliation or actions by third parties, has always been one way of maintaining the belief that all legal systems need to be backed by some coercive power (an idea particularly associated with Hans Kelsen). And, for all the undoubted importance of functional benefits and 'learning', sanctions and coercion continue to play a major role: think of the role played by the 'carrot' of aid and technology transfer and of the 'stick' of trade sanctions in the recent negotiations of the ozone regime. Regime theory has also considered the role of habit or inertia, for instance in explaining why regimes persist after the conditions that underpinned their emergence have long since changed.

But it remains the case that regime theory's most distinctive contribution is to have developed the idea of self-interest and reciprocal benefits and, in general, to have downplayed the traditional emphasis placed on the role of community and a sense of justice. The central challenge was to explain the emergence of co-operation on the basis of realist assumptions—that states are self-interested actors competing in a world of anarchy, that co-operation need not depend on altruism, that it can develop from the calculations of instrumentally rational actors.

International cooperation does not necessarily depend on altruism, personal honor, common purposes, internalized norms, or a shared belief in a set of values embodied in a culture. At various times and places any of these features of human motivation may indeed play an important role in processes of international cooperation; *but cooperation can be understood without reference to any of them* [my emphasis] (Keohane 1988: 380)

The core claim is that regimes are created and that states obey the rules embodied in them because of the functional benefits that they provide. The understanding of co-operation on realist assumptions also explains why labelling becomes tricky and why it is often hard—at least for a European—to separate the 'neo-realist' from the 'neo-liberal institutionalist'.

Functional benefits have always formed one part of explanations for the existence of co-operation between states. They lie at the heart of Vattel's (1758: xiv) conception of the 'voluntary law of nations', as that law is 'deducible from the natural liberty of nations, from the attention due to their common safety, from the nature of their mutual correspondence, [and] from their reciprocal duties'. Hume's description of the emergence of convention and co-operation within domestic society also provides a powerful statement of this idea:

I observe, that it will be for my interest to leave another in the possession of his goods, provided he will act in the same manner with regard to me. He is sensible of a like interest in the regulation of his conduct. When this common sense of interest is mutually expressed, and is known to both, it produces a suitable resolution and behaviour. And this may properly enough be called a convention or agreement betwixt us, though without the imposition of a promise; since the actions of each of us have a reference to those of the other, and are performed upon the supposition that something is to be performed on the other part . . . repeated experience of the inconveniences of transgressing [the convention] . . . assures us still more that the sense of interest has become common to all our fellows, and gives us confidence of the future regularity of their conduct; and it is only on the expectation of this that our moderation and abstinence are founded (Hume (1739) in Cohen 1981: 15)

In addition, many international law textbooks have described the role of international law in predominantly functionalist or purposive terms (Coplin 1966, Schwarzenberger and Brown 1966). Almost all accounts of the role of law describe its political impact in terms of the benefits of order, the costs of violation, and the extent to which it provides an order based on the co-ordination of interests and of patterned expectations. What regimes theorists have done is to give this general idea a much greater degree of specificity and coherence. In the first place regime theory seeks to specify far more precisely what the functional benefits provided by rules and institutions actually are. It stresses their impact in overcoming the assurance problem and affecting the pattern of costs by means of the reduction of uncertainty; the facilitation of communication; the promotion of learning; and the transmission of knowledge and information. Secondly, regime theory seeks to demonstrate in far tighter and more rigorous terms how co-operative behaviour can arise between self-interested actors and thereby to specify the conditions which facilitate the emergence of rules and institutions (for instance the impact of different numbers of players, the importance of issue density and linkage strategies, the critical role of knowledge and information).[6] Its objective has been to move down from generalized discussion of international society to the detailed understanding of the conditions applicable to specific institutions.

4. THE WEAKNESSES OF REGIME THEORY

But the gains have also involved losses and doubts remain whether a sufficiently wide range of factors that explain the dynamics of co-operation can be captured within the terms of rationalist models. Indeed it is interesting to note how many of the criticisms of regime theory that have appeared during the 1980s have involved the re-emergence of older ideas or, at least, the picking up of older, if often unresolved, arguments.

---

[6] For recent, game-theoretically informed developments in this field see Ch. 6, sect. 2, below.

4.1. *Specific Legal Rules and the Broader Structure of the International System*

The first issue concerns the relationship of specific bargains and bargaining processes to the broader international context and to the broader structures of the international system. Now, from one perspective, moves in this direction open up problems for neo-institutionalist approaches to co-operation built on explicitly rationalist foundations. The problem here is that inter-state bargaining is notoriously concerned with relative gains and with the distribution of the costs and benefits of co-operation. It may be true that states have an interest in co-operation in order to maximize their absolute gains. But the competitive and anarchical structure of the state system reinforces concern with the impact of co-operation on a state's relative power political and economic position. States are positional rather than atomistic actors and are often deterred from entering into co-operative arrangements if these entail negative implications for their relative power position.

This argument has been revived recently by Joseph Grieco (1988) but echoes a deep-rooted tradition in realist and mercantilist thought. To quote Rousseau (1782: 160):

Let us add finally that, though the advantages resulting to commerce from a great and lasting peace are in themselves certain and indisputable, still, being common to all States, they will be appreciated by none. For such advantages make themselves felt only by contrast, and he who wishes to increase his relative power is bound to seek only such gains as are exclusive.

The neo-institutionalist response is to argue that their theories take relative gains into account and indeed are based on competitive behaviour between states keenly interested in the distribution of the pie. On this view, states bargain fiercely over the distribution of the costs and benefits of co-operation, but will ultimately accept a settlement which advances their own individual utility. The critics, however, argue more than this, namely that utility is always fundamentally interdependent and that the high degree of 'envy' that exists between states will undermine rationalist models of co-operation.

In an important sense the realist critics overreach themselves. States are not inherently and immutably positional actors obsessed with relative gains under all circumstances (Snidal 1991). The point here, however, is to highlight the way in which the broader structure of the international system, and in particular of the international legal system, can work to overcome this problem. A good deal of the compliance pull of international rules derives from the relationship between individual rules and the broader pattern of international relations: states follow specific rules, even when inconvenient, because they have a longer-term interest in the maintenance of law-impregnated international community. It is within this broader context that ideas about reputation are most powerful and most critical. This can, to a certain extent, be captured by ideas of 'lengthening the shadow of the future', by broadening notions of self-interest and reciprocity, and by trying to trace precisely the processes by which reputation matters. But, as the concern for reputation becomes more generalized and diffuse, it also becomes harder to measure and assess. More importantly, rationalist models of co-operation miss the crucial link between the costs and benefits of specific legal rules and the role of international law as constitutive of the structure of the state system itself—and, one might add, its role as provider of the legal underpinnings of the capitalist world economy, in terms of both detailed rules and fundamental assumptions.

Individual legal rules are important because of their relationship to the legal structure of the state system. As Tom Franck (1990: 196) has put it: 'Nations, or those who govern them, recognize that the obligation to comply is owed by them to the community of states as the reciprocal of that community's validation of their nation's statehood.' The functional benefits of specific rules are, therefore, only one part of the picture. An essential element is the legitimacy of rules which derives from the common sense of being part of a legal community and which serves as the crucial link between the procedural rules of state behaviour and the structural principles which define the character of the system and the identity of the players. Of course the 'power of legitimacy' varies enormously according to the rule and issue involved and such considerations are only one element in decision-making. But they can be an important element. For weak states the achievement of external legal recognition and acceptance as a member of the 'club' is very often a crucial determinant of who holds power domestically: think of the direct political impact of international recognition in cases of civil war or secession. Equally, restraints on intervention and the use of force provide weak states with some measure of external protection. For weak states, then, the legal conventions of sovereignty and the fabric of the international legal order bolster their very ability to maintain themselves as 'states' and provide a powerful incentive to take legal rules seriously, although not always to follow them (Jackson 1987). Just as the structural realists argue that states are 'socialized' into the game of power politics whatever their domestic systems or the inclinations of their leaders, so a parallel process is in operation in the workings of the international legal order. As the newly independent states of the developing world discovered, the acceptance of the basic structures of international law was a necessary corollary of their assertion of independence and their claim to be treated as a sovereign state.

On the other side, rich and powerful states have a double reason for accepting the principles of the legal order. First, such states have a disproportionate stake in maintaining the stability of the status quo, from which they clearly benefit. Second, they have a disproportionate influence over the content and application of international legal rules. As Oscar Schachter (1982: 28) puts it:

International law must also be seen as the product of historical experience in which power and the 'relation of forces' are determinants. Those States with power (i.e. the ability to control outcomes contested by others) will have a disproportionate and often decisive influence in determining the content of rules and their application in practice. Because this is the case, international law, in a broad sense, both reflects and sustains the existing political order and distribution of power.

Once states see themselves as having a long-term interest in participating in an international legal system, then the idea of obligation and the normativity of rules can be given concrete form and can acquire a degree of distance from the immediate interests or preferences of states. Within this society, law exists but is no longer seen to depend on the command of the sovereign. Law is rather the symbol of the idea of being bound and voluntarily accepting a sense of obligation. It is not based on external sanctions or the threat of them but is based rather on the existence of shared interests, of shared values, and of patterned expectations. It is a law of co-ordination rather than subordination. The nature of obligation and the validity and applicability of specific rules can be adduced within the context of the legal system and with reference to the relevant principles, treaties, etc. Being a political system, states will seek to interpret obligations to their own advantage. But being a legal system that is built on the consent of other parties, they will be constrained by the necessity of justifying their actions in legal terms. It is for these reasons that it is important to make a clearer distinction than is common in regime theory between specifically legal rules and the workings of the legal system within which they operate on the one hand, and the wide variety of other formal and informal norms and rules and the processes of negotiation, bargaining, or imposition that underpin them on the other.[7]

4.2. Sense of Community and the Emergence of Co-Operation

The second issue also concerns the importance of a sense of community, but stresses the moral rather than legal dimension. Rationalist models of co-operation may indeed explain how co-operation is possible once the parties have come to believe that they form part of a shared project or community in which there is a common interest that can be furthered by co-operative behaviour. But they neglect the potential barriers that can block the emergence of such a shared project—perhaps because regime theory has been so dominated by understanding co-operation between liberal developed states that enjoy a compatibility of major values and a common conceptualization of such basic concepts as 'order', 'justice', 'state', 'law', 'contract', etc. Robert Axelrod (1984: ch. 4), for example, takes the example of the 'spontaneous' co-operation that arose between the trenches in the First World War. This does indeed show how informal co-operation can emerge in an unpromising situation on the basis of a tit-for-tat strategy. But to what extent did such co-operation not rest upon a prior mutual acceptance of some minimal sense of community and of the other side as legitimate players? Where no such sense of community exists and where one side is convinced that the other has no moral status (or a heavily unequal one), then formal and informal

---

[7] A similar point is made by Kratochwil in Ch. 4, sect. 3, below.

co-operation is unlikely to emerge. The pursuit of holy wars against the infidel, the barbarous behaviour of the imperialist powers in their treatment of indigenous peoples, and the savagery of the fighting on the Eastern Front in the Second World War provide striking examples of where the absence of any shared sense of community has worked to undermine co-operative limitations on conflict based on reciprocity and self-interest.

Once there is a common identification of, and commitment to, some kind of moral community (however minimalist in character) within which perceptions of potential common interest can emerge, then there may indeed be prudential reasons for the players collectively to co-operate. But rational prudence alone cannot explain the initiation of the game, why each player individually might choose to begin to co-operate.[8] This problem might be solved by coercion or the role of a hegemonic power. Or it might be solved by some pre-existing sense of community embodying some common moral purpose.

For many of the classical theorists of international society, this problem was overcome by reliance on the obligations of natural law. For Grotius both the sources and obligatory force of law rested heavily on its natural law foundations. By the time of Vattel, the balance had altered. For Vattel positive law had become the central means of regulating international life in a manner consistent with the realities of the age of *raison d'état*. At the same time, however, the untrammelled freedom of states continued to be balanced by a belief in the residual obligations and restraints derived from natural law. Indeed it is this ultimately unconvincing balance between the voluntary and necessary law of nations that lies at the heart of Vattel's system of law.

For the modern theorists of international society, the problem is recognized but the solution remains ambiguous. The stress on forming part of society or community was one of the most characteristic features of Bull's and Wight's work. Thus for Martin Wight (1966: 96–7), international society

is manifest in the diplomatic system; in the conscious maintenance of the balance of power to preserve the independence of the member

---

[8] I owe this point to Ian Gambles, whose forthcoming doctoral thesis on ethics and modern realism sheds much light on the issues discussed in this section.

communities; in the regular operations of international law whose binding force is accepted over a wide though politically unimportant range of subjects; in economic, social and technical interdependence and the functional international institutions established latterly to regulate it. *All these presuppose an international social consciousness, a world wide community sentiment.* [my emphasis]

For Bull (1977: 13) the subjective sense of being bound by a community was the cornerstone of his definition of international society:

A *society of states* (or international society) exists when a group of states, conscious of certain common interests and common values, form a society in the sense that they conceive themselves to be bound by a common set of rules in their relations with one another and share in the workings of common institutions.

Bull wants to reject any natural law foundations, or, at least, to develop some empirical equivalent to natural law, some set of general principles without which no society could be said to exist —the influence of H. L. A. Hart (1961) is important here. The aim is to identify a conception of international society consistent with self-interest and with the realities of power. Yet, at the same time, there was the awareness that international society could not be understood solely in these terms and had to be rooted within the cultural and historical forces that had helped shape the consciousness of society and had moulded perceptions of common values and common purposes. In other words the dominant line of Bull's thought was to follow Wight (1966: 96): 'International society, then, on this view, can be properly described only in historical and sociological depth.' Great stress was therefore laid on culture and the sense of common interest that developed historically within and across different societies. According to Bull, a common cultural tradition contributes to international society in three ways. First, the existence of a common epistemology, a common language, and a common cultural tradition will facilitate communication between the members of international society. Second, the existence of such a common culture reinforces the bonds of common interest by adding a sense of moral obligation. Third, the existence of a common value system will help ensure that states place the same relative valuation on such objectives as order, justice, peace, etc.[9]

This conception of international co-operation can be related to the arguments of Kratochwil and Ruggie (1986) that international regimes are necessarily intersubjective phenomena whose existence and validity is created and sustained in the interrelationship of their subjects. As they have suggested, the problem is that such a view is at odds with the epistemological positivism of mainstream rationalist regime analysis. It suggests the need for a hermeneutic or interpretivist methodology that seeks to re-create the historical and social processes by which rules and norms are constituted and a sense of obligation engendered. But whilst it may not be easy to measure the normativity of rules in exact terms, we can still try to understand exactly what this sense of obligation consists of, not in general terms but on a specific case-by-case basis: what it is, how it determines the precise nature of the law, and how state practice is to be measured and assessed against it. In other words, precisely what international lawyers spend most of their time doing. In this respect it is the continued *practice* of international law and of the 'invisible college of international lawyers' which is both indicative of this sense of being bound and which gives specific content to legal rules. The role of practice has been usefully stressed by Kratochwil (1989: 61):

Actors are not only programmed by rules and norms, but they reproduce and change by their practice the normative structures by which they are able to act, share meanings, communicate intentions, criticize claims and justify choices. Thus, one of the most important sources of change, neglected in the present regime literature, is the *practice of the actors* themselves and its concomitant process of interstitial law-making in the international arena.

The importance of a shared sense of cultural or moral community in the creation and maintenance of regimes will depend on their scope. If the regimes are primarily intended to secure some minimum degree of coexistence, then common values and a common culture will be of marginal relevance (unless, as argued

---

[9] Much of Bull's work after *The Anarchical Society* was concerned with 'testing' the role of culture by examining the impact on the institutions of international society of the move from a European to a global state system. This is the central theme of Bull and Watson (1984).

earlier, one of the players espouses an exclusivist conception of international life based on notions of its own inherent superiority). Thus states of many different ideologies and cultures have come to see the benefits provided by such basic legal principles as the mutual recognition of sovereignty, the norm of non-intervention, the need to observe treaties, the need to maintain a functioning diplomatic system, etc. A further example might be the non-legal and often informal network of rules and understandings that developed through the course of the Cold War. (But even this was a fitful process in which the idea of a common interest in avoiding nuclear war had to struggle against the exclusivist ideologies of cold warriors in both East and West.) Minimum rules of coexistence of this kind reflect the inherent necessities of a pluralist system of autonomous states: a practical association in Terry Nardin's (1983) terms that is not built around a common vision of the good life.

But as regimes become increasingly global, as the hard shell of the state is increasingly eroded, and as the scope of co-operation is expanded, the picture changes. As co-operation comes increasingly to involve the creation of rules that affect very deeply the domestic structures and organization of states, that invest individuals and groups within states with rights and duties, and that seek to embody some notion of a common good (human rights, democratization, the environment, the construction of more elaborate and intrusive inter-state security orders), then these questions of society and community re-emerge and the validity of models of co-operation that exclude them needs at least to be questioned.

4.3. Justice and Order

This leads to the third issue, which also concerns the adequacy of regime theory's discussion of the normative dimension of inter-national co-operation. Clearly there are many international norms that derive their compliance pull from a shared sense of justice: human rights most notably, but also, for example, norms against armed conquest and the annexation of territory. Rules and norms of this kind do not develop as a result of the direct interplay of state interests or because of the functional benefits which they provide. Rather they depend on a common moral awareness that works directly, if still in fragile and uneven ways, on the minds and emotions of individuals within states. In some cases such ideas can work to disrupt or complicate the functioning of other inter-state regimes (this has always been the realist argument against the promotion of human rights). In other cases, a sense of common moral purpose can work to reinforce inter-state co-operation. The sense in which global ecological interdependence has given greater plausibility to a Beitzian vision of a global moral community may, for example, increase the weight given to aggregrate global utility and lead policy-makers to act against narrow, short-term definitions of national self-interest (Beitz 1979: part III).

This is not at all to say that the creation of such regimes owes nothing to considerations of power and interest. The creation of the post-war human rights regime depended fundamentally on the particular values and interests of the United States and other western states.[10] Equally, the desire to promote the spread of human rights and democracy has always interacted with, and often been dominated by, baser and less noble sentiments (Lowenthal 1991). Finally, there is much to be said for Hume's argument that the *origins* of many moral sentiments depended in the first instance on pragmatic and self-interested calculation (for instance that formal empire no longer paid) but that, over time, the prohibition of conquest and empire came to assume a moral quality.

Once again the importance of specifically legal rules should be stressed. If shared moral concerns are important in the emergence of co-operative behaviour, it is through legal rules that they are predominantly expressed. Indeed one of the virtues of inter-national law is its flexibility and the extent to which it allows new norms and principles to be introduced (often by weak states and sometimes even by individuals or pressure groups), to be given formal expression, and gradually to be hardened into binding rules that are capable of giving rise to specific duties and obligations. The emergence of human rights law is one example, the current process of groping from general principles of environmental management to specific regulatory regimes is another. Of course, this process is in some sense determined by the power and interests of dominant states. But the workings of the legal system provide

---

[10] On this point see also Ch. 7, sect. 6, below.

a degree of autonomy within which the changing normative climate can be given concrete expression. Thus at one end of the spectrum there is a constant and unstable balance between raw power-political behaviour and law-governed behaviour. At the other there is an equally unstable relationship between legal rules as reflective of the actual political interests of states and legal rules as embodying evolving notions of how the international community *should* be organized.

It is certainly the case that many regime theorists have recognized the force of moral obligations—for example Keohane in chapter 7 of *After Hegemony*. But this raises an important difficulty. Can one relax the basic assumption of rational egoism and accept the role of empathetic interdependence, without the overall force of the rationalist project being undermined? Is one not in danger of slipping back into the kinds of older explanations that see co-operation as resulting from a changing mixture of various factors that cannot be encapsulated in a tight and rigorous theory?

There is a further very interesting aspect to the normative question. For a European at least, there is a striking contrast between the concerns of US international relations scholars of the 1940s and those of the 1980s. For all their claims to be uncovering timeless and objective laws of politics, the early post-war realists were passionately commited to a moral project: to uncovering and exposing the dangers of utopianism, and to prescribing the guidelines of rational statecraft, which, although they could never allow states to escape from the dilemmas of the international anarchy, could at least mitigate its worst effects (hence the charge that they were in fact peddling a conservative utopia). But whatever their conclusions, their explicit concern with the deeply problematic relationship between power and morality remains one of the most noteworthy features of their work. The picture of the 1980s is very different. In one sense, there is an implicit moral concern in the work of regime theorists, centred around the assumption that the understanding and promotion of co-operation has an intrinsic value (Keohane 1988: 380f.). There is in fact a good deal of clear prescription: if we understand the conditions under which co-operation is possible, we will be able to promote greater co-operation. At the same time, however, there is also the recognition that not all regimes are benign: 'Since the point is often missed, it should be underlined: although international regimes may be valuable to their creators, *they do not necessarily improve world welfare*. They are not *ipso facto* "good"' (Keohane 1984: 73). Indeed, as the conclusion to *After Hegemony* makes clear, the order created by regimes needs to be subjected to relevant moral standards.

Order and justice are thus seen as separate tracks. First you understand how order is created and then you assess it against some outside normative standards. (The direction of the argument is similar here to that of Bull (1977: ch. 4).) Order is the product of norms whose emergence can be understood in sociological terms and whose impact derives from the functional benefits which they provide. Indeed the term 'norm' is mostly used in regime theory to describe generalized rules of co-operative social behaviour.

The basic question is whether order and justice can in fact be separated in this way. First, is there not a good deal of evidence to suggest that questions of justice and perceptions of equity play a major role in the formation of actors' preferences and in the determination of actors' behaviour? Second, is there not also a good deal of evidence to suggest that successful bargaining outcomes do not depend on the achievement of some notion of optimum allocative efficiency, but rather on the perception that the outcome meets some criterion of justice and equity (Young 1989*b*: 368f.)? As Robert Jervis (1988: 348) puts it: 'Considerations of morality, fairness, and obligation are almost surely large parts of the explanation for the fact that individuals in society co-operate much more than the Prisoners' Dilemma would lead us to expect.' (See also Barry (1989: 357–66).) And finally, the status of the norm of reciprocity raises serious difficulties. It is seen within rationalist and game-theoretic approaches as a given, an ahistorical and acultural norm that is naturally occuring *dans la nature des choses*. But there is a powerful argument that its functioning depends on a pre-existing sense of community, or at least that it is itself reflective of that community. And the more that reciprocity becomes generalized and diffuse, the more it tends to become synonymous with fairness. If this is so, then the validity of separating order from justice is as problematic for the neo-liberal institutionalists as it was for the theorists of international society.

On the one hand, then, notions of justice need to be seen as intrinsic to the process by which order is produced. On the other, the order that is produced tends naturally to reflect the dominant interests of the most powerful states. In terms of future research this suggests two things: first, there is a pressing need to understand a good deal more about how conceptions of a just international order vary between states. The radically divergent perceptions on the nature of order and legitimacy thrown up in the wake of the Gulf War (and in post-Cold War Europe) attest to the complexity and centrality of this question. Second, it is surely important to try and bridge the gap that has opened up between theorists of international co-operation and the increasing number of political theorists who have become more aware of the need to develop theories of justice within an inter-state and global context. In part this involves the creation of appropriate principles of justice. But in part—and this is surely the distinctive task for international relations as a discipline—it means the critical analysis of how such principles can be applied within the political dynamics of the international system, in other words returning once more to the interaction between politics and morality.

4.4. The Domestic Dimension

The fourth and final issue concerns the domestic dimension. Although regime theory grew out of theories of interdependence and transnationalism that stressed the multiple linkages between the domestic and the international, it sought essentially to explain co-operation in third image terms. The need to address the domestic dimension has become a common theme.[11] Clearly, the way in which states bargain and co-operate cannot be understood except with reference to the changing nature of the state and the domestic political system. State interests are not fixed but vary according to the institutional context, to the degree of organization of the contending political forces within the state and wider political system, and to the leadership capacities of the major actors.

Domestic factors are also central to the issues raised in this

---

[11] For a first attempt to shed light on the 'domestic sources of regime formation' see Ch. 12 below.

chapter. Notions of society and community cannot be easily separated from the character of domestic political systems. This was one of the central problems with the Bull–Wight approach to international society. On the one hand, they sought to develop a conception of international society that was focused at the inter-state level, to locate a set of common rules applicable to the workings of a society of states (along lines not so very different from Kissinger's conception of legitimacy). But on the other, the reliance on the role of common values and a common culture almost inevitably opens up questions about the impact of domestic social, cultural, and political factors. In addition, conceptions of fairness and equity are closely related to distinct histories and to specific cultures. This is particularly true when the idea of costs and benefits is extended beyond the purely economic, when, for example, the safeguarding of political autonomy or cultural heritage is seen as having a fundamental value that must be built into co-operative inter-state regimes.

As the primary focus of research shifts from regime creation to implementation, domestic factors become, if anything, even more critical. Various issues and possibilities can be noted. First, there is the role of international rules, and especially international law, in the policy-making process. If the focus is on the subjective sense of being bound, then we need to look in far more detail at how this sense of obligation plays out within the policy-making process. It is, after all, only individual policy-makers who are capable of feeling a sense of obligation. Despite the methodological difficulties there is much that can be done. We can, for instance, build on the work of Louis Henkin (1979) and reconstruct the ways in which international law shaped the policy options that were considered by governments and the extent to which these options reflected the internalization of legal rules. Indeed by looking on the basis of detailed documentary work at the options that were considered but ultimately rejected, we can go some way towards overcoming the dilemma of counterfactuals.[12]

Second, there are specific and often technical linkages between international law and domestic legal systems and the complex processes that underpin the national implementation of inter-

---

[12] Biersteker, in Ch. 13 below, discusses the problem of counterfactuals in detail.

national rules. As Antonio Cassese (1988: 15) has observed: 'It is therefore apparent that international law cannot work without the constant help, co-operation, and support of national legal systems.' If regime theory is seriously interested in questions of compliance and implementation (and in explanations of differing patterns of compliance between different types of states), then it is essential that these technical linkages should be understood and assessed by political scientists.

Third, many of the political costs of violating international rules are domestic. One of the most powerful reasons for complying with international legal rules, even in 'hard cases' in which national security interests are involved, lies in the degree to which the creation of a convincing legal case is essential for ensuring domestic political support. Conversely, it is often the violation of specific international norms and laws that provides the focal point around which domestic opposition is able to mobilize. For all the alleged weakness of international law, it is striking just how often international rules form the basis of claims and political action within states. Equally, given that governments are often not good at blowing the whistle on each other, a good deal of the monitoring of international regimes is carried out by domestic groups acting either within one country or transnationally.[13]

5. CONCLUSIONS

The purpose of this chapter has been to place regime theory within a broader tradition of thought on the possibilities and problems of co-operation in international life that focused on the concept of international society and gave a key role to international law. Seen in this light the charge of faddishness falls away and the way in which the concerns of regime theorists have built on the ideas and concepts of earlier theorists becomes apparent. Moreover, the reformulation of the problem of co-operation within more rigorous rationalist models has brought clear benefits, above all in terms of giving greater precision to the functional benefits of norms, the

---

[13] These points are well demonstrated by Harald Müller's study of 'the politics of compliance' in three security cases. See Ch. 15 below.

concept of reciprocity, and the ways in which co-operation can develop between self-interested actors. But this rigour has been bought at a significant cost. First, the centrality and complexity of the normative dimension has been neglected or downplayed: above all in terms of the importance of a shared sense of community in understanding how the co-operative enterprise can get off the ground, and in terms of the necessity of viewing ethics as intrinsic to the processes by which order is produced. And second, the quest for rigour (and perhaps an excessive desire to avoid the sins of idealism) has led to far too wholesale a dismissal of the need to understand both the specific character and the technical features of the international legal system. It is international law that provides the essential bridge between the procedural rules of the game and the structural principles that specify how the game of power and interests is defined and how the identity of the players is established. It provides a framework for understanding the processes by which rules and norms are constituted and a sense of obligation engendered in the minds of policy-makers. And it provides one way of analysing the linkages that exist between the rules that facilitate order internationally and the domestic political and legal systems of states.

4

Contract and Regimes

Do Issue Specificity and Variations of Formality Matter?

FRIEDRICH KRATOCHWIL

1. INTRODUCTION

This chapter examines two questions that have puzzled regime analysts and their opponents alike. The first concerns the boundaries of regimes. The second concerns the formality/informality dimension of regime norms and its impact upon regime strength. The first question has given rise to the charge that regimes are fuzzy and, by implication, not very useful for understanding international relations, when compared to 'fundamental' concepts such as power and interest (Strange 1983). The second question addresses the extent to which international politics, even in the absence of central institutions, is structured by such means as 'signalling', tacit understandings, or custom, and to what extent formal agreements and the emergence of formal organizations are necessary for the implementation of 'regimes'.

These two questions are not simply two separate problem areas of regime analysis; they are interrelated in various ways as I shall argue below. Without a proper boundary of the regime concept the impact of regimes on decision-making cannot be assessed. Theorists may not only see regimes everywhere, they may also fail to appreciate the true reasons for this phenomenon. By focusing

I gratefully acknowledge the research help by Rey Koslowski as well as the support provided by the Lawrence B. Simon Chair. Nick Onuf, Oran Young, and A. J. R. Groom have read earlier versions of this chapter and provided me with useful criticism. Special thanks also to Volker Rittberger for his comments and his help in seeing this project through.

on epiphenomenal factors such as the rhetoric of actors who invoke norms, we may lose sight of the generative capacity of the traditional structure of international politics. Consequently, the radical disaggregation of those structures in favour of issue specificity might entail significant costs.

Similarly, even if we believe that norms play an important part in politics, the lack of attention to the formality/informality dimension of norms is likely to court disaster. International as well as domestic actors usually do make careful distinctions between norms which are clear and whose duty-imposing character is easily established and other norms such as 'comity' or tacit understandings which carry no such obligations. While I cannot hope in this brief chapter to analyse exhaustively regime strength in its behavioural and normative dimensions, the taxonomy developed below should at least be helpful in clarifying the varying degrees of obligatoriness of regime norms.

Furthermore, when 'regimes' need formal organizations for their implementation, their establishment is not possible without a high degree of domain consensus defining the mission of these organizations. To that extent formality and explicitness become decisive dimensions in establishing functioning regimes. Thus while it is certainly a myopic understanding of formal organizations to assume that their activities neatly coincide with the domain established by their organizational charter, it is also clear that formal bureaucratic structures cannot function in the absence of highly explicit rules. These rules define both the organizational tasks and the standard operating procedures which link technical knowledge to the implementation of goals.

In order to make good on these claims my argument takes the following steps. In the next section (sect. 2) I take up the problem of issue orientation and the boundaries of regimes. I argue that, despite its constitutive nature, the notion of an issue area in the regime debate is woefully inadequate. By misunderstanding regimes as the more or less accurate reflection of power, the links between regimes, knowledge, and legitimacy are obscured.

Frequently, this problem is further aggravated by the tendency to solve conceptual problems of regime analysis by means of stipulative definitions. The result is that the analysis both of issue areas and of regimes proliferates without having any basis in the actual praxis of states. Regimes cannot be construed simply for purposes of facilitating the analysis made by the observer. The analytical usefulness of this concept is only safeguarded when norms and rules are explaining actual decisions of the actors themselves.

In section 3, I address the question of the formality/informality dimension of normative understandings. In this context, I examine both the strength of a regime and the incentives of actors to utilize different modalities of regime formation. By contrast with the usual analysis, which uses only the distinction between formal and informal norms, I argue that, in addition, their explicitness and implicitness, as well as their public or secret form, are important dimensions. Section 4 offers a short summary of the above arguments.

2. ISSUE AREAS, CONTRACTS, AND THE EMERGENCE OF REGIMES

In raising the question of the boundaries of a regime Mark Zacher (1987) argued that certain injunctions guiding state behaviour in an issue area are not properly part of a regime. He had in mind the norms and rules that circumscribe self-help measures, such as the suspension or voidability of treaties (Zoller 1984). This led to his distinction between norms and the issue area, a distinction that follows the classical legal practice of separating the institutional nature of contracting (treaty-making) from the subject-matter which a particular contract or treaty regulates. The paradigmatic example underlying this distinction is the spot contract in which the parties freely enter into mutual promises and agree on an exchange of self-chosen obligations.

But considerable complications arise when we no longer deal with one-shot simultaneous exchanges but with contracts codifying mutual promises for non-simultaneous exchanges. Here questions of enforcement costs, of legitimacy and commitment to broader principles, and finally of a particular identity, significantly modify the conceptual apparatus of understanding contracts. I shall develop these modifications by distinguishing five ideal-typical forms of contracts: the spot contract, the spot contract with sequential performance, the simple incomplete contract (iterative long-term contract), the complex long-term contract (exemplified by the wage contract), and finally a contract imposing obligations concerning an ongoing relationship (exemplified by both marriage and constitutional contracts).

Although these examples are taken from domestic law, the underlying distinctions have considerable heuristic power for the clarification of problems in regime analysis. Given this continuum we can place most regimes in the category of (incomplete) long-term contracts. By demonstrating that a generative logic exists, the problem of issue specificity as a defining dimension of regimes can be dealt with in a systematic fashion. Following this logic we can rigorously examine the emerging properties when we move from one-shot spot contracts to long-term commitments.

In the spot contract the parties create their obligations through a mutual promise and agree on the specific quid pro quo. Performance is usually unproblematic, leaving aside for the moment the complications of mistakes of form, fraud, and misrepresentation, which void the contract *ab initio* or make it voidable. Difficulties are likely to arise if the spot contract entails duties which require sequential performance (Hobbes 1651). Knowing this, the parties must insure themselves against opportunism. This insurance can take various forms. In order to avoid litigation costs, parties in commercial transactions usually utilize escrow accounts, bind themselves beforehand to seek arbitration, or resort to limited acts of retaliation. In the international arena, the equivalent are unilateral countermeasures such as the suspension of treaties (Zoller 1984).

Further complications arise when the contract is made for iterated transactions which defy clear stipulations of all possible contingencies. The longer the considered time period is, the less information is available to the parties and the less able they are to stipulate the conditions for the iterated exchanges (Lewellyn 1931). Consequently, the terms of the contract become inexact. Instead of a direct quid pro quo, the parties have to promise each other to resolve the inevitable disputes in an amicable fashion. In other words, the contract consists now of two distinct parts: one is the commitment to continue the relationship, subject to dispute settlement, the other is the specific quid pro quo of the future bargain.

It is clear that the effectiveness of such incomplete contracts depends increasingly on commonly shared norms that facilitate the specific bargains. The incomplete contract, for example, provides for dispute settlement in a 'businesslike manner', or according to customary principles of equity. However, the parties to such a contract will be able to continue with their undertaking only if they share some common understandings of what these abstract principles mean in particular situations. Here precedent, analogies, saliency and custom are all important in particularizing the shared higher order principles which provide the background for the compromise in any particular round.

Up to now, we still assume the incomplete contract to consist solely of iterated rounds of bargains. Long-term delivery contracts of commodities, providing for periodic renegotiation of prices, are good examples. Another stage in the complexity of contracting is reached, however, when, with the exchange of promises, the relationship between the contracting parties attains a new quality. Consider in this context the wage contract. On the surface, it is a simple incomplete contract. But this appearance is deceptive.

Both Marx and modern organization theory following the transaction cost approach (Coase 1937) have analysed the implications of this contract. For Marx the decisive difference consisted in the commodification and alienation of labour. Work is no longer regulated by the norms and values of social exchange, but is co-ordinated via a medium of exchange in the market. In contrast, modern organization theory is largely concerned with the emergence of formal organizations on the basis of such incomplete contracts.

The transaction cost approach starts with the complete information assumption of classical economics. Consequently, in a perfectly competitive market no firms should exist as the actors could resolve all exchange problems by spot contracts (Williamson 1975). Adducing market failure as an explanation, this transaction cost approach to organizations focuses on the implications of the wage contract which establishes a new relationship among the parties. Labour has now not only a price, but the wage contract amounts to an exchange of money for the acceptance of the employer's *authority*.

From this vantage point we can see now why Marx was right as well as wrong. He was right by pointing to the new dimension of social relations based on such a complex incomplete contract.

The entrepreneur not only buys the worker's labour power but acquires the right of directing his activities. A 'structure' emerges that is characterized by explicit inequality in decision-making power. Employees have to *defer* to the authoritative directives of their boss; they can no longer object to specific commands, or bargain over them, because in the incomplete contract they have committed themselves at least to the presumption of postponing their own preferences.

Last, but not least, 'time' attains new importance. Given that the contract is unspecific as to the concrete activities, what is exchanged is not only labour power and directive control for money, but rather also time for money. Only in his spare time can the employee now direct his own actions. Marx was wrong, however, in assuming that such problems appear only under conditions of capitalism. As we can see, the emergence of formal 'organizations', exemplified here by the firm, is analytically independent of the issue of ownership of the means of production.

Also, contrary to Marx's expectations, labour markets are never institutions in which the commodity, labour, is solely allocated through market exchanges. Precisely because of the special nature of labour, various market 'imperfections' are accepted and sanctioned by law. They range from measures against hazardous activities and injunctions against child labour, to the institutionalization of collective bargaining. In addition, the sphere of authority of an entrepreneur or manager is tightly regulated and enforced. Thus, an employer can buy the time of an employee to do certain types of work, or even to do 'make-work', but he cannot ask, for example, his secretary to do his shirts, or 'to be nice to him', even if this demand falls within the time period contracted for.

Similarly, in international politics the contract among states establishing an international organization delineates a particular domain within which the organization is supposed to exercise its 'powers'. Activities which fall outside the accepted domain consensus become contestable and their legitimacy is impaired. Under such circumstances, charges of politicization of the organization and of its programmes can be made. Actors are then likely to resort to various strategies of exit, voice, and loyalty (Hirschman 1970) in order to re-establish a domain consensus for the organization. Examples include US charges that the labour and educational regimes were undermined by the activities of ILO and UNESCO (Imber 1989). Similarly, the United States withheld funds to the UNO for the same reasons (Kassebaum Amendment).

Consider finally another type of incomplete contract: that of a marriage and the imagery of a constitutional contract. The distinguishing characteristic of this type of incomplete contract is that no commitment to specific exchanges is entailed, even though such exchanges will be part of the ongoing relationship.

The marriage contract is rather a commitment to the relationship as such, 'for better or for worse'. It is limited in neither scope nor time, nor is it governed by a specific authority that comes into existence at its inception (although most traditional societies accepted the authority of the *pater familias*). Also, the marriage contract is, at least in its intentions, not easily revocable if the parties' preferences change. Rather it is conceived as a commitment to become a certain type of person, a 'life-partner' for the other. Aside from the question of intimacy, which becomes thereby possible, the important element for our purposes here is that this relationship entails—in game-theoretical language—the endogenization of individual preferences. The language of contract becomes strained and its relevance is rather limited to the disposal of property in case the couple is unable to sustain this relationship.

Similarly, the constitutional contract entails an extension of the meaning of contract, albeit this extension has been historically of great importance.[1] Despite the fact that the resulting consent theory for political authority has been criticized from Jean-Jacques Rousseau to Don Herzog (1989), political theorists have found it difficult to think about constitutions in other than contractual terms. Consider in this context Rousseau's (1762) own concept of the *aliénation totale* which clearly transcends the institution of contract. Although this alienation superficially concerns the abandonment of claims to property in order to secure valid titles, Rousseau sees the social contract not limited to the protection of property. By contrast with Locke, he stresses the morality and the new identity of the persons when they become members of a political community.

---

[1] On the power of metaphors directing the development of conceptual systems see Lakoff and Johnson (1980).

At this point it seems appropriate to draw the lessons of these examples for the regime debate. First, placing the issue of regimes within the wider framework of contracting, its generative logic demonstrates which factors become relevant when we move from spot contracts to more encompassing undertakings. Knowing which factors are relevant allows for a *conceptual* clarification instead of expecting the answers from the examination of a variety of issue areas, or from purely stipulative or definitional exercises.

Second, our examples derived from the generative logic of contracting also show why questions of *legitimacy* have to be addressed, as they crucially influence the delineation of issue areas (or domains). In order to examine this problem more fully let us begin with the demand-for-regimes argument. In this approach regimes are designed to lower transaction costs. Rational actors are provided with the necessary information that otherwise would not be available to them because of lack of transparency. A car buyer is at a disadvantage as he does not know how the car will perform in the future; his spot contract clearly suffers from the sequential performance difficulty. Without liability rules and warranties market failure occurs and exchanges are impaired.

Analogues to these measures for increasing transparency and lowering transaction costs can easily be found in international relations. They range from the counting and classification rules in arms control agreements, to the rules for empowering for example, the IMF with supervisory functions (conditionality), to the promises not to interfere with national means of verification in the SALT treaties. Although many regimes are likely to contain rules and norms that serve this function, it is difficult to call such provisions by themselves a regime, unless we refer directly to contracting itself as a regime. At a minimum a regime requires a relationship that emerges from long-term iterative contracting. This seems to be required for two reasons.

First, the parties to an incomplete contract must agree not only on rules regulating specific actions, but also on much more general principles which impose upon them duties to settle future disputes. Consequently, it is quite understandable that these principles have been held to supply the 'basic defining characteristics of a regime' (Krasner 1983*a*: 3), or even its 'nature' (Zacher 1987: 178). For example, the various multilateral regimes that developed in the post-war era are not simply nominally definable as involving the participation of more than two participants (Keohane 1990). Their distinct nature was provided by the principles on which they were based. As Ruggie (1991*b*) pointed out, the multilateral regimes of the post-war era were characterized by a commitment to general principles applicable to all, by indivisibility, and by diffuse reciprocity. The importance of these principles was that they gave rise to more specific norms. These prescriptions counteracted the normal presumption derived from 'sovereignty' and the realists' maxims, that each state will be the autonomous judge of all of its interests.

Second, since the relationship established by a regime is not a commitment to a common life, its domain and boundaries have to be specified. In long-term contracts of the simple kind (iterative bargains), a commodity or even an activity (such as fishing or lumbering) usually provide reasonably well-specifiable domains. With the complex long-term incomplete contract, however, when the quality of the relationship changes through the emergence of authority, a new problem arises. As we saw in the wage contract, 'labour' is not quite a commodity even if it takes on certain traits in labour markets. Rather the exchange between employer and employee is governed partially by norms and principles taken from the logic of the market, and partially by other norms. The latter, for example, specify the scope of the employer's authority as well as the concomitant duties of the employee. Thereby, certain exercises of authority are proper and others *illegitimate*.

With the establishment of authority, issues of legitimacy are inevitably raised. In addition, the problem of knowledge and its social acceptability becomes crucial in this context. Thus the partial commodification of labour is not only the result of structural changes in the economy during the industrial revolution. Rather the industrial revolution and the creation of a labour market came about because of a new social consensus on the appropriateness of liberal *laissez-faire* economic doctrines. The emancipation of labour from the practices of a corporatist and stratified status society can only be understood by paying attention to the interaction between legitimacy and technical (economic) knowledge, leading to 'consensual knowledge' (E. B. Haas 1975, 1980).

There remains the last example of the contract for a 'way of life'. As already mentioned, such contracts represent, because of their comprehensiveness and indeterminacy, limiting examples of both 'contract' and 'regime'. Nevertheless, the agreement leading to the Europe of 1992 might fall into this category, as does the compact establishing the Swiss confederation, or the adoption of the American Constitution by the successful revolutionary states.

There still remain a few corollaries which follow from the above argument. First, it is now clear why and how 'issue specificity' is a defining aspect of regimes. Although some regimes can be characterized by certain commodities, such as tin or coffee, other such commodities or activities have not served as the crystallization point for a domain consensus. Textiles or fibres represent a genuine regime, while sardines and shoes do not. It is also clear why certain shared environments, such as outer space, are not simply governed by one regime, and why other comprehensive regimes, such as the oceans (UNCLOS III), are likely to disintegrate in a multiplicity of separate regulations with potentially serious externalities. Precisely because activities in outer space, ranging from remote sensing to space exploration and telecommunications, are subject to differential patterns of consensus, treating them as elements of a comprehensive regime would be seriously misleading. Similar considerations are justified by the likely disintegration of the envisaged comprehensive UNCLOS III regime.

Second, nominalist definitions are unlikely to help us in our attempts to understand and explain actual phenomena. To the extent to which the delineations of regimes have to respect the political praxis of the actors, regimes cannot be introduced by the researcher *ad libitum*. For example, if the members of the international community decide that a particular issue is supposed to be governed by particular norms, a regime emerges, as was the case for fibres (the Multifibre Agreement). On the other hand, even hot issues such as automobiles or electronic gadgets do not define a regime, because these issues are still debated within the larger context of the international trading order. Similarly, although 'outer space' seems to provide clear bounds for categorizing certain issues, it is not useful to conceptualize this collection of activities—even if they are norm-governed—as one 'regime', because varying patterns of consensus inform the regulations of specific uses of outer space.

Ernst Haas (1975, 1980) has pointed out that the way in which issues become aggregated into an issue area has to be an explicit part of regime analysis. Thus, while shared notions such as geography or a particular commodity might be sufficient to serve as a reference for a specific issue, *this* type of issue specificity is not useful in advancing our theorizing on regimes despite its clarity of reference. I think much of the 'fuzziness' of the boundaries of regimes could be eliminated if this distiction between issue specificity as a referential term, and issue specificity as an indicator of *practice* governed by normative consensus were to be kept in mind.

Third, quite different from the demand-for-regimes argument, the rationality constitutive of political actions and their regulation cannot be compressed into one concept of instrumental or strategic rationality. Precisely because both consensual knowledge and legitimacy represent irreducible elements of political action, questions concerning normative arrangements cannot be reduced to simple functional explanations. Hence, attempts to build a science of politics through the elimination of these complicating factors and reducing explanations to instrumental reasons for these particular institutions are bound to fail.

Fourth, as to contract for a common way of life: both the marriage contract and the founding of a political association by means of a covenant show their relatedness to the contractual paradigm by the explicit uptake of the obligations through a historical act. Most political systems, however, lack such explicit covenants. Consequently, contracts have to be construed in order to safeguard the legitimacy of the established order, whose obligations often appear to the members as imposed, rather than freely contracted for.

This last point raises the issue of how such contracts can be implied or derived from certain communicative acts. With that we enter into the discussion of how imputations are made by the actors in their interactions, how these implicit understandings structure expectations, and how, finally, these expectations give rise to *legal* obligations. It is the task of the next section to examine in greater detail the issue of formality of these normative expectations.

3. TACIT, INFORMAL, AND FORMAL AGREEMENTS

The above discussion, based on various forms of an explicit bilateral contract, seems to suggest that regimes have to be based on formally negotiated agreements. But as Oran Young (1983) points out, regimes might be, aside from bargaining, the outcome of spontaneous convergence, or even imposition. The acceptance of the territorial sea together with the *mare liberum* regime is an example of the former; the making of prize law by the British Courts of Admiralty during the late eighteenth and nineteenth centuries is an example of the latter. In addition, consider the problem of Schelling's (1966) tacit agreements which influenced the conduct of hostilities through reciprocal restraint during the Korean War.

These various examples require the examination of three interrelated issues, as well as one definitional clarification. The first issue concerns the conceptual distinctions between informal and formal agreements as well as those between tacit and explicit and public and secret agreements. The second addresses the question of what difference the form of the agreement makes for the character and the strength of a regime. Thirdly, we have to analyse why actors might choose certain forms rather than others in order to secure co-operation. Finally, since 'co-operation' is used in a quite ambiguous fashion, a preliminary definitional clarification is in order. Below I want to begin with the definition and examine the other issues subsequently.

Despite the attention co-operation has received in the discussion of 'co-operation under anarchy' (Oye 1986), the reader of this literature is likely to feel at a loss, given the confusion that surrounds this concept. For example, Axelrod and Keohane (1986) distinguish co-operation from 'harmony', but then go on to define it in terms of the actors' 'anticipated reactions to others' expectations', which seems to make this concept identical to one form of 'power'.

Similarly, the attempt to identify co-operation with purely formal criteria, such as Pareto optimality, is problematic since it cannot distinguish between blackmail and the uptake of a voluntary obligation. In a way, the victim who hands over his billfold to the proverbial gunman co-operates—and the exchange is even

Pareto optimal—but it is quite doubtful whether much can be learned from such a paradigmatic example for fostering co-operative enterprises in international relations. Perhaps 'co-operation' is a cluster term which is characterized by lumping together a variety of instances that might share some similarities but have no common core, as Wittgenstein suggested in elaborating the notion of family resemblance.

At least part of the confusion is the result of the equivocal use of the term in both everyday language and the literature. The term 'co-operation' is used both to refer to an outcome as well as to a process. This usage explains why the actions during a robbery can be lumped together with the process of mutually adjusting choices.[2] In contrast, the example of a Nash equilibrium, i.e. when the actors act independently, instantiates the 'outcome' dimension of this term, despite the fact that no meaningful social action (in Weber's terms) is involved.

It is useful to limit the term to instances of *social action*, i.e. to situations where the participants notice the interdependency of their decision-making and have come to the realization that they can improve their position. Charles Lipson (1991: 500) reminds us that co-operation not only involves predictability and order in mutual choice behaviour, but 'what distinguishes cooperation, whether tacit or explicit, are the subtle forms of mutual reliance and the possibility of betrayal and regret'.

It is these factors of mutual reliance and regret which help us to understand some of the complexities of implicit and explicit, as well as public and secret understandings, and their connection with the strength of regimes. While mutual reliance is necessary for the frictionless exchanges in the pursuit of self-interest, the emergence of resentment in the aftermath of a betrayal raises the issue of what normative force this breached obligation had.

Consider the following cases of mutual reliance and the explicitness of understanding. If Wolfgang wants to listen to classical music, but his room-mate Mick wants to listen to the Rolling Stones, they are likely to interfere with each other's listening pleasure by simultaneously turning up their stereos. Without at least some implicit rule developing through their interaction, such as a schedule: 9–11 hard rock, 1–3 classical music (weekends to

---

[2] I owe this thought to Lisa Moore.

be decided by beer-guzzling duels on Friday nights), they will be frustrated. It is clear that the development of implicit understandings becomes more complicated as more actors are involved. Consequently, agreeing explicitly on such a rule and posting it formally on the bulletin board under the heading 'house rules' will make things considerably easier. Thus, with such a rule fraternity brothers can rely on the explicit and formal norm which preserves peace and sanity and guarantees the achievement of their goals, instead of relying on various rounds of stereo wars, involving trial and error and risking the mutual loss of hearing.

The above example showed two things. First, interests as such are not sufficient for explaining the actual outcome (regimes). Rules often serve an important and independent function in structuring expectations. Second, compliance patterns with rules and norms are crucially affected by the explicitness with which the norms are stated. For instance, when George relies on John's statement that he will be at a particular event, George has reason to feel disappointed when John does not show up. However, the disappointment will become a justifiable resentment if John's statement of intent was prefaced by 'I promise'.

The applications of the lessons from these cases to international interactions are not so far-fetched as it might seem. Co-ordination norms are needed in order to ensure that actors who use, for example, certain bands of the radio spectrum do not interfere with each other's messages. These rules and norms are virtually self-enforcing. Nevertheless, even in such functional areas as telecommunications etc. in which, technically speaking, simple co-ordination norms are at issue, the considerable bargaining casts considerable doubt on the explanation of their spontaneous emergence and unproblematic nature.

The explicitness of an obligation imposed by a norm is, however, even more important in cases in which norms have to overcome prisoners' dilemma situations. Although it is traditional to stress, in this context, the need for enforcement, our discussion shows that the problem of compliance is more complicated. Before any enforcement can take place there must be means of discovery and agreed procedures of establishing the occurrence of an actual violation. Discovering an infraction and appraising its seriousness presupposes, however, the explicit acceptance of obligations and the agreement on appropriate behavioural indicators.

In international politics, the possibility of *secret* formal undertakings raises one further complication. However, it is important
not to mistake 'secrecy' for the tacit (or implicit) character of a
rule. In order to clarify these two points, consider the case of co-
operation based on a treaty. Treaties, or their equivalents,[3] are
formal and explicit undertakings in which at least two parties
exchange promises.[4] In addition, they might be public or secret.
Alliance treaties, duly ratified by Parliament or Congress, are an
example of explicit, formal, and public undertakings. They
come into existence by utilizing certain formulae and practices
constituted by norms, which indicate to the participants, and the
wider public, that a solemn mutual (or multilateral) commitment
has been made.

But as we know from history, alliances often were kept
secret. They could be treated in this fashion because only the
'sovereign' had to ratify them. Under modern conditions, the
'Advice and Consent of the Senate', as well as the constitutionally
necessary implementing legislation, make it difficult to follow such
a practice. Nevertheless, secretive practices are not unknown
even in modern times. The Molotov–Ribbentrop pact concerned
with the dismemberment of Poland is a sorry example. Such
secret deals *are* exceptional in present state practice, precisely
because of the need for democratic legitimization of the government's commitments and the often necessary implementing
legislation.

The regime definition, therefore, has correctly stressed the
'decision-making procedures' as an important element of regimes.
While it has been common to consider procedures of international
conferences or organizations in this context, such an understanding is too narrow. After all, there is no reason to exclude from
regime analysis those procedures which translate the internationally contracted obligations into domestic law and which set

---

[3] Here I have in mind e.g. 'executive agreements' which need no 'Advice and
Consent of the Senate' under the American Constitution.

[4] See in this context the definition of a treaty in the Vienna Convention on
Treaties in Art. 2, 1 (a): '"treaty" means an international agreement concluded
between states in written form and governed by international law, whether
embodied in a single instrument or in two or more related instruments and
whatever its particular designation.'

the standard operating procedures for national bureaucracies implementing the regime.[5]

The above remarks also make intelligible why states sometimes might spend a considerable amount of effort on explicit and public, but *informal*, agreements. The Helsinki Final Act is the most obvious example. One can only speculate why Brezhnev made the Helsinki accords such an explicit part of his foreign policy, while at the same time insisting that Helsinki did not represent a treaty. A rather 'legalistic' explanation is as good as any other that one could think of. First, since international obligations of a state can be acquired not only by formal treaties but by unilateral declarations of state representatives, the absence of formality of a declaration matters little in this respect. Having all nations solemnly declare, so to speak, unilaterally, the inviolability of post-war boundaries added considerable legitimacy to the status quo.

Second, when the West insisted on including a strong human rights component (Principle VII, Basket Three), Brezhnev balked at first, but ultimately swallowed that toad. Since human rights commitments would have required further implementing action on the part of Soviet authorities, no such obligation could be construed from the accords since they were, technically speaking, not treaties. The fact that Brezhnev fundamentally miscalculated the eventual impact of Helsinki's human rights provisions is another matter. He was, after all, not alone in his assessment that through Helsinki the Soviet Union had gained support for the 'final' division of Europe while only having had to pay lip-service to human rights.

Explicit informal agreements which remain secret raise different issues. For instance, the Cuban missile crisis was brought to an end by an explicit, but informal secret agreement between Robert Kennedy and the Soviet Ambassador Dobrynin. Rejecting the Soviet demand for a public commitment to remove US missiles

---

[5] See in this context the complications that arise for statutory construction. In the famous case of *Missouri* v. *Holland* (252 US 416) (1920), which concerned a protective regime for certain migratory birds, set up by the United States and Canada, the US implementing statutes were held constitutional by the Supreme Court, although such legislation arguably violated the presumption of the 10th Amendment, and similar statutes made by the Federal Government for the same purpose (but without the backing of a treaty) had been held unconstitutional before. For a further discussion see Kratochwil (1985).

from Turkey, Robert Kennedy gave private assurances that such an action would follow the Soviet missile withdrawal. Should the Soviets make this part of the negotiations public, however, the United States would disavow the informal deal they just had struck (Kennedy 1971, Garthoff 1989). President Kennedy and his brother obviously believed that they had to take care of possible repercussions of such a deal upon America's allies. Thus, keeping part of the bargain secret remained important. Similarly, decision-makers have an incentive to conceal their commitments from others when the bilateral deal is against some widely shared norms (pre-emptory norms, *ius cogens*). Examples include mutual assistance pacts to commit genocide, to aid terrorists, or to arm insurgents in another country in order to overthrow the existing government.[6]

Rules and norms underlying co-operative ventures can, however, also be implicit or tacit. In accordance with my taxonomy I also distinguish between an informal and formal dimension. The idea of an implicit and formal rule seems to strain our normal understanding. However, customary norms appear to satisfy these conditions. They remain implicit because they are not the result of explicit undertakings and are therefore usually not stated in explicit forms. In addition, the rule underlying a particular practice might be susceptible to a variety of formal statements. Their formal character is nevertheless established by the fact that customary norms are referred to in explanations and justifications of state actions, while informal norms, such as the rules of the game, cannot be adduced for such purposes. Schelling's (1966) discussion of the rules of the game make it clear why these implicit rules are able to guide action but cannot be formally acknowledged.

The above discussion of custom accords with its treatment by the International Court of Justice (ICJ). In the North Sea continental shelf case the Court held that for custom to exist a repeated practice on the basis of at least an implicit obligatory rule is necessary.[7] Thus, a simple regularity of behaviour is not enough.

---

[6] That constitutional mandates are not necessarily sufficient in this case is evidenced by the Congressional debate on the 'secret' war in Central America and on appropriating the funds for the commitments made by the executive.

[7] *Federal Republic of Germany* v. *Denmark*, and *Federal Republic of Germany* v. *Netherlands*, 1969 ICJ 4.

It is also not sufficient to formulate a rule that would account for a regularity, such as the trivial maxim that people have to open their umbrella when it is raining, or that the English drink tea at 5 o'clock. What is required is an interaction in which interests are mutually adjusted on the basis of a rule.

Relying on such a rule can then create obligations not only among the interacting parties but even among non-participants. This change from the requirement of explicit consent to the deference to a customary rule can be defeated only if the actors have persistently objected to it.[8] It needs no further elaboration that both the formulation of the implicit rule underlying a practice and the ascertainment of its 'binding' character often provide considerable puzzles for both social and jurisprudential analysis (D'Amato 1971). In addition, the fact that the underlying rule can often be stated in a variety of forms gives rise to difficulties of interpretation which far exceed those of explicitly stated rules.

The above cases are represented in Table 4.1, which combines the explicit/implicit, formal/informal, and public/secret dimensions of rules and norms underlying interactions. (Since norms which are both implicit and secret do not make sense only six variations are considered.)

Having outlined some of the salient distinctions of the formality/ informality as well as of the explicit/tacit and public/secret dimensions, I do not want to imply that international obligations can

TABLE 4.1. *Dimensions of Agreements*

	Explicit		Implicit (Tacit)	
	Public	Secret	Public	Secret
Formal	treaties	Molotov–Ribbentrop Pact; some classical alliances	custom	*impossible*
Informal	Helsinki Accords	Kennedy agreement on missiles in Turkey during the Cuban missile crisis	spheres of influence; rules of the game	*impossible*

[8] See the pronouncement along these lines of the ICJ in the asylum case (*Colombia* v. *Peru*), 1950 ICJ 266.

only be acquired through bargaining. As already mentioned, unilateral acts such as declarations might bind a state and have consequences for the legality or illegality of its further acts,[9] perhaps even in the absence of reliance by another power.[10] Furthermore, normative expectations can arise through the inter-actions of unilateral measures. This type of interaction is some-times called 'tacit bargaining' and has been recommended by Schelling (1960*b*, 1985) and Adelman (1984) for arms control regimes. Our discussion, however, shows why such proposals quickly run into difficulties when they are conceived of as a panacea for resolving the thorny issues which inevitably plague arms control regimes. True, the quick unilateral fix of detonators on nuclear weapons, undertaken by the Kennedy Administration as an insurance against accidents, as well as unilateral measures to secure control and command capabilities, short-circuit possible long drawn out negotiations. But from this example we are not justified in inferring that all problems of co-operation are usefully conceived in this way.

The main shortcoming of such Nash equilibria is that they are vulnerable to any change in the surrounding conditions. The main advantage of 'nailing things down' with explicitly stated norms is that norms allow one to separate the disagreements on a particular issue from the rest of the ongoing social interactions. Actors who rely on moves rather than on explicit verbal communications about the infractions of specific norms cannot have a discourse about their disagreement (Jervis 1970, Young 1968). They also cannot distinguish between an erroneous action or a deliberate act of upsetting a pattern on which the other relies. Thus while one party has good reason to feel betrayed, the other can claim that no violation of a norm has occurred.

Consequently, the parties cannot set aside their disagreement on a specific issue from their overall relations. Unexpected be-haviour is not an indication of a simple disagreement or even violation of a normative expectation that can be examined further through arguments which are limited to the 'relevant facts'.

---

[9] See the unilateral declaration by a Norwegian official not to contest Danish sovereignty over Greenland which was held to be binding on Norway by the Permanent Court of Justice when the status of Greenland was litigated. *Denmark* v. *Norway*, PCIJ Ser. A/B, No. 53 (Eastern Greenland case).

[10] See e.g. the nuclear test case (*Australia* v. *France*), 1974 ICJ 253.

Rather, unexpected behaviour is taken as an indicator for the
deterioration of trust in the relationship as a whole. As conflicts
become less and less bounded by common understandings, worst-
case analysis is likely to drive out other possible interpretations.
A self-confirming spiral of suspicions and hostilities is likely (Jervis
1976: ch. 3).

Of course such spirals are not unknown even when explicit
communication occurs. The point here is not that inflammatory
rhetoric is less destructive than 'signalling', but rather that the
invocation of norms imposes certain limits on both the style of
argument and the issues over which the parties disagree. Since I
have dealt with the problem of normative arguments in another
context (Kratochwil 1989), these brief remarks might suffice here.

4. CONCLUSION

The purpose of this chapter was the examination of two issues: a
distinction between specific contracts and regimes and the formality and informality of regime norms. I argued that these two
issues are not only interrelated but that the examination of this
link promises to advance both our understanding of regimes and
of the role of formal organizations in the international arena.

My demonstration took two steps. First, by placing regimes
within the wider logic of contracting I distinguished five distinct
forms of contract. Furthermore, I showed that regimes come
closest to the type of long-term incomplete contracts. Since such
contracts, by necessity, cannot specify the particular terms of the
iterative bargains, both the emergence of formal organizations
and the development of institutions ascertaining the validity of
norms and their concomitant obligations are responses to these
complications.

The 'organizational' response solves the problem by substituting
authoritative control within specific domains for iterative contracting
of the parties. But organizations are susceptible to politicization
and the disintegration of a domain consensus. The development
of various modalities and explicitness of norms can therefore be
understood as an alternative strategy.

With this alternative strategy, actors try to profit from co-

operative ventures, while at the same time retaining their autonomy and coping with the uncertainties introduced by longer time
horizons, changing preferences, information costs, and the incentives for acting with guile. The formality/informality, explicitness/
implicitness of norms have important implications for the regime
strength as indicated by the varying degrees of obligatory pulls
regime norms exert. Since actors always act against the background of certain expectations, the existence of norms and their
contestation and interpretation is part of their collective existence.
Thus, rationales and justifications, pleas for exemptions and the
offering of excuses, arguments about the formality or clarity of
certain prescriptions—as disingenuous as they might be—are all
part of a communicative dynamic which we have to take into
account when we want to assess the strength of a regime.

Furthermore, if contestation is not to lead to the demise of
regimes, actors have to institutionalize arenas and occasions for
contestation. This is most clearly done when international trib-
unals or review conferences are created. However, very often
domestic institutions, and particularly domestic courts and regulatory agencies, 'double up' as substitutes for such international
fora (Kratochwil 1985). It is therefore important that regime
analysis shall more explicitly examine decision-making procedures
and more systematically link domestic bureaucratic structures and
international regimes.

A further examination of why certain specific organizational
responses occur, and particular mixes of these alternatives outlined above are chosen, remains a task for further analytical as
well as historical investigation.

5

Crossing the Boundary between Public and Private:

International Regimes and Non-State Actors

VIRGINIA HAUFLER

1. INTRODUCTION

The premiss of this chapter is simple: the activities of private organizations can be similar to the activities of states in establishing the contours of an international regime. This premiss goes against the prevailing focus in International Relations, in which private sector actors only provide the background against which the actions of states are show-cased.[1] Even in regime analysis, which can trace its origins to the transnationalists of the 1970s, much of the current research slights the role of corporations and non-governmental organizations, and concentrates on the decisions of state policy-makers. By doing so, it misses the important contributions of non-state actors to the creation and maintenance of regimes.

There are two ways we can conceive of the relationship between states and non-state actors in regime creation and maintenance. First, states can build an international regime upon the foundation of practices and norms previously laid down by non-state actors. They also can use private sector agencies to implement some of the functions of the regime itself. In other words, the relationship between state and non-state actors within a regime may be instru-

---

[1] This characterization of International Relations, while correct in general, does not apply to the work of some prominent theorists. For example, Susan Strange (1988) consistently puts forth the view that private sector activities have as much to do with the shape of world politics as do states, if not more. See also Stopford and Strange (1991).

mental in nature, with the state dominant. This is a fairly traditional view of the political role of non-governmental organizations.

Second, the relationship between states and non-state actors may be reversed. Private sector actors may construct independent international regimes, or play a relatively equal role with states within a regime of mixed 'parentage'. The focus of this chapter will be primarily a discussion of this second, relatively radical approach. A more complete understanding of the variety of relationships between state and non-state actors may change our idea of the boundary between the public and private spheres.

Regime theory has been firmly linked to the development of hegemonic stability theory, thereby contributing to its state-centric bias. When power in the international system is concentrated in one state, that state, or hegemon, attempts to reduce the costs of its leadership by institutionalizing the framework for negotiation in particular issue areas. The hegemon establishes regimes in order to provide stability to the system as a whole. When the hegemon loses its power, these regimes will weaken and fail (Kindleberger 1981, Krasner 1983c, Keohane 1984, 1989b, Stein 1983, Snidal 1985). Thus, regimes are created and maintained through the efforts of a powerful state. Hegemonic regime theory melds the state-centric focus of neo-realism with a liberal's concern for co-operation and institutions.

Recent research attempts to get beyond the issue of hegemony and examine regimes *qua* regimes. Keohane (1984), for instance, provides evidence that regimes gain value for their members over time, and may be maintained by them even after the hegemon declines in power. Young (1989a), E. B. Haas (1990), and P. M. Haas (1989) examine the ability of private voluntary organizations, formal international organizations, and informal scientific communities to act as catalysts for change within regimes.[2] However, states still remain the creators of regimes, though other forces may affect their continuity.

Overall, regime theorists have left out of their analyses the possibility that states might play only a minor role in a regime. There are four possible justifications for this neglect: (1) the definition of regimes excludes purely private sector activity

---

[2] On the effects of epistemic communities on institutional learning see Ch. 8, sect. 4, below.

from its realm of application; (2) regimes established by private corporations are simply oligopolies or cartels; (3) non-corporate, non-governmental organizations are too weak to have a serious impact on world affairs; and (4) states set the boundaries within which others act, and therefore any attempt to analyse private regimes would not lead to productive theorizing about world politics.

In the rest of this chapter, I will look more closely at these justifications, particularly the first three, which I see as the major barriers to developing a systematic analysis of the relationship between private sector actors and regimes. In the next section (sect. 2), I argue that neither the common definition of 'regime' nor the fundamental assumptions made about regimes suggest that there can be no such thing as a purely private regime. In the following two sections (sects. 3 and 4), I discuss both corporate and non-corporate private regimes, giving examples of private sector activities which contribute to the development and maintenance of regimes. In the concluding section (sect. 5), I will point to the implications and limitations of focusing on the role of non-state actors in international relations, and will suggest avenues for further research.

2. DISTINGUISHING CHARACTERISTICS OF INTERNATIONAL REGIMES

Regimes are not just issue areas or international organizations, nor are they simply patterned behaviour. In this section, I discuss private sector actors in the context of four characteristics of regimes: basic definitional factors; effectiveness; contention; and functions. In each case, I provide examples of private sector activity which contributes to the creation and maintenance of regimes, and perhaps even leads to the establishment of a purely private regime.

The commonly accepted definition of regimes is the one drawn from Krasner's (1983*a*: 2) edited volume: 'Regimes can be defined as sets of implicit or explicit principles, norms, rules, and decision-making procedures around which actors' expectations converge in a given area of international relations.' Principles are beliefs of fact, cause, and right. Norms are standards of behaviour. Rules tell the actors what to do or not to do under specified conditions. Decision-making procedures refer to practice and implementation.

This definition is fairly broad and vague, which has provided a wide scope for criticism of regime theory.[3] On the face of it, though, there is no obvious reason why private actors, such as corporations and non-governmental organizations (NGOs), might not establish principles, norms, rules, and decision-making procedures affecting activities in areas of concern to them. The accepted definition need not be limited to interaction among states alone.

One potential example of a private regime can be drawn from the area of population and family planning programmes. Private voluntary organizations in the field of population issues played a key role in the transnational policy coalition which established an international regime in the mid-1960s. International family planning NGOs, such as the International Planned Parenthood Federation, accept as fact, or principle, that overpopulation is a key element in underdevelopment, and uphold the norm that governments should adopt national population policies consistent with their country's demographics (Sadik 1991, Crane 1993).[4] These norms and principles are now supported by both governmental and non-governmental actors.[5] As yet, there is wide variety and even conflict among participants over the exact details of practice and implementation.[6] However, the international family planning institutions have developed an effective, decentralized

[3] For discussions in this volume of the definition of 'international regime' (or aspects of it) see Ch. 1, sect. 3.1, Ch. 2, sect. 3, and Ch. 4, sect. 2.

[4] While most analysts accept the link between population growth and underdevelopment, there are some economists, such as Julian Simon (1990), who argue that population growth will produce its own solutions through market forces. See also Sadik (1991).

[5] Among the 'shapers' of global population policy are the International Planned Parenthood Federation, the World Council of Churches, the Population Council, multinational dairy companies, US universities, and John D. Rockefeller III, in addition to UN agencies and the US Agency for International Development (Marden, Hodgson, and McCoy 1982: 40).

[6] The excellent analysis by Crane (1993) focuses primarily on the role of international population institutions, including both international governmental organizations (United Nations Population Fund) and national agencies (US Agency for International Development). This regime is now changing, and transnational actors (both IGOs and NGOs) have been reformulating a new, possibly more 'private', regime.

monitoring system. The Population Council, a US-based non-governmental organization, has provided leadership within the regime in research and monitoring of programme effectiveness (Crane 1993). In the past five years, the NGOs have taken the lead in bringing together the population and environmental agendas, reconstructing the regime based on ideas of 'sustainable development'. One population issues analyst argues that further development of this regime will depend on the active participation of other NGOs, such as women's organizations and medical and public health professionals (Crane 1993).

Rittberger and Zürn add another dimension to the debate over regimes by arguing that some minimal level of effectiveness and durability is essential for a useful definition of regimes.[7] In their terms, a regime is a form of regulated conflict management among states which is resilient in the face of deteriorating relationships among the participants (Rittberger and Zürn 1990, Rittberger 1990*b*). For a regime dominated by private sector participants, the ultimate test of effectiveness would be the implementation of norms and rules in the face of opposition from states, since states can press their claims through the use of legitimate force. States also have the ability to draw upon extensive resources not available to many non-governmental actors, such as a national treasury, mobilization of public opinion, and expert staffs.

None the less, when the interests of government policy-makers and influential non-state actors come into direct conflict, government leaders may not always prevail in determining the final outcome. For example, the norms and principles developed by human rights activist groups have contributed substantially to developing the structure of a global human rights regime. Amnesty International and other organizations have been effective in changing the human rights practices of governments and successfully modifying the treatment of political prisoners. The human rights regime directly challenges the sovereignty of governments and the ability of government leaders to utilize force, even against their own citizens, to pursue their interests. A recent assessment of international human rights concludes that 'the proliferation

---

[7] Rittberger and Zürn (1990: 17) persist in the state-centric focus common in the regime literature. According to them, 'international regimes represent the strongest form of cooperation between independent states short of formally giving up part of their sovereignty'.

of non-governmental organizations in the last few decades has resulted in a privatization of diplomacy and the realization that local citizens cannot be excluded from the international system' (Chopra and Weiss 1992: 105).[8]

Regulated conflict management as described by Rittberger and Zürn (1990: 15) also requires some 'object of contention'. Certainly, the relationships among non-state actors may be just as strained as those among states, leading to the need to manage inter-organizational conflict. In the example given above of international family planning, obvious conflicts exist between the interests of religious and non-religious organizations over family planning practices.[9] The Catholic Church does not support artificial intervention to prevent conception, which is a key tool of most family planning programmes. However, the Church today does support 'natural' family planning programmes. This represents an effective compromise between the Catholic Church and population planning agencies, allowing both groups to support population control policies in overpopulated developing nations (Marden, Hodgson, and McCoy 1982, Crane 1993).

We might still doubt the existence of true private regimes based on the functions regimes perform in international politics. Regimes generally provide collective goods to their participants, and perform the valued function of reducing transactions costs, increasing information, and decreasing uncertainty (Keohane 1984, Kindleberger 1981).[10] While the logic of collective action indicates that private provision of collective goods should be rare, it does not discount this possibility entirely (Olson 1965). One classic example is the operation of lighthouses, which are often used as an example of a public good. All ships at sea can enjoy the benefits of the light provided by the lighthouse, while it would be difficult to exclude a ship which had not paid for its services. Ships would have a strong incentive to free-ride. None the less, history shows

---

[8] The mobilization of human rights organizations in the former eastern bloc countries was crucial to the successful overthrow of communist governments. This is possibly the most dramatic example of the power of NGOs in the international human rights regime (Tismaneanu 1992).

[9] The World Council of Churches has been a strong and active supporter of the population planning regime, unlike the Catholic Church (Marden, Hodgson, and McCoy 1982, Crane 1993).

[10] The public goods version of hegemonic stability theory and regimes is not universally accepted. See Gowa (1989).

us many examples of lighthouses which have been operated by private shipowners and insurers; for many years, the British insurer Lloyd's of London operated a system of coastal lighthouses at no cost to individual ships.[11] This demonstrates that private actors can in fact supply a public good; from this, we can conclude there is no reason why a private regime would not be capable of providing public goods. Similarly, private organizations can perform the functions of regimes in reducing transactions costs and providing information. For example, the population issue area demonstrates the key role of private agencies such as the Population Council and the World Resources Institute in researching and publishing the links among demographics, development, and the environment.

Given the above arguments and examples, there are no logical reasons for ignoring the role of private actors in regimes. However, we still need evidence that purely private regimes do indeed exist. We need guidelines to help us distinguish private from public regimes. We can identify a private regime as one in which co-operation among private actors is institutionalized, and in which states do not participate in formulating the principles, norms, rules, or procedures which govern the regime members' behaviour.

We should also distinguish among types of non-governmental actors. The most important distinction is between corporations and private voluntary organizations (PVOs), which have very different goals and resources. In fact, the difference in goals and resources makes it unlikely that PVOs would establish an independent private regime. It is more likely that they would operate through influencing domestic coalitions, public opinion, and increasingly by participating in inter-state negotiations (such as the Rio conference). However, regimes may be established entirely by corporations to pursue their own independent interests,

---

[11] There is a surprisingly extensive debate about whether or not lighthouse services are a public or a private good. Some economists argue that the lighthouse is a classic example of a public good. Once a lighthouse turns on its light, all passing ships can use that light whether or not they have paid for it. However, some lighthouse operators could require payment in advance, and technically would be capable of distinguishing paying from non-paying ships and could cover up the light at the approach of those who had not paid. In other words, the light from the lighthouse could be turned into a quasi-public or purely private good (Snidal 1979, Gowa 1988: 23).

or they may operate through the domestic political system to influence inter-state regimes.

The following section discusses the differences between market structure and corporate private regimes. However, we need to acknowledge that most international regimes are mixed in nature. They are not purely the result of inter-state relations, as depicted in standard regime analyses, nor are they entirely established through private efforts.

3. OLIGOPOLIES, CARTELS, AND CORPORATE PRIVATE REGIMES

The idea of a regime based on interactions among private firms raises crucial questions about the difference between a private regime and an economic oligopoly or cartel. For instance, would one consider the oligopolistic domination of world oil markets by the 'Seven Sisters' oil companies during most of the twentieth century an example of a regime? And would the OPEC cartel be considered a regime?[12]

There are a number of categories into which we can divide the organization of private markets. First, there are standard 'Smithian' *competitive markets*, in which organization among individuals and firms is non-existent. These are not relevant to the discussion here.

Second, there are markets characterized by *oligopoly*, in which only a relatively few suppliers exist, competition is restrained, and there exist high barriers to entry by new firms. Economies of scale and economies of specialization characterize these markets. Among oligopolists, there is often some implicit or explicit agreement over prices. Relations among oligopolists are informal; the largest corporations act as 'price leaders', but their signalling is indirect and often restricted by anti-trust law (Sylos-Labini 1987).

Third, *cartels* are explicit, formal organizations among producers (rarely among consumers). Jointly, these producers have a domin-

---

[12] In Keohane's (1984) analysis of the oil market, he pointedly describes it as a regime only by including strategic interaction among *consumers* of oil products, bringing in the state as an active catalyst in constructing an oil consumers' regime.

ant, even monopolistic, position in the market for a specific commodity. The participants give up a measure of competition among themselves in order to establish strict rules and decision-making procedures for setting prices and allocating market share (Weiss 1987). Cartels have a direct impact on other actors, both public and private, through the mechanisms of price and supply. The cartel may operate through self-enforcement, or through some measure of external enforcement by states.[13]

In oligopolies and cartels, each firm pursues partly shared and partly conflicting goals: high prices and profits as a group through dominating a market, but individually large relative shares of income *vis-à-vis* each other. Pursuing these goals in concert, they agree—with or without formal negotiation—to manipulate the market. In an oligopoly, one might expect to see the same prices charged by all firms on their competing products, so that each firm maintains the status quo in market share, keeps prices and profits high and stable, and discourages the entry of new firms. In a cartel, however, the participants negotiate an explicit formula and set of procedures to reinforce the position of the cartel and its members in the relevant market. For example, the International Steel Export Cartel of the 1930s had four clearly defined guidelines: to protect members' domestic market; set policy for steel exports; divide up member quotas; and cartelize merchants importing steel products (Barbezat 1989). Unlike a regime, no larger principles and norms affected the decisions of this cartel.

The fourth, and final, category describing the organization of private markets is that of *corporate private regimes*. Corporate private regimes exist when firms co-operate over issues beyond price, supply, and market share. Regimes include principles and norms, not just rules and decision-making procedures. Members of a private regime institutionalize agreements among non-state actors and regularly negotiate their conflicts. The firms that are members may be highly competitive with one another, and these markets are not necessarily characterized by oligopoly or economies of scale and specialization. A regime is more than

[13] The OPEC cartel, while extremely effective for a time, suffers today from enforcement problems. OPEC does not fall clearly into the categories proposed here, since the members are governments, not private firms. However, OPEC borders on being a regime, given what might be called a norm of antagonism to Israel and its allies.

simply market structure. For instance, the wave of joint ventures and inter-corporate alliances we see now in many industries does not mean that these are incipient regimes. We would need to see common institutions and practices surrounding more than the production and marketing of products in order to label these 'regimes'.

The history of international insurance provides an example of a private regime (Haufler 1991). Insurance is a highly competitive market in general, with a mix of many small firms, some large multinational corporations, underwriters, reinsurers, brokers, and many insurance support service agencies. Insurers have established a network of institutions to negotiate standard contract terms, provide information on current practices, and supply collective services, such as the Salvage Association to regulate salvage at sea, and the International Credit Insurance Association and the Berne Union to negotiate over credit insurance terms. For centuries, insurers have been active in an international market for property, marine, and political risks insurance.[14]

One area which clearly demonstrates how insurers have developed principles, norms, rules, and decision-making procedures is in political risks insurance—insurance against losses due to war, civil war, terrorism, nationalization/expropriation, and acts of omission and commission by governments. The London insurance market, particularly Lloyd's of London, dominated the international risks insurance business throughout the nineteenth and early twentieth centuries.[15] During the twentieth century, the insurance regime moved through four phases: political risks were defined as uninsurable, then insurable, then forbidden, and currently are insurable in limited ways.

By the turn of the century, insurers had established the principle that political risk was uninsurable. Insurance is based on statistical calculations of probabilities based on historical experience of a particular kind of loss. However, political risks could not be systematically analysed; nothing comparable to a life insurance

[14] Some lines of insurance, such as life and automobile, depend primarily on domestic markets. Only in the past decade have these firms attempted to internationalize their services.

[15] Lloyd's of London is an anachronistic form of organization. It is not a corporation, but a market, in which individual underwriters sell their services with unlimited liability. Today, it is under irresistible pressure to change and modernize.

mortality table could be developed. Therefore, all reputable underwriters agreed that political risk insurance, especially against war, was a gamble, pure and simple.

After the First World War, however, insurance underwriters believed they had developed experience and techniques which would make it reasonable to relax the principle that political risks were uninsurable. They began to insure against the effects of war on trade and investment credits.[16] By the early 1930s, Lloyd's of London and other underwriters went further, and began selling insurance against land war risks and war risks on shipping. They eagerly sold insurance against the 'civil commotion' in Spain in 1936, including full risks against fire damage. By 1937, reports began mounting of large losses, with insurers of land-based war risks suffering the most bruising losses. The new technique of aerial bombardment of cities led to mass destruction of lives and property on a scale not seen before.

The end result of heavy insurance losses in the Spanish conflict was a near total ban on land war risks insurance, implemented and enforced by the London insurance market. Led by Lloyd's of London and supported by the International Credit Insurance Association, insurers around the globe signed the Waterborne Agreement, under which they promised to exclude all land war risks from insurance. In other words, they established the principle that land-based political risks were uninsurable, and acted to uphold a norm of non-supply. The individual insurers could have stopped selling land war risks insurance on their own account, in order to protect the profitability of their firms. Instead, they went further and co-operatively redefined the private sphere of decision-making for all insurance firms. Both competition in other insurance products, and pressure from customers for further land war risks insurance coverage, continued after the establishment of the Waterborne regime. However, members have continuously

---

[16] The British Government, and others, became concerned that the lack of insurance might restrict trade during wartime. By the mid-1930s, most governments had established limited facilities for credit insurance and investment guarantees. In no case, however, did a government directly compete with private insurers, and they consulted with the private sector about how to implement their programmes under accepted insurance principles, norms, and practices.

adhered to its strictures, with few defections from the agreement.[17]

The political risk insurance regime demonstrates the differences among oligopolies, cartels, and corporate private regimes. Four elements distinguish this corporate activity as a regime. First, and most obviously, the insurers did not constitute an oligopoly, nor did they have complete monopoly power. They remained highly competitive, fragmented, and multitudinous. Second, unlike an oligopoly or cartel, the insurers promoted a policy of non-supply of land war risks insurance, demonstrating that they were not solely motivated by profit and market share considerations. Third, they developed and enforced principles and norms, going beyond the standard concerns of market actors. Fourth, they established co-operative institutions in which to negotiate their differences.

We can conclude from this brief example that corporate private regimes do indeed exist. Clearly, we need further research to evaluate the uniqueness and generalizability of this individual case.

4. STATES, NGOS, AND INTERNATIONAL REGIMES

The number and activities of international NGOs operating in world affairs has increased dramatically since the Second World War, from under 3,000 in 1945 to over 13,000 by 1990 (P. Lewis 1992: 4). Some of these are formally organized, while others are informal associations. They include both organizations which promote moral or religious values (such as Amnesty International or the Catholic Church), and international business and political

---

[17] If one insurance company began to sell war risks policies on land-based property, the others would feel compelled to enter and compete in this market too. This is a classic case of incentives to defect from co-operation, and the strength of the regime can be inferred from the fact that the Waterborne Agreement has lasted over fifty years. Currently, some insurers are exerting pressure to relax or eliminate the Waterborne Agreement. Three factors may lead to the weakening of the Agreement: the decline of Lloyd's of London owing to scandal and corruption; increasing competition among insurers for new markets; and sophisticated approaches to setting the terms of political risk insurance contracts to limit underwriting losses and divide the risk among a complex multitude of insurers and reinsurers.

associations (such as the International Chamber of Commerce or Greenpeace). As the number of such NGOs increases, we need to ask questions about their role in international affairs. In the context of this discussion of private regimes, we need to explore further the degree to which NGOs organize their activities and co-operate with one another, and the impact of the 'increased incidence of transnational and transregional coalitions and alliances of NGOs on global issues' (Porter and Brown 1991: 56).[18]

Relationships between NGOs (both corporate and non-corporate) and states can be either independent or instrumental. Traditional regime analysis supplies us with many examples of purely inter-state relations, independent of NGO influence. However, it is probably rare to find a purely private regime, and if one is found, it is likely to be a corporate private regime. Corporations have more resources and influence than social interest groups, and thus are able to establish institutions which are relatively independent of states. They are capable of constraining state behaviour through their market power, as noted in much of the literature on business–government relations.[19] Their position is further reinforced by a prevailing liberal ideology, which cordons off some activities from government intervention. They are also likely to be able to call upon the state itself to enforce their efforts to establish an independent regime. Further research on private corporate regimes will elucidate the opportunities and constraints on independent corporate behaviour within a regime context.

Non-corporate private associations, however, have relatively limited resources and power. Their stated goals may be focused on changing state behaviour, or may directly target individuals. Therefore, they are less likely to establish independent international regimes. Either they will be used as instruments of state policy, or they will 'use' states to implement their own goals. This latter possibility raises complex questions about the nature of the state itself in a world that is increasingly interdependent

---

[18] Porter and Brown (1991: 56) classify NGOs as (1) large, general membership organizations focused on domestic issues; (2) organizations focused on international issues that are part of an international network of affiliated organizations; and (3) think tank organizations without large membership but with influence through research, publications, and law suits.

[19] The classic analysis of the power of business is Lindblom's *Politics and Markets* (1977).

not just on economic matters, but also in political and social realms.

PVOs generally perform two functions: they may contribute to the emergence of norms and principles of behaviour upon which regimes are based; and they can perform the surveillance, information gathering, and enforcement functions of an already established regime.

Global environmental politics provides many examples of the relationship between PVOs and regimes. Peter Haas (1989, 1992*b*) has documented the role of scientists and scientific organizations in developing a Mediterranean pollution control regime. An 'epistemic community' came into being across PVO and state lines, sharing common perceptions and understandings of the problem and the possible solutions. In this case, the private sector played an important role in developing the principles and norms of the regime. In another example, private groups such as the Nature Conservancy forged a crucial link between the international financial system and the environmental movement by developing the idea and practice of debt-for-nature swaps. NGOs developed the principle that economic crisis puts pressure on valuable land; the norm that commercial transactions should be used as the basis for land conservation policy; and the rules and decision-making procedures for negotiating a debt-for-nature swap with indebted-country governments and local environmental groups (H. Williams 1992).[20]

In these two examples, states which had an interest in developing an inter-state regime appropriated the principles and norms of private sector organizations. In many regimes, NGOs also directly implement many regime functions. We can again turn to the family planning example to illustrate how states can utilize private organizations in regime-building.

In its early years, the family planning regime revolved around the International Planned Parenthood Federation, which channelled both private *and* public assistance to private family planning associations in developing countries. It was one of the first voices to call for global population control, and backed this up with a network of national family planning associations (Crane 1993,

---

[20] The US Government later appropriated the idea of debt-for-nature swaps, and used it as the foundation of its Enterprise for the Americas Initiative.

Marden, Hodgson, and McCoy 1982). NGOs such as the Ford
Foundation and the Population Council attempted to create an
'epistemic community' around the idea that population and
development were linked (Sadik 1991, Crane 1993). They developed the norm that governments should adopt national population policies consistent with their country's demographics, which
is supported by both governmental and non-governmental actors.
The Population Council has provided leadership within the regime
in research and monitoring of programme effectiveness (Crane
1993). As yet, there is wide variety and even conflict among
participants over the exact details of practice and implementation.
Most regime members, however, accept that governments should
facilitate personal preferences with regard to family size by
supplying the information and means for individuals to determine
freely the number and spacing of their children (Johansson 1991,
Crane 1993).

In the past five years, NGOs have taken the lead in bringing
together the population and environmental agendas, reconstructing
the regime based on ideas of 'sustainable development'. Since
some donor governments are under pressure from anti-family
planning forces (especially in the United States), the international
population institutions today increasingly provide their services
through the private sector. Furthermore, Crane argues that further
development of this regime will depend on the active participation
of other NGOs, such as women's organizations and medical and
public health professionals (Crane 1993).

A more interesting, and yet difficult, case to make is that NGOs
are not always simply the servants of state policy. Both corporations and non-corporate organizations may influence state
preferences by forming coalitions within the domestic political
system, or by creating transnational coalitions. In Brazil, an
alliance between foreign NGOs and indigenous peoples successfully put the issue of rain-forest destruction on the world agenda.
Furthermore, transnational alliances helped pressure then-President
José Sarney to attempt to change government policies which gave
tax incentives to environmentally destructive agricultural and
ranching interests (Porter and Brown 1991). A report on the
preparations for Earth Summit 1992 stated that the delegates
'were being watched, bullied, cajoled and lectured by an increasingly important group of actors on the international stage . . .

environmental organizations argued tirelessly with delegates over every comma in the texts they were preparing, bombarding them with studies and arranging briefings' (P. Lewis 1992: 4).

To sum up the argument to this point, there are two ways we can conceive of the relationship between states and non-state actors in regime creation and maintenance. States can use non-state actors in developing the normative basis of a regime, or in implementing its programmes. Alternatively, non-state actors can either act independently in establishing a regime, or they may operate on state preferences through domestic or transnational coalitions. In either case, the activities of non-state actors have a large impact on the shape of global politics.

5. REGIMES AND NON-STATE ACTORS: CROSSING BOUNDARIES

Do regimes matter? And, if one believes they do, does it matter whether or not they are private or public regimes? Does it matter that non-state actors are influential in international regimes? In general, the consensus seems to be that regimes matter in areas where participants believe they would be better off with a co-operative solution to a shared problem. They have little impact in areas of fundamental conflict, where actors operate on short-term calculations of interest and power, and the gains to unilateral action outweigh co-operation (Rittberger and Zürn 1990).

There are a number of ways in which non-state actors 'matter'. Private corporate regimes, the most extreme case of private sector activity, can directly affect state interests by changing the policy options available to them, particularly through their market power. Self-organization among corporate actors can either facilitate or obstruct the pursuit of state welfare goals. The existence of private corporate regimes raises anew the problems of transnationalism and interdependence noted decades ago. The central problematic of most analyses of multinational corporations, for instance, is the extent to which the interests of states and firms coincide or conflict, and which one has greater power over outcomes. In other words, corporate private regimes may matter because they are 'bad', changing the costs and benefits of different courses of action for both states and individuals. Therefore, systematic analysis of corporate regimes may tell us about the conditions under which states opt out of or are too weak to affect decisions in particular issue areas.

There is an obverse side to this argument, however. The existence of a private regime may eliminate the need for government intervention, or may act as an instrument to facilitate the development and implementation of national or collective goals. In this case, private corporate regimes or the PVOs may become policy instruments themselves. For example, a sophisticated, well-developed regime in political risks insurance obviates the need for government leaders to consider supporting trade and investment through extensive insurance programmes. Or, as another example, foreign aid programmes can be administered through networks of PVOs in the field of family planning and development, eliminating the need for expensive direct government aid programmes.

The two sets of actors, private and public, have reciprocal influence on each other. The point here is that both private and public agencies today often sit down at the negotiating table together to hammer out agreements concerning such issues as human rights and environmental obligations. Political scientists need to develop further the theoretical framework for understanding the exact relationship between private associations and international governmental organizations (Nadelman 1990).

The discussion above presents some preliminary hypotheses and illustrations concerning types of non-governmental actor and their relations with states in global regimes. Clearly, we need to develop further both the theoretical and the empirical contours of state–NGO relationships. Three tentative lines of inquiry could be pursued. First, we need a better understanding of how issue areas shape the relative power of NGOs. Particular attention should be paid to possible variations in private sector activity across issue areas, to determine the conditions under which private self-organization is likely. We also need to understand how changes within an issue area may weaken a private regime or lead to its incorporation into a public regime. The realist assumption that states set the framework within which other actors must operate may be true for certain areas, but less so for others.

Second, we need to analyse the systematic linkages between domestic politics, NGO influence, and regime formation and change. Private voluntary associations perform important supplementary functions in upholding international agreements and norms, within both private *and* public regimes. They play an important role in developing the norms which undergird inter-state agreements, and are influential in agenda setting and in mobilizing domestic political groups. For instance, once governments agree to a set of rules in an issue area, it provides political activists with a way to monitor and pressure governments for compliance. Greenpeace has been effective in providing surveillance and enforcement in the areas of whaling and sea dumping. In January 1990, Greenpeace obstructed a British ship attempting to dump coal ash in the North Sea, thus enforcing an international agreement Britain had signed prohibiting ocean dumping (Sagoff 1992). A weak empirical base hinders extensive theoretical and conceptual development concerning the role of NGOs and transnational coalitions in regimes.

The third line of inquiry would pursue the relationships between regimes themselves. Increasing technological interdependence, global ecological crisis, and evolving international social norms make it more and more difficult for states to control their environment. Options once available are often now out of reach, and the line between public and private realms of activity has become blurred. Issue areas that once were distinct have begun to overlap in significant ways. The population planning issue area becomes a subset of sustainable development issues, for example. Every regime is embedded in and entwined with others. These changes and linkages have not been thoroughly analysed to date, and would provide a rich area for research.

The transnationalists of the 1970s perhaps were ahead of their time. The end of superpower rivalry and the break-up of the Soviet empire force us to imagine a new kind of world politics. In the future, we may see a further institutionalization of the role of non-governmental actors in international negotiations. This may presage the emergence of a truly global society.

6

Progress in Game-Theoretical Analysis of International Regimes

ANDREW KYDD AND DUNCAN SNIDAL

1. INTRODUCTION

Over the last decade, regime theory has dominated the analysis of international institutions; over a slightly longer period, non-cooperative game theory has enjoyed a tremendous resurgence in the analysis of social, economic, and political phenomena. Both regime and non-cooperative game theory are centrally concerned with problems of competition and co-operation in what international relations scholars refer to as an anarchic environment. These parallels are hardly coincidental, since regime analysis has borrowed some of its intellectual energy from game theory. Understanding the strategic logic of conventions or the importance of the shadow of the future in enforcing co-operation, for example, has been crucial in explaining why regimes matter in international anarchy. Discussions of hegemony, issue linkage, relative gains, misperception, and interdependence have already been significantly informed by game-theoretical considerations. The central purpose of this chapter is to discuss the continuing positive impact of game theory on regime theory through the incorporation of additional and crucial elements including information, beliefs, communication, and domestic politics.

New work addresses two deficiencies in game-theoretical analy-

We thank the participants at the Tübingen conference on 'The Study of Regimes in International Relations—State of the Art and Perspectives', 14–18 July 1991, James Fearon, Mark Levy, Michael McGinnis, Peter Mayer, and Volker Rittberger for comments on earlier drafts of this chapter.

ses of regimes. The first is that earlier game-theoretical work was directed towards general issues of co-operation and was insufficiently attuned to the specific role of regimes as institutions. The goal was to show that co-operation was possible in anarchy and then to trace out the implications of factors such as hegemony for the creation and maintenance of regimes. It was assumed regimes played a role in this co-operation, but that role was not made sufficiently explicit or put at the forefront of the analysis. To be sure, analyses like Keohane's (1984) use concepts from game theory to discuss the role of regimes. But the focus is more on the maintenance of regimes 'after hegemony', rather than on the role of regimes in the development of co-operation. Moreover, the discussion of how regimes are effective is informal. Below we show how relatively recent game theory solution concepts such as trigger strategies, correlated equilibrium, and cheap talk potentially enhance our understanding of the functions of regimes by offering a more detailed explanation of the role played by beliefs, communication, and information in the emergence of co-operation.[1]

A second concern is that game-theoretical models miss key factors relevant to the operation of international regimes. A prime example is domestic politics as an important determinant of regime performance in issue areas as diverse as trade, the environment, and international security. Game models that assume states to be unitary, rational actors seem to suppress this important dimension of the problem. Recent work addresses this critique in two quite different ways. One approach shows that the rational actor assumption is fully consistent with a richer understanding of domestic politics captured implicitly in the preferences of the state as actor; another approach incorporates domestic factors explicitly through analysis of 'two-level' games. Together, they show how game theory contributes both to substantive debates about the importance of domestic politics and to the development of better theory regarding regime operation.

A related purpose of this chapter is to argue for a better balance between theory and substance even as our examples demonstrate the quite different ways that game theory can be applied to regime

---

[1] A 'solution concept' is a rule predicting how rational agents will behave in a game situation. Different solution concepts focus on different aspects of a game situation and therefore may offer different predictions for the same game.

theory. Application of alternative game theory solution concepts to international relations illustrates a methodologically driven relation from game to regime theory. These solution concepts originate in economics and pure game theory, with no regard to international politics. Yet the general problems they address, like the questions in much of game theory and certain areas of economics, have important parallels in international relations. In particular, non-cooperative game theory and industrial organization theory both investigate how actors collude in settings without centralized enforcement and (more recently) where monitoring others' behaviour is difficult. Similarities in such fundamental questions allows for a productive intellectual arbitrage of game-theoretical ideas into international regime theory. The formal analysis helps international theorists sometimes achieve a higher level of analytic rigour. However, this borrowing is not costless. Game theory solutions developed in a purely abstract realm, or with an eye towards different specific problems of oligopolistic collusion, do not come ready-made for application to international relations. There is a significant danger that models will dominate the substantive analysis in ways that distort rather than enhance our understanding of international regimes. Thus we need to scrutinize work in this tradition carefully so that we do not falsely recast international problems to fit game theory models but, instead, successfully adapt game models to the international setting.

By contrast, two-level games analysis uses informal game models to pursue a specific substantive question regarding the interaction between domestic and international politics. This might even be described as an 'interpretative' approach whereby the metaphor and language of game theory are used to expand our understanding of a wide range of cases.[2] As an interpretative device, game theory imposes a structure on the two-level problem by setting clear requirements for evaluating the coherence and plausibility of

---

[2] James Johnson (1991) discusses game theory as an interpretative theory that reconstructs our understanding of strategic interaction in different settings. John Ferejohn (1991*a*) makes a similar point in illustrating the complementarity of interpretivist and rational approaches. Note that this complementarity does not resolve more fundamental issues between rational choice theory and interpretative theory regarding the possibility (or desirability) of scientific generalizations in social science.

any account. In this sense, the inherently tautological nature of game-theoretical analysis (i.e. that conclusions must follow logically from premisses) allows us to distinguish good from bad arguments. Of course, the rational model is very flexible in terms of, for example, attribution of preferences and information to different actors. This means that a clever scholar can reconstruct any single empirical case from a rational actor perspective. However, it is progressively more difficult to reconstruct additional cases using a limited number of comparable and consistent assumptions. Thus a two-level game analysis is more compelling when the same factor (e.g. differences in state autonomy) explains outcomes across different cases than when the explanation relies on multiple factors. The persuasiveness of the explanation will be further enhanced in so far as interpretative two-level analysis is connected to formalizations that produce additional and more tightly specified predictions. We explore this possibility in terms of one recent attempt to extend the formalization of two-level analysis.

Our point is that there is a clear synergy between the different research styles; the understanding of regimes will only be impaired if we dogmatically favour one approach over the other. Game theory has contributed much to regime theory and will contribute much more in the future provided care is taken in using its tools. Our models need to be more carefully attuned to substantive problems just as regime theory needs to be more carefully informed by game theory. We hope the examples and discussion below illustrate these different possibilities for achieving an appropriate balance between rigour and substance, and that our criticisms will help improve work that is already on a productive course.

2. REGIMES, INFORMATION, AND BELIEFS

Because centralized enforcement of agreements is not generally available in international politics, international regime theory emphasizes how regimes affect state behaviour by changing beliefs and expectations about each other's behaviour. This emphasis is reflected in the standard definition of regimes as 'implicit or explicit principles, norms, rules, and decision-making procedures around which actors' expectations converge in a given area of international relations' (Krasner 1983*a*: 2). Informal norms and conventions play a key role in the formation of these mutual expectations, as do formal regime rules that require certain behaviour in certain situations. International institutions provide a forum for the exchange of information, and for learning about others' goals and behaviour. In short, information and beliefs are fundamental to international regimes.

Contemporary game theory has also increasingly investigated the influence of information and beliefs on behaviour. Earlier models assumed 'perfect information' where players knew everything about each other's preferences, capabilities, and past behaviour.[3] Such models contributed to general understanding of international co-operation, but were of more limited value for understanding the informational and co-ordinating roles of regimes. In newer game models, information or 'beliefs' are important because actors are unsure of key elements of their interaction. Actors do not know each other's preferences fully, have different information about the nature of the game between them, and observe each other's behaviour only imperfectly. These variations have an important impact on predicted equilibrium outcomes, on the ability of actors to achieve co-operative agreements, and on their ability to monitor and enforce co-operative outcomes. In this way, these new models open a crucial window on how regimes affect co-operation.

Fairly subtle changes in information can have a large impact on outcomes.[4] Shared beliefs promoted by regimes facilitate the choice among existing (Nash) equilibria by indicating appropriate points of co-ordination.[5] Even more important, regimes create

---

[3] 'Perfect information' is only one of a number of alternative definitions of the knowledge conditions in a game. Others include imperfect, uncertain, and incomplete informations. Rasmusen (1989) offers a useful discussion and typology.

[4] This observation is hardly new and is illustrated in Schelling's (1960*a*) many examples of the role of focal points in driving particular resolutions of conflicts of interests. A recent example is Rubinstein's (1989) 'electronic mail game', where a seemingly minor change from 'common' to 'almost common knowledge' overturns the rational ability to co-operate. The paradox in Rubinstein's model is also instructive in illustrating a game theory equilibrium that he points out is not a compelling solution to his problem. This should warn us of the danger that clever models sometimes lead to analyses that are not substantively insightful.

[5] A Nash equilibrium is an outcome from which no actor has an incentive to deviate provided no one else deviates. The prisoners' dilemma demonstrates emphatically that an equilibrium need not be a good outcome.

new equilibria by fostering changed beliefs among states. In turn, the collective configuration of beliefs may combine with the ongoing provision of information through the regime to enable the decentralized enforcement of co-operation. Conversely, failure to develop and sustain appropriate beliefs may lead to the demise of a regime.

To demonstrate the impact of game theory on the study of regimes, we will examine some recent examples of work in the field. While our purpose is to see the potential of the game theory approach, its limitations should be equally apparent. As always, the greatest danger is that the formal mechanics are so enticing that they are applied insensitively to the substantive problems central to regime analysis.

2.1. Regimes as Information-Providers

A first example is the impact of information on the celebrated result that co-operation is possible when a prisoners' dilemma (PD) is repeated through time through the use of reciprocal strategies exemplified by tit for tat.[6] This model is important for understanding co-operation, but it contains important and possibly limiting oversimplifications. In the model, actors must co-operate or defect totally; in reality, states often co-operate in part and defect in part. In the model, actors know precisely what the other has done; in reality, states often have remarkably vague know-ledge of the other's past behaviour.[7] These two problems interact since it is typically harder to detect small deviations from co-operation than large ones. Moreover, states have greater incentives to co-operate when they can be observed and to shade on agreements when monitoring is difficult. Since the standard repeated PD model fails to capture these features of reality, it cannot convince us that co-operation is possible or, most importantly, explain how regimes facilitate co-operation in the face of such complications.

---

[6] The Folk Theorem shows that, in a repeated prisoners' dilemma with sufficiently high valuation for the future, any outcome is possible provided that it offers each participant at least his individually attainable pay-off. See Fudenberg and Maskin (1986).

[7] US misestimates of Soviet military expenditures (and of the Soviet economy more generally), one of the most closely monitored aspects of the post-war period, illustrate this point decisively.

This shortcoming is largely obviated by recent studies involving continuous strategy choices and uncertainty. Downs and Rocke (1990) show how newer game-theoretical solutions address and accommodate such informational problems in the context of arms races.[8] As in earlier models, when each party can monitor the other's behaviour well, then a range of co-operative arms treaties can be sustained. A proportionate response strategy such as tit for tat can enforce co-operation, as can an abrogation strategy where violation of the agreement by the other side leads to abandonment of treaty terms by the first. But if one or both sides can monitor the other's military capability only imperfectly, these strategies rapidly become ineffective as the quality of information deteriorates. To solve this problem, Downs and Rocke propose a 'trigger' strategy, drawn from the literature on economic oligopoly. Here, each state abides by the treaty only as long as the other is observed exceeding a minimum threshold level of co-operation (the 'trigger'). Since monitoring is imperfect, the trigger is selected to allow for observational error so that co-operation is not too easily ended by faulty monitoring or by minor accidental slips in the level of co-operation. Thus the strategy seeks a middle ground that allows for informational problems while still threatening retaliation to limit the other's incentive to cheat on the agreement. In this way, Downs and Rocke show that robust co-operation can be maintained under a fairly wide range of circumstances.

Although Downs and Rocke focus on tacit and informal arrangements (and do not explicitly discuss regimes), their analysis raises interesting considerations for regime analysis. Most obviously, their emphasis on the quality of information reinforces the importance of this aspect of regimes. In so far as formal or informal regimes improve information quality, they expand opportunities for co-operation. A striking result is that one-sided intelligence gathering cannot always adequately substitute for an information-sharing regime. Indeed, unilateral improvements in the quality of

---

[8] Downs and Rocke also examine the achievement of arms control using a sequential equilibrium analysis. The emphasis there is on one state's uncertainty about the other side's preferences, that is, whether the other is an inherently aggressive state, and on the possibilities for one state initiating co-operation. Here, we discuss their separate analysis of the problem of maintaining co-operative agreements when there are informational difficulties in accurately observing the other state's behaviour.

information may reduce the possibility of co-operation rather than improve it (Downs and Rocke 1990: 212–22).

Comparison of these different strategies suggests that a more nuanced analysis of the content of international agreements and individual state strategies offers an important area for exploration. And it illustrates how game theory approaches offer an important adjunct to traditional analyses of these problems. However, Downs and Rocke's analysis also points out the potential difficulties of translating results from the abstract world of formal models to real international situations. Is it politically feasible or realistic that a state would ignore fairly substantial violations of an international agreement and that such a policy of continued co-operation would be domestically viable in this circumstance? Alternatively, would a precipitous return to an arms race based on the other crossing some artificial threshold be compelling, especially when monitoring is known to be faulty? In addition, game-theoretical thinking raises questions about the credibility of a threat to return to an all-out arms race, thereby sacrificing all future consideration of new or renegotiated treaties. These points do not indicate problems with Downs and Rocke's analysis but rather illustrate the important further questions to which their analysis leads.

Like the game-theoretical approach in general, Downs and Rocke's analysis reflects an inherent tension in game-theoretical analysis of institutions. By stressing the decentralized enforcement of co-operation, regime institutions seem relegated to a secondary or catalytic role.[9] Indeed, Downs and Rocke do not frame their analysis in terms of regimes, stress the importance of 'tacit' over 'formal' bargaining, and do not consider the role (if any) of institutions in the bargaining process. Yet many issues they raise in the verbal discussion around their model are closely connected to considerations of regimes. For example, Downs and Rocke (1990: 205) argue that tacit bargaining works best in tightly circumscribed issue areas such as naval races involving only one

[9] In analyses of domestic politics problems where centralized enforcement is possible, the parallel problem is that institutions tend to be embodied in the rules of the game and are thereby made exogenous to the analysis. A growing cottage industry is trying to endogenize institutions in order to explain them properly within a game-theoretical framework. See Krehbiel (1988) for an excellent overview with respect to legislative institutions.

type of ship, nuclear testing, satellite reconnaissance, or biological or chemical weapons. This claim begs a set of questions about the role of regimes in tightly defining issues[10] and, also, about the circumstances under which linkage provides a stronger basis for co-operation. The answers require a more careful integration of institutions, including informal ones, into game-theoretical analysis.

2.2. Regimes as Correlated Equilibria

A second example of the application of recent game-theoretical work to international relations seeks such an integrated analysis. Michael McGinnis and John Williams (1991, 1992*a*, 1992*b*) use the concept of a *correlated equilibrium* to analyse an iterated PD that has broader relevance for international regimes. Their ambitious attempt to establish the applicability of this solution concept for regime analysis illustrates the tension between formal elegance and substantive relevance. Although we remain sceptical of the usefulness of correlated equilibria in regime analysis, it is too early to evaluate fully the success of this agenda.

A correlated equilibrium is a scheme whereby actors 'correlate' their behaviours through some device (which could be a randomizing mechanism such as a die, or an agent such as an institution) that, selecting on a probability distribution defined over the possible outcomes and that is common knowledge, directs each actor how to behave so that each prefers to follow the dictate of this device under the assumption that others do so.[11] This completely opaque definition is best clarified through some simple examples. Suppose two states face the co-ordination problem presented in Fig. 6.1. There being no obvious resolution of the distribution problem, and a danger that they will pass up joint efficiency gains by not co-ordinating, states might reasonably agree to flip a coin and play {top, left} if it comes up heads but

---

[10] On this point see also Ch. 4, sect. 2, above.
[11] Aumann (1974, 1987) develops the concept in detail and the numerical examples below are taken from Aumann (1987). Note that Nash equilibria are special cases of correlated equilibria and that the probabilities reflect uncertainty that players have regarding each other's choices, not the randomization of mixed strategies. Actors are told only how they should behave, not what others are being told. Forges (1986) develops the related and broader concept of 'communication equilibria'.

2,1	0,0
0,0	1,2

Fig. 6.1 A co-ordination problem

{bottom, right} if it comes up tails. If the row player sees tails he knows column is instructed to play right and so would only lose by choosing anything but bottom (and so forth for the other combinations). This produces a correlated equilibrium that is a compelling outcome not dissimilar to everyday solutions of this problem.

A more complicated and striking case is the chicken game in Fig. 6.2(*a*) combined with a correlation device that proposes various pay-off combinations with the probabilities shown in Fig. 6.2(*b*). This distribution of probabilities provides an expected pay-off of (5,5) whose collective value exceeds that of any Nash equilibrium outcome. The key to this collectively superior equilibrium is that the correlation device does not tell each player what cell has been selected but only what action to take. Thus if row is told to play 'up' she knows only that column has an equal probability of having been told 'left' or 'right.' The correlation equilibrium is self-enforcing, moreover, since row has a higher expected value from following the device's advice than deviating to play 'bottom' (and similarly for column and for the alternative messages from the device). Finally, note that correlation has no impact in the prisoners' dilemma of Fig. 6.3 (where the correlated equilibrium is simply the Nash equilibrium) since both sides always have an incentive to play {bottom, right} regardless of the message offered by a correlation device.

6,6	2,7		1/3	1/3
7,2	0,0		1/3	0

(*a*) The pay-offs   (*b*) The correlation distribution

Fig. 6.2 A correlated equilibrium for chicken

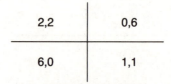

2,2	0,6
6,0	1,1

Fig. 6.3 Prisoners' dilemma

Correlated equilibria work by helping players achieve their common interest in co-ordination (through the correlation of their strategies) while preventing them from pursuing their conflicting interests (by not providing precise information as to the other player's behaviour). Consequently, the solution concept is of declining interest as the co-ordination element of the strategic interaction decreases. In co-ordination games, adhering to a correlated equilibrium is similar to accepting a focal point (Schelling 1960*a*) as a relatively agreeable resolution of the underlying co-operation problem. It has an added advantage that random determination of the outcome can lead to equal expected values for each player and in this sense be 'fairer' than a focal point determined by historical or situational factors favouring one particular player.

Regimes can be usefully interpreted as correlation devices when there is a strong common interest in co-ordination. In Fig. 6.1, for example, a regime could be interpreted as a mechanism for selecting among Nash equilibria. Expectations raised by the regime's decision make adherence to a particular equilibrium a compelling choice for individual states. Regimes governing communication and transportation, and agreements about some industrial, health, and safety standards might be seen as correlational devices in this sense. However, the enforcement of the outcome in these cases relies on direct incentives of the participants and not on the regime's ability to conceal information. For this reason, pure co-ordination regimes, while possibly very important in international relations, are degenerate cases of correlated equilibrium and do not reflect its more interesting enforcement possibilities.

It is harder to imagine a correspondence between regimes and correlation devices when conflicts of interest are more substantial. In chicken, for example, a regime working as a correlation device would be an attractive alternative if no regime could directly enforce the mutual co-operation outcome. But it is difficult to think of an example or even imagine a regime that is able to conceal from one state what it reveals to another, and such secrecy is an essential element of correlated equilibria in more conflictual circumstances. Thus the difficulty in applying correlated equilibria to international relations lies in finding a plausible analogue to the 'correlation device' when state interests diverge.[12]

Our conclusion is that the correlated equilibrium concept needs further development before it can expand our understanding of regimes. The fundamental problem rests with the difficulty in finding a compelling correspondence between the formalization and the substantive issues raised in regime analysis. On this count we would be pleased to be proven wrong by McGinnis and Williams or others. In the meantime, correlated equilibria exemplify, on the one hand, how the formal techniques of game theory can suggest innovative ways to examine problems and, on the other hand, how these innovations sometimes turn out not to be fully persuasive.

2.3. Cheap Talk in International Regimes

If correlated equilibria are a less promising avenue for regime analysis, the related concept of *cheap talk* is very promising.[13] Cheap talk refers to communication that is essentially costless in itself, where verbal communication is a prime example.[14] Its importance for regime analysis is clear: regimes facilitate communication among states and, indeed, are often disparaged as

[12] McGinnis and Williams use a result from Aumann (1987) to claim that Bayesian rational actors can achieve a correlated equilibrium without a device. This interpretation of the result is contestable. Tan and Werlang (1988) show that the common priors assumption needed to achieve correlated equilibria is stronger than that needed for rationalizable strategies or Nash equilibria, and argue that correlated equilibria are unlikely in the absence of explicit correlation devices. Even if McGinnis and Williams's position is correct, moreover, they still do not make clear what role regimes play in helping states to correlate their behaviours.
[13] Matthews and Postlewaite (1989) illustrate the connection between the two concepts in terms of mediated versus unmediated communication. On cheap talk see Farrell (1987) and Farrell and Gibbons (1989).
[14] See Jervis (1970) for the nearly identical concept of 'signals' in international politics.

'mere' talking-shops. Yet many regime theorists have implicitly subscribed to the notion that 'talk' matters without having a persuasive analytical justification. Until recently, game-theoretical applications have focused overwhelmingly on costly signals which are now well understood to have an important impact on outcomes. Deterrence models, for example, show how a willingness to risk nuclear escalation (Powell 1990), or incur costs of mobilization (Fearon 1990), helps one state persuade another not to engage in military expansionism. Deterrence works because only a state that was serious about containing expansion would be willing to incur such risks and costs. Costliness is the essence of such signals. By contrast, cheap talk refers to messages that have no immediate cost—they are just talk—although they have indirect costs in possibly affecting the ultimate equilibrium outcome.

An example of international cheap talk is exploratory, perhaps secret, discussions to end a war, promote arms control, or expand free trade. These initial talks pose no costs to participants, who can walk away from them without penalty. If preliminary negotiations indicate a significant possibility of striking a mutually agreeable bargain, however, discussions move to a subsequent stage perhaps involving an international conference, formal treaty negotiations, or a summit leading to an international agreement.[15] The perhaps surprising result is that the first round of cheap talk can affect both whether an agreement is struck in the second round as well as the terms of the agreement. The reason is that if neither party shows sufficient interest in the first round then no serious second-round bargaining will occur.[16] This gives states an incentive to convey real information about prospects for success so that negotiations move forward. If no one indicates a willingness to

[15] Of course, standard enforcement problems arise in this second stage. In the formal analysis, the second round is based on a specific bargaining structure that is reasonable for economic transactions (e.g. Farrell and Gibbons 1989) but needs further adaptation for international negotiations.

[16] It is substantively more realistic to assume the second round would not occur since formal international negotiations *are* costly among states (even if we ignore the cost of diplomats' salaries and fine living as we do in the first round) because of their international as well as domestic ramifications. Cheap talk is important, however, not because the second round is costly but because of the expectations that actors take into it from the cheap talk round. This impact can be isolated formally by assuming that a (costless) second round occurs and examining the impact of cheap talk on its outcome.

make concessions that will make a deal more likely, then there is no point bargaining. This means that cheap talk is *indirectly* costly, however, because a state that indicates it wants negotiations to continue into a second round is implicitly weakening its bargaining position to assure the seriousness of continued negotiations. Thus 'cheap talk' is a slightly misleading term. While ineffective talk is cheap, effective talk has real and therefore sometimes costly consequences.[17] The important point is that talk can be effective even when not directly costly because it conveys information as to the range of mutually acceptable agreements and helps players co-ordinate on one of them.

James Morrow (1992) demonstrates the relevance of cheap talk to the analysis of international regimes. He proposes a model in which states face a co-ordination problem, sometimes differ on their preferred co-ordination outcome, and have different information regarding their common situation. Their shared interest in a co-ordinated outcome creates incentives to communicate truthfully, but differences regarding where to co-ordinate creates incentives to misrepresent their private information. Morrow exploits this tension to show two separate yet complementary roles for regimes as mechanisms of *communication* and as mechanisms of *co-ordination*. Communication entails sharing information to improve each side's understanding of the consequences of a particular agreement. For example, pooling expertise regarding the costs and effectiveness of various environmental controls can help us formulate a better global environment policy. Co-ordination refers to the selection of a particular agreement from a larger set of possibilities, each of which is preferred to non-coordination but over which states have divergent preferences. For example, states want common technical or safety standards but often differ over which standard to adopt because any particular choice advantages producers from certain states and disadvantages others.

Different regimes emphasize these different communication and co-ordination roles according to the nature of the issue between the two states. The success of regimes does not depend on the

---

[17] If both parties indicate they want to move to a second round, equilibrium pay-offs may not be affected and so talk has no net cost to either. However, talk has expected *ex ante* costs since one side cannot know that the other will also indicate a desire for continuing negotiations or else it could free-ride on the other's request that negotiations continue.

shadow of the future, and greater co-operation can be enforced in a decentralized manner by the beliefs and incentives of the actors in a cheap talk equilibrium. Unfortunately, in so far as there are divergences in the interests of the actors (i.e. it is not a pure co-ordination problem with purely harmonious interests) cheap talk cannot lead to fully efficient outcomes. The reason is that states will provide misleading information to promote their preferred co-ordination outcome and this impairs the communication process whereby states locate jointly preferred outcomes. Nevertheless, cheap talk can still improve the outcome over the pre-existing Nash equilibrium. Finally, Morrow points out that mutually bene-ficial cheap talk regimes may not be adopted because of their distributive consequences. Despite these limitations, cheap talk is important because it demonstrates that regime effectiveness does not rest solely, or even principally, on enforcement capacities.

Cheap talk is compelling for international regimes because it captures much of what goes on in formal and informal inter-national institutions. The conventional wisdom that international organizations are useful because they provide an opportunity for states to communicate takes on an additional dimension here. The exchange of information is more than just talk and can have real effects. At the same time, it is important to point out that cheap talk can also lead to 'babbling' equilibria where the talk is as meaningless and as irrelevant to equilibrium behaviour as cynics claim is the case with most international discussions. Perhaps a better understanding of the positive possibilities of talk will help us better understand why certain institutions are more effective than others. At the same time, the analysis of cheap talk needs greater refinement to include, for example, analysis of more realistic situations where talk is sequential rather than simultane-ous (Matthews and Postlewaite 1989). Game theory, like regime theory, still has a long way to go in explaining how we get more informative communication and better equilibria.

The equilibrium concepts discussed in this section illustrate a new and emerging wave of impact from game theory to regime analysis. Unlike earlier models, recent work explicitly incorpor-ates the information, beliefs, and communication long believed to be crucial by regime theorists. Trigger equilibria demonstrate the importance of information acquisition in maintaining agreements and suggest the superiority of symmetrically available information provided collectively by a regime over unilateral national intelligence gathering. Cheap talk addresses the importance of traditional diplomacy and ongoing international organizations as costless channels of communication. Hopefully, such tools will prompt regime scholars to move beyond general questions of co-operation to more focused analysis of the role of specific institutional arrangements in its generation.

3. RATIONAL STATES, TWO-LEVEL GAMES, AND REGIMES

Game theory can also be important for analysis of the impact of domestic interests on regime outcomes. In the standard rational actor approach, goals such as the pursuit of power or wealth are stipulated, and then state behaviour is derived by maximizing the (often implicit) utility function, subject to environmental constraints presented by limited resources and the activities of other states. This simple framework underlies much international relations theory, formal and non-formal, and is implicit in most of the regime literature. However, the rational or unitary actor assumption has been challenged in ways that may promote fruitful innovation in regime analysis.

Critics argue that the rational actor assumption is inappropriate because coherent pursuit of a unitary national purpose is often thwarted by domestic interests. An extreme form of this argument, associated with the bureaucratic politics literature, is that the complexity of internal decision-making invalidates the unitary actor assumption. A more moderate version is captured in the two-level games approach. This argues that our theories need to incorporate more details about states (including domestic institutions, pressure groups, economic systems) in order to provide a clearer understanding of the domestic constraints on international policy-making. This will lead to a more refined view of international outcomes, either by giving a clearer picture of how state interests are derived from domestic interests, or by clarifying how domestic politics force a departure from rationality at the nation-state level. Of course, such theories will pay a possibly severe price for this greater richness in terms of loss of parsimony and tractability.

This section considers two alternative ways to conceptualize the state as actor and its domestic politics within regime analysis. Formal analysis clarifies the bureaucratic politics argument to show why it is better framed as a debate about the content of state preferences than about rationality itself. This provides a natural linkage to two-level games analysis, which is an ambitious attempt to build a more detailed understanding of the domestic determinants of state behaviour into regime analysis.

3.1. Modelling the State as a Unitary Rational Actor

Recent game-theoretical analysis provides an important response to the bureaucratic politics critique of treating states as rational actors. Christopher Achen (1989) and George Downs and David Rocke (1990) have developed a model of a central decision-maker buffeted by a myriad of competing interests. Provided competing interests can be assumed to be goal-seeking actors—as the bureaucratic politics literature does—their result is that the central decision-maker behaves as if she were maximizing a collective utility function. This analysis invalidates the central complaint of the bureaucratic politics literature that the state cannot be treated as a unitary maximizing agent. But the analysis also reinforces a major argument of domestic politics explanations. In the absence of consensus, we need to know who influences the utility function that the state acts 'as if' it is maximizing. Thus this result is no licence for ignoring domestic politics; however, it is a warrant for treating states as rational actors provided careful attention is paid to assessing their objectives.[18]

Consider Achen's extensive explication of the model. His 'focal actor' model has a single leader who makes the final decision, and many influencers who affect that decision by rewarding the focal actor for making a decision that favours them. Rewarding is costly,

---

[18] In a similiar vein, Nalebuff (1991) shows that certain psychological critiques that rational choice theory cannot handle misperceptions can be remedied by including information and beliefs within a more sophisticated game model. However, it would be wrong to interpret Nalebuff's analysis as showing that psychological models are incorrect or uninformative for international relations. What he shows is that certain anomalies that once appeared to defeat rational explanations now can be incorporated within the theory by expanding and enriching its scope to deal with information.

however, so they can only reward so much. The game is organized sequentially. First, influencers announce schedules of reward on the principle that the more the focal actor's decision favours them, the more they reward her. Then the focal actor chooses among alternatives to maximize her utility, including the rewards promised by the influencers. The result is the same as if the focal actor maximized a weighted sum of all players' utilities. Hence the collectivity, focal actor plus influencers, behaves like a unitary rational actor that maximizes a collective utility function. Achen takes this to be a decisive blow to the bureaucratic politics literature. And indeed he is right: if the focal actor model is a reasonable model for foreign policy, the rationality of the state as actor is assured.[19]

Two caveats are in order. One is that while the focal actor model is appropriate for many foreign policy interactions involving tacit bargaining or executive agreement, it does not adequately represent situations where international agreements must be submitted to legislative approval. (Such situations are central to the two-level games discussed next.) Achen's model explicitly avoids legislative institutions where the 'impossibility' of deriving a collective utility function is well known. This restricts the range of his analysis, in so far as legislative organs are involved in foreign policy, and their special characteristics that frustrate collective rationality come into play. For some applications—treaties between democracies, for instance—a more appropriate model might be a focal actor associated with a spatial legislative model. Different protocols relating to amendments etc. could then be investigated for their impact on international agreement. It is unclear whether this different domestic setting will produce such an elegant and simplifying conclusion.[20]

The second caveat is that domestic politics still matter even when states can be treated as unitary. In order to predict behaviour it is not enough that the actor be rational, one needs an assessment

---

[19] Note that other ancillary arguments used in the bureaucratic politics literature (e.g. 'standard operating procedures', flawed execution of decisions, distortions of information) are not modelled here. However, Achen's model clearly picks up the core bureaucratic politics argument regarding 'pulling and hauling' among interests.

[20] Work on 'structure-induced equilibria' can be seen as trying to solve this problem for legislative institutions (Krehbiel 1988). Although it does not lead to the same simplifying result as Achen's, it produces results which are, in principle, amenable to two-level game analysis.

of the preferences of those in a position to influence the focal
actor. Achen has presented one such model in which the political
power of domestic actors translates relatively smoothly into central decision-maker behaviour. This amounts not to a rejection of
domestic investigation, but to a reassertion of the possibility of
developing a parsimonious framework for including domestic
actors in international politics.

3.2. Two-Level Game Analysis of Regimes

Two-level games also bridge the domestic–international divide to
incorporate a more nuanced analysis of domestic politics into
regime analysis. Regimes that seem attractive on the basis of
supposedly 'national' interests may be blocked by powerful groups
within one or more member states. This possibility is especially
important for understanding regime creation and change, since
influencing ongoing negotiations is easier than forcing a renegotiation of an existing arrangement. But protectionist forces within
GATT countries, and the resultant backsliding on international
commitments, illustrate the ongoing sensitivity of regime performance to domestic factors. The two-level approach seeks a
more refined understanding of these domestic constraints on
international regimes.

In an influential article, Robert Putnam (1988) presents a
framework for analysing the link between domestic and international politics that is particularly apt for analysis of regime
formation. He argues that international relations should be conceived as a two-level game, where statesmen simultaneously play
an international game with other states and a domestic game
with their own polity. An edited volume (Evans, Jacobson, and
Putnam: in progress) applies this metaphor to case studies of
twentieth-century international relations. In a separate paper, Iida
(1992) looks at bargaining with 'win-sets', a central concept of two-
level games, verifying some of Putnam's hypotheses while calling
others into question.

Putnam's metaphor is a game with two levels or boards, one
corresponding to the international level and one to the domestic
level. Statesmen go back and forth between the boards, attempting to win on both of them at once. Only if victory is secured on

both boards is the statesman's goal achieved. The implicit model is of an international bargaining game whose outcome is constrained to fall within the domestic win-sets of both states. (A 'win-set' is the set of options that are ratifiable at the domestic level.) One interesting possibility is that statesmen can manipulate their own and each other's win-sets, through acts targeted at their own and the opposing domestic actors. Hence domestic constraints cannot be simply treated as exogenous. The play of the game can alter them, making agreements possible or impossible as time goes by. Putnam's case study, G-7 negotiations over monetary policy in the late 1970s, provides examples of the stratagems employed and problems encountered.

Two-level analysis provides an instructive example of the value and pitfalls of a more interpretative use of game theory. The novelty of Putnam's analysis lies not in his substantive observation of an interaction between domestic and international politics—as he points out, that is very old stuff—but in the way he invokes game-theoretic imagery and language. His implicit claim is that a more systematic analysis can be based on these clearer concepts and the associated, logically consistent (and perhaps rigorously derived) hypotheses. The special strength of game theory as an interpretative device is that it imposes a stronger coherence test on the analysis. Observed international behaviour must be explained in terms of a strategic interaction between actors whose goals and constraints are consistent with domestic political configurations.

This theoretical perspective is currently being combined with a multiple case study design in a follow-up project (Evans, Jacobson, and Putnam: in progress). Strict falsification is difficult in the isolated case because the open-ended nature of empirical interpretation and the flexibility of game theory provide tremendous leeway for particularistic interpretations through (possibly) idiosyncratic specification of domestic actors and their goals. Any single case can be rationally reconstructed by a sufficiently ingenious proponent of two-level games. It is a much more difficult test to rationally reconstruct a series of cases using empirical interpretations that are theoretically comparable and consistent across cases. Thus a two-level explanation that consistently explained a variety of case studies would be a valuable addition to our understanding of international politics.

Unfortunately, current two-level analysis offers few generalizations that are sufficiently specific to be falsifiable. Without more precise guiding hypotheses, the case studies are individually compelling but insufficiently commensurate with each other to allow their systematic comparison and evaluation of common hypotheses. There are no clear criteria for choosing between (or rejecting) competing explanations. Of course, the common language and framework of the two-level project does facilitate the search for inductive generalization across cases. Nevertheless, a large part of the deductive-theoretical promise of two-level games has been left behind in the execution of the project.[21]

Andrew Moravcsik (1991) points out that more general claims could be specified and investigated even within the metaphorical mode of analysis. One example is how different domestic institutions interact at the international level. Do systems with more trouble ratifying agreements domestically, such as presidential systems with strong legislatures, fare better internationally against parliamentary systems, where the majority party's will is enacted relatively easily? Does party fragmentation help or hurt a country in international negotiations? Can democracies co-operate more easily with each other than with authoritarian regimes, or vice versa? Such questions could be investigated through hypotheses derived informally from the two-level game metaphor of how decision-makers interact with their domestic environment and the international system, and then examined empirically. Hence even without explicitly formalizing the model some general investigations can be based on the two-level game framework.

Further game-theoretical development of the two-level framework is illustrated by Keisuke Iida's (1992) model of the impact of 'win-sets' on international bargaining. This is a good example of formal analysis of problems once thought to be too complex for game-theoretical analysis. Though it inevitably simplifies the problem to some degree, Iida's analysis is rich enough to confirm certain intuitions from the non-formal literature while challenging

---

[21] Because some project papers are still in draft form, subsequent revisions may attenuate our criticisms. In particular, Andrew Moravcsik's introductory chapter that we discuss below is still under active revision. Nevertheless, we expect our basic point will apply to the forthcoming two-level games volume.

others.[22] For example, Putnam hypothesizes that the smaller the win-set (1) the greater bargaining leverage a country will have, but (2) the more difficult it will be to reach agreements. Using a standard game theory bargaining model (Rubinstein 1982) Iida shows that the second proposition depends vitally on the existence of some form of uncertainty between the states. This does not invalidate Putnam's claim, but it identifies the central importance of an unrecognized variable.

Iida then considers two alternative specifications of uncertainty, each with a different substantive interpretation. The first is of uncertainty as risk, where the likelihood of domestic ratification is known by both sides to increase with the attractiveness of the bargain. In this case, Putnam's second hypothesis holds but his first proposition does not always hold. The second specification is of uncertainty as ignorance, where a country has only imperfect information as to the prospects of domestic ratification in the other country. Iida shows that under certain circumstances (where the other player overestimates the probability that your win-set is small), Putnam's first hypothesis holds but the second one does not. This, of course, exactly contradicts the previous case.

The implications are that two-level games need further theoretical refinement, that formalization can expand our understanding of the underlying processes, and that empirical results cannot be properly interpreted without further theoretical refinement. Inevitably formalization misses some of the richness of the informal presentation. For example, the win-set is simply taken as exogenous. In contrast, Putnam and Moravcsik stress the need to treat the win-set as endogenous, not merely to assume its existence, since the effort of central actors to manipulate win-sets is an important part of the two-level story. Thus Iida's work is only a partial formalization of Putnam's theory, but nevertheless provides important insights and challenges to it.

Finally, Iida's paper illustrates how formal game theory is valuable, perhaps essential, for refining less formal or purely verbal arguments. Game-theoretical refinements of the meaning

[22] Another formal analysis that examines a two-level game is Jongryn Mo (1990). His central question is how the bargaining strength and political power of the various domestic parties affect their share of the pie in international bargaining. Hence it belongs more to the second image reversed tradition than to two-level games.

of uncertainty expose aspects of the problem that are disguised in purely verbal analysis. The models allow Iida to trace out the fairly subtle but important impact of different assumptions in a way that even the tightest verbal argument cannot. The price paid in terms of stronger and more specific assumptions is more than rewarded by a deeper understanding of their implications in the argument.

4. CONCLUSION

This chapter has examined different ways that game theory has recently been applied to international regime theory. Some applications are driven by methodology, applying solution concepts from economic and pure game theory to international co-operation. Others focus on substantive problems, using game theory in a looser, more interpretative manner. We conclude by highlighting some of the contributions that this range of game-theoretical approaches has generated for the study of international regimes.

The rarefied assumptions of earlier game-theoretical analysis— unitary actors, complete information, no errors or misperceptions —left it open to criticism of missing or misrepresenting key aspects of international politics. For example, perfect information models overlooked the communication and provision of information that have always been seen as central to international regimes. Recent game-theoretical work addresses such issues directly and thereby refines our understanding of regimes. Iida shows how uncertainty plays a central and insufficiently understood role in two-level bargaining. The cheap talk literature shows how costless signals make co-operation possible by facilitating communication and co-ordination. This result is particularly important because it emphasizes the role for regimes as facilitators and co-ordinators of international co-operation.

Finally, game-theoretical investigations provide a better understanding of how domestic actors are affected by and affect international regimes. Previously, the debate assumed that if domestic actors were important, the state could not be considered a rational actor, and the issue was simply over how important domestic actors are. Achen and Downs and Rocke have taken the debate an important step further by showing that bureaucratic politics need not impede state rationality. But even if the state can be treated as rational, the domestic determinants of its goals must be investigated in order to understand state behaviour. In this way, the two-level games project shows how the reciprocal influences between international and domestic actors can be important. As it progresses, we will have a clearer idea of when domestic factors can be set aside, when they must be brought in, and how to do so.

This progress should not obscure continuing shortcomings in game-theoretical analysis of regimes. There are still too few examples where the game models have been fully tailored to specific substantive questions raised by regime theory. The context of international politics is sufficiently distinctive that there are limitations imposed by borrowing models from the different context of economic theory or the purely abstract realm of game theory. For this reason we have stressed the point that advance in this area will increasingly depend on a closer integration of the analytical tools with the substantive questions and empirical investigations.

PART III

Regime Formation and Change

7

Sovereignty, Regimes, and Human Rights

STEPHEN D. KRASNER

1. INTRODUCTION

There are two distinct lines of argument in the literature on international regimes (Krasner 1991). For the first, which is generally characterized as liberal co-operation theory, the basic challenge for states is to overcome market failure, the situation in which individual rational self-interested policies produce outcomes that leave each state worse off than it might otherwise have been. The challenge is to devise policies that make it possible to reach the Pareto frontier. The exemplary problem is posed by the prisoners' dilemma pay-off matrix.

The solution offered by liberal co-operation theory is institution-building. By changing the incentives facing policy-makers, institutions encourage co-operative behaviour (Keohane 1984, Krebs 1990). International regimes, one form of institution, are a device for overcoming problems of market failure. The success or failure of regime-building can be explained by the extent to which regimes provide information, monitoring capabilities, or focal points that allow states to move to the Pareto frontier; everyone becomes better off at the same time; absolute rather than relative gains matter.

The second line of argument about international regimes, generally characterized as realism, focuses on power and distribu-

I would like to thank Masaru Kohno and Volker Rittberger for their comments on earlier versions of this chapter.

tion rather than information and joint gains. The basic issue is where states will end up on the Pareto frontier, not how to reach the frontier in the first place. Gains for one actor mean losses for another. International regimes are created to promote the interests of particular actors. Regime creation and maintenance are a function of the distribution of power and interests among states (Grieco 1988, 1990, Gilpin 1981, Krasner 1976).

Resolution of the debate between liberal and realist perspectives is not likely to depend on which approach best explains the same body of empirical data; rather it will depend on whether market failure or distributional issues best describe the range of issues involving international politics. Some prominent issues can clearly be characterized as market failure problems: in international trade, the first best policy for each state is to impose an optimal tariff, but if all states pursue such a policy, they will be worse off than they would have been had each adopted free trade. Other issues are more clearly distributional: in international wars victorious powers have usually been in a position to impose terms on their defeated adversaries which involve changes in territorial boundaries and political regimes.

Human rights have been defined in many different ways. This chapter understands human rights as issues involving the relationship between rulers and ruled. Human rights involve limitations on the scope of authority which a state can exercise over individuals. Can the state, for instance, cut off a hand if an individual commits theft, punish women or couples for exceeding a specified number of births, discriminate on the basis of race, gender, ethnicity, or sexual proclivity, ban or encourage abortion, sanction slavery, prescribe religious practices?

Despite being thought of as a quintessentially liberal issue, international human rights regimes cannot easily be understood from a liberal perspective. If all states were committed to the same conception of human rights, there would be no need for an international regime; each state acting on its own initiative would defend a shared conception of the appropriate relationship between rulers and ruled. This would be harmony (Keohane 1984). International regimes for human rights are designed to encourage some states to adopt policies that they would not otherwise pursue. The question of whether states adhere to such regimes is not a function of the extent to which a regime enhances information and discourages cheating by other actors; rather it is a function of the extent to which more powerful states in the system are willing to enforce the principles and norms of the regime.

The following pages examine four cases involving human rights or the relationship between rulers and ruled—religious practices in the seventeenth century, the slave trade in the nineteenth century, minority rights in Central Europe in the late nineteenth and early twentieth centuries, and liberal individual rights in the late twentieth century. The abolition of the slave trade was a success. The protection of minority rights was a failure. For religious practices and liberal individual rights the outcomes are more ambivalent. Religious toleration in the seventeenth century and liberal individual rights in the twentieth century were accepted in some polities but not in others. The differences in outcomes in these four cases are best explained by the capabilities and commitment of those states that supported each of these regimes. Only when powerful states enforced principles and norms were international human rights regimes consequential.

The claim that the creation and maintenance of human rights regimes is better understood from a realist rather than a co-operation perspective cannot be a general test of these two approaches. Because human rights regimes are attempts to alter relations between rulers and ruled within polities, they are not likely to be responses to problems of market failure. If all states were prepared to accept the principles and norms of the regime, there would not be any need for the regime in the first place. Human rights practices would be self-enforcing within each state; the implementation of human rights in one polity is not likely to be dependent on monitoring behaviour in others.

Moreover, liberal co-operation theory and realism are not the only approaches for understanding international regimes, even if they are the most prominent. Both realism and liberal co-operation theory, as they have been developed in the United States, are state-centric perspectives. They assume that states are the basic actors; they pay little attention to sub-state actors. The most powerful consequences of international human rights regimes, however, may be the way in which they enhance the capabilities of particular groups or individuals within states. For instance, the Helsinki Final Act of 1975 made it easier for dissident groups in Eastern Europe to place pressure on their own governments.

Treaties on international refugees enhanced the scope of authority of some national bureaucracies while narrowing that of others (Thomas 1991, Hartigan 1992). The European human rights regime has been institutionalized within national legal systems as well as in the European Court of Human Rights (Forsythe 1983: 52, 57, 59). In the recent American literature on international regimes, approaches which emphasize the impact of non-state actors have not been explored as systematically as state-centric orientations of either the liberal or realist variety.

2. SOVEREIGNTY AND HUMAN RIGHTS

Sovereignty is a system of political order based on territory. The territorially grounded nature of sovereignty distinguishes it from other forms of political order such as tribes, in which authority claims are made over people rather than space, and ancient empires, which had fluid frontiers rather than unambiguous boundaries. The defining principle of the sovereign state system is that external actors are denied any authoritative powers within a given territory; if foreign institutions, such as the Catholic Church, were able to make authoritative decisions about the behaviour of individuals in a variety of territories, then it would not be a sovereign state system. Within a given territory, political authority may be organized in any number of ways: authority can be concentrated at the centre or federalized; it can be conferred through inheritance or elections; the franchise can be limited or universal. It is the exclusion of external authority, not the organization of internal authority, which defines sovereignty as a distinct mode of political organization.

There are two prominent norms that follow from the principle of exclusive control within a given territory. The first is the norm of non-interference in the internal affairs of other states. This norm was explicitly developed during the nineteenth century, most vigorously by the states of the Western Hemisphere, and has been enshrined in many major international agreements during the twentieth century. The second is the norm of self-help. Self-help means that every state has the right to conduct its foreign policy as it sees fit. In external as in internal affairs each state can set its own policy.

Exclusive territorial control, non-interference, self-help—these are the trinity that define a sovereign state system. They are the basic principles and norms of the sovereignty regime. Specific rules and decision-making procedures flow from them.

The sovereignty regime is, however, neither logically consistent nor self-reinforcing. The norms of self-help and non-interference are contradictory in theory and potentially in practice as well (S. Hoffmann 1984: 11). If each state has the right to set its own policies, then it can pursue any objectives that it chooses, including policies that involve interference in the internal affairs of other states. Self-help implies that a state can determine its own affairs even if that entails undermining the political regime of another country, assassinating its leader, or corrupting its electoral process. The norm of non-interference implies that all such activities are illegitimate.

Human rights is one issue area where the conflict between self-help and non-interference can be manifest. In the contemporary world, human rights have been defined primarily, although not exclusively, in liberal democratic terms. In a more general sense human rights can be thought of as questions involving the relationship between rulers and their subjects or citizens. Can the sovereign enslave subjects with blue eyes? The principle of non-interference in internal affairs implies that this or any other practice, no matter how heinous it might appear to 'enlightened' minds, ought not to be the concern of other states. In contrast, the principle of self-help implies that other states can do whatever they want, including making the abolition of any such practice part of their foreign policy agendas.

When there is a clash between non-interference and self-help in an issue area as close to the core of any polity as the scope of state authority over subject or citizen, how is it resolved? Does one norm always predominate? Does non-interference, for instance, always trump self-help, or vice versa? How can the variation in outcomes be explained?

For the four cases examined in this paper—the support for religious toleration, the abolition of the slave trade, the protection of minorities in Central Europe, and the promotion of individual rights—the most important explanation for the variation in outcomes is the relative power and interests of states. The slave trade was abolished because the major European powers, especially

Britain, vigorously monitored and enforced the regime. The protection of minority rights failed because the dominant powers were unwilling to enforce treaty provisions which they themselves had signed. Religious toleration was only successfully imposed in the seventeenth century in areas where local rulers were too weak to resist, although over time religious freedom came to be widely accepted among the advanced democratic capitalist countries of the West. Ultimately issues associated with religious practices were resolved not by an extension of state power but by capitulation: religious questions were either removed entirely from the state's portfolio (which is what is meant by religious freedom), or their importance was deflated. Individualistic human rights have been only fitfully and incompletely accepted; the most powerful advocates of universal human rights, such as the United States, do not have the resources or inclination to compel or entice recalcitrant states to accept such practices.

3. THE PEACE OF WESTPHALIA AND RELIGIOUS TOLERATION

The issue of religious tolerance plagued the western world until the twentieth century. This was not simply a manifestation of the concern that individuals have with their own salvation, it also reflected the relationship between religion and political stability. Because sectarian doctrines and practices have been used to legitimate political regimes, threats to these doctrines could also be threats to the state, but state efforts to destroy dissident sects could precipitate civil strife.

Early Christians, including Christ, preached toleration and the separation of Church and State. This doctrinal commitment did not long survive Constantine's conversion. Once Christianity became the official religion of the Roman Empire, both Church and State attempted to suppress other creeds. During the Middle Ages and into the sixteenth century Christian Europe was generally intolerant, often more so toward heterodox Christians than to Jews, Muslims, and pagans.

The leaders of the Reformation, which split Christendom more deeply than any earlier schism, did not accept other creeds. After some initial vacillation, Luther rejected toleration. In 1525 he advocated suppression of the Mass because it was a blasphemy. By 1530 he supported the death penalty for Anabaptists. In 1532 he urged the Great Elector of Brandenburg to expel Zwinglians because they disagreed with Lutherans about certain doctrinal matters. In 1536 he supported the expulsion of Jews from Saxony. Toleration for unregenerate Jews was a position which Luther never seriously considered and in the 1540s he wrote violently anti-Semitic tracts. Calvin also totally rejected toleration of any dissident sect (Kamen 1967: 41, 79; Haile 1980: 287–94).

The religious disputes precipitated by the Reformation contributed to intense military and political conflict in Europe. In England, religious disagreement undermined the mutual expectations that had undergirded the British political system. The old order had been based on a shared understanding between the Parliament and the King. The King had the responsibility to defend the realm. The Parliament had the obligation to provide resources. So long as King and Parliament had the same views about what the defence of the realm meant, as had been the case for instance under Elizabeth I, this system worked. It did not work, however, when Parliament suspected that the King was pursuing a foreign policy agenda motivated by his own religious convictions, rather than advancing the interest of England (Ferejohn 1991*b*). The results were the brutal British civil wars of the seventeenth century, the end of the Stuart dynasty, and the removal of two monarchs.

In England both Hobbes and Locke were a response to the disorder, devastation, and chaos produced by the civil wars. Hobbes sought to eliminate discord by justifying complete obedience to the sovereign. Once consent was granted, he maintained in the *Leviathan*, it could not be challenged. Religious, and other, strife would be abolished by fiat. Hobbes's solution did not work, but Locke offered a more viable strategy, religious toleration. He argued in his *Letter Concerning Toleration* that 'neither Pagan, nor Mahometan, nor Jew, ought to be excluded from the civil rights of the commonwealth because of his religion' (quoted in B. Lewis 1992: 49). Civic tranquility would be achieved not by extending the reach of the sovereign, but by limiting it, by removing religious issues from the purview of the state.

The most dramatic strife and disorder, however, occurred not

in Britain, but on the Continent. Germany, that is, the Holy
Roman Empire of the German nation, had the most fragmented
political order in Europe. The major political institutions of the
Empire included the Emperor, who was elected by the seven
electors (composed of three prelates and four major secular
princes), the Imperial Diet (which had three separate councils
composed of the electors, the principalities, and the cities), two
imperial courts of law, some fifty imperial cities, about one
hundred principalities, several thousand imperial knights living on
small estates in the South and West, and a number of ecclesiastical
states (Gagliardo 1980). The Habsburg monarchs, committed
Catholics and the rulers of Austria among other dominions, were
the dominant force in the Empire, and, with the exception of the
years 1742–5, they held the office of Emperor from 1438 until
the Empire was abolished by Napoleon in 1806. Their power,
however, was circumscribed by other political actors, by the
contorted institutional arrangements of the Empire, and by the
Reformation.

The Reformation weakened the political legitimacy of the
Emperor and the Empire. The Holy Roman Empire had been
represented as the successor to Rome, the secular arm of
Christendom. Despite long-standing disputes between the Emperor
and the Pope, the Empire was closely associated with the Catholic
Church. Three out of the seven electors (the archbishops of Trier,
Mainz, and Cologne) were Catholic prelates. The Habsburgs were
themselves Catholic. The Reformation, which was centred in
Germany, challenged the legitimating myth that had helped to
support the unity of the Empire and the position of the Emperor.
Religious disorder was a challenge to the state as well as the soul.
As one historian has written: 'Religious disorder meant chaos, and
chaos in turn meant dissolution of all established political and
social order. . . . Throughout the history of Christianity in the
West religious challenges to authority had been accompanied by
political challenges' (Mosse 1970: 170).

Religious dissension in the Empire culminated in the Thirty
Years War. The war began in Bohemia, then a Protestant area
that was ruled by the Habsburg monarch of Austria under a
separate title as King of Bohemia. The Habsburgs had attempted
to turn back the Reformation in Bohemia. Resistance from the
local population had first led to a grant of limited religious

toleration in 1609, the Letter of Majesty issued by the Emperor Rudolf II. When the new King Ferdinand, however, more vigorously pursued the agenda of the Counter-Reformation, a revolt broke out in Prague in May of 1618. The Bohemians deposed the Catholic Ferdinand and chose in his stead the Great Elector Frederick, the Protestant ruler of the Palatinate (Beller 1970: 308–12).

These events initiated thirty years of strife in Germany. All of the major European powers were drawn into the conflict. But religion was not the only cause of the Thirty Years' War. Alliances were not simply formed along religious lines. Because of the threat posed by the Habsburg family, which ruled not only Austria and the Empire but Spain as well, Catholic France allied itself with the Protestant princes of Germany and the Protestant ruler of Sweden. After 1635 Protestant Saxony was allied with Catholic Austria. Religious strife, however, contributed to the general disorder and exacerbated the conflict.

Germany was devastated by the war. Armies were undisciplined. Many cities and towns along the Rhine were pillaged many times. Starvation and disease were widespread. The rural population might have sunk by 40 per cent, the urban by 33 per cent (Beller 1970: 345 f., 357). Battle deaths for the great powers have been estimated at 2.1 million, the third most costly war in history, and a figure that was not exceeded until the First World War (Tilly 1990: 165 f.). While France and Sweden emerged as the military victors, all of the major European powers were exhausted by the struggle and anxious to contain religious conflict.

At the time the Peace of Westphalia was negotiated in 1648, religious conflict had embroiled Europe for almost 150 years. Power was divided between Protestant and Catholic monarchs. Religious divisions did not correspond with security interests. Neither side was in a position to win a decisive victory.

The Peace of Westphalia, which was composed of two separate treaties, the Treaty of Münster between the Emperor and the Catholic monarchs and the Treaty of Osnabrück between the Emperor and the Protestant monarchs, sought to restore order in part by establishing a regime, at least for Germany, that would contain religious strife by defining the relationship between subjects and rulers in an international agreement.[1] These efforts to

---

[1] The treaties are printed in Parry (1969: 119–269, 273–356).

establish principles, norms, rules, and decision-making procedures for religious practices were an attempt to create a human rights regime; that is, to define the relationship between the state and its subjects or citizens, to constrain the internal freedom of action of legitimate political authority.

The peace provided that religious practices were to be restored to the situation that existed on 1 January 1624. Where there was agreement between ruler and subject on religious practices as of that date these were to continue unless they were changed by mutual consent. Catholic orders were to stay Catholic; Lutheran orders were to stay Lutheran (Treaty of Osnabrück, v. 12–v. 22). Dissenters (Catholic or Lutheran), who did not have any rights of religious practice in 1624 and who wanted to move or were ordered to move, were to have the freedom to do so and were given five years to sell their property (Treaty of Osnabrück, v. 29 f.). Catholic and Protestant magistrates were admonished to forbid any person from criticizing or impugning the religious settlement contained in the agreement and in the earlier Treaty of Passau (Treaty of Osnabrück, v. 41).

Those Catholics who lived in Lutheran states or Lutherans who lived in Catholic states, who did not move or were not ordered to move, were to be given the right to practise their religion in the privacy of their homes, and to educate their children at home or to send them to foreign schools, even if they had not had such rights in 1624. Subjects were not to be excluded from the 'Community of Merchants, Artizans or Companies, nor depriv'd of Successions, Legacies, Hospitals, Lazar-Houses, or Alms-Houses, and other Privileges or Rights' because of their religion. Nor were they to be denied the right of burial or charged an amount for burial different from that levied on those of the religion of the state (Treaty of Osnabrück, v. 28).

Cities with mixed Lutheran and Catholic populations (Augsburg, Dinkelsbühl, Biberach, Ravensburg, Kaufbeuren) were to have freedom of religious practices for Catholics and Lutherans (Treaty of Osnabrück, v. 24). In the first four of these cities offices were to be divided equally between adherents of the two sects (Treaty of Osnabrück, v. 3, 7).

The peace provided that Catholics and Lutherans should be equally represented in the assemblies of the Empire. Religious issues were to be decided by consensus (Treaty of Osnabrück, v.

41). Representatives to the imperial courts of law were to be divided by religion. If the judges split along religious lines, then a case could be appealed to the Diet. If there were cross-cutting cleavages with respect to religion then a case could not be appealed (Treaty of Osnabrück, v. 45).

Rights given to Lutherans and Catholics were also extended to Calvinists (Treaty of Osnabrück, vii). In the case of a situation in which the religion of the ruler of a particular territory changed from one Protestant sect to another (from Lutheran to Calvinist or vice versa) the new ruler was to have the right of worship of his own religion, but he was prohibited from attempting to change the religion of his subjects or the status of churches, hospitals, schools, and revenues. The new ruler was enjoined from giving 'any trouble or molestation to the Religion of others directly or indirectly' (Treaty of Osnabrück, vii).

The Peace of Westphalia was very far from being a general endorsement of religious toleration. The two treaties mentioned only the Catholic, Lutheran, and Calvinist persuasions. There was no tolerance for other groups (Treaty of Osnabrück, v. 28). The King of France was obligated to the Catholic religion and to 'abolish all Innovations crept in during the War' in those territories that were ceded to France by the treaty (Treaty of Münster, lxxvii). In Catholic Austria, the Habsburg rulers offered no tolerance for Protestants.

In sum, the Peace of Westphalia was deeply concerned about one form of human rights, religious belief and practice. The treaties were attentive to relations between individuals and the state (Gross 1979: 196). The peace constrained behaviour in the weaker German states, even specifying the division of offices in some imperial cities. All signatories were prohibited from arbitrarily changing the religion of their subjects and the distribution of Church resources.

Outside of the weaker German states, however, princes were free to deal with dissenters in any way they saw fit. Some rulers, such as Frederick William, the Great Elector of Brandenburg (1640–88), were tolerant because their territories contained such a diversity of religions that it would have been politically costly if not suicidal to try to enforce uniformity (Kamen 1967: 192). France practised limited toleration under the Edict of Nantes, issued by Henry IV in 1598, which gave Protestants equal standing under the law, the right to practise in certain parts of the country, and access to public offices, although they had to pay taxes to support the Catholic Church. The edict was revoked, however, by Louis XIV in 1685 after its specific provisions had been dismembered piecemeal over the previous seventy years, more by private actors, especially the Catholic Church, than by the crown (Maddox 1987: 46 f.). In Hungary, which had experienced reasonably tolerant policies by the end of the sixteenth century, the repression of non-Catholic sects became the order of the day by the end of the seventeenth century. Britain rejected religious toleration after the Restoration.

Only in the very far reaches of British North America, in Rhode Island and Pennsylvania, was religious toleration endorsed as a basic principle of the polity (Kamen 1967: 193–207). Roger Williams and John Clarke, the founders of Rhode Island, were both dissenters who had left Massachusetts. Williams argued that their must be a wall between the Church and the State, lest the Church be corrupted. Clarke asserted that the use of force to coerce religious beliefs or practices disrupted civil life and forced men to become hypocrites and liars. William Penn, who established Pennsylvania, also argued that coercion destroyed authentic religious experience. Penn, elaborating on Quaker doctrine, maintained that no individual had any authority over the conscience of another. Penn, however, went on to found a theocracy. Only those who acknowledged God would not be molested. Only Christians could hold public office. Labour was prohibited on the Sabbath (Adams and Emmerich 1990: 3–6).

With the founding of the new republic, the United States became the first country to embrace not just religious toleration, with its implication that there was some dominant sect, but religious freedom, the principle which excludes religious practices from the portfolio of state concerns. In a series of debates in Virginia in the 1780s, the position of Madison and his allies, which rejected the right of the state to tax for the purpose of supporting religious activities, triumphed. In his *Memorial and Remonstrance against Religious Assessments*, Madison argued that each individual had the right to determine how to render homage to the Creator. Article VI of the Constitution prohibited the use of religious tests for office-holders. This was a significant achievement because prior to 1787 almost all of the colonies had required religious oaths that limited office-holding to Christians. After the Constitution was adopted most state governments also eliminated religious oaths (Adams and Emmerich 1990: 11–13). In 1790 George Washington wrote to the Jewish community of Newport, Rhode Island, that: 'The citizens of the United States of America . . . all possess alike liberty of conscience and immunities of citizenship. It is now no more that toleration is spoken of, as if it was by the indulgence of one class of people that another enjoyed the exercise of their inherent natural rights' (quoted in B. Lewis 1992: 49).

The issue of religious practice was, then, a matter of central concern to states in the seventeenth century, the question of non-intervention notwithstanding. The Peace of Westphalia specified elaborate rules for regulating religious behaviour in the weaker German states and the Imperial Diet and law courts. Stronger states, however, were free to do as they pleased, and their practices varied, although nowhere in Europe did full toleration become the accepted norm.

Nevertheless, the Peace of Westphalia was a step on the path that culminated in the endorsement of religious freedom by the secular, democratic, capitalist states of the West. The Peace of Westphalia did help to reinforce the norm that when a new sovereign took over a territory the religious practices of the inhabitants would be respected. In 1814, for instance, when Belgium was given to the Netherlands, the Prince of Orange made an explicit commitment to religious equality. When the King of Sardinia ceded territory to the Canton of Geneva in 1822, Geneva agreed that the rights of Catholics would be protected (Macartney 1934: 158 f.).

More importantly, the Peace of Westphalia provided support for religious toleration and freedom which ultimately became accepted practice in the West through changes in national policies that reflected a recognition that religion was too contentious an issue for state involvement. The United States, where the Constitution was signed by members of six different Christian denominations, was the first state to fully embrace religious freedom (Adams and Emmerich 1990: 8 f.). The purpose of secularism was to 'prevent the upholders of any doctrine from using the state. After the long and bitter struggles of the wars of religion, Christians gradually came to the conclusion that only in this way would it be possible for adherents of rival or even merely different churches to live side by side in reasonable peace' (B. Lewis 1992: 50). International regimes, which inevitably transgressed the norm of non-intervention, could reinforce and encourage, but could not compel or dictate, because the external enforcement of religious toleration is a daunting task involving extensive resource commitments, something that states have been loath to do unless civil strife in one country has threatened the political tranquility of others, as was the case in the wars of religion of the sixteenth and seventeenth centuries. As the contemporary Middle East demonstrates, the acceptance of religious freedom is hardly universal.

4. THE ABOLITION OF THE SLAVE TRADE

The abolition of the slave trade across the Atlantic, a precursor to full emancipation, was a product of principles and norms that were supported by the most powerful states in the international system, especially by the dominant naval power in the nineteenth century, Great Britain. Britain coerced, badgered, cajoled, and threatened other countries, notably Portugal and Brazil, into accepting an end to the slave trade and played the major role in enforcing and monitoring the international regime which it had itself created through a series of international treaties.

Britain outlawed slavery for its own-flag vessels in 1807 (Ray 1989: 409). During the Napoleonic Wars Britain used her navy to capture slave ships from enemy states, France and the Netherlands, justifying such action in terms of her rights as a belligerent. Slaves on these ships were set free, usually in Sierra Leone (Bethell 1970: 10). Near the end of the conflict Sweden and newly liberated Holland signed treaties with Britain abolishing the slave trade. Napoleon, hoping to curry favour with Britain, abolished the slave trade after his return from Elba, a commitment which Louis XVIII, who owed his crown to Wellington's triumph at Waterloo, was obliged to honour. By 1815 Britain, Russia, Austria, Prussia, France, the Netherlands, Sweden, and the United States had agreed to prohibit the transatlantic slave trade. In 1817 Spain agreed to abolish the slave trade north of the equator and in 1820 to abolish it completely. Portugal had accepted a ban on the trade but only north of the equator (Bethell 1970: 11–15, 20).

Despite these commitments, the slave trade was so lucrative that large numbers of Africans continued to be transported across the Atlantic. Britain made the major effort to enforce the ban on slaving. Between 1818 and 1820 Britain signed treaties with a number of European countries that gave British warships the right to search and seize vessels suspected of engaging in the slave trade. In 1831 France, which had not enforced its own prohibition of the slave trade, was pressured by Britain into signing a treaty that allowed for mutual search and seizure of vessels suspected of transporting slaves. This treaty eliminated the French flag as an option for those engaging in the slave trade (Bethell 1970: 20, 96).

Portugal and Brazil, which declared its independence in 1822, were the most recalcitrant slave-trading countries. Brazilian agriculture was heavily dependent on slave labour. Immediately after abolishing the slave trade for British shipping in 1807, Britain began to put pressure on Portugal, whose colonies in Africa and South America were both a major source and a target of the slave trade. Portugal at first totally rejected British initiatives. However, Portugal had a close and highly asymmetrical relationship with Britain. When France invaded Portugal in late 1807, the Portuguese royal family was forced to flee to Brazil under British protection. In 1810 Portugal signed a commercial treaty with Britain which provided in part that Portugal would co-operate with Britain in bringing about the gradual abolition of the slave trade. Britain, however, conceded to Portugal the right to continue slave trading within her African territories. In 1815 Portugal signed an agreement with Britain agreeing to abolish the slave trade north of the equator, a commitment of limited consequence since much of Portugal's trade between Africa and Brazil was south of the equator. In 1839 Britain unilaterally authorized its navy to board and seize suspected slavers that were flying the Portuguese flag. This came after long and unsuccessful efforts to sign a bilateral treaty with Portugal authorizing such seizures. The slaves were to be released in the nearest British port, and the disposition of the ships was to be decided by British admiralty courts; the crews of such ships, however, were to be returned to their own countries for trial (Bethell 1970: 7–9, 13, 164).

After Brazil gained independence, Britain focused its attention on it. In exchange for recognition by Britain, Brazil agreed in 1826, despite strong opposition from many members of its parliament, to a treaty which stipulated that the slave trade would be abolished by 1830. The treaty designated the slave trade as piracy after that date, providing Britain with legal grounds for seizing slave-trading ships on the high seas (Bethell 1970: 60 f.). Despite the agreement, slave trading continued between Brazil and Africa, even growing in the 1830s beyond what it had been before the treaty was signed (Bethell 1970: 60 f., ch. 3).

Confronted with the continuation of the slave trade some twenty years after it should have been abolished under the 1826 treaty, Britain acted unilaterally. Slaving had already been declared piracy, giving British ships the right to board and seize suspected slavers on the high seas. In 1850, British warships entered Brazilian ports and seized and burned a number of vessels that were suspected of engaging in the transport of slaves. In the course of these actions the British were frequently fired upon from Brazilian forts. It is difficult to imagine a less ambiguous violation of sovereign control and non-interference (Bethell 1970: ch. 12).

Nevertheless, these pressures were effective. Confronted with British naval power and the antipathy of other advanced states, Brazil passed and enforced legislation that was designed to end the slave trade. One Brazilian leader speaking to the Brazilian Chamber of Deputies in 1850 recognized that Brazil was the only country actively resisting the anti-slave regime and stated that 'with the whole of the civilised world now opposed to the slave trade, and with a powerful nation like Britain intent on ending it once and for all, can we resist the torrent? I think not' (quoted in Bethell 1970: 338).

The abolition of the slave trade, and ultimately of slavery itself, was an exceptional triumph for human rights and freedom. It was a triumph that was made possible in large measure because of the commitment and power of Great Britain. Britain took the lead in initiating a series of international treaties in the early part of the nineteenth century which committed states to abolishing the slave trade. Brazil was the most important defector from this system, refusing to enforce its own treaty obligations, which were scorned if not explicitly repudiated as a product of British coercion. Britain used naval power, including entry into Brazilian territorial waters and the destruction of Brazilian ships, to force

Brazil to end the slave trade. Self-help, Britain's commitment to ending international commerce in human beings, triumphed over non-intervention.

5. THE PROTECTION OF MINORITIES

In the late nineteenth and early twentieth centuries systematic efforts were made to create an international regime that would protect the rights of national minorities, especially in Central and Eastern Europe. Provisions for the protection of such rights were included in a number of treaties that were guaranteed by the great powers, most notably the Berlin Treaty of 1878. After the First World War extensive minority rights provisions were written into a number of peace treaties and a monitoring and enforcement mechanism was established within the League of Nations.

These efforts were an abject failure. National governments ignored their obligations to protect the rights of minorities within their own borders. Neither the major powers nor the League of Nations acted to enforce the regime. After the Second World War attempts to guarantee the rights of defined national minorities was virtually abandoned, replaced by a liberal emphasis on purely individual human rights.

Ethnic conflicts in Central Europe in the wake of the collapse of the Soviet empire have infused new life into the issue of whether rights should be protected for individuals or groups. The conundrum, however, which doomed earlier efforts to create a minority rights regime to defeat, remains: the cost of enforcing any minority rights regime is likely to outweigh the benefits for would-be enforcers. In the absence of domestic commitment to minority rights, external management is likely to be extremely expensive in terms of both life and treasure, while the direct security benefits to potential intervenors are limited. The abolition of the slave trade, which required British naval action against much weaker opponents, was much less costly than long-term military involvement in hostile foreign territory. Only if there are domestic divisions within oppressor states which could be activated and strengthened by an international regime or economic sanctions (usually much less costly than military intervention) are minority rights regimes likely to be effective.

During the nineteenth century minorities were defined primarily, although not exclusively, as religious minorities. European attention was focused on the collapsing, multi-religious and multi-ethnic, Ottoman Empire. Efforts to protect Christians within the Ottoman Empire can be traced back as far as unilateral commitments by European monarchs in the thirteenth century and explicit treaty agreements between the Porte and France, Austria, and Russia in the seventeenth and eighteenth centuries (Macartney 1934: 161–3).

As the Ottoman Empire fell apart during the nineteenth century, the major European powers intervened more actively. In the treaties granting independence to states that were formed out of the Empire, clauses for the protection of religious minorities were included. For instance, in 1830 Great Britain, France, and Russia concluded a protocol guaranteeing the independence of Greece which stated that the signatories, to preserve Greece from 'the calamities which the rivalries of the religions therein professed might excite, agree that all the subjects of the new States, whatever their religion may be, shall be admissible to all public employments, functions and honours, and be treated on a footing of perfect equality, without regard to difference of creed, in their relations, religious, civil or political' (Macartney 1934: 164 f.). When Moldavia and Walachia secured their independence in 1856 the western powers sought to guarantee equal treatment for adherents of all creeds, including Jews.

Nineteenth-century efforts to guarantee minority rights reached their climax at the Congress of Berlin of 1878. At the conference, convened to deal with the consequences of the Balkan wars of the mid-1870s, the representatives of the great powers agreed that the acceptance of religious toleration would be one of the conditions of recognition of new members of the international community; such stipulations were included in the treaties regarding Romania, Serbia, Montenegro, and Bulgaria. The treaty signed with the Ottoman Empire provided that the Porte would protect the rights not only of religious minorities but also of a number of ethnic minorities, including the Armenians (Claude 1955: 2; Macartney 1934: 166 f.).

These measures were ineffectual. The Ottoman Government

supported a number of massacres against the Armenians, the first of which occurred in 1894. Others followed, despite protests from the western powers. Article 44 of the Treaty of Berlin of 1878 prohibited Romania from engaging in religious discrimination against Jews of Romanian citizenship, but Romania evaded this obligation by declaring that no Jew could be a citizen. The major Western European powers basically did little or nothing to enforce the minority rights provisions of the treaties that were signed as a result of the Congress of Berlin (Macartney 1934: 170; Claude 1955: 5; Sharp 1979: 171).

Despite the failure of the nineteenth-century system, efforts to establish and protect minority rights were vigorously renewed at the end of the First World War. Guarantees took several forms. Austria, Hungary, Bulgaria, and Turkey were defeated states and protections were written into their peace treaties. Poland, Czechoslovakia, Yugoslavia, Rumania, and Greece were new or enlarged states. They signed minority rights treaties with the Allied and Associated Powers. Albania, Lithuania, Latvia, Estonia, and Iraq made declarations that were similar to the rights in the minority treaties as a result of pressure that was brought upon them when they applied to join the League of Nations. Germany assumed obligations for minority rights in the Geneva Convention, a bilateral treaty signed with Poland which established an elaborate minority rights system for Upper Silesia and gave an important role to the League (Claude 1955: 16; Jones 1991: 45).

The rationale for the protection of minority rights was that stable domestic orders were necessary for international peace, an obvious conclusion that could be drawn from the experience of the First World War, which had been precipitated by the assassination of the Archduke Ferdinand by a Serbian nationalist. Collective security, the Wilsonian vision that informed the effort to create a peaceful international order, was based upon the existence of democratic states. The relationship between minority rights and collective security was more important than any effort to guarantee the rights of minorities for their own sake. The treaties sought to resolve the minority problem by making minorities loyal citizens of the states in which they happened to live. The issue of national self-determination would be resolved not by allowing fissure, which was inherently problematic where ethnic groups were mixed together, but rather by reconciling minorities to a secure place within existing states. If minorities were ill-treated they could generate disorder within their countries of residence and threaten international peace, especially if their co-nationalists controlled an independent state and came to their assistance (Macartney 1934: 275, 278, 297; Claude 1955: 14).

The protections offered to minorities were elaborate. For instance, the Polish Minority Treaty provided that 'Poland undertakes to assure full and complete protection of life and liberty to all inhabitants of Poland without distinction of birth, nationality, language, race or religion' (Art. 2). Religious differences were not to affect public or professional employment (Art. 7). Where there were a considerable number of non-Polish-speakers they would be educated in their own language in primary school, although the state could mandate the teaching of Polish (Art. 8). Jews would not be obligated to perform any act which violated the Jewish Sabbath, including not holding elections on Saturday (Art. 11). The treaty was made part of the fundamental law of Poland.[2]

Monitoring and enforcement of the minority treaties that arose after the First World War was much more institutionally elaborated than had been the case for the provisions of the nineteenth-century treaties, which left enforcement entirely in the hands of the great powers. The various treaties and other declarations designated the Council of the League of Nations to assume the responsibility for supervision and implementation. The Permanent Court of International Justice was given the right to make binding decisions. Any member of the Council of the League could submit a case to the Court. However, the members of the Council did not want to resort to the Court; during the 1920s they devised a procedure for handling minority cases which provided for the Minorities Section of the Secretariat to receive petitions from any source. If a petition was found to have merit and the issue could not be resolved informally then it could be brought to the Council. The accused state had the right to participate in any such proceedings and could veto any Council decision (Claude 1955: 20–8; Sharp 1979: 174).

The minorities regime established after the First World War was a clear violation of the norm of non-interference. As a condition of full participation in the international community, the smaller

---

[2] The text of the treaty can be found in Macartney (1934: 502–6).

states of Central and Eastern Europe were compelled to accept limitations on their internal sovereignty that included issues as detailed as the days of the week on which elections could be held. Clemenceau, in a covering letter conveying the Polish Minorities Treaty, argued that the provisions of the treaty were consistent with diplomatic precedent. He stated that:

This Treaty does not constitute any fresh departure. It has for long been the established procedure of the public law of Europe that when a State is created, or even when large accessions of territory are made to an established State, the joint and formal recognition of the Great Powers should be accompanied by the requirement that such States should, in the form of a binding international Convention, undertake to comply with certain principles of Government. . . .

In this connection I must also recall to your consideration the fact that it is to the endeavours and sacrifices of the Powers in whose name I am addressing you that the Polish nation owes the recovery of its independence. It is by their decision that Polish sovereignty is being re-established over the territories in question, and that the inhabitants of these territories are being incorporated in the Polish nation. It is on the support which the resources of these Powers will afford to the League of Nations that the future Poland will to a large extent depend for the possession of these territories. There rests, therefore, upon these Powers an obligation, which they cannot evade, to secure in the most permanent and solemn form guarantees for certain essential rights which will afford to the inhabitants the necessary protection, whatever changes may take place in the internal constitution of the Polish State . . . (quoted in Macartney 1934: 238).

The second paragraph of Clemenceau's note is a much more compelling explanation for the minorities treaties than the first. The provisions for minority rights were imposed on the weaker states of Central and Eastern Europe by the victorious allied powers. The importance given to minority rights after the First World War reflected the configuration of power at that historical moment. Two of the multinational empires—Austria-Hungary, and the Ottoman Empire—had been destroyed entirely by the war. The third, Russia, was in the hands of new revolutionary leaders. Guarantees of minority rights were never voluntarily accepted. The peace was dictated by the liberal states of Western Europe, and by the United States (Claude 1955: 17).

The victors did not accept any restrictions on their own internal sovereignty. Britain refused to allow any issues related to Wales or Ireland to become a matter of concern to the League. Italy refused to accept any provisions regarding minorities, despite the fact that the peace settlement placed a large number of German-speakers in the South Tyrol within Italy's new borders. Questions related to the treatment of Afro-Americans in the United States were completely off the agenda (Macartney 1934: 252, Sharp 1979: 181–3).

The regime for the protection of minorities established within the League failed as badly as its nineteenth-century precursor. The minorities states viewed the regime as an infringement on their internal sovereignty. Their leaders maintained that the failure to impose similar obligations on all states violated the principle of the sovereign equality of states. They pointed out that Germany and Italy were not obligated in similar ways (Claude 1955: 32–5). By the time that Poland formally renounced its obligations toward minorities in September 1934, when its representative declared that without a uniform and general system Poland would no longer co-operate with international bodies, the minorities treaties were already a dead letter (Claude 1955: 30). The victorious powers of the First World War had created a regime for the protection of minority rights but they were not willing to enforce it. The League established an institutionalized procedure for dealing with minority questions, but without the backing of the major powers these decision-making procedures were vacuous. There could not be a more graphic, chilling, and unambiguous demonstration of the failure of the effort to protect minorities after the First World War than Nazi Germany and the Holocaust. At the conclusion of the Second World War, only very limited efforts were made to accord special protections to designated minority groups. Rather, individual human rights became the focus of attention of the international community.

The creation of the minorities regime after the First World War was a triumph of the principle of self-help over non-intervention. The regime was imposed on the newly created states of Central and Eastern Europe by the more powerful allied victors, but the regime was ineffectual because its creators were not willing to provide the resources that would have been necessary to enforce it. The minority states had accepted the regime in the first place only because they needed international recognition and support when they were first established. Once recognition had been offered, the allies had exhausted their stock of cheap leverage. Because the allies were unwilling to accept external monitoring of their own treatment of minorities (Catholics in Northern Ireland, Afro-Americans in the United States), there was little chance that the norms and principles of the regime would be voluntarily accepted by the states of Central and Eastern Europe or by a significant segment of their populations. Over time the minorities states increased their ability to resist external pressures from their larger western neighbours who could not or would not dedicate the resources that would have been needed to defend the regime, a choice that reflected not only the cost of enforcement but also the fact that in the inter-war period the rise of German power, not the disintegration of Central and Eastern European states, posed the major threat to the security of France and Britain.

6. THE CONTEMPORARY WORLD AND HUMAN RIGHTS

In the contemporary world there has been a great deal of concern about human rights. It is not, however, clear what human rights are. While all issues associated with human rights have involved the relationship between rulers and ruled, diplomats from differ-ent states have articulated different visions even while signing the same documents. Western liberal conceptions based upon the autonomy of the individual hold the leading position, but they are not hegemonic. The prominence of western conceptions reflects the distribution of power—political and economic—in the international system.

The most obvious manifestations of contemporary concerns with human rights are found in various declarations adopted by the United Nations. The preamble to the Charter of the United Nations reaffirms fundamental human rights, the dignity of the individual, and the equality of men and women. These individual-istic values which had been initiated by the French and American revolutions were endorsed by the community of nations (Vincent 1986: 92 f.).

The Universal Declaration of Human Rights was adopted by

the UN General Assembly in 1948 after three years of debate. The Declaration specifies personal rights such as protection against racial, sexual, or religious discrimination; legal rights such as the presumption of innocence and equality before the law; civil liberties such as freedom of religion, opinion, movement, association, and residence, including the right to leave any country and 'to seek and enjoy in other countries asylum from persecution' (Art. 14); family rights, including the right to marriage, equal rights for both spouses in marriage, and full consent to marriage; subsistence rights such as the right to food; economic rights such as the right to own property, to work, to enjoy 'periodic holidays with pay' (Art. 24), and to social security; social and cultural rights such as the right to an education, including the admonition that 'elementary education shall be compulsory', and that 'higher education shall be equally accessible to all on the basis of merit' (Art. 25); and political rights such as universal suffrage. The Declaration was designed to provide substance for Article 55 of the Charter, which states in part that the United Nations shall promote 'universal respect for, and observance of human rights and fundamental freedoms for all without distinction as to race, sex, language, or religion'. Two covenants dealing with social and economic, and civil and political rights were passed in 1966. While these generally endorsed and elaborated the Universal Declaration there were exceptions, such as the failure to mention the right to private property and the addition of the right of self-determination (Donnelly 1986: 607; Forsythe 1983: 8 f.).

In the contemporary world both statesmen and analysts have articulated different, and often competing, versions of human rights. The ideals expressed in the Universal Declaration were most strongly informed by western liberal conceptions about the nature of the ideal polity. The individual is the basic unit. Rights adhere to individuals, not to some collective group. The state should be the creature of its citizens.

Liberalism is not, however, the only contemporary conception of human rights. In Islam, rights are a corollary of duties that are owed to God. It is difficult to reconcile the notion of individual freedom on which human rights in the West are based with the Islamic doctrine that human actions are the subject of God's will. Inalienable rights belong only to Allah and to Allah's agent, the state; they are not held by individuals. The individual is understood only as part of a larger community of believers. Islam does not recognize any fundamental conflict between the individual and the state, which is seen as an agent of God. The judiciary stands not against the arbitrary exercise of power by the state, but rather the judge is understood to be the legal secretary of the ruler.

There is no right of private property in Islam, only a right of use, because all belongs to God. Women are regarded as the wards of men. By law they receive only half the inheritance of men. In court, a woman's testimony is only worth half that of a man's. Women cannot hold political or legal office.

Islam did provide some protection for the followers of other monotheistic religions, Christianity and Judaism. They could form self-governing communities, but they could not hold office or marry Muslim women. They had to pay a special tax and were required to wear distinctive dress. In contrast, those who did not believe in revealed scriptures could be killed or enslaved. There was no freedom for a Muslim to give up the faith (Arzt 1990: 205–10; An-Na'im 1987: 3–17).

Analysts of African societies have argued that human rights can be more effectively understood in the context of a community. Individuals cannot be viewed in isolation from their larger social context. For African society, the extended family is the basic building-block of the society, not the atomistic individual. Within the extended family there are substantial rights and obligations. Land in traditional African society is held communally. The community has an obligation to provide subsistence to everyone (Cobbah 1987).

Aside from different cultural traditions, different conceptions of human rights have informed debates between the more advanced market economy countries, whose spokesmen have tended to focus on political and civil rights, and the Third World, whose representatives have emphasized economic and social rights. The Third World has stressed decolonization, elimination of racial segregation, and economic aspects of self-determination as important components of human rights. In 1977 the General Assembly of the United Nations passed a resolution affirming that it was impossible to have civil and political rights without first providing for economic, social, and cultural rights. During the first two decades of the existence of the United Nations, debate focused almost exclusively on political and civil rights. Once the

Third World secured a majority of votes in the General Assembly, discussion focused on economic and cultural rights (UN Doc. No. ST/HR/4/Rev. 4, 18; Vincent 1986: 79–91; Donnelly 1981).

The institutional arrangements for monitoring and enforcing declarations and covenants concerning human rights are more elaborate than in past historical periods. During the nineteenth century there were no formal public international organizations committed to protecting human rights. Enforcement and monitoring rested with individual states, British suppression of the slave trade being one clear example.

Nevertheless independent oversight is still limited. National states have guarded their sovereign prerogatives. The UN declarations recognize that enforcement is in the hands of national states. The UN Human Rights Commission is composed of states. For most of its history it looked into the activities only of pariah states —South Africa, Israel, and Chile under Pinochet. Individual states report on their own practices to the Commission. While some of these reports are accurate others are propagandistic or irrelevant, some simply listing constitutional provisions. The most powerful states in the system have not been subject to much international pressure (Forsythe 1983: 46; Donnelly 1986: 610).

States have been reluctant to accuse other states of human rights violations because of the danger that their own sovereign control would be undermined. Despite the fact that six treaties provide that disagreements over human rights issues can be brought to the International Court of Justice, the Court has not been very active. States must explicitly agree before a case can go to The Hague. Even those states that have agreed to the jurisdiction of the Court in general have been reluctant to sue other states lest the situation reverse itself at some future time (Forsythe 1983: 57; Falk 1981: 153).

In sum, there have been several conflicting visions of what constitutes human rights in the contemporary world. At the present moment the commanding vision is the one associated with a western liberal, capitalist, democratic, individualistic conception of the polity. In large part this domination reflects the economic, institutional, and political power of the West: the industrialized market economy countries control most international capital, dominate international financial institutions such as the World Bank and the IMF, and possess a preponderance of military power.

7. CONCLUSION

Human rights have been on the agenda since the beginning of the modern state system. In the modern world, like the world of the seventeenth century, there has been intense international discussion about the relationship between ruler and ruled. Since 1945 there has been an explicit effort to construct an international human rights regime. It has not, however, been the first effort. The Peace of Westphalia contained detailed rules about issues related to religion for parts of Germany. Largely at the instigation of Great Britain a regime, manifest in various international treaties, was established during the first half of the nineteenth century to abolish the slave trade. Elaborate formal commitments to protect minorities in Central and Eastern Europe were made in the late nineteenth and early twentieth centuries.

The persistent effort to introduce human rights regimes, that is, to establish principles and norms for the relationship between rulers and ruled, and the tension such efforts have caused, reflects an inherent contradiction in the meta-regime of sovereignty. A political order based upon sovereign states implies both the right of self-help and the norm of non-interference. But if states have the right to pursue whatever policies they choose, there is nothing to prevent them from interfering in the internal affairs of other countries. While such interference has often been carried out directly, it has also been manifest in various human rights regimes which have reflected the values and preferences of the most powerful states in the system at a particular historical moment. France and Sweden could force stipulations regarding religious practices on the defeated Holy Roman Empire. Britain could pressure states into abolishing the slave trade. The major powers of Western Europe could force the smaller states of Central and Eastern Europe to accept provisions for the protection of minorities. The western liberal democracies could formulate universal declarations on human rights that largely reflected their own values.

The articulation of principles and norms is one thing; their enforcement is quite another. Of the four human rights regimes examined in this chapter only the abolition of slavery was fully implemented. This success in part reflected a widespread abhorrence in the western world of the slave trade. Nevertheless, abolition would not have occurred as quickly without the naval power of Great Britain, which was prepared to act on its own to monitor and enforce the regime.

The practice first of religious toleration and then of religious freedom, reflected in the Peace of Westphalia, was gradually accepted in the West not because of pressure from an international regime but because individual national states ultimately removed religious issues from the portfolio of their concerns. Religion was so volatile and disruptive that political tranquility could only be achieved by restricting the scope of state activity. Efforts to protect the minorities of Central and Eastern Europe were a total failure because the more powerful states in the system were not willing to enforce the norms and rules which they had themselves initially imposed. Contemporary human rights declarations have largely, but not exclusively, reflected the preferences of western liberal democracies, but these states have only episodically been willing to commit substantial resources for monitoring and enforcement.

These episodes suggest that realist rather than co-operation perspectives provide a more compelling understanding of the content and success of international human rights regimes. This is hardly surprising given the nature of the issue which such regimes address. Human rights regimes do not attempt to rectify market failures, the exemplary problem for liberal co-operation theory. Rather they are an effort to alter the relationship between rulers and their subjects or citizens. This may make some rulers better off, but it will also make others worse off. If all rulers were prepared to accept the principles and norms articulated in international human rights regimes, there would be no need for the regimes in the first place.

Human rights regimes involve distributional issues whose resolution will depend heavily if not exclusively on the power and interests of states. The principle of self-help, which is based on national capabilities, has trumped the principle of non-intervention, which requires voluntary constraint. The content of human rights issues that were at the forefront in various historical periods reflected the concerns of those states which possessed a preponderance of economic and military power. Monitoring and enforcement depended on the policies adopted by the great powers.

Realism does not, however, provide a full account of the creation and implementation of human rights regimes. As John Ruggie (1983*b*) has argued in other settings, social purpose, which cannot be explained by the distribution of power in the international system, has determined the content of various regimes. Neither realism nor liberal co-operation theory systematically addresses the consequences of domestic divisions, which can impact on the success of human rights regimes by creating transnational alliances. Regimes are likely to be more effective if they enhance the position of support groups within target states than if no such support groups exist in the first place. Realism is the right first cut for understanding international efforts to alter the relationship between rulers and ruled, but it is not the last cut.

8

Epistemic Communities and the Dynamics of International Environmental Co-Operation

PETER M. HAAS

1. INTRODUCTION

Encountering unprecedentedly large environmental disasters in the 1960s, governments engaged in a paroxysm of international regime formation. Seventy-six multilateral environmental treaties have been signed since the 1972 United Nations Conference on the Human Environment (UNCHE), and environmental regimes have been growing increasingly sophisticated in their approach to managing ecosystems. How can this phenomenon be explained? International relations theorists from at least three schools of thought have sought to formulate general propositions to describe and explain the creation and transformation of regimes under a variety of international political conditions or domains specified by each school.

In this chapter I elaborate four different *regime patterns*—styles of collective management and lesson-drawing associated with regime creation, persistence, and change—derived from theorists from the schools of thought of neo-realism, institutionalism, and cognitive approaches, and evaluate their hypotheses in light of one hard case study, efforts of the Mediterranean countries to protect the Mediterranean Sea from pollution. Respectively, these schools of thought offer power-based, interest-based, and knowledge-

I am grateful to Ernst B. Haas, M. J. Peterson, Thomas Risse-Kappen, Volker Rittberger, and Olav Schram Stokke for comments on earlier drafts. The usual disclaimers apply about their responsibility for this chapter. This chapter was written with the support of NSF Grant SES-9010101.

based explanations of regimes.[1] For theorists of regimes, one of the most striking elements of this regime is the way in which it persisted, and grew in substantive scope, despite the collapse of the power-based factors which contributed to its creation. While each theory is able to explain phases or parts of the regime, none alone is sufficient to explain its full twenty-year history. Understanding the formation of, and changes in, the regime requires the use of variables which emphasize the distribution of material capabilities and institutional constraints within which states seek to co-ordinate their policies and behaviour, such as applied by neo-realists and institutionalists, as well as knowledge-based variables as applied by cognitivists.

I argue that the knowledge-based factors which help explain the regime's substance and persistence also help to explain the regime's evolutionary pattern. A path-dependent model which utilizes knowledge-based variables and a transnational level of analysis is further required to explain the full history of the Mediterranean Action Plan (Med Plan), because the knowledge introduced during one phase helped shape actors' perceptions of their preferences and opportunities during subsequent phases. By identifying the source of ideas and knowledge which regimes carry we can endogenize our understanding of regime change within the reflective patterns which regimes may have helped establish earlier in time, rather than leaving the explanation of regime change up to such exogenous mechanisms as imperial overreach, technological change, and transformations of public consciousness (Adler and Haas 1992, Kratochwil and Ruggie 1986).

Because the extant theoretical literature is inspired by different ontological commitments, each body of thought addresses only one way of explaining regimes. Each is confined by the choice of actors and mechanisms which it deems appropriate for pursuing its research programme within the boundaries of its historical period of experience and inquiry. Neo-realist authors, for instance, primarily restrict themselves to studies of the post-Westphalia system, focusing on inter-state relations grounded on efforts to promote national preferences, as constrained by the international distribution of material capabilities. Since the 1970s, most North

---

[1] In Ch. 10 below Young and Osherenko report the results of a test of various 'theories of regime formation' originating in these three schools of thought.

American neo-realists have self-consciously applied a positivist and mechanistic approach to explaining regimes, out of a belief that patterns of human behaviour obey mechanical laws. Consequently, neo-realists neglect the influence of non-state actors and of the potential for international influence based on non-material factors.

Institutionalists have focused on the broad institutional factors which may influence states and other international actors in their ability to negotiate joint outcomes which are mutually beneficial. Such studies focus on the context within which regimes emerge and persist, including such factors as norms, and organizational rules and practices that prescribe behavioural rules, constrain activity, and shape expectations. These studies have been largely confined to the period following the Second World War, and presume the existence of mutual interests. However, they seldom address the origins of such interests, or their accuracy.

Cognitivists, in turn, have focused on the role of prevailing forms of reason by which actors identify their preferences, and the available choices facing them. New regime patterns may result from new information and as a consequence of self-reflection by various actors. Cognitivists treat actors as reflective organisms, rather than as inert matter which obeys universally applicable and unchanging mechanical laws, as the neo-realists and institutionalists treat them. Consequently, dynamic and autopoietic models are seen as more applicable for capturing regime dynamics and patterns of human behaviour over time (Maturana and Varela 1980). More sensitive to historical context than the other two traditions which aspire to offer universal theoretical propositions, most cognitivist studies of epistemic communities, for instance, have been limited to the period since the Industrial Revolution, during which the authoritative form of policy-relevant understanding which policy-makers accept has stressed the role of scientific study, and been articulated and disseminated by experts and professionals.

2. PROBLEMS OF ENVIRONMENTAL REGIME CREATION

International concern about international environmental degradation and transboundary pollution exploded in 1972 at the UNCHE, and returned in the late 1980s (World Commission on Environment and Development 1987). Following a host of heavily publicized accidents in the late 1960s and 1970s, widespread domestic concern with transboundary pollution arose in the industrialized countries. Dozens of international regimes were established to deal with such diverse problems as protecting regional seas from pollution, controlling acid rain, protecting stratospheric ozone from depletion, and conserving species; overall, the dominant focus was on the control of transboundary pollution (Caldwell 1990, Carroll 1988, Kiss 1983, Kiss and Shelton 1991, Rummel-Bulska and Osafo 1991, Young 1989*a*, 1989*b*, Sand 1991, and P. M. Haas 1993). In marine pollution control regimes, principles involve the acceptance that human emissions are responsible for environmental contamination. Principles are becoming increasingly comprehensive, focusing on the protection of ecosystems rather than discretely controlling individual pollutants or sources of pollution. Norms typically enjoin states to curb their activities which cause environmental degradation. Rules take the form of pollution control limits and environmental quality standards, typically in the form of 'black' (banned) and 'grey' (controlled) lists, and prescriptions to notify neighbours in cases of emergency situations. These too are becoming increasingly comprehensive in light of the growing ecological sophistication of the principles of the regimes. Decision-making procedures take the form of yearly or two-yearly intergovernmental meetings to review the activities of international secretariats, authorize new projects, and hash out differences in national approaches to environmental policy (Boczek 1986, Kiss and Shelton 1991: 154).

Such outcomes are surprising to many theorists because, typically, it is difficult to obtain widely satisfactory arrangements in environmental issues. The management of international transboundary environmental problems requires countries mutually to adjust their policies towards sources of transboundary pollution, because otherwise they will be unable to achieve desirable levels of national environmental quality, and may also force their companies to sustain higher production costs which will make their economies less competitive internationally. Governments need international co-operation to achieve domestic ends, but are reluctant to participate unless they can be sure that other significant polluters will actively participate in the regime as well. Thus, the difficulty of obtaining international policy co-ordination also inhibits the pursuit of environmental protection domestically.

Active environmentalism in the North gave rise to a problem of international harmonization. On the one hand, leaders recognized that joint action was necessary. On the other hand, the potential for high adjustment costs for countries asked to adopt more stringent measures made regime creation difficult. By the 1970s, when serious efforts for international environmental protection began, the political problem further involved co-ordinating the discordant policies, instruments, and policy philosophies that had developed in individual countries. Many industrialized countries had already adopted approaches to cope with domestic resources, such as rivers, lakes, and the atmosphere. Many developing countries have not yet established environmental policies, and those that have been adopted are generally narrower in scope than in the developed countries, and tend to focus on the management of specific resources, instead of trying to integrate environmental considerations in all development planning, such as is increasingly the case in the industrialized countries. Many less developed countries (LDCs) also fear that environmental policy co-ordination with industrialized states can threaten to retard short-term economic growth by introducing new production and operating costs.

Simply awarding property rights would not have worked. First, new authors accept that transaction costs are sufficiently low for Coase's Theorem to successfully yield a Pareto optimal solution. Moreover, it is particularly difficult to apply the concept of property rights to environmental commons, where market signals still provide incentives for individuals (or states) to overuse the shared resource (Ostrom 1990: 13; Wijkman 1982; Ruggie 1972).

'Regimes' is a convenient shorthand and research heuristic for investigating the process of international efforts to co-ordinate diffuse national environmental protection policies. Regimes are institutions which condition national behaviour and choice (Krasner 1983*a*: 2). The real utility of the regime concept is to focus analysis on the multidimensional factors which lead states to engage in regularized patterns of behaviour. The definition demands attention both to cognitive studies of the beliefs which influence the creation and change of internationally shared norms and principles and national interests, as well as to power-based studies of the distribution of international capabilities which shape the creation of rules and decision-making procedures (Aggarwal 1985: ch. 2; Odell 1990).

How countries can successfully co-ordinate their environmental policies and create environmental regimes may be understood through a study of the Med Plan. Of the marine pollution cases, the Mediterranean has one of the longest histories, and is suitable for demonstrating various regime patterns. It is a fruitful setting for studying the process of compromise by which regimes are created, as the Med Plan emerged out of significant differences in preferences of countries with highly disparate levels of material power. It is also a case which fits the domains of most of the theoretical propositions about regime patterns, and thus allows for theory-testing (Eckstein 1975, George 1979, George and McKeown 1985). Such conditions should make it an easy case for power analysts, because of French regional dominance throughout much of the 1970s. But their explanation fails to explain the period fully; failing to satisfy an easy case suggests serious shortcomings for the approach more generally. For institutionalists it should be a hard case, because of the serious North–South power disparities and political conflicts in the region. Their limited explanatory success is suggestive for further constructive work in the area by which common technical understandings and bureaucratic politics may ameliorate political suspicions between states. Finally, for cognitivists, the existence of such major political cleavages would make the influence of cognitive factors more unlikely; their relative utility in this instance thus strengthens their general value for understanding international regimes.[2]

3. APPROACHES TO UNDERSTANDING ENVIRONMENTAL REGIME PATTERNS: INTERESTS, POWER, AND KNOWLEDGE

Most regime analysis has been broken into the three convenient, discrete categories of regime creation, persistence, and transfor-

---

[2] The existence of an epistemic community does not make the Med Plan an easy case for cognitivists. Its existence is merely a necessary condition for the theory to be applied to the case. A more general historically grounded theory to explain the domain in which epistemic communities are likely to be found is still needed to elaborate fully this line of explanation. For a first thrust in this direction see P. M. Haas (1992*b*).

mation. Underlying these different categories are singular regime patterns, or styles of collective management and lesson-drawing associated with regime creation, persistence, and change. Particularly for environmental issues, it is often more reasonable to see these three categories as part of a broader pattern, or as part of a dynamic path of co-operation in which nation states accumulate and assimilate rapidly evolving information in an effort to manage collectively a shared problem marked by disagreements over preferences. In this formulation a major concern for regime analysts is the extent to which participants actually modify their behaviour in line with regime obligations. This element, which Oran Young (1992) terms 'effectiveness', is largely neglected by most neo-realists and institutionalists.[3]

Different schools of thought describe and analyse discrete patterns. Although much analysis is devoted to explaining specific events, such analysis is grounded in broader research programmes aimed at explaining recurrent patterns of behaviour. Specific events are generally chosen for study because of their relevance to this broader theoretical enterprise. The theoretical whole should be greater than the sum of its empirical parts. While individual analysts often focus on one feature or characteristic of the pattern, each school of thought ties the features together into different, yet distinct, syndromes or patterns of regime characteristics. Analysts typically explain the variation in each characteristic in terms of their tradition's preferred independent variable, be it the distribution of power, state interests, institutional features, consensual knowledge, or involvement of epistemic communities. Thus, for each school of thought, discrete patterns exist of covarying regime features.

Each regime pattern includes a characteristic set of features. These include the political process by which it is created and maintained, the regime's substance, compliance effects on participating countries (effectiveness), and institutional learning.

Regimes are developed, maintained, and changed through a *political process* which may be based on state leadership or institutional bargaining. A regime's *substance* relates to the types

---

[3] Regarding a minimum of effectiveness as a defining feature of international regimes, the Tübingen group has naturally paid more than usual attention to this issue. See Ch. 1, sect. 3.1, above and Ch. 14, sect. 2, below.

of policies which are collectively endorsed. In turn this has two dimensions: scope and strength. Many environmental regimes vary in the scope of the rules, from controlling discrete substances to entire uses of a shared resource. Regimes also vary in terms of the strength of their rules: the stringency of the demands on states to comply. These may vary from weak, in the case of largely exhortatory regimes, to very strong, in the case of regimes where the use of specific substances is banned. Compromises between scope and strength can be easily imagined. Regime substance also varies in terms of the actual policy instruments which governments choose to endorse collectively.

In turn, each pattern entails a different set of *compliance effects* on participating countries. Schematically these effects can be analysed for activist countries whose environmental policies are initially more advanced than those of other countries (leaders), and for countries with weaker overall efforts (laggards).

Each pattern also has an attendant style of *institutional learning*, which pertains to the way and extent to which participating countries modify the regime in light of new information. In the context of regimes, 'learning', as I use it here, is a political process through which collective behaviour is modified in light of new collective understanding (Breslauer and Tetlock 1991). It is an international process which can influence collective behaviour and which is unrelated to the more commonly studied distribution of material sources of influence. For analytic purposes, to understand better the role of learning in shaping regime patterns, a major independent variable is new information, a major intervening variable is the mode of information-processing at the state level, and the dependent variable is the regime pattern.

It is analytically important to distinguish three discrete dimensions of institutional learning. First is the extent of learning. Two types of learning are possible along this dimension. States may modify policies in a discrete area of activity, or they may come to link two areas of activity which had previously been managed independently. Because environmental issues interact with so many other international issues and regimes, investigating the linkage element is important for understanding the conditions under which more holistic and comprehensive environmental and other international policy choices are reached.

This distinction is not the same as a second dimension, which refers to the type of learning which may occur. Recent students of institutional learning have distinguished between whether simple lessons are drawn or complex ones; whether new styles of information-processing are applied to existing puzzles.[4] Simple learning ('adaptation' in E. Haas's terms) may be best measured by whether institutions develop new organizational tasks following the acquisition of new information. Complex learning ('learning') may best be measured by the number of references to necessary measures undertaken in other associated areas when states are seeking to establish regime rules within a given domain.

Thirdly, learning may occur in a variety of ways. Institutional adaptation to environmental challenges need not be cognitive (Heclo 1974, Rose 1991, P. M. Haas 1990: 58–63). A dominant actor may compel other states to accept its preferred policies, while using new information as a justification. Policy change may occur by states emulating or imitating successful public policies adopted elsewhere. No interaction is required in this form. Learning may also occur through an infection model, where one state's policies are adopted elsewhere following the exchange of information and experience among regime participants. The system-wide replacement of one set of bureaucratic actors endowed with a dominant policy paradigm by another may have a similar effect. Learning may also be cognitive, as policy-makers and others jointly reflect on their experiences and modify their means and/or ends. Linkages between issues may be forged on the basis of tactical, fragmented, or substantive connections. Tactical and fragmented linkages are likely to persist so long as they serve the short-term political needs of the coalition for whom the linkages are useful. Substantive linkages, on the other hand, will probably persist until the scientific basis for the connection is rejected (E. B. Haas 1980).

Three master variables are typically invoked by major schools of thought to explain regime patterns.[5] Regime patterns are generally understood analytically in terms of the systemic distribu-

---

[4] See Argyris and Schon (1978), Nye (1987), Breslauer and Tetlock (1991), E. B. Haas (1990), P. M. Haas (1990: 58–63). Argyris and Schon speak of single and double loop learning, Nye of simple and complex learning, E. B. Haas of adaptation and learning, but the distinction is roughly equivalent in all usages.

[5] For a related attempt to classify theories to account for *compliance patterns* see Ch. 15, sect. 2, below.

tion of material power resources, the distribution of state interests (or preferences), and knowledge (Krasner 1983*a*, Young 1993). To some extent an excessively dry distinction is drawn between power and knowledge. The control of knowledge and meaning is surely an important power resource (Cox 1987). Still, most neo-realists and Marxist-informed scholars focus on material capabilities as the major source of power and influence. These variables reflect a kaleidoscope of forces which may influence regime patterns and their dynamics; different regime patterns result from different configurations of forces. Comparative studies of environmental regimes have demonstrated that it is impossible to explain regime dynamics in terms of any single variable (Young and Osherenko 1993, P. M. Haas 1993).[6]

The distribution of power is the major variable for most international regime analysts, including analysis by realists, neo-realists, Marxists, and dependency theorists, and is mechanically invoked to identify correlates of regime patterns. States deploy power resources in pursuit of their preferences. Regime patterns are thus subject to the distribution of power between states. Most realists and neo-realists also identify power as a major objective of nation states.

Realists define power in terms of material capabilities. Material capabilities may be concentrated globally, as is argued by world system and hegemonic stability theorists, or be issue-specific. More issue-specific measures of resources which confer influence are often more appropriate for analysing environmental issues because the basis of power is often unclear when managing pollution. Environmental issue-specific power resources include such factors as controlling enough of a resource for the country to possess a virtual unit veto over collective decisions affecting it, having enough capacity to affect unilaterally the quality of a shared resource, controlling enough trade so that unilateral environmental restrictions would have serious economic consequences for trading partners, and having a strong reputation for diplomatic skill and scientific competence.

Purely power-based approaches are limited by their inability to explain how countries are likely to respond to circumstances where state interests are not manifestly clear, or are intimately

---

[6] See also Ch. 10 as well as Ch. 11 below.

intertwined with other issues, and where the utility of orthodox policy levers is unclear. In many environmental cases in particular, information about the extent of pollution, its sources, and the necessary means to eliminate it is not sufficiently available or developed to allow a government to formulate rationally a set of objectives.

Institutionalists focus on interests and analyse the context or setting under which co-operation may be valued and pursued by states out of self-interest. Such analysts typically focus on the institutional context in which decisions are taken, seeking to specify features which may promote the possibility of joint gains being realized through regime creation. Actors are generally portrayed as egoistic, rational utility-maximizers, with complete information. Their interests are thus given, and largely invariant. Alternatively, analysts may take actors' statements of their preferences at face value as accurate depictions of their objectives. Knowledge is generally seen to play a minor role, although it can be a source from which actors recognize new interests, or appreciate a change in institutional context.

Co-operation can also be understood in terms of knowledge. Scholars who emphasize perceptions, cognitive processes, and interpretative approaches to understanding international relations commonly stress the role of ideas and knowledge in shaping the perceptions, beliefs, expectations, and preferences of major actors (P. M. Haas 1992c).[7] Such theorists argue that interests are often unknown, or incompletely specified. Consensus about policy-relevant understanding can contribute to shaping regime patterns. Interests are identified subject to consensual knowledge, and the decision to deploy state power is conditioned similarly. Recently, it appears that such explanations have growing utility, as there has been an emergent environmental regime pattern, driven not only by state power, but by the application of scientific understanding about ecological systems to the management of environmental policy issues with which decision-makers are unfamiliar. The role of scientific or expert understanding in international policy co-ordination is documented for security and economic issues as well as environmental issues (P. M. Haas 1992c).

[7] For a discussion of cognitive approaches towards explaining regime dynamics see also Ch. 9 below.

Scientific knowledge may be best operationalized in terms of *epistemic communities*. Consensual knowledge does not emerge in isolation, but rather is created and spread by transnational networks of specialists. Under conditions of complex interdependence and generalized uncertainty, specialists play a significant role in attenuating such uncertainty for decision-makers. Leaders and politicians are typically in the dark about the sources of pollution, extent of contamination, interaction between emissions and water quality, the costs of clean-up, and the likely actions of their neighbours. Such conditions are particularly puzzling in technical issues which pose low probability but high-risk outcomes and where specific state interests may be hazy.

Under such circumstances perceptions may be false, leaders lack adequate information for informed choice, and traditional search procedures and policy-making heuristics are impossible. Information is at a premium, and leaders look for those able to provide authoritative advice to attenuate such uncertainty, and consult them for policy advice and/or delegate responsibility to them. Subsequent discussions and policy debates are then informed and bounded by the advice which leaders receive. International negotiations may then be viewed 'as a process for reducing uncertainty' (Winham 1977: 96) as well as a process of deferring to specialists regarded as possessing a reputation for expertise in the domain of concern. Such experts' influence is subject to their ability to avoid widespread internal disagreement, and their influence persists through their ability to consolidate political power through capturing important bureaucratic positions in national administrations, from which they may persuade other decision-makers or usurp control over decision-making.

In environmental issues, many of these experts have been members of an ecological epistemic community. Epistemic communities are networks of knowledge-based communities with an authoritative claim to policy-relevant knowledge within their domain of expertise (P. M. Haas 1992c). Their members share knowledge about the causation of social or physical phenomena in an area for which they have a reputation for competence, and a common set of normative beliefs about what actions will benefit human welfare in such a domain. In particular, they are a group of professionals, often from a number of different disciplines, who share the following set of characteristics:

1. Shared consummatory values or principled beliefs. Such beliefs provide a value-based rationale for social action of the members of the community.
2. Shared causal beliefs or professional judgement. Such beliefs provide analytic reasons and explanations of behaviour, offering causal explanations for the multiple linkages between possible policy actions and desired outcomes.
3. Common notions of validity: intersubjective, internally defined criteria for validating knowledge.
4. A common policy enterprise: a set of practices associated with a central set of problems which have to be tackled, presumably out of a conviction that human welfare will be enhanced as a consequence.

Such characteristics may be identified through interviews and studies of specialized publications of technical advisers before their entry into policy-making.

Members of epistemic communities involved in environmental regimes have subscribed to holistic ecological beliefs about the need for policy co-ordination subject to ecosystemic laws. Thus, they promote international environmental regimes which are grounded on policies that offer coherent plans for the management of entire ecosystems, sensitive to interactions between environmental media (such as air and water), sources of pollution, and contending uses of the common property resource, rather than being limited to more traditional policies for managing discrete activities or physical resources spaces within fairly narrow time horizons.

4. ENVIRONMENTAL REGIME PATTERNS

Four regime patterns can be identified from the interplay of variables analysed by neo-realists, institutionalists, and cognitivists.

4.1. *Neo-Realism and Follow-the-Leader*

Neo-realists such as Kenneth Waltz (1979), Robert Gilpin (1981), Joseph Grieco (1990), and David Lake (1988) argue that in the absence of centralized authority, collective behaviour is shaped by the strongest country. Co-operation and effective management are likely to emerge only from the concentration or balance of international power, not from technical concerns. In the absence of compulsion to co-ordinate their efforts, governments act principally to insulate their domestic sphere of policy-making, thereby acting to reduce the influence of any other groups on their actions (i.e. international organizations, other governments, or multi-national corporations), as well as eliminating any forms of international obligations they may accept in order to protect the environment. To the extent that non-state actors are considered, they are generally believed to have little long-term influence on how such state patterns of action are developed. When co-operation occurs, it is led by a hegemon, and predominantly reflects the hegemon's concerns.

Neo-realists predict that regimes are only likely to emerge when a systemic concentration of material power resources exists. Regimes will persist so long as such a power concentration exists; regimes will decline with the diffusion of international power. Such authors argue that environmental regimes will be created by a dominant country which leads other countries to accept a regime which it prefers. The regime is created by the strongest party and other countries are compelled by that country to join and comply. The regime persists as others emulate the dominant country, or are compelled by the dominant country to co-ordinate their policies. The regime persists until the hegemon's control over tangible resources declines, after which the regime collapses. The actual substance of the regime is a projection of the dominant country's particular preferences. Its preferences often vary, from broad and inchoate foreign policy (such as funnelling assistance to one's allies or opening up new diplomatic channels) to efforts to get other countries to conform with the dominant country's past policy experience in order to create a level playing-field.

The regime may be either strongly or weakly regulatory, depending upon the dominant country's prior domestic experience. For instance, US–Mexican environmental arrangements impose stronger US regulatory standards on the less environmentally rigorous Mexicans, while the US–Canadian acid rain regime is primarily a joint research operation, owing to US preferences which are laxer than Canada's.

The level of regime effectiveness will depend upon whether the dominant party's environmental policies are more or less stringent than those of other countries. In either case the dominant party presses smaller countries to modify their policies so as to accommodate its own preferences. Politically weaker laggard countries have to improve their policies. Politically weaker countries with initially more stringent measures, however, may be less prone to abandon them and to approach a lower hegemonic preference, because of established domestic routines and expectations among domestic groups which the more stringent standards have fostered. Other countries' compliance varies by the dominant party's willingness to supervise and compel others to enforce the regime rules, because of the constant temptation to defect and the need for a centralized authority to oversee arrangements.

Learning is likely to be fairly limited because foreign-policy makers in the dominant country tend to be more concerned with political or economic considerations than with technical ones. Learning will be simple rather than complex. The only policy and linkage learning likely to occur involves modifying the dominant country's security and economic objectives in light of technical lessons about the environment which may inhibit the pursuit of existing foreign policy objectives. Other countries may be forced to accept the policies of the dominant country, or they may learn by copying policies in the hegemon; for instance, many USEPA regulations are applied elsewhere in the world (Brickman, Jasanoff, and Ilgen 1985). Environmental issues are only likely to be linked tactically to other issues, owing to the absence of serious input from ecological scientists to negotiations and the reluctance of states to accept policies which may circumscribe national autonomy or sovereignty, or which may be expensive to implement.

US leadership has been crucial in shaping global atmospheric regimes. The United States exercised significant influence in negotiating the 1992 climate change treaty, and successfully pressured the European Community to water down the treaty's strength to reflect the relatively weaker existing US domestic energy conservation and carbon dioxide emission policies. Similarly, the relatively weak 1985 Vienna Convention for the Protection of the Stratospheric Ozone Layer which established the stratospheric ozone protection regime was also strongly shaped by US leadership and opposition to European efforts to control CFC production (Benedick 1991, P. M. Haas 1992*a*).

4.2. *Inseitutionalism and Bargaining Patterns*

Contractual institutionalists who are informed by social choice approaches focus on bargaining structures through which regimes are created and maintained. Such authors as Robert Axelrod, Robert Keohane (1984, 1989*b*, Axelrod and Keohane 1986), Elinor Ostrom (1990), Arild Underdal (1982), and Oran Young (1989*a*, 1989*b*, 1993) exemplify this tradition. They assume a common area of interests, and seek to specify institutional factors which may encourage actors to overcome their reluctance to co-operate. Individuals are deemed to be constructive, information-seeking actors. The policy question is how to provide them with sufficient incentives—of which information is one—to ensure they produce outcomes beneficial to the international community, such as preserving the environment. Power is not as important an explanation as is the opportunity for finding joint gains from co-operation. States' recognition of their preferences is essential for successfully applying bargaining techniques, as well as under-standing states' behaviour in collective negotiations.

Institutionalists believe that regime creation efforts are further inhibited when a large number of parties is involved in environ-mental protection and that the regimes emerging under such circumstances are likely to be very weak and transitory in charac-ter. Conversely, smaller numbers would increase the possibility that institutional bargaining could lead to more stringent and durable regimes (Baumol 1971, Olson 1965).

Institutionalists expect to find negotiated regimes whose sub-stance merely reflects the measures tolerable to the least enthusi-astic party; in essence, the least common denominator (LCD). Arild Underdal (1982) has formulated this behavioural pattern as the 'law of the least ambitious program' (see also Saetevik 1988). Consequently, collective measures are often far too diffuse and weak to significantly improve environmental quality. Such behavioural patterns are widely evident in the management of international fisheries, and obtained in collective efforts to protect the North Sea and the Baltic from pollution until 1987.

LCD regimes are largely formalizations of the least stringent existing national efforts. Such regimes would typically lack serious compliance measures, and regulatory standards would tend to be extremely weak. In regions where countries have no standards or only weak ones, the regime will be correspondingly modest. If states have stronger standards, the weakest one will serve as the regime norm. Since national obligations are meagre, compliance is a relatively minor matter. As with *follow-the-leader*, backsliding by states with stronger measures is unlikely because of domestic conditions. Some simple emulatory policy-learning may be possible, but more sophisticated institutional learning is unlikely because governments are driven by experience and a reluctance to accept new obligations, and joint decisions reflect the views of the least enthusiastic party.

Some alternatives to the LCD option exist. Stronger regime patterns are possible if negotiations occur within a setting of institutional bargaining, or if certain institutional design factors obtain. Oran Young characterizes institutional bargaining as the setting in which regimes are created and maintained through bargaining between several distinct types of actors, including states and NGOs, in an organizational context and subject to uncertainty about the costs and benefits of co-operation (Young 1989*b*, 1993). While actors are seeking to obtain their own preferences, they may not be fully certain as to what they are. Under such circumstances Young expects that actors will have only a weak regard for distributional effects.

In institutional bargaining, leadership can come from a country, entrepreneurial individual diplomats, or non-state actors, including international organizations, NGOs, or epistemic communities. Such a leader can help identify compromises from which everyone may benefit. With the use of such techniques as stressing uncertainty, monitoring, iterated games, promoting equity and integrative bargaining over debate on distributive and efficiency issues, and the introduction of such 'selective incentives' as side payments, political pressure, education, and the like, designers may create and maintain regimes through bargaining which exceed the LCD model.

Robert Axelrod, Robert Keohane, Elinor Ostrom, and Oran Young identify other institutional factors by which negotiated regimes may exceed the limited scope of LCD regimes (see also Kremenyuk 1991). They observe that stronger, long-lasting regimes are possible when it is easy to monitor and verify actors' compliance with major behavioural obligations, numbers of participants are relatively small, actors are engaged in iterated games, and actors are encouraged to consider long-term effects of their actions (the shadow of the future). Regimes may persist past hegemonic decline if participants come to appreciate the value provided by the regime, and realize that continued co-operation is preferable to a relapse into policy disorder (Keohane 1984).

Other work informed by the social choice tradition suggests that, to the extent that regimes are created without the exercise of hegemony, their substance will be largely informational or will provide insurance. Moreover, only regimes which perform this function will be likely to persist beyond hegemony (Keohane 1983, 1984, Axelrod and Keohane 1986). Even with a greater need for information about the quality of the environment and about other countries' pollution control activities in issues such as the environment that have a high degree of issue density, these authors suggest that countries will only support environmental institutions which conduct monitoring, administer pollution control facilities, or pay clean-up costs from a joint insurance fund. The creation of regulatory or policy-promoting bodies is extremely unlikely. These theorists' explanations are challenged by the highly regulatory nature of many of the environmental regimes which have been established over the last twenty years.

Institutional bargaining may contribute to movement away from the LCD over time, subject to domestic-level pressures. As national environmental pressures mount, governments are forced to try and persuade their neighbours to adopt stronger measures as well, creating a ratcheting element in the LCD process. Important domestic pressures include the division of powers between the federal and state levels, legal traditions, administrative organization and expertise, relations between the judiciary and administration, and a country's research system and its input into public policy (Brickman, Jasanoff, and Ilgen 1985, Hoberg forthcoming).

Regimes resulting from bargaining will demand stronger compliance from laggards than from leaders. Because the regime will probably end up with measures which are weaker than in the strongest country, little accommodation is required by the leader.

But laggard countries will have to beef up their measures to comply with the regime. Leaders may even have their efforts inhibited or retarded by other countries, who would urge them to go slowly in their adoption of more rigorous standards that could introduce incompatibilities between national systems which they are trying to harmonize. For instance, Sweden's efforts to reduce sulphur dioxide emissions from cars were slowed by up to two years by the EC's reluctance to adopt similar measures for the Community (Boehmer-Christiansen 1984).

Environmental regimes which provide incentives for states to participate are likely to be more effective than ones which do not. Major factors which encourage state compliance include regime features which create a stable bargaining environment, so that ongoing negotiations are possible and future expectations of rewards are created; which enhance national concern, so that governments are held accountable by their populations for complying with international obligations; and which offer improvements in state capacity, so that states are rewarded for their participation and find it easier to comply with their obligations (Haas, Keohane, and Levy 1993).

Learning in institutional bargaining is possible. New policies may be identified and adopted, and some issue linkage is also possible. Because actors are engaged largely in integrative bargaining involving exploratory forays to determine the exact shape of the bargaining Pareto frontier, new scientific findings and consensual knowledge may lead actors to link substantively issues in a regime. Many processes of learning are possible within international institutions: through demonstration effects laggard countries may gradually come to emulate stronger policies applied elsewhere; and information may be exchanged by experts, leading environment ministers to adopt new measures. While policies may be imitated by other countries, most countries will remain strongly conditioned by the fear of unreciprocated policies and hence fail to adopt new policies which would threaten competitiveness.

Such an approach may have significant value for understanding European environmental negotiations, where many countries have already adopted domestic environmental measures and there are clear reasons for harmonizing national efforts. It is difficult to apply institutional insights to issues where countries with strong domestic environmental protection measures are reluctant to engage in meaningful international discussions, such as the United States during the 1980s.

Limits exist for the applicability of institutional bargaining techniques. If issues are not widely regarded as generating collective outcomes for all, such techniques are unlikely to be effective. Even if actors share common aversions (i.e. play an assurance game), there will be eventual distributional squabbles—perhaps in a second game—which, if actors rationally anticipate, means that they will be unwilling to engage in constructive bargaining to resolve even the first, easier problem (Ostrom 1990: 42 f.; Bates 1988).

4.3. Epistemic Communities and Modified Follow-the-Leader

A focus on epistemic communities suggests that the patterns predicted by neo-realists and institutionalists require modifications. Cognitivists stress that the international system is often far more indeterminate than assumed by scholars from other traditions. Thus, uncertainty is pervasive and states' interests are often unclear. Under such circumstances epistemic communities may significantly influence the patterns which regimes assume.

Epistemic communities are likely to be found in substantive issues where scientific disciplines have been applied to policy-oriented work and in countries with well-established institutional capacities for administration and science and technology. Only governments with such capacities would have need of the technical skills which epistemic community members command, and such professionals would only be attracted to governmental service when they believed that their policy enterprise could be advanced. Crises or widely publicized shocks are probably necessary precipitants of environmental regime creation, but crises alone cannot explain how or which collective responses to a perceived joint problem are likely to develop.

Under conditions of uncertainty, when the international power is concentrated in one state, and when epistemic communities have successfully consolidated influence in the dominant state, then *follow-the-leader* may be modified in light of the policy beliefs of the epistemic community. The regime would still be created through the intercession of the hegemon, but its substance would reflect epistemic consensus. In other respects this pattern would be similar to follow-the-leader: other countries' behaviours remain subject to the influence of the hegemon. The regime's persistence would still covary with hegemonic tenure, unless the hegemon promoted the involvement of epistemic community members in other governments, in which case the regime would be likely to continue through the pattern of *epistemically informed bargaining* discussed in the following section. Modified hegemonic leadership environmental regimes are likely to be more comprehensive in scope than straight hegemonic ones, owing to the shaping influence of the ecological epistemic community. Substantive institutional learning is possible as policies and linkages can be informed by the ecological insights of the epistemic community. Such learning may occur through persuasion and bureaucratic clout exercise by members of the epistemic community in countries where they have consolidated their bureaucratic influence, and by emulation and other patterns in other countries. The development and modification of the international regime for stratospheric ozone protection since 1985 fits this pattern (P. M. Haas 1992*a*).

4.4. Epistemically Informed Bargaining

Cognitivists argue that when epistemic communities are widely spread, even in the absence of leadership by a strong state, environmentally effective regimes are possible. Environmental regimes in this instance emerge through institutional bargaining, as described by institutionalists. Regimes are most likely to be created following widely publicized environmental disasters which mobilize the demands of the public and of experts for governmental action. Regime negotiation and maintenance would be characterized by conference diplomacy, with many countries seeking to resolve shared problems subject to the technical advice which they receive from their own experts, NGOs, transnational scientific networks, and international organizations. Non-state actors play an important role.

As epistemic communities obtain and consolidate influence in different governments, national preferences and policies will come to reflect the epistemic beliefs. International organization secretariats can play a key role in such patterns as sources of information and new policy ideas, as well as buffering political differences between the parties. Epistemic communities have often lodged themselves in international organizations as well, in particular UNEP.

The negotiated regime would then reflect the causal and principled beliefs of the epistemic community. National positions would vary according to the extent of penetration by epistemic communities, or the sensitivity of policies in that country to policies in a country already influenced by the epistemic community. In most cases this would make epistemic environmental regimes more stringent and comprehensive than other forms of environmental regimes owing to the more sophisticated vision of ecological problems which ecological epistemic communities hold. Regimes will be regulatory. Regimes will persist until the epistemic community's shared body of knowledge collapses. Both leaders and laggards might modify their policies in light of the new regime as a bandwagoning process develops, leading to gradual, progressively increasing changes in national policies to accommodate evolving scientific understanding about how ecosystems work. As with other patterns, anticipations of material rewards from the regime (i.e. capacity-building provisions) would also encourage states to comply with the regime.

Learning would reflect lessons imparted by the epistemic community. Policies and linkages may be quite sophisticated, reflecting the quality of its beliefs. The extent to which such lessons are accepted and converted into new policies in different countries, as well as regime compliance, are subject to the ability of members of the epistemic community to occupy key bureaucratic slots and to persuade others of their preferred policies. They may encourage governments to undertake new patterns of economic development based on more complex and integrated visions of ecological interactions, organize issues in novel ways, and make decision-makers aware of possibilities for mutual gains from co-operation which they had not previously recognized.

Learning in this context may be quite complex, in the sense that policy-makers recognize or appreciate new connections between issues which were previously regarded as distinct. Epistemic communities may lead policy-makers to reflect on their objectives and to link issues in novel ways, subject to an ecological understanding of global ecological dynamics and a dawning recognition of extensive interplay between environmental protection and other state concerns. As such actors intercede in policy-making, they may change national attitudes towards environmental protection, thereby overcoming the antipathy to institution creation and international co-operation. Decision-makers would become more likely to link issues based on their substantive connections. New institutions would be created by bargaining and by the gradual insinuation of such groups into international secretariats and national bureaucracies, rather than by state leadership.

The epistemic community pattern may well have differential impacts on developed countries (DCs) and less developed countries (LDCs). DCs, with greater familiarity and ability to evaluate external advice, will be more likely to defer to transnational scientific advice. Conversely, many LDCs are highly suspicious of technical advice and information from abroad, and will only defer to scientific advice which is provided through domestic channels. The development of indigenous scientific capability reinforces the authority of those scientists providing advice to decision-makers.

4.5. Applicable Domains for Theory-Based Predictions about Regime Patterns

These three theoretical approaches to the study of international regimes offer different hypotheses concerning regime patterns under different conditions. Before using the Med Plan for testing their utility, it is first necessary to summarize the appropriate domain for each set of hypotheses.

Neo-realists predict patterns of *follow-the-leader* under conditions of concentrated systemic power, and much weaker and transitory regimes under other conditions. Institutionalists expect to see LCD regimes in cases with large numbers of actors and where the institutional techniques as identified by institutionalist authors are not applied. When they are applied, they expect to see the regime pattern of *bargaining*, regardless of the distribution of power or knowledge.

Cognitivists modify these hypotheses under conditions when epistemic communities are present. With a high concentration of systemic power, cognitivists expect to see *modified follow-the-*

leader, and *epistemically informed bargaining* under conditions of diffused power.

The Med Plan falls within the domains of these three traditions: from 1970 to 1975 regional power was concentrated; from 1976 to 1980 regional concentration of power overlapped with an epistemic community; and since 1980 the epistemic community has existed in the absence of significant concentration of capabilities. It would be a mistake to consider the special case of a parsimonious theory which successfully explains one period or set of regime features as justification for generalizing that parsimonious theories are more useful than more complex ones (Ostrom 1990). More complex theories are necessary to explain the dynamic evolution of environmental regimes which may demonstrate different patterns at different points in time.

5. THE MEDITERRANEAN ACTION PLAN AS AN EVOLVING REGIME

The regime was established in 1975, with the adoption of the Mediterranean Action Plan, and grew in stringency and scope. In 1976 the umbrella Barcelona Convention was signed, as well as protocols banning dumping of wastes at sea and organizing co-operation in cases of oil spill emergencies. In 1980 a protocol was signed which regulates land-based sources of pollution, banning emissions of a set of widely used toxic compounds, and requiring common standards for the emissions of a broader set of less toxic materials. In 1982 a protocol for specially protected areas was adopted. All treaties rapidly entered into force. Control measures for twelve pollutants or groups of pollutants have been adopted since 1985, and efforts are under way to develop common standards for all the substances on the 1980 protocol.

Co-ordinated research and monitoring activities have been sponsored by UNEP for the region since 1976, involving training hundreds of North African scientists and technicians and providing them with new laboratory equipment. A Regional Co-Ordinating Unit was established in Athens in 1982, which now has a two-year budget of 13.2 million dollars. A Regional Oil Combating Centre was set up in Malta in 1976. An integrated planning unit was established in 1977 in France to generate prospective models of regional growth trajectories, called the Blue Plan, and to encourage more comprehensive views of economic planning. A Priority Action Programme was established in 1979 in Yugoslavia to study more concrete projects of immediate interest to the developing countries, including soil protection, water resource management, fisheries and aquaculture management, human settlements, tourism, and 'soft' energy technologies. A Coastal Areas Management Programme was established in 1990 to promote development planning in accordance with local environmental conditions. A centre for dealing with specially protected areas was established in Tunis in 1985.

Thus, a vibrant regime has come into being, which is seen by well-regarded local scientists as reversing the decline of Mediterranean water quality. The Mediterranean is probably no dirtier than it was twenty years ago, despite a doubling of the coastal concentration of industry and population. By 1990 a much more comprehensive regime existed than existed originally. Originally designed to control discrete sources of pollution, the regime is now aimed at encouraging more comprehensive coastal zone management. Following the elaboration of the regime, many national pollution control efforts have progressed as well, including the construction of sewage treatment plants in twelve large cities, drafting of new environmental legislation region-wide, the application of environmental impact assessment type procedures to economic planning in five countries, and introducing measures to modify their existing environmental standards and techniques in order to control the broader list of substances in the Med Plan (P. M. Haas 1989, 1990: ch. 5).

1970–1975: Concentrated Power without Epistemic Community

From 1970 to 1975 France was the regionally predominant power. It controlled a large proportion of trade which would be affected by environmental regulations, had the most highly developed marine science capability, had a strong reputation for diplomacy, and regarded the Mediterranean as a region in which French foreign policy should hold sway.

Preparations for UNCHE alerted government officials to the new issue of the environment, and Jacques Cousteau sounded public alarms about the impending 'death' of the Mediterranean Sea. Yet decision-makers were highly uncertain about their possible range of action. They lacked specific information about the extent of contamination, its causes, and the sea's ability to sustain pollution, as well as about the range of possible policy responses. Fisheries directors approached the General Fisheries Commission of the Mediterranean to collect information about the causes and extent of marine pollution in the Mediterranean, and to draft a treaty for regional protection. The FAO delivered an interim report in 1972 demonstrating that pollution was fairly extensive, and required immediate action.

France convened a conference in 1972 to promote a regional convention to control oil spills which resembled extant French policy commitments. However, many LDCs were suspicious of French motivations, and along with Italy and Spain deputed UNEP in 1974 to direct efforts on a draft treaty and regional action plan. France consistently opposed the inclusion of substances or policy instruments in the regime which did not mirror existing French programmes, although France was ultimately unable to determine the regime unilaterally.

Little learning of any sort occurred during this period, as information on regional pollution was scarce. Few states had yet established national authorities with regulatory responsibilities, and only France, Israel, and Yugoslavia adopted even general marine pollution control laws for oil and dumping. The environment remained isolated from other political issues of regional concern.

1975–1980: Concentrated Power and Epistemic Community

French regional dominance persisted until 1980, but the Med Plan's second phase was distinguished by the mobilization of a regional ecological epistemic community. France was the primary source of funding for Med Plan activities, and strongly pressed its preferences at international meetings. While France maintained a predominant share of tangible power resources, it was unable to compel others to follow its preferred policies, and ultimately made concessions to others at negotiations conducted during French hegemony.

French efforts at control were stymied by the UNEP secretariat.

The secretariat refused French offers to conduct monitoring unilaterally, to draft treaties, and to house the headquarters unit. Instead, it drafted documents which endorsed the control of a broader range of pollutants than France preferred as well as supporting monitoring and research in other countries. LDCs were subsequently much more willing to participate and support regional talks when they were held under UNEP's auspices. The Land-Based Sources Protocol eventually covered radionuclide emissions and pollution transmitted through rivers and the atmosphere, over French and Italian objections. While the quality of the marine science was surely not as high as if it had all been done in France, expanding scientific participation served the political function of expanding the constituency for pollution control.

UNEP's leadership efforts were conditioned by a regional ecological epistemic community. By 1975 UNEP (which had only recently been created) had obtained control over drafting procedures from the FAO, and proceeded to develop a more comprehensive set of policy proposals than FAO had anticipated. UNEP was staffed much more heavily with ecologists, and the officials responsible for the Mediterranean were members of the ecological epistemic community. They hoped to develop comprehensive region-wide measures for promoting environmentally sensitive styles of economic development. The members came from a variety of professional backgrounds—engineering, marine science, and law—but all were enamoured with the holistic policy philosophy emerging out of UNCHE and had been galvanized into a common policy enterprise of protecting the environment. They wanted to control a broad range of sources of Mediterranean pollution, and incorporate environmental considerations into national economic planning. Stjepan Keckes, a Yugoslav oceanographer, devised a plan to involve a network of Mediterranean marine scientists in regional pollution monitoring and policy design, in order to promote their broader vision of ecological planning. The epistemic community already existed in the region; Keckes's plan was to mobilize it through continued involvement in the collective negotiations, by financially supporting monitoring and research, and by disseminating its findings regionally. Through a consulting mission for UNEP in 1974 and 1975 Keckes became familiar with most of the major figures.

Its influence was gradually felt on the negotiations through a deliberate UNEP strategy of concurrent environmental assessment and environmental management. Research on environmental quality occurred while regime negotiations were being conducted. Thus, the scientists involved in the research had an improved access to policy-makers, and the negotiations were forced to take note of ongoing improvements in technical understanding about the sources and extent of pollution. Moreover, as many of the littoral countries established new environmental ministries or environmental protection agencies, members of the epistemic community were hired to staff the new bodies, in part because few professionals had the relevant experience, and in part because their professional profile had been enhanced through UNEP's monitoring programmes. By providing such resources, UNEP deepened its transnational bond with the region's marine scientists, which was already based on shared concern about regional pollution. Even if they did not share UNEP's holistic vision, they did support the control of specific substances with which they were familiar. Key environmental policy posts in Israel and Greece were already filled by people sympathetic to UNEP's cause, and indeed believed with UNEP in the need for coherent, ecologically sound regional development.

Through UNEP the regional ecological epistemic community was mobilized and involved in regional discussions after 1976. While France remained dominant, it was unable to prevail in all of its objectives. The regime's substance was regulatory, banning the use of nine proscribed groups of substances and establishing limits and permit-setting procedures on the use of thirteen other groups. The actual substances covered reflected the shared understanding of the epistemic community about potential threats to the environment, which was well in excess of the more limited desires expressed by all individual countries.

National policy-learning occurred during this phase. Israel, Greece, Algeria, and Spain converted co-ordinative environmental agencies into regulatory authorities, and Greece, Libya, and Morocco adopted new legislation governing oil pollution and marine dumping. Linkages remained weak, though, as only France adopted legislation requiring environmental impact assessments for new development projects, an administrative requirement reflecting a new appreciation of the connection between environmental protection and other economic and development objectives. Participating states began to consider the linkages between national development activities, population growth, and environmental quality through Med Plan projects such as the Blue Plan, but few countries other than France expressed strong interest in the projects or their conceptual base during this period.

From 1980 Onwards: Diffuse Power and Epistemic Community

By the early 1980s much of France's dominance had passed, as the North African states were able to diversify their trade dependence from France to the EC, and acquired a much greater marine science capability from participating in the Med Plan. The regime persisted, as it became self-funding through annual governmental contributions which were proportional to their regular UN assessments, a new protocol establishing marine protected zones for endangered species was adopted in 1982, twelve control measures were adopted for previously targeted pollutants, in 1985 the parties called for a reorientation from pollution control to coastal zone management, and a more comprehensive coastal zone management programme was established in 1990.

The regime was largely maintained and modified through a process of *epistemically informed bargaining*. While countries continued to engage in institutional bargaining to develop joint measures, national policy-making was increasingly shaped by the epistemic community. Its members drafted national policies, and, on delegations, encouraged officials from foreign ministries to endorse UNEP's efforts for more stringent controls. Over time most of the countries introduced more stringent environmental protection measures, and supported the development of universal regulatory standards for specific polluting substances.

The Med Plan remained significant for both leaders and laggards (defined in terms of the stringency of their national policies) during this period. Countries in which the epistemic community had consolidated its influence have moved toward convergent policies. The effectiveness of the regime is not due entirely to its provision of capacity-building equipment and training, as institutionalists suggest. Countries such as Algeria and Egypt did not come to support the Med Plan until their governments received advice from domestic scientists that coastal pollution was an environmental hazard, even though they had already been receiving capacity-building assistance from UNEP and other international organizations for several years.

The regional leader, France, wound up by improving its marine pollution control efforts in accordance with the Med Plan. It also continued to support the regime financially and diplomatically throughout the 1980s. In France and Italy many Mediterranean pollution control efforts preceded the Med Plan, but the trajectories of public activity steepened following the Med Plan. In each country rates of environmental investment and public enforcement of existing measures grew more vigorous in the late 1970s (for France) and late 1980s (for Italy). The laggards also improved their environmental protection efforts in light of the Med Plan. Greece, Algeria, and Egypt all embarked on vigorous new public administrative campaigns to integrate environmental considerations into traditional coastal zone development and economic planning. Similar shifts are evident for Israel and Spain, although the data are less thorough. Algeria and Egypt adopted more comprehensive environmental policies. Following their participation in Med Plan discussions, and the epistemic community's capture of key environmental policy units within their national administrations, policy reversals occurred in both these countries during the early 1980s. Algeria further strengthened the legal standing of its environmental agency, and passed a sweeping environmental protection law in 1983, requiring environmental impact assessments on new projects. While the state infrastructure and capacity to implement such measures remain weak, the legal changes are none the less dramatic. Egypt also strengthened the environmental ministry in 1982, and applied more stringent domestic environmental policies in 1983.

However, movement during this period has been slow, owing to the inability of many of the developing countries to enforce the measures actively. In the absence of major resources and in a world-wide recession these are difficult to accomplish. In April 1992 the World Bank and European Community announced a new programme to promote sustainable development in the Mediterranean countries. The division of institutional responsibilities between the Med Plan Regional Co-Ordinating Unit and these other organizations is still being worked out, but such an institutional shift may overcome the financial bottle-necks which had inhibited the North African countries from fully implementing the domestic projects developed to enforce their Med Plan obligations.

National and institutional learning have been fairly comprehensive since 1980, reflecting the epistemic community's causal beliefs, as seen by the new linkages between environment and economic development which many of the region's governments have acknowledged. During the 1980s most countries adopted stronger domestic environmental standards for marine pollution, and environmental concerns were increasingly linked to other concerns, domestically and internationally. Domestically, environmental impact assessments were required in Israel, Greece, Algeria, and Egypt. Internationally, most states became more active participants in UNEP projects involved with integrated planning and developing alternatives to coastal development activities which threatened marine quality, and endorsed new projects for comprehensive coastal zone management and sustainable development. These new policies reflect the broader concerns of the ecological epistemic community, involving more comprehensive coverage of sources of pollution, and developing more comprehensive planning procedures to harmonize state developmental and environmental objectives. While some governments have merely borrowed standards from the USEPA or the World Health Organization, the need for such emulation was prompted by epistemic community members, and the information was transmitted through the epistemic community network. In other countries members of the epistemic community were responsible for actually finding the figures elsewhere and applying them in the countries where they were responsible for formulating and enforcing environmental policy.

The Med Plan and the Three Approaches towards Understanding Regime Patterns

The evidence from the Med Plan suggests that insights from each of the approaches are useful for understanding regime patterns. The first phase was largely one of institutional *bargaining*, with leadership exercised by UNEP, as predicted and explained by institutionalists. French diplomatic and financial support during the first phase was important for regime creation, as neo-realists would suggest. The French failure to control the regime, despite its unparalleled control over resources, challenges neo-realists' explanations grounded solely on the distribution of power. The second and third phases were periods of *epistemically informed bargaining*, as explained by the cognitivist approach. France failed to control the regime, and continued to support it even after its dominance had receded, contrary to neo-realist expectations. The number of substances controlled by the regime is larger than the simple summation of the concerns of individual countries, contrary to institutionalists' predictions. Moreover, the regulatory nature persisted despite the diffusion of power. Compliance by both the leaders and the laggards has persisted, contrary to the expectations of analysts based on the international distribution of power. The full effectiveness of the regime is less than cognitivists expected solely on the basis of the influence of the epistemic community, which, however, is due to the absence of national resources to implement national obligations fully.

Most striking is the rapid strengthening of the regime over twenty years. The evolving regime reflects the altered preferences of the large number of countries in which the epistemic community successfully consolidated bureaucratic power. Knowledge about the behaviour of ecosystems, as imparted by the epistemic community, led states to change their preferences for types of environmental protection. Epistemic community members usurped bureaucratic power, and persuaded colleagues of the need for more sweeping national environmental policies and support for co-ordinated region-wide measures. As the number of countries grew in which it held influence, support for a more comprehensive regime grew as well. Changes in national preferences reflecting more stringent environmental demands occurred during a period of declining systemic concentration of power. The regime's comprehensive substance clearly reflects the holistic beliefs of the epistemic community, which they successfully imparted to the regime despite the opposition of France and a number of LDCs to specific elements.

To a large extent the epistemic community's influence is irreversible, as its involvement in the region's institutions—both in national administrations and on the Med Plan secretariat—will persist unless there is a full-scale purge—and even then their policies would be likely to endure, owing to the various established patterns of behaviour which they have induced in domestic industries.

6. CONCLUSION

The addition of epistemic communities to explanations of international regime patterns yields novel insights into the patterns by which environmental regimes are created, persist, and change. More thorough and effective environmental protection has occurred than explanations based solely on the distribution of power and interests typically suggest. Theories which focus on the static impact of material power resources and institutional factors on regime patterns are incapable of explaining broader patterns of regime change over time. While accurately capturing brief periods of the Med Plan, they failed to explain the broader developments over time. More broadly, these approaches are unable to explain behaviour which transforms or exceeds the initial conditions from which it emerged.

A focus on epistemic communities provides the final benefit of endogenizing knowledge-based sources of regime change. As a consequence of the regime's activities, new sources of information and new actors became available to states for articulating the extent of information relevant to the regime's policy domain. The ecological epistemic community was initially found in just a few organizations: Israel, Greece, and UNEP. A weak regime was established through a combination of the epistemic community's influence on its own governments, through the diplomatic efforts of those governments, through UNEP's organizational actions, and regular international bargaining. Once established, the regime helped to identify members of the ecological epistemic community as authoritative sources of information about environmental protection, and also helped to strengthen LDC scientific capacity, thus deepening epistemic community members' domestic power base, as well as providing institutional incentives for LDCs to support the regime. As epistemic community members consolidated their influence in their respective governments, most notably Egypt and Algeria, their governments came to adopt stronger domestic marine pollution control measures, and to support a more stringent and comprehensive regime. As a sufficiently large power bloc was amassed in the region, the epistemically influenced governments and UNEP were able to press for a more comprehensive regime which reflected their own policy preferences. Through this political process the shared understanding of the ecological epistemic community about the way ecosystems operate was introduced to regional environmental policy-making, and institutional learning occurred through the intercession of the ecological epistemic community. The regime's rules became stronger and more sophisticated, and also became linked to rules about economic development.

Alone, epistemic communities do not fully explain regime patterns, as outcomes are clearly the result of power exercised by parties on behalf of the ideas and preferences imparted by the epistemic community, and institutional resources are also important for an effective regime. Yet, without heeding the knowledge controlled and transmitted by the epistemic community the analyst is unable to capture the change over time in the regime's substance, strength, and effectiveness. Learning is a critical process by which regime patterns change over time, and epistemic communities are important actors for shaping what learning occurs, and moulding the path by which regimes evolve.

9

Cognitive Factors in Explaining Regime Dynamics

CHRISTER JÖNSSON

1. INTRODUCTION

According to a commonly accepted and oft-quoted definition, an international regime can be understood as 'principles, norms, rules, and decision-making procedures around which *actor expectations converge* in a given issue-area' (Krasner 1983*a*: 1; my emphasis). It is noteworthy that this definition points to the subjective, cognitive world of decision-makers rather than any 'objective' reality. Other authors have reiterated that regimes 'exist primarily as participants' understandings, expectations or convictions about legitimate, appropriate or moral behavior' (Puchala and Hopkins 1983: 62). The ontology of regimes, Friedrich Kratochwil and John Ruggie (1986: 764) argue, rests upon a strong element of intersubjectivity.

Issue areas—a key component of the cited definition of international regimes—may also be understood in cognitive terms. Neither issues nor the linking of issues into issue areas are inherent in international subject-matters but are human artefacts which vary over time and across actors. 'When governments active on a set of issues *see* them as closely interdependent, and deal with them collectively, we call that set of issues an issue area' (Keohane and Nye 1977: 65; my emphasis).[1]

In view of the fact that the key concepts are defined in such terms, it is surprising that cognitive theory does not figure more

---

[1] On the notion of issue area see also Ch. 4, sect. 2, above.

prominently in regime analysis. Instead, structural explanations of regime dynamics have predominated the field, the theory of 'hegemonic stability' assuming an almost 'hegemonic' position. In fact, several regime analysts have explicitly questioned the value of cognitive theory. The Tübingen group dismisses cognitive theory for not having produced testable hypotheses.[2] Similarly, Robert Keohane (1988: 392) criticizes what he calls 'reflective' approaches—a label which includes cognitive theory—for the lack of a clear research programme. Stephan Haggard and Beth Simmons (1987: 511) are sceptical of cognitive theories because of their problematic predictive value.

In this chapter I shall accept the challenge of these and other regime analysts and explore to what extent cognitive theory offers hypotheses and a research programme which might enrich regime theory. Let me state from the outset that cognitive theory, in my opinion, should be seen not as a substitute for, but as a useful complement to, existing regime theory. Specifically, I do not share Keohane's (1988) view of rationalistic and cognitive approaches as mutually exclusive categories.

Cognitive theory does not assume irrationality but explores the *limits* of human rationality. It rests on a conception of man as selectively responding to and actively shaping his environment. There has been a gradual shift of emphasis away from cognitive balance theories viewing man as a 'consistency seeker' to attribution theories viewing man as a 'problem solver' or 'intuitive scientist'.

No longer the stimulus–response (S–R) automaton of radical behaviorism, promoted beyond the rank of information processor and cognitive consistency seeker, psychological man has at last been awarded a status equal to that of the scientist who investigates him. For man, in the perspective of attribution theory, is an intuitive psychologist who seeks to explain behavior and to draw inferences about actors and their environments. (Ross 1977: 174)

While proceeding from an assumption of similarities between scientific and common-sense inferences, modern cognitive theory has brought certain explicable judgemental heuristics and biases into focus. The purpose of this chapter is to discuss the relevance of some of these to the study of international regimes.

[2] See Ch. 11, n. 5, below.

2. COGNITION AND INSTITUTIONS

Ernst Haas is one prominent advocate of increased emphasis on cognitive factors when explaining regime dynamics. Focusing on 'choice based on perception and cognition' and 'change in perception', Haas (1980: 360, 361) contends that 'institutionalized collaboration can be explored in terms of the interaction between changing knowledge and changing social goals'.

There have been calls for the study of the nexus of institutions and cognition from other quarters as well. In her book on 'institutional thinking', Mary Douglas (1987: ix) notes: 'A theory of institutions that will amend the current unsociological view of cognition is needed, and a cognitive theory to supplement the weaknesses of institutional analysis is needed as well.'

Another 'institutionalist', Stephen Krasner (1988: 74), points to the interrelations between cognition and institutions when he introduces the concept of 'vertical depth', referring to the extent to which the institutional structure defines the individual actors. Krasner emphasizes that this concept reflects an epistemological stance that views reality as a social construct:

In an uncertain or even unknowable external environment, meaning does not simply present itself in the form of some objective social reality. It is contingent on individual cognitions and possibly, with regard to the depth of institutionalization, on the extent to which these cognitions are determined by the immediate institutional environment within which the individual functions. (Krasner 1988: 75)

A final point of departure: I concur with Stephen Krasner's (1983*b*: 357, 358) argument against unqualified structuralism to the effect that 'causal relationships may vary across periods of regime creation, persistence, and dissipation', specifically that 'once a regime is actually in place, it may develop a dynamic of its own that can alter not only related behaviour and outcomes but also basic causal variables'. In the same vein, I shall discuss the varying significance of cognitive factors in explaining regime creation, persistence, and change, respectively.

3. REGIME CREATION

What are the cognitive prerequisites for international co-operation, including regime creation? International co-operation is rarely, if ever, the result of harmony or identity of interests, but typically grows out of *bargaining situations*, that is, situations characterized by the coincidence of diverging and converging interests as well as interdependent decisions (Schelling 1960*a*: 5 f.; Axelrod and Keohane 1986: 226). Bargaining situations represent dilemmas, that is, choices between incompatible alternatives where neither alternative is optimal but each has both desirable and undesirable consequences.

As we know all too well, the conflictual elements frequently take the upper hand in international bargaining situations. The game-theoretical conception of co-operation under anarchy emphasizes that co-operation is typically a *risky* option. The actor following a co-operative strategy is vulnerable to losses inflicted by defecting partners. Moreover, positive actions tend to be more ambiguous than negative ones. 'The ambiguity of beneficial actions centers around the extent to which ulterior, manipulative purposes may be served by them' (Jones and Davis 1965: 259). Especially in international relations, it is difficult to find an action that incontrovertibly conveys a co-operative or con- ciliatory intent. Concessions and accommodative gestures are frequently interpreted as tactical tricks, designed to drive a wedge into one's coalition or lull one's vigilance (Larson 1988: 286 f.).

A first question in connection with the creation of regimes is thus how the co-operative aspects of a given bargaining situation come to prevail over the conflictual aspects. One common answer, which looms large in both game-theoretical and other discussions, points to the need for *trust* between the co-operating parties. Indeed, trust has been characterized as 'the belief on which cooperation is predicated' (Gambetta 1990*b*: ix).

While most analysts—from game theoreticians to social anthro- pologists—attest to the necessity of trust in achieving lasting co-operation, few have subjected the concept to closer scrutiny.

The importance of trust pervades the most diverse situations where cooperation is at one and the same time a vital and a fragile commodity: from marriage to economic development, from buying a second-hand car to international affairs, from the minutiae of social life to continuation of life on earth. But this very pervasiveness seems to have generated less analysis than paralysis: in the social sciences the importance of trust is often acknowledged but seldom examined, and scholars tend to mention it in passing, to allude to it as a fundamental ingredient or lubricant, an unavoidable dimension of social interaction, only to move on to deal with less intractable matters. (Gambetta 1990*b*: ix–x)

A recent cross-disciplinary symposium devoted to the concept of trust reached a degree of convergence on a definition in terms of expectations or subjective probabilities. Trust can be understood as an agent's theory of how another agent or group of agents will behave in the future, based on the target agents' current and previous claims, either implicit or explicit, about future behaviour (Good 1990: 33; Gambetta 1990*a*: 217).

Trust, in this view, is basically a cognitive phenomenon. A few additional observations on trust, thus understood, are in order. Trust is predicated on ignorance or uncertainty about other actors' behaviour (Gambetta 1990*a*: 218). It concerns expectations that have a bearing on one's own action. That action, in turn, must be chosen *before* one can monitor the actions of those others, or independently of one's capacity ever to be able to monitor them (Dasgupta 1990: 51; Gambetta 1990*a*: 217). Hence, 'trust is a peculiar belief predicated not on evidence but on the lack of *contrary* evidence' (Gambetta 1990*a*: 234).

Fundamentally, trust is a device for coping with the freedom of others. It is premised on the fact that agents have a degree of freedom to disappoint our expectations (Dunn 1990: 80; Gambetta 1990*a*: 218 f.). Thus trust implies a willingness to enter into dependent positions, to increase one's vulnerability to others whose behaviour is not under one's control (B. Williams 1990: 8; Lorenz, 1990: 197).

Trust is essential whenever we want to move beyond 'specific reciprocity' (tit for tat) to 'diffuse reciprocity' (Keohane 1986*a*). In the absence of trust co-operative arrangements, such as regimes, will be difficult to attain. The parties will either 'defect' in game-theoretical terms or spend a lot of time and energy on fashioning safeguards designed to minimize the risks of being a victim of opportunistic behaviour (arms control negotiations over the years are a good example of the latter) (Lorenz 1990: 202).

One pertinent question is thus: what kind of conciliatory behaviour is likely to minimize suspicion and elicit trust? First, actors are generally more likely to infer that their opponents' concessions are sincere—and hence are more likely to reciprocate—if the concessions are perceived to be *voluntary* and relatively *costly* to the other side. Conversely, to the extent that the concessions are seen to be accidental, the result of domestic or external pressure or something the other side had a unilateral interest in doing anyway, they are less likely to be reciprocated (Larson 1988: 292; Pruitt 1981: 38).

This hypothesis is related to the 'augmentation' and 'discounting' principles, formulated by attribution theorists. The augmentation principle holds that 'if for a given effect, both a plausible inhibitory and a plausible facilitative cause are present, the role of the facilitative cause will be judged greater than if it were alone presented as a plausible cause of the effect' (Kelley 1971: 12). In other words, when an effect occurs in the presence of an inhibitory cause, the perceived force of the facilitative cause is *augmented*.

Applied to international co-operation, the augmentation principle suggests that the other side's action 'will be viewed as expressing a stronger disposition the greater the risk or cost associated with taking that action' (Pruitt 1981: 125). For instance, the Soviet decision to withdraw from, and agree to the neutralization of, Austria in 1955 was perceived as a genuinely conciliatory gesture, since it involved the risk of raising popular expectations in Eastern Europe that the Soviets might withdraw and condone neutrality. As noted by Deborah Larson (1987: 48), American policy-makers were impressed by the Soviet willingness to incur such risks and felt compelled to reciprocate.

Conversely, the discounting principle indicates that 'the role of a given cause in producing a given effect is discounted if other plausible causes are also present' (Kelley 1971: 8). Hence, a co-operative action will produce less trust if it can be seen as deriving from role requirements or can be attributed to weakness (Pruitt 1981: 126). Conciliatory gestures may be dismissed because the other side is perceived to have a unilateral interest in making them whether or not they are reciprocated.

For example, Soviet conventional troop cuts in 1955, 1956, and

1958 were not viewed in Washington as indications of Soviet good intentions. Rather, they were assumed to be motivated by the urge to modernize Soviet forces and transfer much-needed manpower to industry and agriculture (Larson 1988: 293). Hence the unilateral Soviet measures were not reciprocated and did not result in any arms control agreement.

Finally, conciliatory behaviour is more likely to elicit trust if it is repeated despite lacking reciprocity. This notion underlies Charles Osgood's (1962) GRIT (graduated reciprocation in tension reduction) strategy, designed to facilitate negotiation between bitter, long-term adversaries. Osgood recommends that the initiator of co-operation make a series of conciliatory actions spread over different issue areas or geographic areas, stating publicly that the moves are intended to reduce tension. Not assuming immediate reciprocation, GRIT prescribes continual incremental concessions over a period of time, even though the other side does not respond. This, presumably, will foster greater trust and convince the other side of good faith. A series of moderately risky concessions, not easily dismissed as the product of self-interest or hostility, would finally succeed in persuading the adversary to reciprocate and thus set into motion a spiral of tension reduction.

Soviet behaviour prior to the signing of the Austrian State Treaty in 1955 has been cited as one example of the successful application of GRIT (Larson 1987). The Soviet Union then made a series of unilateral concessions in various areas of East–West confrontation. In an unexpected policy reversal, Moscow in February 1955 abandoned its previous linkage of an Austrian settlement with the conclusion of a German peace treaty. In April the Soviet Union signed a bilateral agreement with Austria for the withdrawal of Soviet troops and the elimination of Soviet economic enclaves. On the eve of the final Four Powers negotiations on Austria, Soviet negotiators tabled a disarmament proposal that moved towards the western position in a number of important respects, and the Soviet Government announced that a high-level mission would visit Yugoslavia. Consistent with GRIT, the Soviets explained publicly that their objective in signing the Austrian State Treaty was to reduce tensions.

Trust, in short, refers to the co-operating parties' perceptions of each other and their mutual relations. But the cognitive prerequisites of co-operation also include perceptions of the issue area in question. In the game-theoretically inspired literature, it is mainly a matter of perceived pay-offs. The more substantial the gains from mutual co-operation and the less substantial the gains from unilateral defection are perceived to be, the greater the likelihood of co-operation.

However, co-operation depends not only on perceived pay-offs of given alternatives. A number of bargaining theorists have proposed that an agreement often requires a *formula*, a shared perception or definition of the problem (Zartman and Berman 1982: 95). In this view, 'the development of common perceptions becomes more important than the exchange of concessions' (Winham 1977: 97). Ernst Haas (1990: 162) alludes to the import-ance of a 'core anchoring concept' in regime formation, a notion that appears more or less synonymous with formula. The signifi-cance of the convergence around a formula is that it facilitates the bargaining process. Of course, a formula may eventually, but does not necessarily, turn into a principle upon which a regime is founded.

In 1970, for example, the United Nations General Assembly adopted the famous formula of the seabed as 'the common heritage of mankind'. In mammoth negotiations on the law of the sea throughout the decade, negotiators then faced the task of giving substance to the 'common heritage' formula in an inter-national regime for the seabed (Sebenius 1984: 8). In the end, however, this formula failed to translate into a regime principle.

As this example suggests, a formula may be of a *metaphorical* nature. Linguists and cognitive theorists alike have pointed to the metaphorical nature not only of our language but also of our knowledge structures. Indeed, our penchant for pictorial and metaphorical thinking has been suggested as the principal differ-ence between human and artificial intelligence, between the human mind and the computer.

'The essence of metaphor is understanding and experiencing one kind of thing in terms of another' (Lakoff and Johnson 1980: 5). We typically conceptualize the unfamiliar in terms of the familiar, the non-physical in terms of the physical, the less clearly delineated in terms of the more clearly delineated. We tend to structure the less concrete and inherently vaguer concepts (like those for mental processes) in terms of more concrete concepts (like those for physical processes) with a clearer experiential basis

(Lakoff and Johnson 1980: 59, 112, 115). For instance, many of the terms used to characterize intellectual activity are based on the metaphor of seeing with the eye—'observe', 'see', 'view', 'point of view', 'outlook', 'focus', 'perspective', etc. (Miller 1979: 166; Lakoff and Johnson 1980: 48). Also, abstract political phenomena are strikingly often treated in metaphorical terms by practitioners and theoreticians alike (Miller 1979: 163).

When they cover whole areas rather than discrete events or phenomena, metaphors tend to be systematic. Coherent systems of metaphorical concepts and expressions may develop around a basic metaphor. For example, the basic metaphor 'time is money' has entailed a series of expressions, such as 'wasting or saving time', 'living on borrowed time', 'having time to spare', and the like (Lakoff and Johnson 1980: 7–9, 46–51).

By drawing attention to some aspects and, by the same token, concealing others, metaphors influence our ways of perceiving and interpreting reality. They define problems and imply possible solutions.

The very systematicity that allows us to comprehend one aspect of a concept in terms of another . . . will necessarily hide other aspects of the concept. In allowing us to focus on one aspect of a concept . . . a metaphorical concept can keep us from focusing on other aspects of the concept that are inconsistent with that metaphor. (Lakoff and Johnson 1980: 10)

Though systematic, metaphors are often unconscious. Systematic metaphors 'appear natural, as indeed they are. They also appear to be uniquely necessary, which of course they are not' (Chilton 1989: 11). For every metaphor there are alternative metaphors. Finding new solutions to a problem often requires being guided by alternative metaphors.

Hence, in considering the creation of an international regime, one should not underestimate the role of a formula consisting of a systematic metaphor which makes the actors view their common problem in a new light. International co-operation can be facilitated by 'frame restructuring', to use a term suggested by Donald Schön (1979).

Schön (1979: 255) argues that the essential difficulties of policy-making may have more to do with problem setting than with problem solving: 'When we examine the problem-setting stories told by the analysts and practitioners of social policy, it becomes apparent that the framing of problems often depends upon meta-phors underlying the stories which generate problem setting and set the directions of problem solving.' Policy innovation requires questioning of these pervasive, tacit 'generative metaphors' and consideration of alternative metaphors—'frame restructuring', in short.

One of the examples adduced by Schön is instructive though unrelated to international co-operation. Product development researchers, considering how to improve the performance of a new paintbrush made with synthetic bristles, were puzzled as to why the new brush delivered paint in a discontinuous, 'gloppy' way. After having unsuccessfully tried a number of different bristle improvements, someone suggested, 'A paintbrush is a kind of pump', thereby redirecting attention to the spaces between bristles, through which paint is forced onto the surface. Thinking of the brushes as pumps, the researchers noticed that the natural brush formed a gradual curve when pressed against a surface whereas the synthetic one formed a shape more nearly an angle. By concentrating on the bending shape of the synthetic brush the researchers in the end managed to produce a smoother flow of paint. Paintbrush-as-pump served as a generative metaphor. By analogy, the building of an international regime in a given issue area may be aided by a new generative metaphor (such as the 'common heritage' one in the law of the sea).

Mary Douglas (1987: 45–53) similarly proposes that institutions are founded on analogies or metaphors. 'To acquire legitimacy, every kind of institution needs a formula that founds its rightness in reason and in nature' (Douglas 1987: 45). These analogies confer natural status on social relations. Noting that 'some meta-phors work catalytically to promote collective action, and others do not', Douglas (1987: 50, 52) concludes—without adducing much supportive evidence—that institutions founded in nature are the most robust. In line with the reasoning above, I would rephrase her thesis and argue that 'generative metaphors' need to allude to familiar phenomena with a common experiential basis to be effective as the basis for international regimes.

Historical analogies are examples of such captivating phenomena of special relevance to international affairs. Policy-makers tend to be influenced by events that are recent, that they experienced firsthand, or that occurred when they were first coming to political awareness (Jervis 1985: 22). Such prototypical events assume a metaphorical quality and in extreme cases are elevated to become myths.

Hence international co-operation frequently requires the replacement of old historical lessons of conflict with newer lessons of co-operation. For example, the lessons of the late 1930s—sometimes referred to as the 'Munich syndrome'—long had a detrimental effect on East–West arms control negotiations. The Cuban missile crisis in late 1962 created a new precedent and taught new lessons which could overshadow the negative 'appeasement' lessons. The crisis, which brought the superpowers to the brink of war, provided a dramatic illustration of the common US–Soviet interest in avoiding a nuclear catastrophe and had a salutary impact on the arms control negotiations, first manifested in the Limited Test Ban Treaty of 1963 (Jönsson 1990: 133–5).

A final caveat: the creation of an international regime typically involves cross-cultural interaction. This may be an obstacle to finding a common generative metaphor or historical lesson. People of different cultures may be 'speaking of different things even while uttering the same words' (Bozeman 1960: 9). Various cultures may impart distinctive ways of putting ideas together, associating causes and effects, seeking knowledge and understanding, using evidence and reasoning. Metaphors and historical analogies are particularly susceptible to differing interpretations and associations across cultures.

Stephan Haggard and Beth Simmons (1987: 511) have referred to 'the recurrent structural fallacy' of expecting similar responses to the same structural constraints by all actors and ignoring cultural varieties. One may perhaps even raise the question: which types of cultures value, and which do not value, co-operation generally? Aaron Wildavsky (1987, 1989), for example, has proposed a fourfold categorization of political cultures: collectivist, egalitarian, individualist, and fatalist. Axelrod's (1984) much-debated work can be read as a demonstration that individualism does not exclude co-operation. One may hypothesize that only fatalist cultures are principally opposed to co-operation (Thompson, Ellis, and Wildavsky 1990: 35).

Such reservations aside, the cognitive prerequisites of regime creation identified above are the development of trust, on the one hand, and the convergence around a formula or generative meta-phor, on the other. Let us turn, next, to cognitive factors and regime persistence.

4. REGIME PERSISTENCE

First, it should be noted that the cognitive factors associated with regime creation have a bearing on regime maintenance, too. The significance of trust, for example, remains beyond the forming of a regime. It has been said that 'trust, like other moral resources, grows with use and decays with disuse' (Dasgupta 1990: 56). A regime makes for increased contact which, in turn, facilitates communication. Within a regime a special language is usually forged which permits more sensitive interpretation and greater certainty as to the intent behind any communication. When transactions become embedded in a network of personal relation-ships, the level of shirking, cheating, and dissimulation decreases (Krasner 1988: 82 f.; Good 1990: 44 f.; Lorenz 1990: 208).

Yet 'there may well be distinctive logics to regime initiation and regime maintenance' (Lipson 1983: 236). Regimes, in Krasner's (1983*b*: 357) words, 'may assume a life of their own'. From a cognitive perspective, regimes will eventually colour the partici-pants' perceptions and thinking. Once established, international regimes become *explanans* in addition to *explanandum*.

This is the essence of Krasner's (1988) institutionalist perspec-tive, according to which the preferences and basic self-identities of individual actors are conditioned by enduring institutional structures. Mary Douglas (1987) is a vocal advocate of the view that institutions direct and control cognitive processes. Drawing on Emile Durkheim's and Ludwik Fleck's theories about the social control of cognition, she argues that institutions influence our processes of classifying and recognizing, remembering and forget-ting. Institutions, in brief, 'perform the same tasks as theory' (Douglas 1987: 59).

In Foucauldian terms, a regime establishes a dominating or hegemonic discourse which 'gives specific definition and order to a public space or realm of action' (Keeley 1990: 92). It specifies relevant phenomena and issue areas and endorses certain language, symbols, modes of reasoning, and criteria of truth and meaning.

Categorization is basic to human thought and perception. According to conventional wisdom, categories exist in the world independent of people and are defined only by common properties. They are assumed to be abstract containers, with things either inside or outside the category. However, recent studies of conceptual categories in anthropology, linguistics, and psychology have accumulated evidence in conflict with conventional wisdom (Lakoff 1987). Categorization is not independent of who is doing the categorizing and on what basis. Categories do not exist 'in the world' but have to do with the world as we interact with it. Institutions bestow sameness and assign disparate items to classes and load them with moral and political content (Douglas 1987: 63).

By the same token, institutions establish selective principles that highlight some kinds of events and phenomena and obscure others. Institutions produce 'public memory' and 'structural amnesia' (Douglas 1987: 70).

Let me exemplify by referring to a regime I have myself studied (Jönsson 1987). The first international aviation regime, created in 1919, amplified the memory of the First World War, which demonstrated beyond doubt the military value of aircraft. Protection against incursion from the air therefore became the principal consideration of national policy-makers, and the Paris Convention of 1919 endowed each state with 'complete and exclusive sovereignty over the airspace above its territory'. The earlier discussions about freedom of the air, modelled on Grotius' *mare liberum* doctrine, became 'unthinkables and unmemorables', to use Douglas's (1987: 76) terms. The focus on sovereignty entailed placing the international aviation issue area in a *national* frame. In order to establish an international air service, a state had to negotiate with the foreign governments concerned for the right to overfly and land. Commercial airlines became national enterprises, 'flag carriers'. 'Political frontiers had been built in the airspace where physical boundaries could never be' (Cooper 1947: 22). The first aviation regime, in short, induced thinking of international air transport as an aspect of inter-state relations rather than a transnational business venture.

Mary Douglas, following Fleck, maintains that institutions create 'thought collectives'. 'The individual within the collective is never, or hardly ever, conscious of the prevailing thought style which almost always exerts an absolutely compulsive force upon his thinking, and with which it is not possible to be at variance' (Fleck, as quoted in Douglas 1987: 13). Thus institutions establish the range of discourse and available options.

Fleck's 'thought collective' bears a certain resemblance to Peter Haas's (1989, 1990) 'epistemic community', although Haas emphasizes the role of knowledge-based communities in the creation rather than the maintenance of regimes. Haas (1990: 55) defines an epistemic community as 'a professional group that believes in the same cause-and-effect relationships, truth tests to assess them, and shares common values' and underlines that its members share a common interpretative framework and a common vocabulary. Regimes may be created by, but may also create, epistemic communities, thus understood.

By influencing perceptions and thought patterns and by giving rise to 'thought collectives' or 'epistemic communities', institutions tend to perpetuate themselves. In a world of 'habit-driven actors' (Rosenau 1986), who act upon habitual memories, beliefs, and expectations, past choices constrain future possibilities. The persistence of international regimes is related to such 'path dependence' (Krasner 1988: 67). An early precursor of 'path dependence' theory, Niccolò Machiavelli (1532: 21), put it thus:

It must be considered that there is nothing more difficult to carry out, nor more doubtful of success, nor more dangerous to handle, than to initiate a new order of things. For the reformer has enemies in all those who profit by the old order, and only lukewarm defenders in all those who would profit by the new order, this lukewarmness arising partly from fear of their adversaries, who have the laws in their favour; and partly from the incredulity of mankind, who do not truly believe in anything new until they have had actual experience of it.

Machiavelli's idea that established interests, habitual thought patterns, and human resistance to the new and unfamiliar tend to perpetuate old orders has been repeated by latter-day students of international regimes:

Social practices and convergent expectations frequently prove resistant to change, even when they produce outcomes that are widely understood to be undesirable or suboptimal. Existing institutional arrangements, such as the international agreements pertaining to coffee or Antarctica, are familiar constructs while new arrangements require actors to assimilate alternative procedures or patterns of behavior and to accept (initially) unknown outcomes. Additionally, planned changes in regimes require not only the destruction of existing institutions but also the coordination of expectations around new focal points. (Young 1983: 96)

These notions of path-dependent thinking and behaviour are firmly grounded in cognitive theory. It is a well-established fact that beliefs tend to be resistant to change. Robert Jervis (1976: 291–6) has identified several psychological mechanisms which may account for the human tendency to maintain images and beliefs even in the face of discrepant information. Actors may (1) fail to see that new information might contradict their beliefs; (2) see the information as discrepant but reject its validity; (3) discredit the source of discrepant information; (4) admit puzzlement with new information; (5) engage in bolstering—seeking new information that supports initial beliefs; (6) engage in undermining—adducing additional elements to weaken discrepant information; (7) engage in differentiation—splitting the object by sloughing off the parts that are causing attitudinal conflict; and/or (8) invoke transcendence—the opposite mechanism from differentiation, where elements, instead of being split down, are built up and combined into larger units. Moreover, change is impeded by the frequently noted tendency over time to escalate perceived utility as a result of the 'investment' or accumulated expenditure incurred in the pursuit of an object (Edmead 1982).

In sum, established international regimes will colour the perception and thinking of participants. The prevalent bias will be towards path dependence and resistance to change. Thus cognitive factors contribute to an explanation of regime persistence.

5. REGIME CHANGE

If states and other international actors are, in fact, habit-driven, how then can change occur? James Rosenau's (1986: 864) somewhat circuitous answer is that 'the readiness to learn is part of an actor's habit pool and, as such, is susceptible to activation under certain conditions'. This points to *learning* as a key cognitive variable in accounting for regime change.[3]

Learning is a common but also a controversial concept in the social sciences. In psychology there have been two major families of learning theories, stimulus–response and cognitive. Earlier definitions emphasized the role of reinforcement—reward and punishment—in producing behavioural or cognitive change, excluding changes resulting from other processes than reinforcement (Kimble 1968: 114).

The emphasis on reinforcement is easily associated with some kind of authority, and a major preoccupation of students of learning has been with the experimental manipulation of a variety of variables. However, in connection with international regimes, we normally think of 'a learning process in which each party is both teacher and student' (Zartman and Berman 1982: 19). Mutual learning through interaction is what may elicit regime change.

Also, learning is commonly understood as a process that is experienced by individuals. Yet, as George Modelski (1990: 7) argues, the concept of learning is broad enough to be extended to social systems and cultures as well: 'For what we have in each of these three cases is a network—the brain and nervous system, the social structure, and the cultural system—which experiences change through rearrangement of its connections as the result of past (reinforced) stimuli.' Social learning is generally considered to be slower and more constrained than individual analytic learning (Nye 1987: 381).

Definitions of learning typically say nothing about the kinds of behavioural changes that qualify as indicators of learning. For example, they do not imply that learning necessarily leads to improved behaviour; there is positive as well as negative learning.

Regime analysts who have proposed learning as a key variable accounting for regime change understand the concept in terms of cognitive change in response to new information. Joseph Nye (1987: 379) emphasizes that 'the alteration of beliefs by new information does not always increase effectiveness' and points to

---

[3] For an analytical distinction of different dimensions of institutional learning see Ch. 8, sect. 3, above.

misread lessons of history and inappropriate analogies as examples of negative learning.

Ernst Haas (1990: 24) similarly views learning as 'the elaboration of new cause–effect chains more (or less) elaborate than the ones being questioned and replaced', and admonishes that learning 'may imply progress or regress, depending on the normative commitment of the observer or the preferred reading of history'.

Nye and Haas see eye to eye also with regard to distinguishing between what Nye labels simple and complex social learning:

Simple learning uses new information merely to adapt the means, without altering any deeper goals in the ends–means chain. The actor simply uses a different instrument to attain the same goal. Complex learning, by contrast, involves recognition of conflict among means and goals in causally complicated situations, and leads to new priorities and trade-offs. (Nye 1987: 380)

Haas's (1990: 3) terms 'adaptation' and 'learning' roughly correspond to simple and complex learning, respectively. Adaptation refers to incremental change occurring as a result either of altering means of action or of adding new ends without worrying about their coherence with existing ends. Learning, in Haas's terminology, is reserved for radical change involving questioning and redefinition of underlying values and ultimate purposes. Causal relationships are specified in new ways, and new nested problem sets are constructed.

'Adaptive behavior is common, whereas true learning is rare.' This leads Haas (1990: 37) to conclude that 'the very nature of institutions is such that the dice are loaded in favor of the less demanding behavior associated with adaptation'. This is in line with the reasoning above about institutional thinking as an aspect of regime maintenance. Institutions incarnate habit-driven behaviour and therefore favour adaptation over learning (E. B. Haas 1990: 173).

Also, Nye's and Haas's two types of learning can easily be associated with the distinction between regime change and changes within regimes (Krasner 1983a: 3 f.). A regime change is characterized by alteration of principles and norms, which implies complex or 'true' learning. Changes in rules and decision-making procedures without altered principles and norms, on the other hand, are referred to as changes within regimes; these involve simple learning or adaptation.

Is perhaps 'learning' just another word for 'regime change'? And does a focus on learning invite circular reasoning? That would be a premature conclusion. One can well imagine learning without concomitant regime change. Also, if we are to believe structural theory, regime change may occur without learning. Regimes may be imposed rather than negotiated (Young 1989*a*: 84–9); regime change may be the result of declining hegemony. Learning, in short, can be posited as an intervening variable between structural change and regime change.

Under what circumstances, then, can we expect complex learning which, in turn, may lead to regime change? Nye and Haas agree that a widespread sense of dissatisfaction with the old regime and a dramatic crisis usually trigger a learning process (Nye 1987: 398; E. B. Haas 1990: 27 f.). In addition, Haas (1990: 164) identifies two major conditions underlying successful international learning:

First, there must be a relatively stable coalition of like-minded states whose professed goals do not differ fundamentally from government to government. And, second, there must be sufficient consensual knowledge available to provide the rationale for the novel nesting of problems and solutions. *Both* conditions must be met. The existence of either, by itself, does not permit learning.

Let me return to my international aviation example. The 'unrestricted sovereignty' regime created after the First World War ushered in a period of intensive bilateral 'horse trading' between governments for air rights. Air transport privileges were frequently used for gaining ends that had little to do with aviation (Jönsson 1987: 29–31). Most governments assumed 'the role of feudal baron who levied private tribute on all the commerce passing along the highroads within his grasp' (Warner 1945: 25). When the future of civil air transport was again put on the international agendas toward the end of the Second World War, there was widespread dissatisfaction with the old order and a general willingness to release international air transport from its cocoon of multiple national restrictions.

The eventual 'Chicago–Bermuda' regime diluted the principle of airspace sovereignty by combining it with the principles of international regulation and certain 'freedoms of the air'. This also implied an enhanced role of airlines at the expense of governments and the establishment of new multilateral organizations. Thus, an element of complex learning seems to have occurred.

To be sure, there was no immediate international consensus after the Second World War concerning the future aviation order. On the contrary, the first post-war years saw acrimonious clashes, especially between the Americans and the British. Yet the eventual bilateral compromise at Bermuda in 1946 managed to combine US competitive and British regulatory principles. Ever since the 1944 Chicago conference it had been obvious that only such a compromise could guarantee the orderly and mutually profitable development of international air commerce. Other countries, most notably Canada, had in fact proposed solutions along these lines. Therefore, the Bermuda agreement was supported by most aviation nations; it came to represent 'not merely a bilateral agreement between the two major air transport nations, but a general philosophy on the way in which the economic regulation of the industry should be achieved' (Wheatcroft 1964: 70). In the end, a stable coalition of like-minded countries and consensual knowledge—E. Haas's prerequisites of learning —emerged.

A final observation about learning and regime change concerns the tendency toward 'lumpy' learning, to use Nye's (1987: 398) expression: 'Large groups or generations may learn by crisis or major events which serve as metaphors for organizing diverse sets of experience.' Drawing on an analogy with evolutionary theory, Krasner (1988: 77–80) uses the term 'punctuated equilibrium' to characterize such cycles of long institutional stability and sudden change. In evolutionary theory the term denotes a process in which long periods of stasis are broken by relatively short episodes of rapid speciation. The analogy is especially suggestive today, when the institutional stability of the Cold War period is replaced by accelerating change and flux. In a longer view, a pertinent question for further research is whether international regimes tend to change together after periods of regime persistence and stability, and whether such patterns reflect lumpy social learning. And to what extent are social learning and institutional change associated with wars and upheavals, as Robert Gilpin (1981) has suggested?

6. CONCLUSION

Theories and models are like floodlights which illuminate one part of the stage but, by the same token, leave other parts in the shade. They sensitize us to certain aspects of a phenomenon or problem while desensitizing us to others. My purpose in this chapter has been to shed light on aspects of international regime dynamics which have been left in the dark by traditional theories. Cognitive theories and hypotheses 'explore what structural, game-theoretical, and functional approaches bracket' (Haggard and Simmons 1987: 509).

At the same time, my floodlight has left other aspects of international regimes in the dark. As I stated initially, I view cognitive theory not as a substitute for, but as a useful complement to, existing regime theory. I share Keohane's (1988: 393) hope that constructive competition and dialogue will eventually produce a synthesis between 'rationalistic' and 'reflective' approaches. And I agree with Haggard and Simmons (1987: 513) that 'the resolution of the debate between structuralists and cognitivists will depend on tests that allow a confrontation between the two approaches without violating the epistemological tenets of either'.

Then Keohane and Nye's (1977: 58) advice to 'seek explanation with simple models and add complexity as necessary' is worth heeding. If it yields satisfactory explanations, there is no need to add complexity to a simplified model. If it does not, complexity may be added gradually by relaxing the simplifying assumptions of the original model step by step. Hence, cognitive theory becomes useful whenever neither the 'structural' theory of hegemonic stability nor 'functional' game theory offers satisfactory explanations of regime creation, persistence, and change.

First, these theories have the virtue of parsimony yet are essentially *static*. They fail to take the dynamics of political *processes* into account. Elsewhere (Jönsson 1987), I have argued the need to develop a process model of regime evolution. Cognitive theory, I posit, may contribute to this development.

Second, whereas the strict rationality criterion of these theories assumes a relatively unambiguous reality, ambiguity is the point of departure for cognitive theory. What is real, is ultimately what human beings perceive to be real. By understanding how people think about the ambiguous world, therefore, we can get a richer understanding of the processes underlying regime creation, persistence, and change.

I do not claim to have covered all aspects of cognitive theory that may be of relevance to a better understanding of regime dynamics. My essay should be seen as suggestive rather than exhaustive. Using the warp of regime dynamics, I have tried to weave together disparate threads from the literature on institutions, cognitive processes, language, and social learning. The ensuing pattern no doubt needs refinements and additions. But I hope to have demonstrated that cognitive theory may contribute to the production of a richer texture.

Testing Theories of Regime Formation

Findings from a Large Collaborative Research Project

ORAN R. YOUNG AND GAIL OSHERENKO

1. INTRODUCTION

Can international actors agree on a plan to reduce the threat of global climate change? Will they be able to secure and extend the international trade regime? Why do actors in international society reach agreement on some issues, yet fail to achieve consensus on other, seemingly similar, problems? While negotiators working on a convention on biological diversity and another on climate change became enmeshed in a complex effort to find formulas to satisfy both northern industrialized states and developing southern states, we initiated a project to search for the underlying determinants of success or failure in regime formation. We sought to learn from regimes created early in the century that remained stable over decades, as well as from more recent international arrangements to address transboundary air pollution and ozone depletion.

Both scholars and practitioners engaged in international negotiations have offered a wide range of explanations for success or failure in efforts to reach agreement on rules, norms, and decision-making procedures to deal with common problems—to reap joint gains or avoid mutual losses. Yet few have conducted sustained empirical tests of the principal hypotheses dealing with processes of regime formation. This chapter reports the findings of a large collaborative research project in which we have made a start towards filling this gap.[1] The Ford Foundation provided the

---

[1] For a very similar endeavour see Ch. 11 below.

primary funding for the two-year project organized by the Institute of Arctic Studies at Dartmouth College.[2]

In this project, fourteen scholars from four countries joined forces to develop a template of hypotheses based on the literature relating to sustained international co-operation and to conduct five in-depth case studies of the formation of regimes as a means of testing these hypotheses. Three distinctive attributes set this project apart from many others dealing with regime formation. The project combines the methodology of structured or focused case studies with a carefully crafted set of hypotheses formulated in advance of the empirical work. The case studies are drawn from the experience with sustained international co-operation in the Arctic; for the most part, they involve issues relating to natural resources and the environment. The multinational research team, including analysts from Canada, Norway, Russia, and the United States, not only agreed to use a common set of hypotheses, but also succeeded in transcending cultural and disciplinary differences to produce integrated case studies.[3]

2. THE SCOPE OF THE PROJECT

We began our research with a single question: what are the determinants of success or failure in efforts to form international regimes dealing with specific issues? As the project developed, however, we came to understand that the concept of regime formation requires unpacking to make it analytically tractable as a dependent variable. At least three aspects of regime formation are worthy of differentiation. There is, to begin with, the simple question of whether a regime forms or, in other words, whether the efforts of those involved in the process of regime formation succeed or fail. A second aspect deals with the issue of timing. How long does it take to reach closure on the terms of a constitutional contract establishing a regime, and why does the

---

[2] Those who worked on the case studies include Alexander Arikainen, Margaret Clark, Anne Fikkan, Peter M. Haas, Natalia Mirovitskaya, Gail Osherenko, Ron Purver, Artemy Sagirian, Elen Singh, and Marvin S. Soroos.

[3] For a complete treatment of the project and its case studies and findings, consult Young and Osherenko (1993).

process take much longer or go through more stages in some cases than in others? Additionally, there is the matter of a regime's substantive content. We want to know not only whether and when a regime forms, but also how to account for the contents of a regime's principal provisions. These are analytic distinctions; it does not make sense to deal with any one of these concerns to the exclusion of the others. Still, it is appropriate to point out that the findings reported here have more to tell us about the first and second of these issues than about the third.

2.1. Theoretical and Methodological Perspectives

In thinking about the determinants of success or failure in efforts to form international regimes, analysts have generally directed their attention to the exercise of power, the interplay of interests, and the influence of knowledge.[4] For the most part, they have produced explanations of regime formation highlighting the role of one or another of these sets of factors. To test the adequacy of these explanations, we began by distilling a set of explicit hypotheses from the existing literature on regime formation. In the process, we developed an interest in the impact of apparently unrelated contextual factors in bringing regimes into being. The resultant theoretical template guided the work of those conducting the case studies that form the heart of our project. To facilitate the work of the research team, we grouped these explanatory arguments into four broad categories: power-based hypotheses, interest-based hypotheses, knowledge-based hypotheses, and contextual arguments (the full template can be found in the Appendix to this chapter).

The practice of using structured or focused case studies to test and refine theory-based arguments is not without its limitations or, for that matter, its critics. There is a danger of skewing the results through a biased selection of cases, producing *ad hoc* interpretations of historical events, and manipulating information to conform to theoretical expectations, to name a few of the pitfalls. Yet, carefully conducted case studies have substantial advantages in the

---

[4] See also Ch. 8, sects. 3 and 4, above, where Haas examines the predictions of these three 'schools of thought' with respect to 'regime patterns'.

search for evidence regarding the extent to which theoretically grounded ideas about international co-operation accurately and adequately explain regime formation. While the results of a single case may be suspect, the opportunity to compare conclusions across a number of well-chosen cases increases our ability to test specific hypotheses and to refine theories of regime formation for consideration in future research. When hypotheses state necessary or sufficient conditions, single contrary cases suffice to disconfirm the hypothesized relationships. For hypotheses framed as measures of association, the evidence from the case studies can only be characterized as more or less consistent with the hypothesized links. Overall, we regard the findings of this project as a challenge to those seeking to refute, refine, or extend our conclusions in their own research on regime formation.

2.2. *The Universe of Cases*

We examined five cases, including: the regime for the Svalbard Archipelago worked out in the context of the Paris Peace Conference in 1919; the regime for North Pacific fur seals initiated in a four-nation treaty in 1911; the polar bear regime established under the terms of a 1973 agreement among the five ice states; and the regime to protect stratospheric ozone emerging in several stages during the 1980s. For comparison, the fifth case focuses on the failure to develop a regime to deal with Arctic haze, an increasingly important transboundary air pollution problem of particular relevance to the Circumpolar North. In analysing this case, the author contrasted the failure to establish an Arctic haze regime with the successful development of an air pollution regime initiated in the 1979 Geneva Convention on Long-Range Transboundary Air Pollution (LRTAP) and fleshed out in a series of protocols dealing with sulphur dioxide, nitrogen oxides, and volatile organic compounds.

Taken together, these cases convey a strong sense of both the richness and the diversity of the institutional arrangements that belong to the category of international regimes. The arrangement for the Svalbard Archipelago, a stewardship regime in which a single member plays the role of trustee for the concerns of the broader community, stands as testimony to the proposition that the absence of a centralized structure of authority in international society (Bull 1977) does not preclude the development of mechanisms that serve to promote the common good. The polar bear agreement establishes a co-ordination regime that commits its members to act in accordance with a set of common rules and procedures, while leaving each member free to implement these rules and procedures in its own way.[5] The fur seal regime and the protection system for stratospheric ozone involve more complex arrangements. The regime for fur seals evolved over time into a users' club coupled with a co-operative mechanism for arriving at collective decisions regarding the consumptive use of seals. The ozone regime, which began as a co-ordination arrangement, has developed into a co-operative management system with the addition of the 1990 London Amendments to the 1987 Montreal Protocol.

None the less, we found ourselves dealing in each case with a process of regime formation that featured efforts to reach agreement on explicit, though not necessarily legally binding, statements setting forth the major provisions of regimes.[6] In some cases, the process has been long and drawn-out—it took more than twenty years of intermittent negotiations to produce the four-party treaty on fur seals of 1911. Sometimes the provisions included in the final agreement differ dramatically from those under consideration in earlier phases of the negotiations—the deliberations on Svalbard before the First World War, for example, centred on the idea of *terra nullius* coupled with a proposal for the establishment of an international administrative apparatus. In other cases, the outcome is an open agreement to which additional members are permitted to accede as they see fit—the LRTAP protocols on sulphur dioxide (SO_2), nitrogen oxides, and volatile organic compounds fit this model. In still other cases, a regime develops in stages through a continuing series of negotiations

---

[5] The significance of co-ordination regimes in international society raises questions about Keohane's (1990: 733) observation that 'regimes are usually accompanied by organizations'.

[6] There is a rapidly growing literature on 'soft law' in international society or, in other words, prescriptions that take the form of legal rules but that are not expressed in the form of legally binding treaties or conventions. For a discussion of 'soft law' regimes see Thacher (no date). Some effective international agreements are even more informal. On the conditions under which actors are likely to prefer informal prescriptions see Lipson (1991), as well as Ch. 4, sect. 3, above.

punctuated by partial or interim agreements—the ozone regime evolved from the framework provisions of the 1985 Vienna Convention to the substantive arrangements set forth in the 1987 Montreal Protocol and, more recently, the 1990 London Amendments. In every case, however, the process of regime formation centred on efforts to negotiate the terms of a package of mutually acceptable provisions to be set forth in a constitutional contract.[7]

3. SINGLE-FACTOR ACCOUNTS

Considered separately, the case studies included in our project cannot confirm the hypotheses in the theoretical template. But taken together, the results of these studies enable us to proceed with some confidence to identify hypotheses that are disconfirmed and to focus on those that have received sufficient support to make them interesting as subjects for further investigation. The hypotheses as first derived from theory and formulated for this project appear in the Appendix to this chapter. In the course of the empirical phase of the project, the research team made some adjustments and elaborations to the hypotheses. These are discussed in the text and account for minor differences between the Appendix and Tables 1–4, which tabulate the conclusions from the five cases. This section provides an accompanying narrative. To save space, only the most important findings are mentioned here (Young and Osherenko 1993).

3.1. Power-Based Hypotheses

None of the cases offers strong support for the proposition that success in regime formation requires the participation of a single dominant party or, in other words, a hegemon. In four of the cases, researchers found no evidence of a *single* state making use of superior material resources to obtain or impose its preferred

---

[7] A constitutional contract is an explicit agreement setting forth the rules of the game for a given social practice. Such contracts may, but need not, be codified in legally binding instruments like treaties or conventions. For a well-known account of constitutional contracts by a political economist see Buchanan (1975: ch. 4).

TABLE 10.1. *Power-Based Hypotheses about Regime Formation*

Hypotheses	Fur seals	Svalbard	Polar bears	Ozone	Haze/ LRTAP	Summary
Hegemony	D	D	D	M	D	4D/1M
Other configurations of power	—	C	C	–	C	3C

Note. A dash indicates that the hypothesis is not addressed in the case study.

Key
 C = consistent with hypothesis
 D = tends to disconfirm hypothesis
 M = results mixed

outcome. While power was important in each of the cases, we have found that it is often better understood as a source of bargaining strength in the interactive processes highlighted by the interest-based hypotheses. Power in the material sense may even come to be regarded as an obstacle, as in the polar bear case, where American negotiators took care to avoid derailing negotiations by any display of dominance (see Table 10.1).[8]

After rejecting the pure form of *hegemonic stability theory*, however, the authors of the case studies searched for and found different configurations of power that come into play in regime formation. The ozone case suggests the value of exploring the idea of *issue-specific hegemony* or the ability of a single state to play a dominant role with regard to a specific issue, even when it does not possess a preponderance of material resources across the board. Several of the cases suggest that *middle powers* can assume key roles in regime formation. Germany played a central part in negotiating the 1985 SO_2 protocol to LRTAP; Canada played a pivotal role in creating the polar bear regime and may do so again in the future with regard to a regime to deal with Arctic haze. On the other hand, the results of the cases are mixed with regard to the idea that a *symmetrical distribution of power* or a *(bipolar) balance of power* facilitates the process of regime formation. While bipolarity, for example, may have hindered efforts to form a co-operative arrangement to deal with Arctic haze, it did not block

[8] In this regard, our findings parallel those of a well-known group of European scholars working at the University of Tübingen. See Rittberger and Zürn (1991*a*).

agreement on the terms of the Geneva Convention dealing with transboundary air pollution in Europe or the provisions of the management regime for polar bears. In fact, there is evidence in these cases that a desire to find areas in which East and West could co-operate encouraged formation of these regimes.

One of the most provocative results of our study with regard to power arises from the role of *surrogate negotiators* in the Svalbard case. There, a group of 'great powers', acting as the victors of the First World War, were able to assert their authority to forge a regime in which they themselves had no intense interest. These surrogates used their position as victors—having fought a costly war, they were not particularly dominant in material terms at the time—to legitimize their role in deciding the fate of Svalbard. Is the role of surrogates a mere aberration occurring only in the unusual circumstances following the Great War? Or does the case of Svalbard offer a useful model for the future? These questions are certainly relevant today as the United Nations Security Council assumes a higher profile in handling international problems.

3.2. Interest-Based Hypotheses

Among the four central sets of ideas we tested (those pertaining to power, interests, knowledge, and context), the case studies consistently emphasized factors affecting interest-based behaviour in the context of interactive decision-making. With regard to the specific hypotheses tested, the role of individual leaders received such strong support that we now believe it constitutes a necessary condition for regime formation. A second group of hypotheses received enough support to suggest that they tap important (though not strictly necessary) conditions for the formation of regimes. Our cases tended to disconfirm a third group of hypotheses (see Table 10.2).

One or more individuals emerged as leaders in each of the five cases, and the *leadership* they provided proved to be important in the formation of the regime. In addition, both the lack of strong and consistent leadership in earlier attempts to form a regime for Svalbard and the absence of leaders to push for a regime to deal with Arctic haze strengthen the case for leadership as a necessary

TABLE 10.2. *Interest-Based Hypotheses about Regime Formation*

	Hypotheses	Fur seals	Svalbard	Polar bears	Ozone	Haze/LRTAP	Summary
Necessary condition	Individual leadership	C	C	C	C	C	5C
Important conditions	Equity (more important than efficiency)	C	M	C	C	C	4C/1M
	Salient solutions	C	C	C	M	C	4C/1M
	Availability of effective compliance mechanisms	C	C	C	C	N	4C/1N
	Integrative bargaining	M	C	C	C	C	4C/1M
	Veil of uncertainty	M	C	C	D	C	3C/1M/1D
	Exogenous shock or crisis	M	D	C	C	C	3C/1M/1D
Disconfirmed hypotheses	All parties participate	C	D	C	D	—	2C/2D
	Common good prevails	—	D	M	D	—	1M/2D
	High priority on all agendas	D	D	D	D	M	1M/4D
	Low priority on all agendas	—	D	D	D	D	4D
	Technical over political issues	D	D	D	D	—	4D

Note. A dash indicates that the hypothesis is not addressed in the case study.

Key
C = consistent with hypothesis
D = tends to disconfirm hypothesis
M = results mixed
N = no clear test

condition for regime formation. As the project evolved, we came to understand that leadership on the part of individuals—not some amorphous leadership exercised by governments on behalf of states—plays a key role in regime formation. One of the clearest and strongest findings of the project is that leadership is a cross-cutting factor. Leadership is both affected by and affects power relationships; it also shapes the values and ideas discussed in connection with knowledge-based hypotheses.

The authors of the case studies found the typology of leadership —differentiating among structural, entrepreneurial, and intellectual leadership—useful.[9] All five case studies identified one or more individuals as entrepreneurial leaders (Stanovnik of the ECE in the transboundary air pollution case; Tolba, Lang, and Benedick in the ozone case; numerous individuals in the polar bear case; Jordan in the fur seal case, and Wedel-Jarlsberg in the case of Svalbard). Sometimes an individual identified as an entrepreneurial leader also played a role as a structural leader (for example, Benedick, Bohlen, Wedel-Jarlsberg). An individual with exceptional entrepreneurial skills (such as Bohlen in the final negotiation of the polar bear agreement) may head the delegation of a powerful state engaged in institutional bargaining. In other cases, heads of delegations are properly regarded as structural leaders (for example, Clemenceau in the Svalbard case).

Members of the research team had difficulty testing the original version of the hypothesis about *equity* because we initially juxtaposed efficiency and equity rather than addressing the presence and importance of equity as distinct from efficiency. The issue at stake here, we now believe, arises precisely when it is necessary to make trade-offs between the pursuit of efficiency and the achievement of equity. To be specific, the hypothesis should state that institutional bargaining cannot succeed unless it produces an outcome that participants can accept as equitable, even when the adoption of equitable formulas requires some sacrifice in terms of efficiency. In this connection, the ozone and LRTAP cases are

[9] Structural leaders seek to translate the possession of material resources into bargaining leverage. Entrepreneurial leaders use negotiating skill to foster integrative bargaining and put together deals that would otherwise elude parties engaged in institutional bargaining. For their part, intellectual leaders develop systems of thought that shape the perspectives of those engaged in institutional bargaining (Young 1991*a*).

particularly interesting because they eventuated in regimes only when parties were willing to accept some reduction in efficiency in order to obtain equity. Efficiency alone would dictate arrangements encouraging deeper cuts in the consumption of CFCs or in SO_2 emissions on the part of those able to make such cuts at the least cost. But formulas featuring across-the-board or equal cuts on the part of the participants proved (with a few exceptions) more defensible on grounds of equity, and it seems apparent that a willingness to accept such formulas played an important role in producing successful outcomes.

In all the case studies, authors found evidence that a *salient solution* (Schelling 1960a: ch. 3) broke through potential blockages in the negotiating process. The common factor underlying the impact of salience is simplicity, in the sense of uncomplicated formulas that advocates can explain to policy-makers in straightforward terms and that journalists can encapsulate in headlines for public consumption. Frequently, the salient solution is also a formulation that breaks an impasse over a tricky distributive issue. Sometimes this involves avoiding the issue altogether, as in the polar bear and Svalbard cases. The salient solution in the polar bear case was one that avoided jurisdictional questions and defined the geographical coverage of the regime's rules in historical terms, thereby avoiding the complications of legalistic terminology. In the Svalbard case, the entire agreement is contained in ten short articles, compared with the fifteen chapters and seventy-five articles of the 1912–14 drafts. The complexities of administration are eliminated by the simple device of assigning sovereignty to Norway and delegating to Norway the tasks allocated in earlier drafts to a more cumbersome tripartite commission. In other cases, the salient solution is distributive in nature, but it offers a formula that is easy for policy-makers to grasp and that is intuitively appealing to the general public. In the fur seal case, the salient solution involved the coupling of a total ban on pelagic sealing with a simple formula for sharing the proceeds of the harvest in a way that satisfied all the parties.

Authors of four of the five case studies found evidence of the *availability of compliance mechanisms* which the parties at the time regarded as clear-cut and likely to be effective. These cases tend to confirm the important role of compliance mechanisms in institutional bargaining. The Arctic haze/LRTAP case offered no clear test of the hypothesis. Despite near-unanimity regarding the need for compliance mechanisms, however, the specific methods used to obtain compliance differ substantially. They range from decentralized systems of implementation (for example, the polar bear regime) through reliance on the stewardship of a single member (for example, Svalbard) to conscious efforts to increase transparency in order to minimize the likelihood of unreported violations (for example, the transboundary air pollution arrangements).

Four of the cases produced evidence consistent with the hypothesis that *integrative* or *productive bargaining* plays a prominent role in successful processes of institutional bargaining. Three of these cases also confirmed that a *'veil of uncertainty'* contributed to the process by making it difficult for individual participants to foresee how the operation of particular provisions would affect their interests over time. The mixed results of the fur seal case highlight the fact that institutional bargaining is seldom wholly integrative or distributive but rather constitutes a hybrid involving both types of bargaining.

We suspect that a measure of integrative bargaining or, in other words, a negotiating climate favourable to contractarianism is a necessary condition of regime formation. However, the complexity associated with the presence of numerous distributive as well as integrative issues in specific cases makes it hard for researchers to reconstruct the level of effort directed towards handling each type of issue and to determine the relative importance of integrative as opposed to distributive bargaining. In evaluating the importance of a veil of uncertainty, it is also difficult to separate regime formation and regime effectiveness. The evidence suggests that regimes may emerge even when the veil of uncertainty is thin or diminishing but that the resulting regimes are apt to be less effective.

Three of the five cases are consistent with the idea that *shocks or crises exogenous to the negotiating process* are important in the regime formation process.[10] The polar bear case study examines a 'manufactured crisis' in elucidating the role of non-governmental organizations (NGOs) and the media in creating at least the

[10] The fact that the positive evidence comes from the more recent cases suggests the value of examining the possibility that the growing role of the media has enhanced the effects of exogenous shocks or crises in regime formation.

appearance of crisis. In the ozone case, the 'discovery' of the Antarctic 'ozone hole', along with other scientific alarms, 'jump-started' stalled efforts to go beyond the general framework of the 1985 Vienna Convention. The Arctic haze case study compares the evolution of the LRTAP regime following the publicization of forest death (*Waldsterben*) in Europe with the absence of any comparable sense of crisis or shock regarding Arctic haze.

Yet the authors of the Svalbard and fur seal case studies found no specific shock or crisis associated with formation of the regimes in question (although the changes wrought by the First World War surely played a role in the case of Svalbard). We conclude that while the occurrence of an exogenous shock or crisis is not *necessary* for regime formation, it does help in some cases to promote agreement on the terms of a constitutional contract. The cases also suggest that further research to determine the effect of crisis on the substantive provisions of regimes would be fruitful. Evidence is mixed on whether crises do more than speed regime formation or, in other words, on whether the heightened attention by media and the public to the issues leads to stronger terms or a more effective regime.

3.3. Knowledge-Based Hypotheses

Four of the case studies found evidence consistent with the general proposition that values and scientific knowledge influence regime formation independently rather than simply contributing indirectly to the exercise of structural power or to the definition of the interests of state actors. Only the Svalbard case study found cognitive factors largely irrelevant to regime formation.[11] The fact that the four cases confirming the importance of *knowledge and values* all deal with natural resources or environmental issues leads us to ask whether such regimes differ markedly from others with regard to the knowledge factors involved in institutional bargaining (see Table 10.3). Certainly, environmental regimes rely heavily on the development of science coupled with changing values regarding the human use of natural resources, whereas a

---

[11] For a systematic treatment of cognitive factors in explaining regime formation, persistence, and change see Ch. 9 above.

TABLE 10.3. *Knowledge-Based Hypotheses about Regime Formation*

Hypotheses	Fur seals	Svalbard	Polar bears	Ozone	Haze/ LRTAP	Summary
Values/ideas matter	C	—	C	C	C	4C
Consensus emerges (Cooper)	C	D	D	N	M	1C/2D/1M/1N
Presence of epistemic community	—	D	D	C	M	1C/1M/2D

Note. A dash indicates that the hypothesis is not addressed in the case study.

Key
  C = consistent with hypothesis
  D = tends to disconfirm hypothesis
  M = results mixed
  N = no clear test

regime designed to resolve jurisdictional questions, such as the Svalbard regime, is not so dependent on scientific knowledge.

We suspect, however, that the role of scientific knowledge and values in forming regimes that do not deal with natural resources or the environment is not irrelevant but merely more subtle and difficult to trace. For example, where did the idea of forging a stewardship regime for Svalbard come from, following two attempts in the previous decade to employ the traditional concept of *terra nullius*? The idea of demilitarization, which became an important element of the Svalbard regime, may have owed something to the establishment of neutralized states in the cases of Switzerland in 1815 and Belgium in 1839 (Black *et al.* 1968). But its application to an area that had previously been 'no man's land' was a unique adaptation of an idea borrowed from prior experience with different situations.[12] It seems unlikely, then, that the Svalbard regime could have come into existence without the infusion of the ideas of restricted sovereignty and demilitarization, together with the values they embody.

[12] Many observers regard Antarctica as the first demilitarized zone. But the evidence suggests that the demilitarization of Svalbard provided a model for the Antarctic Treaty in this regard.

As to the specific knowledge-based hypotheses in our template, the results are mixed. Two cases (Arctic haze/LRTAP and fur seals) offer some support for the hypothesis advanced by Cooper (1989) and others that international co-operation emerges easily and almost spontaneously once a common or widely shared understanding of the problem, its causes, and its solutions emerges, and conversely that no regime will emerge in the absence of such *consensual knowledge*. But other cases tend to disconfirm this hypothesis. Though scientific convergence clearly helped in developing the polar bear regime, this did not eliminate the need for hard bargaining among the principals. Strikingly, the Montreal Protocol calling for sharp reductions in the production and consumption of CFCs emerged prior to the achievement of scientific consensus on several critical points.

While the ozone case study argues that an *epistemic community* played an important role in regime formation, the results of the other cases are more equivocal on this matter. The Svalbard, fur seal, and polar case studies found no conclusive evidence of the impact of an epistemic community. In the case of transboundary air pollution, such a community did develop. But by that time, the general public's activism on transboundary air pollution in Europe had become a more significant factor than the epistemic community in motivating governments to co-operate at the international level. Overall, the cases suggest that epistemic communities— when they arise—deal with the relevant technical and scientific issues and that this effort precedes the main phase of institutional bargaining conducted by diplomats who confirm the work of the scientists and resolve remaining controversial issues.

3.4. Contextual Factors

One of the most striking findings of this project is the identification of a class of factors that appear to play a major role as determinants of regime formation but that have not received systematic attention in the scholarly literature. Our cases strongly suggest that any explanation of regime formation will be incomplete in the absence of a discussion of the relevance of natural and human events unfolding outside the issue area to which the regime pertains. These *contextual factors*, as we have chosen to call them,

TABLE 10.4. *Contextual Factors of Regime Formation*

Hypotheses	Fur seals	Svalbard	Polar bears	Ozone	Haze/ LRTAP	Summary
Contextual factors	C	C	C	N	C	4C/1N

Key
  C = consistent with hypothesis
  N = no clear test

create windows of opportunity in which regimes may form (see Table 10.4).

The range of contextual factors extends from broad shifts in values and ideas (for example, a growing environmental consciousness) to political trends (for instance, periods of thaw in the Cold War) and even to specific events (for example, the outbreak of war or changes of officials occupying key positions). Only in the ozone case did we find little evidence of contextual factors enhancing regime formation, though even then the electoral success of the Green Party in Germany during 1986 altered the German position on CFCs in a manner that increased prospects for success in regime formation. The strong evidence in four cases suggests that a more systematic analysis of contextual factors can make an important contribution to the explanation of regime formation and to our understanding of institutional bargaining more generally.

4. MULTIVARIATE ANALYSIS

There is an understandable tendency among students of regime formation to concentrate on formulating hypotheses that focus on bivariate relationships involved in the formation of international regimes. Especially when cast as necessary or sufficient conditions, these hypotheses are powerful in the sense that they direct attention to relationships that are invariant across an entire universe of cases. They can be stated in a clear and precise manner. Equally important, they are comparatively easy to test. Every case should conform to the expectations raised by such hypotheses, a fact that makes it possible to engage in testing without resorting to the deployment of statistical techniques. Given the fact that the numbers of truly comparable cases are always small in dealing with such international phenomena as regime formation, the appeal of hypotheses stating necessary or sufficient conditions from the point of view of testing is not just understandable, it is almost irresistible.

Our research suggests that this way of thinking about the determinants of regime formation does have merit. Though we do not hold out great hope for the identification of conditions that by themselves are sufficient to bring about the formation of regimes, we continue to think some factors are so central to the process of regime formation that they can serve as a basis for propositions stated in the form of necessary conditions. The hypothesis concerning the necessary presence of one or more individual leaders able to exercise entrepreneurial skills merits attention in this context. The hypotheses dealing with equity, salient solutions, and compliance mechanisms also received strong support from the case studies. None the less, we are now convinced that it will not do to confine scholarly attention in this field to a search for bivariate relationships governing the process of regime formation. Those who proceed in this manner will not only find that most of their hypotheses are disconfirmed, but they will also fail to develop a clear picture of the complex process of regime formation. Surely,

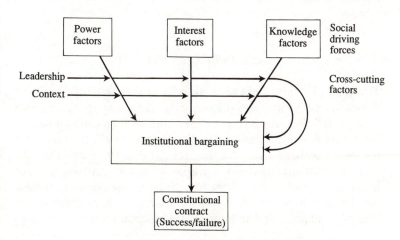

Fig. 10.1 A multivariate model of regime formation

this is an unsatisfactory outcome; there are compelling reasons not to leave the study of regime formation here.

Reflecting on these epistemological concerns, we have concluded that the appropriate response is to construct a multivariate model of the *process of regime formation* in international society. Fig. 10.1 depicts the key components and linkages of such a model. The independent variables or forcing functions in this model all feed into a process of institutional bargaining, which may or may not eventuate in success in the sense of agreement on a set of provisions that are articulated in the form of a constitutional contract. We have labelled the driving social forces in this model, any one of which may carry the bulk of the weight in specific cases of regime formation, power factors, interest factors, and knowledge factors. At the same time, several cross-cutting factors, which we have named leadership and context, ordinarily come into play in directing or channelling the operation of the driving social forces in specific cases. That is, leadership and context exert their influence on the process of institutional bargaining not directly but indirectly through their capacity to determine how power is exercised, the mix of integrative and distributive bargaining, and the ability of participants to bring knowledge to bear on an issue.

A review of our case studies has led us to place strong emphasis on two sets of considerations arising in connection with this multivariate model: (1) substitution effects, and (2) interaction effects.[13]

4.1. Substitution Effects

There are, we now believe, a number of differentiable paths or routes along which institutional bargaining can move towards success. In other words, regime formation in international society can follow any of a number of tracks that are, in effect, substitutes for one another. Thus, we do not dispute the view that the presence of a dominant power can on occasion be a critical factor in the process of regime formation. But our cases point to several other routes to success in international regime formation. In the case of Svalbard, the Big Four operating as surrogate negotiators

---

[13] For considerations along somewhat similar lines see Ch. 11, sect. 3, below.

through the mechanism of the Spitsbergen Commission played a critical role, although it would hardly be accurate to describe any one of them as a dominant power in this case. With regard to fur seals, progress became possible when the participants acknowledged that the efforts of individual parties to exercise power in a process accentuating distributive bargaining to the exclusion of integrative bargaining could not succeed. As to polar bears, the efforts of the scientific community to reach consensus regarding the need to protect bears and their habitats surely played an important role in preparing the ground for the diplomats to agree on the provisions of the polar bear regime within the span of a few days at the Oslo meeting in November 1973. In a sense, the fact that success in regime formation can occur along any of a number of paths is encouraging. It helps to explain why those engaged in institutional bargaining do succeed in producing positive results with some frequency, despite the operation of an array of well-known collective action problems that plague the bargaining process.

4.2. Interaction Effects

Even more interesting is the occurrence of interaction effects among the driving social forces and between these forces and the cross-cutting factors. Whereas students of regime formation have often sought to demonstrate the primacy of power factors, or interest factors, or knowledge factors in the formation of international regimes, we have become convinced that some of the most illuminating insights into the process of regime formation arise when we direct our attention to the interactions among these factors. The growth of knowledge and, for that matter, the emergence of epistemic communities can play a critical role both in identifying and framing the issues at stake and in shaping the way participants understand their interests, even when the actual process of regime formation is properly construed as a form of integrative bargaining. This, we now believe, is an important realization in making sense of the creation stories of the polar bear regime, the transboundary air pollution regime, and the regime for the protection of stratospheric ozone. In all three cases, scientific concerns played a key role in defining the problem and bringing it to the attention of policy-makers and diplomats who then proceeded to negotiate the terms of an international regime with their counterparts.

Contextual developments, to take another example, can stimulate the emergence of the political will needed to tackle an issue as an exercise in integrative bargaining or problem solving rather than as an exercise in bringing structural power to bear in the form of bargaining leverage. The rise of the conservation movement, with its emphasis on ideas such as managing resources scientifically to achieve maximum sustainable yield, made it much easier to come to terms with the fur seal problem in 1911 than it had been in the 1890s, when efforts to tackle the problem stalemated over jurisdictional issues. The window of opportunity created by improved relations between Norway and Sweden and Russia's incapacity at the end of the First World War coupled with the existence of a political forum in the form of the Paris Peace Conference made it relatively easy to devise a pragmatic solution to the problem of governing Svalbard, which had proven intractable in the pre-war era. The desire of several key players to demonstrate the feasibility of transcending the confines of the Cold War in the context of the Conference on Security and Co-Operation in Europe (CSCE) process clearly facilitated efforts to reach agreement on the terms of the 1979 Geneva Convention on Long-Range Transboundary Air Pollution.

The simultaneous operation of several different types of leadership constitutes yet another mechanism through which the forcing functions involved in regime formation can interact. The case of transboundary air pollution, for example, highlights the interplay of structural leadership, in the form of Brezhnev's effort to propel the issue to the forefront as a means of breathing life into the CSCE process, and entrepreneurial leadership, in the form of Stanovnik's efforts to devise mutually agreeable formulas and to broker the interests of the various participants. Similar comments are in order regarding the case of the Montreal Protocol, where Benedick wielded considerable influence as the chief negotiator for the United States, while Tolba played a crucial entrepreneurial role in articulating the emerging scientific consensus concerning ozone depletion and disseminating this consensus among the participants in the ozone negotiations.

In one sense, the prominence of these interaction effects poses difficulties for the analyst of regime formation. The methodological problems involved in separating out the contributing factors and assigning weights to each in an effort to explain or predict regime formation are formidable, especially in light of the fact that the available universe of cases is too small to support the use of techniques of multivariate statistics. Yet the study of these interaction effects not only offers the promise of a more accurate understanding of the process of regime formation, but it also provides opportunities for analysts to engage in intriguing detective work as they endeavour to understand the synergy generated by the interaction of two or more driving social forces and crosscutting factors. The importance of coming to terms with these interaction effects in the quest for an improved understanding of regime formation also reinforces our conviction that the use of comparative and focused case studies constitutes an appropriate methodology for the study of this subject. It is difficult to see how the complexities of these interactions can be grasped in the absence of the richness and detail that can be obtained from in-depth case studies.

5. ANALYSIS: RESEARCH PRIORITIES

If the argument we have presented in the preceding sections is persuasive, where should students of regime formation in international society direct their attention in future research? In this concluding section, we provide a brief account of issues needing further attention and areas that have struck us as particularly likely to repay additional research as we have reflected on pre-existing theories of regime formation in the light of the sustained empirical research reported in this chapter.

First and foremost, we need to ask whether our findings are artefacts of the set of cases we have examined. These cases all deal with issues involving natural resources and the environment; even within this domain, we do not claim that our cases constitute a representative sample. It is therefore natural to enquire whether various forms of selection bias have coloured our results. Do environmental cases differ from those involving issues of security or economics because they are more technical and less political in nature? Do our Arctic cases fail to tap some of the political difficulties posed by the North/South split in contemporary efforts to form regimes to deal with climate change or to protect biological diversity? The way to answer these questions, in our judgement, is to engage in systematic studies of additional cases using the theoretical template we have devised. We are eager to see others take up this challenge and prepared to revise our findings should the work of others make this necessary. For the moment, however, we believe the burden of proof rests with those who assert that our findings are biased as a consequence of our choice of cases.

Turning to more substantive matters, there is much to be done to strengthen the analytic tools available for understanding the dynamics of institutional bargaining (Young 1989*b*). Bargaining of this sort, which dominates the critical stages of the process of regime formation in international society, differs from the process envisaged in most formal models of bargaining (Young 1975), both because it takes place in the absence of complete information regarding the contours of the contract zone and because it normally features efforts to reach consensus or to form coalitions of the whole in contrast to winning coalitions.

Some of the consequences of these attributes are easy to identify. Integrative, in contrast to distributive, activities are more prominent in institutional bargaining than in the bargaining occurring in the world of economic or game-theoretic models.[14] Negotiating texts play a major role in institutional bargaining but not in the processes envisaged in the formal models. Although leadership emerges as a phenomenon of great importance in institutional bargaining, there is no place for leadership in the economic and game-theoretic models. None the less, we do not yet have a well-developed model of institutional bargaining in the sense of a logically interrelated set of propositions spelling out the links between the relevant dependent variables (for example, success or failure in regime formation, the timing of regime formation, and the content of regime provisions) and a set of clearly defined forcing functions. Undoubtedly, there are numerous opportunities to expand our understanding of institutional bargaining through

[14] As Schelling (1960*a*: 21) says in discussing game-theoretic work on bargaining, 'we shall be concerned with what might be called the "distributional" aspect of bargaining'.

analyses of individual factors in the absence of a model of this type. Yet we are convinced that efforts to construct such a model should be accorded a high priority among those desiring to maximize our ability to explain or predict regime formation in international society.

The findings of our case studies also suggest a number of research priorities relating to the principal clusters of explanatory variables we have examined. We have laid to rest the argument derived from hegemonic stability theory that the participation of a single actor dominant in the material sense is necessary for regimes to form in international society. Yet this certainly does not license the conclusion that power-based arguments are unimportant in explaining or predicting the process of regime formation. On the contrary, it frees us to return to a serious examination of the role of power without the blinkers imposed by the idea of hegemony. The cases of Svalbard and transboundary air pollution, for example, suggest that progress toward regime formation is facilitated by the emergence of a small group of actors prepared to take action to forge the provisions of a constitutional contract. Perhaps these groups bear a resemblance to what students of collective action, following Schelling's (1978: ch. 7) lead, have called 'k-groups' (Axelrod 1984).

The cases of fur seals and polar bears suggest that the process of regime formation goes more smoothly in the presence of a rough parity of power among parties, at least in the issue area encompassing the prospective regime. The case of ozone, on the other hand, leads us to ask if and when initiatives on the part of an issue-specific hegemon (i.e. an actor possessing exceptional material resources with regard to the issue at stake) are important in the process of regime formation. These are merely initial impressions that may merit further analysis in a non-hegemonic study of the role of power in the formation of international regimes. More systematic work in this area, we now believe, is likely to turn up a number of other relationships of interest to those desiring to understand the process of regime formation in international society.

It now seems clear, as well, that there is a need for a much more careful analysis of stages in processes of regime formation. Partly, this is a matter of clarifying the distinction between institutional bargaining as such and the stage of pre-negotiation, including the emergence of an issue on the active policy agenda and the jockeying for position that occurs in connection with framing the issues and identifying the participants for an exercise in institutional bargaining (Sebenius 1983). In part, it is a matter of differentiating stages in the bargaining process itself, both in the sense of distinguishing unsuccessful stages from successful stages, as in the case of Svalbard, and in the sense of recognizing distinct phases in the evolution of a complex regime, as in the case of ozone. The development of these distinctions, it seems to us, will make it possible to sort out some of the differences that currently separate those who study regime formation. A reading of the polar bear, transboundary air pollution, and ozone cases, for instance, suggests to us that knowledge-based factors can and often do play a role of considerable significance in the early stages of regime formation but that they decline in importance as the negotiators begin to hammer out the actual provisions of a regime. It may even make sense to consider the role of hegemony in the cognitive or Gramscian sense (Cox 1983) in the formulation of the problem during the early stages of regime formation, despite the lack of support for arguments pointing to the role of hegemony in the material sense in connection with institutional bargaining as such.

Our research has led us to believe also in the need to seek a better understanding of two factors that we did not grasp or only dimly perceived when we were formulating the hypotheses to be tested in this project. These are what we would now characterize as the cross-cutting factors of leadership and context. Leadership in the sense of efforts on the part of individuals to circumvent or solve collective action problems surfaced as an important consideration in all our case studies. Once we distinguish among structural, entrepreneurial, and intellectual leadership, moreover, it is easy to see how the actions of leaders can play a role in bringing power-based, interest-based, and knowledge-based factors to bear on the process of institutional bargaining. Leaders are, in effect, transmitters who act to focus underlying social forces (i.e. power, interest, and knowledge) on the issues at stake in specific instances of institutional bargaining and to guide the impact of these forces on the process of regime formation (Young 1991*a*). Our cases have led us to think that leadership in one or more of its forms constitutes a necessary condition for regime formation in international society. But there is clearly a need to devise more specific hypotheses about the role of leadership and to test them in the light of future case studies dealing with regime formation.

Turning to context, we have come to believe that institutional bargaining is a highly constrained process that occurs at the surface of the sea of international and transnational relations. Those engaged in institutional bargaining, and especially in its final stages, have strong incentives to distance themselves from the intrusions of contextual factors. But there are clear indications in our case studies that context can and often does impinge on all phases of the regime formation process. Sometimes the impact of context is direct and dramatic, as in the case of Svalbard, where the First World War broke out within weeks of the 1914 conference in Oslo and where the Paris Peace Conference took up the issue in 1919 despite the fact that the question of Svalbard had not figured in any way in the war. At other times, the role of context is more subtle and harder to pinpoint, as in the case of fur seals, where the independent emergence of the scientific conservation movement (Hays 1968) appears to have played a role in shifting the problem from a jurisdictional issue to a question of managing a shared resource. Conventional models of bargaining either abstract away context or attempt to assimilate it in the process of specifying contract zones or pay-off spaces. Our research suggests that this will not do for those seeking to understand institutional bargaining. We are greatly in need of more suitable ways to factor context into our efforts to explain and predict the course of regime formation in international society.

Drawing these threads together, we have concluded that those interested in regime formation should accord high priority to what we have labelled multivariate analysis. No doubt, there is much still to be gained from efforts to clarify the role of individual factors, like leadership and context. But it now seems apparent that regime formation is a complex process that does not lend itself well to analyses that focus on single factors and seek to formulate propositions taking the form of necessary conditions. At this stage in our search for understanding, we need to devote considerable time and energy to what we called substitution effects and interaction effects in the preceding section of this essay. Can we move beyond the general notion of substitution effects to specify distinct tracks regarding regime formation and to say something about the factors that determine which of these tracks is likely to be followed in specific cases? Can we trace the linkages between knowledge and interests (for example, new knowledge may lead to the redefinition of interests) and between power and interests (for example, power may play a role in determining what gets treated as the 'national interest') as they affect processes of regime formation?

It seems clear in this connection that the model depicted in Fig. 10.1 is no more than a beginning in this realm. While it identifies variables, it says little about the linkages between or among them. The challenge now is to proceed step by step to specify the character of these linkages. There is an important sense in which progress towards a fuller understanding of regime formation in international society can be measured in terms of the development of this model from its present status as a simple 'wiring diagram' towards a construct in which the nature of the relationships between variables is fully specified.

APPENDIX

Template of Hypotheses to be Tested

A. POWER-BASED HYPOTHESES

Basic premiss. Institutions, including international regimes, are structured by and reflect the distribution and configuration of power in international society.

1. *Hegemony.* The presence of an actor possessing a preponderance of material resources (i.e. a hegemon) is a necessary condition for regime formation in international society.

2. *Other power-based hypotheses*
    (a) A *bipolar* or *bimodal distribution of power* (producing a balance of power) is necessary for success in regime formation.
    (b) The greater the degree of *symmetry* in the distribution of power, the more likely efforts to create regimes are to succeed.
    (c) The existence of a *small group of great powers* in a given issue area (i.e. a directorate) enhances prospects for regime formation.

B. INTEREST-BASED HYPOTHESES

Basic premiss. Social institutions, including international regimes, arise from the interaction of self-interested parties endeavouring to co-ordinate their behaviour to reap joint gains that may, but need not, take the form of public goods. It follows that the availability of joint gains or, in other words, a contract zone or zone of agreement constitutes a necessary (though not sufficient) condition for the formation of international regimes.

Efforts to construct theories about the resultant interactions address the following question: why do actors in international society succeed in forming international regimes to reap feasible joint gains in some cases but not in others? The processes leading to success or failure are ordinarily conceptualized as bargaining or negotiation; the hypotheses of interest to us identify determinants of success or failure in the resultant institutional bargaining.

1. *Integrative bargaining and a veil of uncertainty.* Institutional bargaining can succeed only when the prominence of integrative bargaining and/or the presence of a veil of uncertainty make it easy for the parties to approach the problem under consideration in contractarian terms.

2. *Equity.* The availability of institutional options that all participants can accept as equitable (rather than efficient) is necessary for institutional bargaining to succeed.

3. *Salient solutions.* The existence of a salient solution (or a focal point describable in simple terms) increases the probability of success in institutional bargaining.

4. *Exogenous shocks or crises.* Shocks or crises occurring outside the bargaining process increase the probability of success in efforts to negotiate the terms of international regimes.

5. *Policy priority*
   (a) Success in regime formation can only occur when the issue at stake achieves *high priority* status on the policy agenda of each of the participants.
   (b) Alternatively, it is easier to form a regime when the subject-matter is *not high on the political agendas* of the parties.

6. *Common good.* A willingness to set aside narrow national interests in favour of some broader conception of the common good is necessary to achieve success in regime formation.

7. *Science and technology*

    (a) The greater the tendency for parties to *concentrate on scientific or technical considerations* as opposed to political issues, the greater the likelihood of successful regime formation.

    (b) The greater the *role of negotiators with scientific or technical competence* in relation to those with political credentials, the greater the likelihood of successful regime formation.

    (c) It is easier to form a regime when the issues at stake are *highly technical*.

8. *Relevant parties.* All parties with an interest in the problem must participate in the negotiations for regime formation to succeed.

9. *Compliance mechanisms.* The probability of success in institutional bargaining rises when compliance mechanisms that the parties regard as clear-cut and effective are available.

10. *Individuals as leaders.* Institutional bargaining is likely to succeed when individual leadership emerges; it will fail in the absence of such leadership.

C. KNOWLEDGE-BASED HYPOTHESES

Basic premiss. Shared beliefs, understandings of causal mechanisms, and values among the relevant parties as well as identifiable communities (including epistemic communities) and advocacy organizations that arise to propagate this knowledge are important determinants of regime formation.

    Two alternative accounts of how cognitive factors influence regime formation are identifiable in the literature.

1. *Scientific convergence.* Agreement or consensus within the scientific community regarding causal relations and appropriate responses is a prerequisite for regime formation. (Values are less important, though not irrelevant, to this hypothesis than to the next hypothesis.)

2. *Epistemic communities.* A group of individuals (whose membership usually transcends national boundaries and includes both scientists or experts and policy-makers) who share a common view regarding causal mechanisms and appropriate responses and who have a common set of values emerges in conjunction with the issue in question. In order for a regime to form, some mechanism (possibly an international organization but in some cases a less formal network) arises to link the members of this group. The resulting epistemic community is able not only to promote

its own preferred arrangements but also to prevent opposing views and values from becoming influential or dominant at the domestic level in each of the relevant states.

D. CONTEXTUAL FACTORS

National and world circumstances and events seemingly unrelated to the issue area under consideration play a major role in determining if and when international co-operation to address a particular problem or issue area occurs and in shaping the content of any regime that forms.

Integrating and Contextualizing Hypotheses

Alternative Paths to Better Explanations of Regime Formation?

MANFRED EFINGER, PETER MAYER, AND GUDRUN
SCHWARZER

1. INTRODUCTION

Although a lot of effort has been put into the study of international regimes since the mid-1970s, to date no comprehensive regime theory has crystallized. This is not surprising, given the relative novelty of the subject and the diversity and complexity of the research questions that it involves: under what conditions do international regimes come about? which factors determine the specific features and the scope of the regime that forms? what are the forces that cause regimes to change in specific ways? how do regimes bear upon actors and structures in the international system?

In this chapter we will be concerned with the first of these questions only: how can the formation of international regimes be explained? The determinants of regime formation are certainly one main focus of the regime literature and quite a number of promising hypotheses have been advanced and discussed in this connection (Haggard and Simmons 1987, Young 1989*b*, Rittberger and Zürn 1990). Usually these hypotheses point to some individual

For helpful comments on an earlier version of this chapter we are indebted to Helmut Breitmeier, Volker Dreier, Reinhard Meyers, Volker Rittberger, Klaus Dieter Wolf, and Michael Zürn, as well as various participants of the conference on 'The Study of Regimes in International Relations—State of the Art and Perspectives', Tübingen, July 1991. The empirical research we refer to in this study has been funded by the Deutsche Forschungsgemeinschaft (German Science Association).

variable such as the presence of leadership or the pay-off structure alleged to be crucial for the emergence of a regime in a given issue area. The considerable productivity displayed in this field is not without risks, though. Especially, students of international regimes must be careful not to mix up explaining particular instances of regime formation with selecting from the fund of pertinent hypotheses the ones that are compatible with the empirical facts of the case under consideration—a proceeding which might appear the more attractive the larger and the more impressive the fund. Of course, a hypothesis that is consistent with the empirical observations in a particular case can serve as an explanation of that case only to the extent that it has been tested and confirmed independently of that case. Yet, when it is part of the practice of explaining regimes not to give up hypotheses that sometimes, though not always, give rise to false predictions, but to put them back into the fund (since for the next case they might prove useful again), testing in any strict sense is not taking place.

Even if the individual scholar normally will be aware of this danger and seek to avoid it, for example by concentrating on developing and refining a particular approach, more or less neglecting the alternatives, the practice just described does bear much resemblance with what is going on in the study of regime formation as a collective enterprise. From this point of view, the variety of *unrelated* hypotheses and ideas put forward in this field no longer appears as an asset, but rather as an indication of a stage in theory-building that regime scholars should strive to overcome in the long run. This is not to argue for a 'freeze' in the production of innovative hypotheses shedding light on the conditions under which regimes come about; still, there can be no doubt that it is desirable that, at some time, the present pluralism of hypotheses should be replaced by a single, well-tested and confirmed theory of regime formation, however simple or complex.

One possible way of approaching such a paradigmatic theory is stringent testing and subsequent *elimination* of rival hypotheses (or theories).[1] Since the single-variable hypotheses that are advanced

---

[1] Although we do not strictly distinguish theories from hypotheses, in this chapter we will tend to use the term 'theory' exclusively for the desired set of—still hypothetical—propositions about the conditions of regime formation, which have been corroborated in numerous tests and hence, for the time being, can be assumed to be capable of explaining cases of regime formation adequately.

in the study of regime formation are seldom (if ever) meant as deterministic statements, we are confronted with the question of how often predictions must fail in order that we can safely abandon the hypothesis concerned. A given hypothesis is presumably best judged not in isolation, but in the context of a parallel test of a number of competing hypotheses against a multiplicity of cases. However, competition and subsequent elimination of available hypotheses should not be seen as the highway to theory (in the above sense). First, it is by no means certain that any of the single-variable hypotheses advanced by students of regime formation so far would receive such strong empirical support that we would feel encouraged to consider it the (nucleus of the) desired theory of regime formation. In fact, given the rather simple nature of our hypotheses we would be surprised if this were the case. Second, we cannot be sure that a single hypothesis would eventually stand out clearly. The differences in performance might be too slight to justify favouring one of them over all the others.

Despite these caveats, in this chapter we will first (sect. 2) pursue such a course by confronting a handful of hypotheses specifying conditions of regime formation with thirteen issue areas in international politics. In most, but not all, of these issue areas regimes have been set up. Both the cases and the hypotheses stem from the Tübingen project on international regimes.[2] The results of this hypotheses test (though not a strict one in statistical terms) will nourish our scepticism as regards competition and elimination of available single-factor hypotheses as a strategy to achieve theoretical progress in the study of regime formation.

At the same time, however, two alternative strategies will come into sight which here are called 'integration' and 'contextualization', respectively, and which, in our view, hold more promise in this respect. Both strategies seek to overcome the present 'anything goes' in the explanation of regime formation, not so much by clearing our store of hypotheses (strategy of elimination) as by introducing a measure of order into it. Both aim at a composite theory of regime formation involving a number of explanatory variables, although the logical form of the target theories will be different. While *integrating* basically consists in joining several independent variables assumed to interact in the production of the

---

[2] For a brief description of this project and references see Ch. 1, sect. 1, above.

relevant outcomes (i.e. regime formation *or* continuation of unregulated conflict management), *contextualizing* proceeds by relating well-defined subsets of the universe of objects (defined as types of issue areas), on the one hand, and hypotheses well tested and confirmed for these subsets, on the other. Section 3 of this chapter will be devoted to an explication and discussion of these two strategies.[3]

2. TESTING HYPOTHESES ON INTERNATIONAL REGIME FORMATION

2.1. The Cases

In the Tübingen project international regimes are conceptualized as a form of co-operative and rule-guided conflict management. In order to learn more about the causes (and effects) of regimes, particularly though not exclusively in the context of East–West relations in Europe, case studies about the development of conflict management in thirteen issue areas have been carried out. A regime was said to be present in a given issue area if two conditions were met: (1) the actors in the issue area (*de facto* states) had agreed upon a set of principles, norms, rules, and procedures to govern their behaviour with respect to the conflict(s) in question, and (2) the rules thereby created had proved effective in the sense that they were, by and large, complied with by the actors.[4] Thus, a uniform and comparatively demanding definition of 'international regime' was applied to all cases. The period of inquiry covers the post-war era until 1990. Out of the thirteen case studies nine deal with issues in East–West relations (CSCE region) and four with issues in West–West relations (OECD region); all emerged after the Second World War. In the following, the cases will be briefly introduced in chronological order (for a synopsis see Table 11.1).

1. The conflicts between the western powers and the Soviet Union about the *status of Austria* arose in 1946/7. At that time

---

[3] For an effort quite similar in purpose to ours see Ch. 10 above.

[4] For a discussion of the pros and cons of the underlying 'substantive' definition of 'regime' see Ch. 1, sect. 3.1, and Ch. 2, sect. 3, above.

TABLE 11.1. *Case studies of the Tübingen Project on Regimes*

	CSCE region (East–West)	OECD region (West–West)
Issue areas with regime	Status of Austria Access to and status of Berlin Intra-German trade Confidence- and security-building measures (CSBM) Marine environment of the Baltic Sea Long-range transboundary air pollution (LRTAP)	Status of the Saar Constitutionalism in Western Europe Marine environment of the North Sea
Issue areas without regime	Scientific-technological exchange Reduction of conventional forces in Europe (CFE) Working conditions of foreign journalists	Co-operative arms control in Western Europe

Austria, like Germany, was divided into four zones of occupation and was waiting for the former allies to carry out their promise made during the war to restore her independence, which she had first lost as a result of the annexation by Nazi Germany in 1938. However, under the conditions of the Cold War each side was now anxious to avoid the country's coming under the influence of the other. After eight years of negotiations the Four Powers finally signed the Austrian State Treaty in 1955 and agreed to withdraw their troops. Since then the international regime thus created has secured Austria's neutral position between the two blocs as well as its political independence from Germany (Schwarzer 1992*b*).

2. The *Berlin* case represents an issue area characterized by often dramatic, unregulated conflict behaviour that lasted from 1948 until the mid-1970s. Western access to and the status of the city were the most severely disputed issues. However, after the

formation of an international regime based on the Quadripartite Agreement, the parties to the conflict adhered to specific rules concerning access and status matters, with the result that Berlin was no longer the scene of spectacular East–West crises (Schwarzer 1990*b*).

3. The issue area of *intra-German trade* came into the open in 1948, when West Germany responded to the Berlin blockade by suspending trade with the Soviet occupation zone. In the following years the position of the Federal Republic was to commit herself to maintaining, or even expanding, trade with the GDR only in exchange for guaranteed access to West Berlin, a concession which the eastern side was not prepared to make, however. The issues remained on the agenda until the mid-1960s. Only then did the mode of dealing with the conflicts inherent in the intra-German trade relationship change significantly, leading to established trade practices which qualify as a regime (Zürn 1990, 1992: ch. 3).

4. The conflict about the *Saar*, a German region at the French border, became manifest in 1949, when the new West German state refused to put up with the quasi-annexation of that area by France in the years after 1945. In 1954 the two states concluded a treaty that most likely would have formed the basis of a regime regulating the conflicts about the political and economic status of the Saar. However, in 1955 a large majority of the local population rejected the agreement in a referendum, thus expressing their will to return to Germany. As a result France gave up her claims to the territory and the conflict disappeared. Although the Saar regime that was projected in the 1954 accord did not materialize in its entirety, the referendum as an integral part of this accord was implemented, paving the way not only to a regulation, but to a solution of the Franco-German conflict over the Saar. Therefore, in the context of this study, the case will be treated as an instance of successful regime formation (Schwarzer 1992*a*).

5. The issue area of *co-operative arms control in Western Europe* arose soon after the end of the Second World War. The conflicts, mainly separating France and West Germany, but on occasion also these two states and their (future) Anglo-Saxon allies, centred on the conditions of West Germany's rearmament, the status and control of her troops, and the issue of her membership in NATO. An agreement spelling out norms and rules could be reached and was incorporated into the Western European

Union Treaty in 1954. However, no regime can be said to have crystallized in this way, because fundamental obligations were disregarded by some states (particularly France) when they turned out inconvenient for them. Nevertheless, over time the conflicts became less salient and eventually vanished altogether (Efinger 1991*b*).

6. The term *constitutionalism in Western Europe* stands for the 'club' regime that evolved among Western European states between 1949 (foundation of the Council of Europe) and 1953 (entry into force of the European Convention on Human Rights). Under the impression of the Second World War and in response to the threat emanating from the formation of a phalanx of people's republics in Eastern Europe, the international regime spelled out rules which were designed to protect and promote the democratic practices of its participants. Thus, an attempt was made to take precautions against member states falling back into totalitarian or authoritarian forms of government (List 1992).

7. The issue area of *scientific-technological exchange* between East and West has existed since the 1950s. Throughout all these years it has proved impossible to agree upon a set of principles, norms, rules, and decision-making procedures pertaining to the conflicts about the conditions for the transfer of technology as well as the freedom versus control of scientists. In the early 1970s a bilateral effort was made by the United States and the Soviet Union to come to terms with one another on these issues, but it failed to result in an international regime (List 1990*b*).

8. The *reduction of conventional forces in Europe (CFE)* was an issue area in East–West relations from the 1950s onwards. The objects of contention were the military options on the one hand and the admissible quantities of arms and troops on the other. Attempts at regime formation failed for more than thirty years. Only since the conclusion of the CFE Treaty in November 1990 could a conventional arms control regime be said to be in the making. However, these latest developments being beyond our period of inquiry, we treat this case as one in which no regime was established (Schrogl 1990).

9. By the end of the 1960s, East and West in principle acknowledged the need for *confidence- and security-building measures in Europe (CSBM)*. The conflicts in this issue area between East and West centred mainly on the issue of which kinds of measures

would in fact be confidence-building. The Helsinki Accord of 1975 provided for a few rather clear injunctions, but subsequently these rules were more often disregarded than complied with. It was ten more years before, at the Stockholm conference in 1986, a CSBM regime was finally put into place (Efinger 1990, Rittberger, Efinger, and Mendler 1990, Efinger and Rittberger 1992).

10. Also at the end of the 1960s, the issue area *protection of the marine environment of the Baltic Sea* appeared on the East–West agenda. This was at a time when consciousness of the ecological vulnerability of the seas arose world-wide and led to increasing efforts to regulate, and particularly to reduce, the disposal of hazardous pollutants into the seas. From the mid-1970s on, one can speak of a marine environment protection regime embracing the (then) seven littoral states of the Baltic Sea (List 1990*a*, 1991: ch. 3).

11. The issue area of *long-range transboundary air pollution (LRTAP)* has existed since the beginning of the 1970s. At that time the Scandinavian countries became aware of the damage that was being done to their natural environment by the acid rain that they involuntarily imported from Great Britain and other countries in Western and Eastern Europe. By the end of the 1970s, the problem was much better understood and negotiations began between almost thirty states (most of them being importers or exporters of air pollution or both). All states signed the ECE (Economic Commission for Europe) Convention on Long-Range Transboundary Air Pollution of 1979. But only in 1984/5, when eighteen states signed the sulphur protocol assuming the obligation to reduce their sulphur emissions by 30 per cent by 1993, was an 'acid rain regime' founded (Schwarzer 1990*a*).

12. The question of how to protect the North Sea appeared on the agenda of the littoral states at the beginning of the 1970s. Various conferences and conventions dealt with the critical issues (i.e. controlling pollution from different sources), but only in the mid-1980s did the regulations reach a density and extension sufficient to constitute an international regime for the *protection of the marine environment of the North Sea* (List 1991: ch. 2).

13. The *working conditions of foreign journalists* represent an issue area reflecting the ideological differences that separated East and West in the Cold War era. The major objects of contention in this issue area can be traced back to different notions about how

the domestic and international flows of information should be organized. The issues appeared on the agenda of East–West diplomacy as part of Basket Three of the CSCE negotiations. However, up to 1990, the few norms and rules the two sides were able to agree upon were far too weak to qualify as an international regime (Mendler 1990).

2.2. The Hypotheses

The hypotheses we confronted with these cases have been derived from various approaches of international relations theory concerned with the explanation of international co-operation. We have classified them as: (I) power-structural and (II) other systemic hypotheses, (III) problem-structural hypotheses (i.e. hypotheses referring to issue characteristics), and (IV) situation-structural hypotheses (based on rational choice theory).[5] All hypotheses are stated in such a way as to allow us as unambiguously as possible to decide whether they are supported by a given case or not. Often they take the form of biconditionals, i.e. they specify necessary and sufficient conditions of regime formation. Each hypothesis is given a roman numeral (I–IV) indicating the general class or 'family' it belongs to. Hypotheses belonging to the same family are distinguished by arabic numerals. Lower-case letters (a–d) are used to refer to special implications of hypotheses as well as to the elements of more complex hypotheses, both of which we will from now on also refer to as 'sub-hypotheses'. In the language of this chapter only hypotheses, but not sub-hypotheses, in principle entail predictions for any given issue area.

Power-Structural Hypotheses (I)

Systemic analyses seek to explain outcomes with reference to characteristics of the international system. The feature of the

---

[5] These four classes certainly do not cover all approaches that are presently applied in the study of international regime formation. For example, we did not try to evaluate cognitive or second image theories of regime formation. In our view, these approaches have failed so far to come up with the sort of clear-cut hypotheses we needed for the kind of test we had in mind here. (But see now Ch. 9 above and Ch. 12 below.) In any event, this pre-selection must not be forgotten when interpreting the outcome of the subsequent competitive test of hypotheses.

international system that is most often held crucial in this regard is the distribution of power (defined as control over resources). Traditionally, power-structural approaches refer to the overall power of actors in the system (measured in terms of military capacity, size, etc.). However, it has also been suggested that attention should be focused on the resources pertaining directly to the particular issues at stake (Keohane and Nye 1977). Applying this distinction to the two most prominent power-based theories of regime formation, the theory of hegemonic stability (Krasner 1976, Keohane 1980) and the balance-of-power doctrine, we end up with the following four hypotheses:

H I.1 (*a*) If the distribution of overall power among the states concerned[6] is such that one of these states holds a hegemonic position, an international regime is established in the issue area.

(*b*) If none of the states concerned holds a hegemonic position, no international regime is established in the issue area.[7]

H I.2 As H I.1 except for the underlying concept of power, which here is to be understood in terms of resources specific to the issue area concerned.[8]

[6] The formula 'the states concerned' (here and in the following hypotheses) first of all refers to the parties to the conflicts constituting the issue area. In some cases, however, they will also include actors who do not themselves take an interest in the objects of contention as such, but in the way the respective conflicts are dealt with by the parties immediately involved. In the Saar case, for example, it would have seemed quite inadequate to disregard the role of the United States, even though the US Government did not take sides in this dispute.

[7] A state was assumed to be a hegemon within a given group of states if its power resources were at least twice as large as those of the second most powerful state in this group. Power was measured in terms of the GNP per capita, the size of the military forces, and the (non-)possession of nuclear weapons. As sources of information we used various UN publications, studies by Shoup (1981) and Flora *et al.* (1983), 'The Military Balance', and the SIPRI Yearbooks. According to our index the United States held a world-wide hegemonic position from the end of the Second World War until the mid-1960s. (All operationalizations in this chapter have been developed in a joint effort by the Tübingen project on international regimes involving, besides the authors of this chapter, Martin List, Martin Mendler, Volker Rittberger, and Michael Zürn.)

[8] Obviously, the issue-area specific power structure (IAS) had to be determined for each case separately. Not all kinds of issue areas lend themselves equally well to such a perspective. In particular, environmental and human rights cases pose problems in this respect that we have not been able to solve yet. (For an interesting attempt to define power resources specific to environmental issue areas see Ch. 8,

H I.3   (*a*) If the distribution of overall power among the states (or groups of states) concerned is roughly symmetrical, an international regime is established in the issue area.

(*b*) If the distribution of overall power among the states (or groups of states) concerned is asymmetrical, no international regime is established in the issue area.[9]

H I.4   As H I.3 except for the underlying concept of power, which here is to be understood in terms of resources specific to the issue area concerned.

Other Systemic Hypotheses (II)

Integration theory (Deutsch *et al.* 1957) suggests that a group of states is the more likely to be integrated the wider the spectrum of transactions taking place within this group. It does not appear unreasonable to assume a similar relationship to hold at lower levels of inter-state co-operation as well. Reinterpreted in a regime context this hypothesis may be stated as follows:

H II.1 (*a*) If the density of transactions between the states concerned is high, an international regime is established in the issue area.

(*b*) If the density of transactions between the states concerned is not high, no international regime is established in the issue area.[10]

The premiss of the normative-institutional approach is that international organizations or other international institutions bear upon regime formation as fora for the interactive development of

sect. 3, above.) As a result, hypotheses H I.2 and H I.4 could be tested against only part of our cases, i.e. mainly the economic and security issue areas.

[9] Our index yielded the following regularities: the overall power structure (OPS) of issue areas was asymmetrical if one superpower was involved. Issue areas involving both superpowers were symmetrical from 1970 on and asymmetrical in earlier periods. In the other cases we first grouped the states concerned according to the main cleavage in the issue area and then compared the aggregated power resources of the two groups.

[10] Trade relations were used as indicator for the density of transactions and measured following Russett's (1967) lead. The density of transactions within a given group of states was classed as high when it exceeded the average density within the CSCE region by at least a factor of 2.

consensual principles and norms and as models or focal points for new institutions (Rittberger and Zürn 1990: 42 f.). Thus, a mechanism is accentuated that resembles the processes that neo-functionalism has labelled 'spill-over':

H II.2   (*a*) If the issue area belongs to a policy area[11] already structured by international institutions and widely accepted norms, an international regime is established.

      (*b*) If the issue area belongs to a policy area as yet not structured by international institutions and widely accepted norms, no regime is established.

Challenging the 'anti-holistic' perspective on international politics that is widespread in regime analysis, some have suggested that the *overall* condition of East–West relations, and in particular the politico-psychological 'climate' marking the superpower competition at a given point in history, is crucial for the prospects of efforts to regulate East–West conflicts co-operatively:

H II.3   (*a*) If the overall relationship of the superpowers is friendly, an international regime is established, provided the issue area falls under 'East–West relations'.

      (*b*) If the overall relationship of the superpowers is rather hostile, no international regime is established, provided the issue area falls under 'East–West relations'.[12]

The state of the overall relationship of the superpowers may affect the patterns of co-operation among western countries as well. At a time of increased East–West tensions the western allies may tend to stick together more closely, whereas in times of *détente* concerns

---

[11] By 'policy areas' we understand sets of issue areas whose distinguishing feature is the kind of value to be allocated. A list of policy areas might include: security, human rights, economy, technology, communication, environmental protection, etc. (Beller *et al.* 1990: 30–3; Efinger, Rittberger, and Zürn 1988: ch. 5).

[12] For a discussion of the role of this factor in various areas of US–Soviet security co-operation see George (1988: 697–700). Quantitative data on the evolution of the overall superpower relationship not being available for the whole period of inquiry, we established a sequence of phases with different levels of superpower hostility on the basis of a number of qualitative historical accounts of East–West relations (e.g. D. Caldwell 1981, Halliday 1983, Wassmund 1982). Only two of the phases qualified as friendly, 1969–75 and 1985–90, whereas all others were classed as rather hostile, regardless of the more subtle differences holding between them.

for relative gains may prevail, undermining the willingness of parties to a conflict to strike mutually advantageous bargains:

H II.4   (*a*) If the overall relationship of the superpowers is rather hostile, an international regime is established, provided the issue area falls under 'West–West relations'.

       (*b*) If the overall relationship of the superpowers is friendly, no international regime is established, provided the issue falls under 'West–West relations'.

Problem-Structural Hypotheses (III)

Several studies have argued that, besides the characteristics of the international system and its units, issue (area) properties might serve as a basis for theorizing about international politics (Mansbach and Vasquez 1981). Various issue typologies have been proposed in this connection (Efinger, Rittberger, and Zürn 1988, Efinger and Zürn 1990). In particular, the special nature of the issue (area) may account for the way the respective conflicts are dealt with. The Tübingen project constructed a four-part typology of conflicts, attributing to each type a particular propensity for being managed by an international regime (Rittberger and Zürn 1990: 29–35). Slightly reformulated (in order to allow for testing on the basis of a small sample) this hypothesis reads:[13]

H III   (*a*) If the conflicts in the issue area[14] are conflicts of interest about absolutely assessed goods, regime formation takes place soon after the issue area has formed.

      (*b*) If the conflicts in the issue area are conflicts about means, regime formation takes some time, but causes no major difficulties.

      (*c*) If the conflicts in the issue area are conflicts of interest about relatively assessed goods, regime formation either is a lengthy, difficult process or does not occur at all.

---

[13] For an explication of the four types of conflict see Ch. 1, sect. 4.1, above.

[14] Sometimes not all the conflicts in the issue area are tokens of the same type. In such cases the prediction was based on the type of conflict that, among the types actually represented in the issue area, was least conducive to regime formation according to hypothesis H III.

(*d*) If the conflicts in the issue area are conflicts about values, no international regime is established.[15]

Situation-Structural Hypotheses (IV)

There are several approaches to the analysis of international co-operation and regimes seeking to make systematic use of game-theoretic reasoning (Snyder and Diesing 1977, Oye 1986, Ch. 6 above). Here we are interested in arguments linking pay-off structures, which are functions of the actors' preferences regarding a given set of issues, and the prospects of regime formation. Drawing from the work of Ullmann-Margalit (1977) and Harsanyi (1977), Michael Zürn (1990: 166–77) has constructed a typology of problematic social situations[16] and associated it with the following hypothesis:

H IV (*a*) If the situation that the states concerned are involved in comes under the co-ordination game type, an

---

[15] To allow for a clear decision whether the hypothesis was consistent with a given case or not, the vague temporal qualifications in sub-hypotheses H III*a–c* had to be quantified. For this purpose we ordered our regime cases by length of the regime formation process (beginning with the regime that was established the soonest) and used the resultant sequence for the following operationalization: provided the antecedent (if-clause) of the respective sub-hypothesis is true, a case supports H III*a* if and only if it belongs to the first third (length of regime formation process up to 8 years), H III*b* if and only if it belongs to the second third (9 to 15 years), and H III*c* if and only if it belongs to the third third or is one of the non-regime cases (no regime 15 years after the formation of the issue area). Our proceeding is thus analogous to the use of the median in categorizing variables.

[16] This typology consists of (1) co-ordination games, (2) dilemma games, and (3) Rambo games. As in all problematic social situations, in situations corresponding to *co-ordination games* strict individual rationality can yield a suboptimal collective outcome. What is particular to co-ordination situations is that once the actors start behaving in such a way that the resulting pay-offs are Pareto optimal, this collective behaviour is stable, because it constitutes a Nash equilibrium (i.e. a constellation of behavioural choices that none of the players can deviate from unilaterally without harming herself). In *dilemma game situations* the collective optimum is not a Nash equilibrium and is thus inherently unstable. There are incentives for both actors to deviate from the collective optimum, although both will lose if both follow these incentives. In *Rambo game situations* one actor can afford not to co-operate and still get his most favoured outcome unless the other is willing to end up worse off than he could do (Rittberger and Zürn 1990: 39 f.).

In the meantime (i.e. after completion of the case studies of the Tübingen project) Zürn (1992) has further developed his approach by, *inter alia*, subdividing the class of co-ordination games (see Ch. 1, sect. 4.2, above) and adding various qualifications to his (sub-)hypotheses.

international regime is established in the issue area in question.

(b) If the situation that the states concerned are involved in comes under the dilemma game type, an international regime is established, provided that other exogenous factors[17] exert a favourable influence.

(c) Otherwise no regime is established in situations coming under the dilemma game type.

(d) If the situation that the states concerned are involved in comes under the Rambo game type no international regime is established within the issue area in question.

2.3. Results

The Appendix to this chapter displays how the hypotheses held up against the evidence of our case studies, i.e. in which cases a hypothesis yielded a true prediction and in which it did not. If we take our hypotheses at face value, i.e. as strictly general statements, the results are not at all difficult to summarize. In principle, such a statement is falsified by a single counter-example, i.e. by a single false prediction it has given rise to. A quick check of the Appendix reveals that, for each hypothesis, there is at least one case that it is unable to explain, and usually there are many of them.[18]

---

[17] Four kinds of exogenous factors were taken into account in this study: the problem structure (regarding conflicts of interest about absolutely assessed goods and conflicts about means as favourable), the density of transactions (H II.1), the normative-institutional environment (H II.2), and the number of actors (regarding a small number of actors as favourable). Zürn (1990: 173–7) mentions two more factors supposed to be relevant, which, for different reasons, we could not include in this study: (1) we faced insurmountable difficulty measuring the length of the shadow of the future (*discount factor*); (2) we felt that Zürn's reference to favourable conditions at the subsystemic level (*domestic factors*) was not sufficiently backed by actual hypotheses (but see now Ch. 12 below). Another problem we had to solve was how to deal with those dilemma cases where some exogenous factors were favourable, whereas others were not. Also, it was not clear how to weight the various factors. Obviously, there are opportunities for further theoretical refinement of this approach. We chose the 'salient solution' not to attribute any particular weightings to the factors and to assume a wholly favourable influence if at least two factors were on the favourable side.

[18] Even if we no longer insist on the unity of our hypotheses and examine the sub-hypotheses *per se* (testing twenty-four hypotheses instead of ten), the situation does not generally improve. Most of the statements still cannot not be maintained,

Two things seem necessary, therefore. First, we must relax the as yet strict generality of our hypotheses by interpreting them as probabilistic statements. (It has already been mentioned that hypotheses in the study of regime formation are usually not intended as deterministic statements.) Consequently, H II.1, for example, is to be read: 'Regime formation *tends* to occur if and only if the density of transactions between the states concerned is high', and H III*d* as: 'Regime formation is *unlikely* if the conflicts in the issue area are conflicts about values', etc. In addition, we determine that a given case supports a hypothesis if and only if the outcome on the dependent variable that was likely to occur according to this hypothesis actually occurred in that case.[19]

Second, we must find a way to evaluate the relative performance of our hypotheses that is both adequate to the probabilistic (not strictly general) form of these hypotheses and provides a simple criterion of superiority. For this purpose, we make use of a measure for bivariate prediction success, ∇ (read 'del'), which was introduced by Hildebrand, Laing, and Rosenthal (1977: ch. 3). ∇ is a very flexible measure and can be used whenever a hypothesis predicts that certain events or states of affairs will not coincide. Our hypotheses, taking the form of either (sets of) conditionals (if A then B) or biconditionals (B if and only if A), meet this requirement.[20]

Roughly, the measure of prediction success, ∇, reflects the extent to which we can avoid making wrong predictions by relying

---

although it is clear that the hypotheses vary significantly as to the ratio of prediction successes and failures and, in this sense, did not fare equally badly in the test. Moreover, the four sub-hypotheses that are *not* refuted *stricto sensu* (H II.4*b*, H III*d*, H IV*b*, H IV*d*) actually could be used to make predictions in so few cases (between one and five) that we would be very reluctant to draw any further conclusions from this fact.

[19] This decision rule was chosen mainly for two reasons: (1) it allows for assessments of probabilistic hypotheses on a case-by-case basis, and (2) it does not affect the pattern of confirmation and disconfirmation of hypotheses as represented in the Appendix.

[20] Both conditional and biconditional hypotheses essentially rule out certain constellations of events or facts. Thus, in a 2 × 2 table (cross-classifying two variables with two categories each) conditional and biconditional hypotheses specify particular 'error cells', i.e. cells which are assumed to remain empty and therefore indicate prediction errors when filled. Conditional and biconditional hypotheses are distinguished by the number and the position of the error cells they specify: while conditional hypotheses have only one error cell (A, but not B), biconditional ones have two (A, but not B, and B, but not A).

on our hypothesis. A more precise (but also more opaque) interpretation is that ∇ measures prediction success in terms of the proportional reduction of (likely) prediction errors which we achieve in virtue of the knowledge of the state of the independent variable when using our hypothesis (Hildebrand, Laing, and Rosenthal 1977: 70).[21] Obviously, our hypothesis H I.1, for instance, would be no good if knowing whether there were a hegemon in the issue area in question would not at all improve our chances of not erring when predicting the value of the dependent variable, i.e. stating whether regime formation will take place or not. Conversely, if that knowledge, in combination with our assumption that H I.1, suffices to reduce the likelihood of our making a false prediction to zero, the prediction success of this hypothesis could be called perfect. In the latter case ∇ would assume the numerical value 1, while in the former case the measure would equal 0. ∇-values between 0 and 1 (if multiplied by 100) give the percentage of errors that knowledge of the state of the independent variable allows us to avoid. A hypothesis may even be misleading, however, in the sense that knowing whether or not A leads to an *increase* in the rate of prediction errors. In this case ∇ falls below zero. A negative ∇-value for a biconditional hypothesis of the form 'B if and only if A', while it indicates that the hypothesis is a prediction failure, at the same time lends support to another biconditional hypothesis: '*not* B if and only if A'.

In this chapter we use ∇ mainly as a descriptive device to summarize the results of confronting our hypotheses with our cases. In other words, we focus on the properties of our sample and do not attempt systematically to apply methods of statistical inference which require a far greater number of cases. For example, we will not calculate confidence intervals for the ∇-values of the whole population. Given the restrictions in expanding the sample size at will that even research teams face in this field, however, we hold that it is not unreasonable to base an (albeit preliminary) assessment of the quality of hypotheses about the

---

[21] As the baseline of comparison Hildebrand, Laing, and Rosenthal (1977: 40, 70) employ a prediction rule that has the same scope and precision as the theory under consideration and produces an identical number of the same predictions, but on a random basis (i.e. every case has the same chance of being selected for a given prediction).

TABLE 11.2. *Prediction Success of Hypotheses*

Rank	No. of hypothesis	Description of hypothesis	∇
1	IV	Situation structure	0.84
2	II.4	Superpower relationship (West–West)	0.55
3	III	Problem structure	0.45
4	II.1	Transaction density	0.37
5	I.3	Symmetrical power distribution (OPS)[a]	0.18
6	II.2	International institutions	0.16
7	II.3	Superpower relationship (East–West)	0.04
8	I.1	Hegemonic position (OPS)	−0.05
9	I.4	Symmetrical power distribution (IAS)[b]	−0.14
10	I.2	Hegemonic position (IAS)	−0.62

Notes. [a] OPS = overall power structure
     [b] IAS = issue-area specific power structure

formation of international regimes on the evidence of a rather limited number of cases. (In fact, most other studies in regime formation are even worse off in this respect.)

Table 11.2 ranks our hypotheses by their prediction success in terms of ∇. Accordingly, the most striking results of our test appear to be:

1. The prediction success of our hypotheses varies considerably (∇ assuming values between 0.84 and −0.62).

2. There is one hypothesis, the situation-structural hypothesis H IV, which clearly holds more promise than the others of serving as a basis for successfully predicting and thus explaining regime formation.[22]

3. Three other hypotheses besides have displayed a considerable predictive capacity: the West–West variant of the hypothesis referring to the state of the overall relationship of the superpowers

[22] In fact, H IV is the only hypothesis significant at the 0.05 level (the significance level of all other hypotheses being below 0.1). However, when we simplify the problem-structural hypothesis, H III, by lumping together categories *a* and *b* as well as categories *c* and *d* and the respective dependent variable categories alike, we obtain another hypothesis, H III′, also significant at that level. Incidentally, H III′ also achieves the rather high ∇-value of 0.59 (H III having achieved only 0.45), which is reached by no other hypothesis except H IV. Still, it is by no means clear that we should give up H III in favour of H III′, as we would thereby not only gain greater prediction success, but also sacrifice a good deal of precision (as a logical consequence of the now broader dependent variable categories).

(H II.4), the problem-structural hypothesis H III associating conflict type with the likelihood and facility of regime formation, and the hypothesis tracing back regime formation to the density of transactions among the states concerned (H II.1). Among these hypotheses the problem-structural hypothesis H III, in our view, deserves most attention, because its lesser prediction success as compared to H II.4 is compensated for by its unusually great precision.[23]

4. In general, systemic hypotheses appear to be less efficient prediction devices than the other hypotheses, the exception being H II.4. Accordingly, *explanations* of particular instances of regime formation on the basis of these systemic hypotheses would seem to be more questionable.

5. In particular, power-based systemic hypotheses have done rather badly in our test. Only one of them, H I.3, proved at all helpful in reducing the rate of prediction errors in comparison with the random baseline ($\nabla > 0$), while the other three power-structural hypotheses (including the theory of hegemonic stability in both its variants) did worst of all hypotheses examined. However, it has already been mentioned that a negative ∇-value achieved by a biconditional hypothesis, 'B if and only if A', supports the other biconditional hypothesis, 'not B if and only if A'. It could be argued, therefore, that there is one power-structural hypothesis with a considerable prediction success, namely the reverse of H I.2: 'An international regime is established in the issue area if and only if none of the states concerned holds a hegemonic position in terms of issue-specific power resources' (H I.2′).

Actually, this hypothesis achieves a ∇-value of 0.57, which makes it appear the second most promising of all hypotheses under consideration. However, while it does not seem impossible to add *ex post facto* a theoretical argument for this result (but then again: when would this ever be impossible?), the very moderate number of cases should warn us not to put too much emphasis on *a posteriori* findings of this kind.[24] The Appendix reveals that the

[23] That the higher ∇-value of H II.4 as compared to H III is attributable to the lesser precision of that hypothesis is demonstrated by the prediction success of H III′ (see n. 22), which exceeds that of H II.4.

[24] Hypothesis H I.2′ cannot be reduced to symmetry hypotheses such as H I.3, or rather H I.4, and therefore can hardly borrow the theoretical arguments that have been given in favour of such hypotheses. From an institutional bargaining perspective (Young 1989*b*) it might be argued that hegemons relying on their superior capabilities lack the flexibility and openness that is needed to make

number of actual applications of H I.2 (and, consequently, of H I.2′) has been even more reduced as a result of the occasionally insurmountable difficulty researchers had in assessing the distribution of issue-specific power resources.

Closing this section, we briefly turn to the prediction performance of the individual sub-hypotheses. Logically, it is possible that an elementary hypothesis forming part of a more complex one predicts considerably better (or worse) than the complex one does in its entirety. If a hypothesis such as H I.1 identifying hegemony as a necessary *and* sufficient condition for regime formation has not received support from the evidence of our cases, the same evidence might still suggest that hegemony could be necessary for a regime to emerge. (An analogous consideration, of course, applies to hegemony as a potential sufficient condition.) Accordingly, for each of our biconditional hypotheses there are two conditional hypotheses stating a sufficient and a necessary condition for regime formation, respectively. However, calculating the ∇-values for both the sufficient condition and the necessary condition derivatives of our hypotheses, we found only minor changes in prediction performance as a result of this operation. In particular, the rank order of hypotheses (for both derivatives) remained virtually unaffected, altogether only three hypotheses swapping places with neighbouring ones. We conclude, therefore, that our sample of cases does not support the expectation that we might be able to 'rescue' (or 'damage') some of the hypotheses under consideration by using such a decomposition technique.[25]

bargaining processes succeed. But, if the point that theory makes amounts to saying that hegemons are an obstacle to regime formation, we should expect that the relatively high ∇-value of H I.2′ is mainly due to its conditional implication: 'If there is a hegemon in terms of issue-specific resources, no regime will be established.' This conditional, however, achieves only $\nabla = 0.4$ (as compared to 0.57 for the complete biconditional hypothesis).

[25] As to our four-part hypotheses H III and H IV, we found that decomposing the hypotheses into sub-hypotheses led, especially in the case of H III, to a considerable differentiation in ∇-values (ranging from -0.36 in H III*a* to 1 in H III*d*). Yet, we hesitate at this stage to draw any conclusions as to the predictive and thus explanatory capacity of the respective sub-hypotheses. For the four-part hypotheses the reduction in cases for which predictions are made is inevitably even greater than for the biconditionals. And the numerical properties of ∇ are (and must be) such that if there is only one actual test case a single correct prediction suffices to make ∇ assume 1, i.e. indicate perfect prediction success of the hypothesis. In this context, it does seem noteworthy, however, that the situation-structural sub-hypothesis H IV*b* (dilemma game under favourable additional conditions) in five predictions did not produce a single error.

3. PROGRESS IN THE STUDY OF REGIME FORMATION BY MEANS OF INTEGRATION AND CONTEXTUALIZATION OF HYPOTHESES?

In the introduction to this chapter we expressed reservations concerning the prospects of single-variable hypotheses competition as a means of approaching the desired theory of regime formation. However, do the results of our test not make these doubts seem rather unjustified? After all, there *is* a hypothesis, the situation-structural hypothesis H IV, that not only stood out clearly from the rest, but also did extremely well in absolute terms. Still, arguing this way would be missing the point. In a sense there is indeed no alternative to a comparison of the prediction performance of hypotheses in any attempt to achieve or rather demonstrate theoretical progress. Of course, we will accept any proposed theory of regime formation only to the extent that it is superior to other proposals and that it has proved to be so. What we were sceptical about, however, was confronting different *single-factor hypotheses* with one another as a strategy to gain ground theoretically by selecting one approach as a natural candidate for the desired theory of regime formation. And *these* doubts indeed could not have been removed by the preceding hypothesis competition, its most impressive result being that a *composite, multivariate hypothesis* (H IV) has demonstrated far greater prediction success than the other ones relying on single variables. It seems worth while, therefore, dwelling a little longer on this hypothesis and its properties.

3.1. Integrated Theories

We regard the superiority of the situation-structural hypothesis as an indication of the usefulness of a strategy of theory-building that, in the opening section of this chapter, we have referred to as 'integration of variables'. A theory of regime formation may be called integrated if it can be considered (at least in part) the result of a combination of two or more distinct variables and if these variables (or at least some of them under some conditions) are supposed systematically to interact with one another, i.e. to share in the production of a certain result.

The concept of interaction is a rather vague one, and it is therefore expedient to clarify our use of the term by trying to give a formal criterion of theories *with an interaction component*: accordingly, a theory T states the existence of interaction phenomena if and only if there is a set of variables S such that T predicts an outcome on the dependent variable (here: regime formation) for each combination of values of the elements of S. (Here we presuppose that there is no hierarchy among the variables in S, and in particular that there is no single variable the value of which determines whether or not another variable in S has a bearing on the predicted outcome.) T may be called purely interactional if the interaction component, i.e. the set of variables S, is stated to be relevant for the whole universe of cases (issue areas in international relations); if S is hypothesized to influence outcomes only under specified conditions (in particular types of issue areas) T may be called partially interactional.

In this sense the complex situation-structural hypothesis H IV is an integrated theory, as it is—partially (by virtue of sub-hypotheses H IV*b* and *c*)—interactional. Provided the situation of the states concerned corresponds to a dilemma game, H IV entails a prediction for each of the possible thirty-two combinations of the categories of the four variables: density of transactions (high/not high), presence of institutions and norms (yes/no), type of conflict (value/means/absolutely/relatively assessed goods), and number of actors (small/large) (see n. 17 above and accompanying text).

Our criterion for interactional (components in) theories is neutral as to how these predictions are derived. In the case that the individual variables to be integrated are themselves supposed to be associated with regime formation, we may begin by assuming that their interaction is additive in the sense that factors favourable to regime formation increase the likelihood of regime formation in the presence of any other factors whatsoever. Of course, it is quite conceivable that such additivity does not, or does not always, exist in social reality, and we must be prepared to adjust our theories accordingly. At any rate, as far as the situation-structural hypothesis H IV is concerned, the assumption of additivity did not prevent a high degree of prediction success in our test.

In a given case, not all factors as specified by the integrated theory can be expected to be favourable (or unfavourable) to regime formation. Favourable and unfavourable aspects of a situation then may or may not neutralize one another. Here the question arises how to weight the various interacting variables. (In the case of H IV no specific weights were assigned.)

Yet another problem of integrative theory-building (and actually the most fundamental one) is which variables to integrate in the first place. Variables may be selected on the basis of the performance of single-factor hypotheses in tests such as the one we have reported in the preceding section. In this case the degree of prediction success of the individual hypotheses (or the value of some other measure of association) may be consulted when trying to weight the integrated variables. Such a purely inductive approach, however, runs the risk of soon degenerating into a practice where theoretical reasoning is more or less replaced by adding and subtracting variables the substantial relationship of which remains totally obscure. We therefore favour a more deductive approach where the choice of variables is controlled (albeit not determined) by an underlying model or set of core assumptions. In turn, these core assumptions may then also be found helpful in developing a causal interpretation of the correlational success of the integrated theory (Dessler 1991). Michael Zürn (1992) in his situation-structural theory of regime formation has followed such a deductive course by seeking consistently to relate the variables thought relevant to a rational choice framework.

3.2. Contextualized Theories

Our set of hypotheses includes yet another model to be considered in an attempt to transcend the stage of single-factor hypotheses. The second most successful hypothesis in our test in terms of predictive capacity, H II.4, differs from most other propositions we examined in that it is a hypothesis that claims a certain relationship to exist only under specific conditions: regimes are expected to form if and only if the superpower relationship is rather hostile *on the condition that* we are studying an issue area in West–West relations. Thus, H II.4 specifies a *context* ('West–West relations') in which a particular factor ('overall state of the superpower relationship') is supposed to take effect (Salmore *et al.* 1978: 194).

Conditional hypotheses such as H II.4 state the determinant of regime formation for a well-defined subset of the universe of cases or, in other words, for a certain type of case (here: issue areas in West–West relations). Thus, they are essentially incomplete, assuming that the purpose of a theory of regime formation is to account for the occurrence (or non-occurrence) of regime formation in any issue area whatsoever in international relations. Yet, of course, conditional hypotheses may be supplemented by other conditional hypotheses such that they jointly cover the whole universe of cases; in other words, they may form part of contextualized theories.

A *contextualized theory* is characterized by two components: (1) a typology of issue areas (the context variable), and (2) a set of hypotheses such that every hypothesis is applicable to at least one type of issue area *and* there is one and only one pertinent hypothesis for every type of the typology.[26] Thus, contextualized theories break up into a plurality of conditional hypotheses (or partial theories) each designed for only a limited range of issue areas, and the unity and coherence of such a theory is due solely to the unity of its object: the emergence of regimes in the international system. Theoretical progress as compared to the present situation in the study of regime formation (see sect. 1 above) would not necessarily or primarily rest on a reduction of hypotheses but on the assignment of explicit ranges of applications to them. Provided that a partial theory is well tested and confirmed within its range of application it can legitimately be used to explain regime formation in issue areas belonging to the respective subset of the universe of cases. Progress would not depend on our ability to devise partial theories that together cover the *whole* universe

---

[26] The hierarchical relationship between the context variable and the various context-specific explanatory variables distinguishes contextualized theories from integrated ones characterized by a non-hierarchical interaction component. However, the boundary between contextualized and integrated theories is certainly blurred (although one always *could* devise some formal criterion of distinction). Thus, 'contextualized theories' are conceivable whose context-specific hypotheses are as such integrated. Even a partially integrated theory such as H IV might be regarded as a borderline case, as the variable 'type of social situation' (co-ordination/dilemma/Rambo game) is clearly prior to the 'other exogenous factors' forming the interaction component of this complex hypothesis. At the same time, it differs from fully-fledged contextualized theories in that it does not entail specific conditional hypotheses for all the types of problematic social situations it refers to (both H IV*a* and H IV*d* being unconditional hypotheses).

of cases. However, this is what the strategy of contextualization aims at ultimately.

The intuitive idea behind this approach is that different kinds of international regimes (e.g. regimes in economic and regimes in human rights issue areas) may have different kinds of causes and, therefore, may have to be explained on the basis of different approaches as well. The formation of international regimes, in other words, may be an instance of 'equifinality' (George, Farley, and Dallin 1988: 11).

Again, when pursuing this strategy in practice we may try applying primarily inductive, exploratory techniques.[27] In accordance with the logic of contextualization we will begin by attributing the mixed success of at least some of the hypotheses advanced to account for regime formation to *overgeneralization* (beyond their appropriate ranges of application). We may then develop a typology of issue areas and test each of the hypotheses for each of the contexts thus defined. Examples of such typologies (Kohler-Koch 1989a: 62 f.) are scope (number of issues), number of actors, 'conflict formation' (i.e. West–West, East–West, or North–South macro-political context) (Senghaas 1988), 'issue area' (security, economy, system of rule) (Czempiel 1989, 1981), and superpower participation. The strategy can be said to have been successful if for each type we find at least one adequate hypothesis. If we find appropriate conditional hypotheses for only some of the types, we face the choice of trying out another typology or extending our set of hypotheses in order to fill the remaining gaps. It is clear that this kind of research is hardly feasible without the availability of a sufficiently large data base on international regimes (or, rather, issue areas in international politics). Once more, there is the problem of the theoretical 'obscurity' of results produced more or less by trial and error: *why* should this hypothesis be true just for this type of issue area? On the other hand, such results—to the extent that they are well established empirically—may also stimulate and thus promote theoretical reasoning.[28]

[27] Context variables do not differ essentially from what in the statistical language are called control variables.

[28] On a small-scale basis we experimented with inductive contextualizing by confronting our hypotheses with a number of subsets of our cases which we produced by applying several typologies of issue areas: conflict formation, 'issue area' in Czempiel's (1989) sense, number of actors (small/medium/large), type of conflict, and type of problematic social situation. As a result, we found for some

While an inductive approach to contextualization starts out from the construction of issue area typologies, a more deductively oriented approach focuses on the theoretical background of a hypothesis in order to define the limits of its applicability. Thus, it may be argued that the theory of hegemonic stability (H I.1) will predict outcomes adequately only in economic issue areas, or in issue areas with a large number of actors, or in issue areas for which both are true.[29] The drawback of this approach is that in this manner we will not systematically 'fill' a complete typology of issue areas and thus cover the whole universe of cases. Instead, a patchwork of partial theories will result and we will still not know where we stand. Besides, in the overlap zones of types belonging to different typologies, the problem of competing hypotheses the interrelationship of which is unclear will crop up again. On the other hand, reconstructing theoretical backgrounds of hypotheses can be done in the absence of a large sample of case studies, making this approach a feasible option for the individual researcher as well. At least this applies to the initial steps of this approach, for eventually any theory, whether partial or comprehensive, will have to withstand the test of the empirical evidence that is provided by as many cases as possible.

4. CONCLUSION

In this chapter we have proposed and, to some extent, analysed two strategies which students of regime formation may pay attention to when trying to achieve theoretical progress in their field. Both strategies presuppose that there is still considerable space for

hypotheses in certain contexts some moderate changes in ∇-values. In view of the heavily reduced number of applications, however, we do not think there is much point in reporting figures here.

For an attempt at generating conditional hypotheses on the basis of the same sample making systematic use of theoretical anomalies see Rittberger and Zürn (1991a: 171–7).

[29] Actually, the ∇-value of hypothesis H I.1 rises from -0.05 to 0.29 if it is applied to economy cases exclusively. Restricting the universe of cases to issue areas with a comparatively large number of state actors (more than ten) results in an even lower ∇-value (-0.27). In our sample there are only two cases which both belong to the economic sphere and are characterized by a large number of actors. For these cases H I.1 yields one true and one false prediction ($\nabla = 0$).

such progress. At the same time, however, they recognize the work that has been done in this field by trying to build on the rich fund of approaches and hypotheses that have been proposed by regime theorists in recent years. Both strategies rely on the intuition that regime formation, like most other social phenomena, cannot be explained monocausally, i.e. on the basis of single-factor accounts. To some extent, the results of a simultaneous test of various single-variable hypotheses have lent empirical support to this intuition, the validity of which can never be demonstrated cogently, however. Both strategies, which are associated with characteristic conceptions or forms of theories, might help clarify an idea that has been voiced now and again in the study of regime formation: that different approaches to explaining international regimes may be regarded as complementary.[30] Finally, it has to be emphasized that neither of the two strategies is an algorithm. Like any other item on a research agenda they are only as helpful as the researchers using them are committed, ingenious, and lucky.

APPENDIX

Cases and Hypotheses Confronted

In the tables that follow, pluses stand for true predictions, minuses for false ones. From the position of the sign in the row (top or bottom) the value of the independent variable can be inferred. For example, the bottom position of the minus in the row of hypothesis H I.1 in the CSBM column shows that in this issue area no state (before 1990) held a hegemonic position in terms of overall power. That the sign is a minus and not a plus has nothing to do with the value of the independent variable, but shows that the outcome on the dependent variable could *not* be correctly predicted on the basis of hypothesis H I.1 (this hypothesis *inter alia* declaring the presence of an OPS hegemon a necessary condition of regime formation). The abbreviation 'n.p.' (no prediction) is entered where the hypothesis does not imply a prediction for the case concerned; 'n.a.' (no answer) is entered when the author of the case study felt unable to establish the value of the respective variable (power structure etc.) for his or her case.

Changes over time in the value of the independent variable, or the truth

[30] See e.g. Ch. 2, sect. 5.1, and Ch. 9, sect. 6, above.

value of the antecedent of the hypothesis, are reflected by compart-mentalized cells and resulted in an increase in cases for the respective hypothesis. No conclusions can be drawn, however, from the spatial relationship of compartments in different cells of the same column as to the temporal relationship of the respective changes on the independent variables. For example, it cannot be inferred from this table that in the CSBM case both the overall power structure (OPS) and the issue area structure (IAS) changed from asymmetry to symmetry *simultaneously*.

Hypothesis	CSBM regime	CFE (no regime)	Arms control in W. Europe (no regime)	Saar regime
I.1a I.1b Hegemony (OPS)	−	− / +	−	+
I.2a I.2b Hegemony (IAS)	−	−	−	− / −
I.3a I.3b Symmetry (OPS)	+ / +	+ / −	+	−
I.4a I.4b Symmetry (IAS)	− / −	+ / − +	+	−
II.1a II.1b Transaction density	−	+	−	+
II.2a II.2b Institutions	+	−	+	+
II.3a II.3b Superpower rela-tionship (E–W)	− / +	+ / − +	n.p.	n.p.
II.4a II.4b Superpower rela-tionship (W–W)	n.p.	n.p.	−	+
IIIa Absolute IIIb Means IIIc Relative IIId Values	+ / −	+	+	−
IVa Co-ordination IVb } IVc } Dilemma game IVd Rambo game	+	+	+	+

Hypothesis		Baltic Sea regime	North Sea regime	Austria regime	LRTAP regime
I.1a	Hegemony (OPS)	+		+	
I.1b			–		–
I.2a	Hegemony (IAS)	n.a.	n.a.		n.a.
I.2b				–	
I.3a	Symmetry (OPS)		+		+
I.3b		–		–	
I.4a	Symmetry (IAS)	n.a.	n.a.	+	n.a.
I.4b					
II.1a	Transaction	+	+		
II.1b	Density			–	–
II.2a	Institutions	+	+		+
II.2b				–	
II.3a	Superpower rela-	+	n.p.	–	
II.3b	tionship (E–W)			–	–
II.4a	Superpower rela-	n.p.	+ / +	n.p.	n.p.
II.4b	tionship (W–W)				
IIIa	Absolute			–	
IIIb	Means	–	+		–
IIIc	Relative			–	
IIId	Values				
IVa	Co-ordination	+			+
IVb	} Dilemma game		+		
IVc				–	
IVd	Rambo			+	

Hypothesis	Scientific technological exchange (no regime)	Intra-German trade regime	Berlin regime	Constitutionalism regime	Foreign journalists (no regime)
I.1a Hegemony (OPS)		+	−		
I.1b	+		−	−	+
I.2a Hegemony (IAS)	−	+	+	n.a.	n.a.
I.2b					
I.3a Symmetry (OPS)	−		+	+	−
I.3b	+	−	+		
I.4a Symmetry (IAS)	+	−	−	n.a.	n.a.
I.4b					
II.1a Transaction		+	+	+	
II.1b Density	+				+
II.2a Institutions				+	−
II.2b	+	−	−		
II.3a Superpower relationship (E–W)	−	−	+	n.p.	−
II.3b	+		+		+
II.4a Superpower relationship (W–W)	n.p.	n.p.	n.p.	+	n.p.
II.4b					
IIIa Absolute				+	
IIIb Means				+	
IIIc Relative		+	+		
IIId Values	+				+
IVa Co-ordination		+	+	n.a.	
IVb } Dilemma game					
IVc					
IVd Rambo	+				+

12

Bringing the Second Image (Back) In

About the Domestic Sources of Regime Formation

MICHAEL ZÜRN

1. INTRODUCTION

Assessments of the state of regime theory usually conclude with a complaint about the neglect of domestic sources of international regimes. Regime formation and change, according to this criticism, cannot be understood without consideration of the societal forces that either benefit from, or are harmed by, international co-operation.[1]

In contrast, Robert Keohane (1984: 25 f.), following the lead of Kenneth Waltz (1979), has argued that systemic explanations are generally superior to subsystemic ones because of their parsimony. Accordingly, analysing the domestic sources of regime formation

For comments on an earlier version of this chapter I am especially grateful to Robert O. Keohane, Peter Mayer, Harald Müller, Thomas Risse-Kappen, Volker Rittberger, Frank Schimmelfennig, Gudrun Schwarzer, and Klaus Dieter Wolf. I also benefited from the discussion about the draft of this chapter presented at the conference on 'The Study of Regimes in International Relations—State of the Art and Perspectives', Tübingen, July 1991. Finally, I am grateful to the Deutsche Forschungsgemeinschaft (German Science Association) for the provision of the funding for this study.

[1] See the early critique of Strange (1983) and the more recent assessments of regime analysis by Young (1986) and Haggard and Simmons (1987: 513). In the German-speaking community both Hüttig (1990) and Efinger *et al.* (1990) have identified the lack of solid studies on the national level as a major weakness of regime analysis. Domestic politics might be important for both understanding regime formation and accounting for regime consequences. For instance, the basic claim of regime analysts that international institutions matter could probably be best substantiated by showing that they have an impact on domestic politics. (See Ch. 15 below.) In this chapter I will focus, however, on regime formation only.

may be an effort in vain because one can always be confronted with a more parsimonious explanation at the systemic level. From a different point of view, Gerd Junne (1990: 357) suspects that a careful examination of domestic politics would undermine the whole regime approach by discrediting the notion of state actions as being governed by international institutions.

The aim of this chapter is to show that 'second image analysis',[2] in principle, can be integrated into regime analysis without undermining the whole approach and without violating the principle of parsimony. In section 2, I will therefore offer a conceptualization which takes into account the difficulties of explaining regime formation at the actor level. Offering such a conceptualization, however, is hardly sufficient. In addition, it is necessary to show that domestic politics does indeed matter for regime formation. In section 3, therefore, some propositions drawn from the literature are reformulated in accordance with the conceptualization offered and, subsequently, are confronted with the evidence on regimes in the CSCE region studied by the Tübingen project.[3]

The procedure will lead to the following preliminary findings about the domestic sources of regime formation. First, a state actor's foreign policy will result in regime formation when the state tries to correct dissatisfying outcomes in an issue area by utilizing economic and informational resources, and when it displays an orientation towards reciprocity accompanied by the readiness to make one-sided concessions. Second, such a regime-conducive foreign policy is most likely to emerge in states with a corporatist domestic structure. Third, this is most likely to happen in such states after a change in domestic power constellation has taken place, and when the degree of routinization of the pre-established policy is not very high.

---

[2] 'According to the second image [of international relations], the internal organization of states is the key to understanding war and peace' (Waltz 1959: 81). In slight modification of this definition, I will use the term 'second image' to refer to *all* actor properties affecting regime formation, whereas the terms 'domestic' and 'subsystemic' refer solely to aspects of internal organization of actors. Besides Waltz's *Man, the State, and War* the volume *Bringing the State Back In*, edited by Evans, Rueschemeyer, and Skocpol (1985), is, of course, the *locus classicus* referred to in the title of this chapter.

[3] For a brief description of this project and references see Ch. 1, sect. 1, above.

2. CONCEPTUALIZING THE DOMESTIC SOURCES
OF REGIME FORMATION

Consider the following statement about international regimes: 'The takeover by Gorbachev of the Kremlin has resulted in the formation of East–West security regimes.' There might be much truth in this account, but it is theoretically unsatisfactory. One reason for this is that it relies on a fact about a single actor to explain an *inter*action between two or more actors. Thus, the statement implicitly declares the other regime participants to be totally inconsequential. This objection points to a more general difficulty plaguing any attempt to explain regime formation on the basis of domestic sources: the dependent and independent variables are located on different levels of analysis.

The Gorbachev-factor type of explanation of regime formation is dissatisfying for yet another reason. It points to an idiosyncratic condition (Mikhail Gorbachev's coming to power) which does not allow for generalization at all. In a more sophisticated version 'Gorbachev' would stand for a more general condition, that is, regime formation would be assumed to occur when a specific power constellation prevails within the participating countries. Given the considerable scope of many international regimes (some of which are almost global in membership), however, a second image analysis of regime formation is confronted with a second difficulty: too often it will not be feasible by virtue of the informational costs it imposes on the researcher.

2.1. Difficulty 1: Dependent and Independent Variables are on Different Levels

The outbreak of war, the foundation of formal international organizations, and the formation of international regimes are all outcomes of interactions. In international relations, it is not individual action, but the interplay of at least two actors which produces the outcomes to be explained. For most analysts, therefore, the use of systemic variables in order to explain interactive outcomes appears quite natural. Accordingly, the most often cited hypothesis in regime analysis, the 'theory of hegemonic stability', traces international regime formation back to a systemic state of affairs, that is a hegemonic power distribution. To be sure, there seems to be no obstacle in principle to explaining the *compliance* of a given state with the prescriptions of a given regime with reference to characteristics of the domestic politics in that state. But that is clearly something different from explaining regime formation. Regimes can be complied with only if they are already there, but what we want to know about are the domestic sources of their *formation*.

The difficulty of explaining regime formation at the actor level leads to a first conceptual proposition: a subsystemic explanation of international interaction requires the introduction of an inter-mediary variable which I propose to call *foreign policy type*.[4] For the purpose of illustration, recall Stephen Krasner's (1983*a*: 5) basic conceptualization of regimes as 'intervening variable' between the 'basic causal variables' and the observable 'related behaviour' in international politics. My thesis is that, if the category 'basic causal variables' is now specified by 'domestic politics', then one more intervening, or more broadly 'intermediary variable', the 'foreign policy type', becomes necessary (see Fig. 12.1).

---

domestic politics → foreign policy type → regime formation → related behaviour

Fig. 12.1 Foreign policy type as an intermediary variable

This conceptualization splits the original intractable question about the domestic sources of regime formation into two analytical tasks, both of which are tractable: first, regime-conducive foreign policy types have to be identified, and, second, the domestic sources of regime-conducive foreign policies have to be discovered. The rationale of this procedure is that it can reveal links between domestic structures and international co-operation which otherwise are not visible.

[4] The problem parallels that of devising a subsystemic explanation of war, which, like regime-building, is an interaction phenomenon. And also, quite similarly to what I am proposing in this chapter, it has been suggested that war may at least in part be explicable in terms of specific types of foreign policy. However, little research has been devoted to this issue so far (Vasquez 1987: 369).

2.2. *Difficulty 2: Violation of the Principle of Parsimony*

Now suppose that one has found non-idiosyncratic descriptors for a foreign policy type that regularly leads to regime formation. Another question then arises: did domestic conditions of the state in question or its position in the international system cause this foreign policy? This question is intricate because almost any conceivable observed behaviour of a state might be caused by domestic sources as well as by constraints located in the environment in which it acts. It is often argued that a theory relying on the constraints which are imposed on the states by the international system is more parsimonious and for this reason preferable. Accordingly, only if the systemic explanation does not suffice should additional theories referring to the subsystemic level be called upon.

There are several strategies for defending this view. For the purpose of distinguishing these strategies, it might be helpful to conceive of the observed behaviour of a state as a result of a two-stage filtering process (Elster 1985: 9). First, the systemic filter reduces the number of possible choices and, thus, reduces the opportunity space for the state. Domestic politics represents the second filter determining the choice of one form of behaviour from among the remaining alternatives.

According to Waltz (1979), the strength of systemic explanations of state behaviour rests on the fact that, in international politics, the first filter already reduces heavily the opportunity space of the states, leaving them without notable alternatives. From this point of view, any adequate explanation must necessarily focus on the systemic level. This argument, however, presupposes that structures are strong determinants of behaviour in international politics compared to other social systems.

For those who are not convinced of this *a priori* superiority of systemic theories about international politics, and who assume that both filters are of some importance for explaining foreign policy, Keohane (1984: 24 f.) offers additional, more practical justifications for withholding or at least postponing a subsystemic analysis. He asserts that it is very difficult to find relevant subsystemic variables explaining foreign policy which are not as idiosyncratic as the already mentioned Gorbachev factor.

In contrast, I submit that subsystemic level analysis is not *per se* less theoretical than its systemic counterpart and that sometimes even the converse is true. Consider for example the present debate on the prospects for peace in Europe after the end of the Cold War. Systemic theorists explain the 'stable peace' in Western Europe as well as the 'long peace' between East and West with bipolarity and its disciplining effects and, consequently, expect a gloomy future now that this structure has broken down (Mearsheimer 1990). Actor-oriented theorists explain the 'stable peace' in Western Europe by the spread of democracy and the rule of law and, consequently, expect a bright future for the whole of Europe (Senghaas 1990). Either expectation may prove to be wrong, yet the underlying theories are not different in terms of generality. In turn, an institutionalist account of both the so-called 'long peace' and the 'expected future' of politics in Europe (Rittberger and Zürn 1991*b*) represents a systemic explanation that is certainly less parsimonious than the actor-level 'spread of democracy creates peace' argument.

There remains, however, the problem of the amount of information needed to make predictions about regime formation on the basis of domestic conditions. The question arises of how it is possible to explain, at the actor level, the formation of regimes in which often dozens of actors participate. Is it necessary to know and to categorize the foreign policies and the properties of all actors in the issue area? If the answer to this question were yes, the informational costs of testing pertinent hypotheses (which can be seen as another aspect of parsimony) would be insurmountable and the likelihood of identifying domestic factors which hold for all (or most) of the state actors acting in the issue area in question would be extremely low.

In order to cope with this second difficulty of subsystemic regime analysis, I suggest focusing exclusively on those states in the issue area who play a prominent role in the process of institution-building. Thus, a procedure for finding out these *prominent states* is needed. Consider an issue area which so far is not governed by an international regime. Suppose, in addition, that some actors are satisfied with the outcomes in the issue area, while others are not. The dissatisfied actors basically have two options: they can actively seek to change things by initiating the setting up of an international regime or they can resort to internal adaptation (Haftendorn 1989). *Regime initiation* is attempted when a state actor, either individually or as a representative of a group of states, puts forward a proposal for regulating the conflicts in an issue area or prompts the convening of an international conference about the issues. *Internal adaptation* occurs if a dissatisfied actor defines away the original goals, or states verbal complaints without further activities aiming at change, or attempts to withdraw from the issue area in question. All these options require internal adjustments when measured against the original goals. Of course, the actors satisfied with the status quo are likely to resist such initiatives, fearing they can only lose if the mode of conflict management changes in the issue area. Therefore, they may engage in a behaviour which can be called *regime prevention*, that is, a state actor, either individually or as a representative of a group of states, insists on unilateralism for principled reasons, or denies the need for international management of the issues in question, or rejects proposals for international management of the issues in question without suggesting feasible alternatives.

For the study of the domestic sources of regime formation I suggest focusing only on attempts of regime initiation and regime prevention. The in-depth analysis of issue areas usually points to such prominent states. Focusing on those states is a pragmatic means of reducing the informational costs of subsystemic analysis and is thus a heuristic decision which ultimately can be justified only by the success of the whole procedure.

2.3. The Second Image of Regime Formation

In section 2.1 the concept of *regime-conducive foreign policy type* has been introduced. The purpose of this variable is to allow the study of the relationship between domestic politics and foreign policy on the one hand, and the relationship between foreign policy and the prospects for regime formation, on the other. Of course, for the construction of foreign policy types it is necessary to have a clear-cut definition of foreign policy in the first place.

To begin with, the question emerges: what kind of actors are under consideration? For the purpose of this study, I want to restrict the use of the term 'foreign policy' to state actors. That is to say, foreign policy is conducted by the decision-makers of a national government which legitimately governs a territorially defined political community. Speaking of state actors in terms of decision-makers of a national government does not presuppose a unitary actor. It does not rule out contradicting or competing actions by different branches of the same government, each legitimized to act in the so-called national interest.

Foreign policy is most often defined as the development and pursuit of some preferred goals (with regard to the authoritative allocation of values) through the selective use of foreign-policy instruments. This formulation conforms quite well to the general use of the term. Yet, there is one important disadvantage to this kind of definition. As George and Keohane (1980: 221) have aptly emphasized, goals and 'interests can be seen as application of values in context: values applied in the light of situations as they appear to people involved in them'. Thus, a certain choice of behaviour can be seen as resulting from values and perceptions of decision-makers; consequently the values have to be conceptualized as independent variables. That is to say, in order to keep the opportunity open for explaining foreign policy in terms of the decision-maker's values and belief systems which are translated into interests in specific contexts, one should exclude them from the definition of the dependent variable (Carlsnaes 1986: 104–16).

Thus, *foreign policy* is better defined in terms of observable actions of a state towards political units beyond its territorial jurisdiction than in terms of the motives for such actions. It is assumed that certain kinds of foreign policy are regime-conducive, whereas others are working against regime formation. For this reason the term *foreign policy type* is reserved for typologically distinguishable courses of foreign policy.

Foreign-policy interests of states can then be seen as influencing their foreign policies towards greater or less regime-conduciveness. That is to say, interests are conceptualized as existing prior to foreign policy. Yet, foreign-policy interests are, as well as the observable course of action, a result of properties of state actors. Therefore, foreign-policy interests may serve as an intervening variable between actor properties and foreign policy.

The ideas developed so far are summarized in Fig. 12.2. Therein, *positional characteristics* represents a heading for all properties of a state actor that can be assessed only in relation to other actors in the international system. Thus, the relative amount of available power resources, the relative economic strength, the

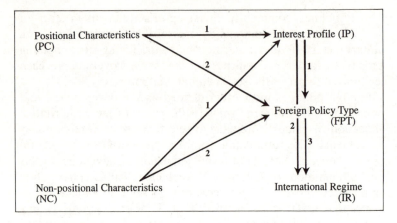

Fig. 12.2 The second image of regime formation

kind of interdependence, and the roles occupied in international institutions can all be seen as examples of positional characteristics.[5]

As opposed to positional properties, *non-positional characteristics* can be determined without knowing anything about other state actors. Non-positional characteristics may be properties of a state's polity and politics, its economy and culture, and its decision-makers that may influence foreign policy.

Both positional and non-positional characteristics can have effects on both *foreign-policy interests* (arrows PC 1 and NC 1) and *foreign policy* (arrows PC 2 and NC 2). Reasoning corresponding to the logic of the arrows PC 1 and NC 1 resembles the 'generic rational choice approach' (Elster 1985: 3). This approach assumes rational choice of a course of behaviour on the basis of domestically defined interests *vis-à-vis* possible outcomes of interaction. If the interests of an actor are explained (arrows PC 1 and NC 1), its course of behaviour (arrow IP 1) and the outcome (FPT 3) can be deduced from the rational choice assumption. According to this

---

[5] Positional characteristics of an actor are different from systemic factors. They are not system properties but characteristics that result from an actor's position in the international system. Some but not all systemic explanations can be reformulated in terms of positional characteristics. For example, the theory of hegemonic stability has an actor-oriented equivalent stating that states clearly superior in economic and in military terms to all other states in the system strive for the creation of a liberal world order, whereas the theory of bipolar stability is difficult to phrase in terms of positional characteristics.

view, foreign policy is clearly dependent on actor interests. Alternatively, it can be assumed that foreign policy is best explained in terms of positional or non-positional state characteristics as such without any reference to interests at all.

Both models can be applicable depending on the circumstances. When foreign policy is the result of a *deliberate* strategy by *one* identifiable decision unit acting rationally (*state as rational actor*), there is almost a strict one-to-one relationship between interest profiles of the decision unit and the resulting behaviour. Consequently, in this case it is most profitable analytically to focus on interest profiles. When the course of foreign policy, however, is more or less *emergent* as the result of an uncoordinated interplay among different governmental units or as wholly dictated by the environment (*state as a social institution*),[6] the focus on foreign policy types is more safe.

For this chapter, I have chosen regime-conducive foreign policy types rather than interest profiles as the intermediary variable between actor characteristics and regime formation. That is not to say that the emergent strategy model is generally more adequate for analysing international politics. Two reasons account for this decision. First, given the preliminary character of second image analysis of regime formation, it seems sensible to concentrate on the variable which is easier to observe. Second, as long as 'regime-conducive interests profiles' and 'regime-conducive foreign policy' have no perfect one-to-one relationship, it seems advantageous to start out with the variable which is 'closer' to the ultimate dependent variable in the model. That is to say, it is easier to 'discover regime-conduciveness' by first focusing on that foreign policy type which, according to my second image model of regime formation, is closer to regime formation than interest profiles. After regime-conducive foreign policy types are identified, it is still possible to prove in a second step that the choice of certain foreign policy types can be accounted for to a large extent on the basis of interest profiles. To put it differently: the main goal of this chapter is to identify *foreign policy types that are regime-conducive*. Thus,

---

[6] For an insightful classification and the respective definitions of organizational strategies on the continuum between the poles of purely deliberate and purely emergent strategies see Mintzberg and Waters (1985). For an explication of the conceptual poles 'state as an actor' versus 'state as a social institution' see Skocpol (1985).

the original question about the domestic sources of regimes should be split up into two parts: (1) What type of foreign policy is regime-conducive? (2) What kind of actor characteristics (including ultimately interest profiles) lead to a regime-conducive foreign policy?

3. GENERATING SOME HYPOTHESES

In the remainder of this chapter it will be shown that the suggested conceptualization of the domestic sources of regime formation may eventually lead to meaningful, general, and potentially predictive statements. The procedure adopted in order to generate hypotheses consists of three steps. First, I chose three academic subfields which seemed to be the most promising for deriving hypotheses relevant to the second image of regime formation: comparative foreign policy analysis, regime analysis, and game-theoretic explanations of social co-operation. Second, I chose general statements from these fields (hypotheses regarding dependent variables different from the ones in this study) displaying a minimal degree of fit with my conceptualization of the second image of regime formation. Third, the chosen statements were confronted with the cases studied in the Tübingen project in order to generate hypotheses about the domestic sources of regime formation. For this purpose, I developed a questionnaire and distributed it to the authors of the case studies in this project.

The empirical basis for the remainder of this part of the chapter consists exclusively of the case studies about conflicts and regime formation in East–West (eight cases) and some West–West issue areas (four cases), which are now listed in alphabetical order:

1. access to and status of Berlin (Berlin): a regime came into existence during the mid-1970s;
2. confidence- and security-building measures (CSBM): a regime was eventually set up in the mid-1980s;
3. constitutionalism in Western Europe (Constitutionalism): a regime was established in the early 1950s;
4. conventional forces reduction in Europe (CFE): unregulated conflict management until 1989 with a regime coming into existence after that;

5. co-operative arms control in Western Europe (Arms Control): conflict management without a regime dominated all the time;
6. international status of Austria (Austria): a regime terminating the conflicts formed in the mid-1950s;
7. intra-German trade (Trade): a regime came into existence in the mid 1960s;
8. long-range transboundary air pollution in Europe (LRTAP): a regime was established in the early 1980s;
9. marine environment of the Baltic Sea (Baltic Sea): a regime was established in the mid-1970s;
10. marine environment of the North Sea (North Sea): a regime was established in the mid-1980s;
11. scientific and technological exchange (Science): dominated by unregulated conflict management all the time;
12. status of the Saar (Saar): a regime was in place for a short period of time with conflict resolution following immediately.[7]

When the issue areas to be studied in this project were selected, attention was not at all focused on the subsystemic level. Thus, in order to find the domestic sources of regime formation no sophisticated research techniques such as systematic pair comparisons or the careful selection of deviant cases could be applied. In addition, the categories used in the questionnaire were by no means conclusively operationalized. Therefore, the study should be regarded as an exploratory data analysis in order to generate hypotheses which appear worth testing in subsequent studies. This should be kept in mind when the findings are examined.

3.1. Attempts at Regime Initiation and Regime Prevention

I start by identifying the *prominent state actors* in the issue area in question: these are all state actors which have made an attempt at initiating regime formation, whether successful or not, as well as

---

[7] Ch. 11, sect. 2.1, above contains a more detailed description of the cases. Although both chapters refer to the same data, my sample consists of one fewer case since I did not receive the answers to my questionnaire for the case study about the working conditions for foreign journalists. All the data used in this chapter stem from the questionnaire. I would like to thank Manfred Efinger, Martin List, Kai-Uwe Schrogl, and Gudrun Schwarzer for the patience needed to answer my numerous questions.

TABLE 12.1. *Attempts at Regime Initiation and Regime Prevention*

Successful regime initiators	Unsuccessful regime initiators	Successful regime opponents	Unsuccessful regime opponents
Austria 1953 (Austria)	FRG 1950 (Trade)	FRG 1970 (LRTAP)	France 1952 (Saar)
FRG 1952 (Saar)	Norway 1970 (LRTAP)	GB 1970 (LRTAP)	GB 1980 (LRTAP)
FRG 1963 (Trade)	Sweden 1970 (LRTAP)	GDR 1970 (Science)	GDR 1963 (Trade)
FRG 1968 (Berlin)	USA 1945 (Austria)	France 1950 (Arms Control)	
FRG 1980 (North Sea)	USA 1950 (Arms Control)	USA 1970 (LRTAP)	
FRG 1982 (LRTAP)	USA 1970 (Science)	USSR 1970 (LRTAP)	
Finland 1972 (Baltic Sea)	USA 1973 (CFE)	USSR 1973 (CFE)	
Norway 1982 (LRTAP)	USA 1975 (CSBM)	USSR 1975 (CSBM)	
Sweden 1972 (Baltic Sea)	USSR 1945 (Austria)		
Sweden 1982 (LRTAP)			
USA 1968 (Berlin)			
USA 1984 (CSBM)			
USA 1989 (CFE)			
USSR 1953 (Austria)			
USSR 1989 (CFE)			

Note. The date accompanying the name of each state actor indicates the year in which the attempts was started. An attempt may have gone on for many years. An attempt is regarded as successful if within six years a regime came into existence. The abbreviations and names in parentheses refer to the issue areas in which the attempt was launched.

all state actors which have actively attempted to prevent regime formation, whether successful or not. The procedure reduces the informational costs of subsystemic analysis by concentrating on a comparatively small number of states and time points which have to be taken into account.

Yet, it should be recalled that the units of analysis depicted in Table 12.1 are the *foreign policies* of these prominent state actors and not the state actors themselves. For this reason, a state actor may be referred to more than once in the same issue area. For example, 'USA 1984' stands for a successful regime initiation in the issue area 'confidence- and security-building measures in Europe', and 'USA 1975' represents an unsuccessful regime initiation in the same issue area. This differentiation is based on the idea that a first attempt at regime initiation in this issue area during the mid-1970s (Helsinki Accords), which turned out to be a failure, can be analytically separated from a second attempt in the early 1980s (Stockholm conference), which proved to be more successful.

3.2. Regime-Conducive Foreign Policy Types

An attempt to initiate regime formation does not necessarily meet with success. Thus, the inquiry aimed at identifying those foreign policies which increase the likelihood of regime formation. For this reason, taxonomies of behaviour from different research fields were utilized and modified so as to allow for a description of foreign policies in issue areas. The goal was to find out which type of foreign policy most often accompanies successful regime initiation as opposed to unsuccessful regime initiation and attempts to prevent regime formation.

In the questionnaire different taxonomies for describing the foreign policy of prominent actors in the studied issue areas during attempts at regime initiation or regime prevention were offered. Thereby, a typology constructed of two of these taxonomies turned out to be helpful in identifying regime-conducive foreign policy types.

The first of these taxonomies is based on the game-theoretical strategies used in computer tournaments. Such tournaments were carried out by Axelrod (1984) in order to find out which type of strategy is most successful in inducing co-operation when the players are engaged in iterated prisoners' dilemma games. In these tournaments the tit-for-tat strategy was most often successful. It is now assumed that an issue-area specific foreign policy of the tit-for-tat type may also induce regime formation.[8]

The numerous strategies submitted for use in the tournaments can be categorized on the two criteria of 'ratio of uncooperative to co-operative moves' and 'degree of reciprocity'. An *uncooperative strategy* is thus characterized by permanent uncooperative behaviour which does not significantly change even when the other side makes concessions. An *unfriendly tit-for-tat strategy* is a course of behaviour that is, by and large, conditional on the other side's behaviour, yet more often uncooperative in the sense that co-operative moves by other actors are less regularly responded to in the same manner than uncooperative moves. A *trial-and-error strategy* is an unconditional mix of co-operative und uncooperative moves. A *friendly tit-for-tat strategy* is a behaviour that is, by and large, conditional, but more often co-operative in the sense that uncooperative moves by other actors are less regularly responded to in the same manner than co-operative moves. A *co-operative strategy*, finally, is characterized by permanent co-operative behaviour which does not significantly change even after numerous defections by the other side.

The second interesting taxonomy of foreign policies is based on observations about the style of foreign policy, that is the instruments utilized and the way they are employed. A *softliner style* uses exclusively economic and informational resources and employs them exclusively as positive incentives. A *bargainer style* also uses exclusively economic and informational resources but employs them as both carrots and sticks. A *protector style* uses all kinds of available resources and employs them predominantly as positive incentives. A *hardliner style* uses all kinds of available resources and employs them as both positive and negative incentives.

Both taxonomies consist of property assignments to the unit of

---

[8] The tit-for-tat strategy in international politics is discussed among others in Axelrod and Keohane (1986) and Patchen (1987). Larson (1987), Zürn (1990), and Downs and Rocke (1990) emphasize that in the real world, for psychological reasons, a more friendly strategy is more conducive to co-operation than pure tit for tat. Those more friendly strategies, while still reciprocal basically, do not in every case require the player to sanction defective behaviour. See also Ch. 6, sect. 2.1, above.

analysis which are independent of each other. Therefore, they can be combined to allow for more complex characterizations of foreign policies. In order to keep the resulting typology manageable, its game-theoretic branch is at first reduced to two categories: *faithfulness*, consisting of friendly tit-for-tat and mainly co-operative courses of action, and *betrayal*, which includes the uncooperative and the unfriendly tit-for-tat strategies (as well as the trial-and-error course of action).

For the limited purposes of this study, the other taxonomy can also be reduced to only two categories. It seems to be most practicable to distinguish only *soft* styles (including both softliner and bargainer style categories as defined above) from *hard* styles (including both protector and hardliner styles as subtypes). The resulting 2 × 2 typology of regime-conducive foreign policy types is displayed in Table 12.2. In this table the highest number (FPT 4) indicates the most regime-conducive foreign policy type, whereas the lowest number (FPT 1) indicates a foreign policy type clearly least regime-conducive.

TABLE 12.2. Foreign Policy Types (FPT) and Regime-Conduciveness

	Hard	Soft
Betrayal	FPT 1	FPT 2
Faithfulness	FPT 3	FPT 4

Although the data generated by the questionnaire allow only for tentative conclusions, the results as regards regime-conducive foreign policy types are very encouraging. The average FPT score of all the successful attempts at regime initiation is 3.6 (coming very close to FPT 'soft faithfulness'), the average FPT score of all unsuccessful attempts at regime initiation is 2.4 (lying between 'soft betrayal' and 'hard faithfulness'), and the average FPT score of all attempts at regime prevention is 1.2 (that is to say, regime prevention is most often pursued through the FPT 'hard betrayal'). Thus, 'soft faithfulness' appears to be the foreign policy type that most often initiates regime formation successfully. Incidentally, 'soft faithfulness' also seems to be an adequate description of the US policies preceding the formation of international economic

TABLE 12.3. *Foreign Policy Types in CSCE and OECD Issue Areas*

FPT 4 Soft faithfulness	FPT 3 Hard faithfulness	FPT 2 Soft betrayal	FPT 1 Hard betrayal
Austria 1953 (Austria)	**FRG 1968** (Berlin)	FRG 1950 (Trade)	*France 1950* (Arms Control)
FRG 1952 (Saar)	USA 1945 (Austria)	*FRG 1970* (LRTAP)	*France 1952* (Saar)
FRG 1963 (Trade)	USA **1968** (Berlin)	*USSR 1975* (CSBM)	*GDR 1963* (Trade)
FRG 1980 (North Sea)	USA 1970 (Science)		GDR 1970 (Science)
FRG 1982 (LRTAP)	USA 1984 (CSBM)		GB 1970 (LRTAP)
Finland 1972 (Baltic Sea)	USA 1989 (CFE)		GB 1980 (LRTAP)
Norway 1970 (LRTAP)	USSR 1945 (Austria)		USA 1970 (LRTAP)
Norway 1982 (LRTAP)	USSR 1953 (Austria)		USA 1973 (CFE)
Sweden 1970 (LRTAP)			USA 1975 (CSBM)
Sweden 1972 (Baltic Sea)			*USSR 1973* (CFE)
Sweden 1982 (LRTAP)			*USSR 1970* (LRTAP)
USSR 1989 (CFE)			

Key
Bold type denotes a successful attempt at regime formation
Roman type denotes an attempt at regime formation without success
Italic type denotes an attempt at regime prevention

regimes after the Second World War. I conclude this section by stating with some confidence that the typology offers considerable help in analysing regime-conducive foreign policy types (see Table 12.3).

3.3. *Explaining Regime-Conducive Foreign Policies*

So far, the thrust of this chapter has been the identification of 'regime-conducive foreign policy types' as one possibility for introducing a second image perspective into regime analysis. This leads to the following finding:

F I   A foreign policy is most regime-conducive if a state actor tries to correct dissatisfying outcomes in an issue area by utilizing mainly economic and informational resources (soft style) *and* by displaying an orientation towards reciprocity accompanied by the readiness to make one-sided concessions intermittently or even over a longer period of time (strategy of faithfulness).

'Soft faithfulness' appears to be the foreign policy type most conducive to regime formation, whereby 'faithfulness', in the cases used for this study, was even a necessary condition. Successful regime initiation (bold type in Table 12.3) was always preceded by a regime initiator's foreign policy coming under either the soft-faithfulness type (ten cases) or the hard-faithfulness type (five cases). In contrast, both unsuccessful attempts at regime initiation (roman type in Table 12.3) and especially attempts at regime prevention (italic type in Table 12.3) were not accompanied by these kinds of foreign policy.

Considering the apparently very high regime-conduciveness of foreign policies which can be characterized as soft faithfulness, it is possible to ask for the domestic conditions under which such a type of policy prevails. Of course, answering this question means nothing other than spelling out the domestic sources of regime formation. For this purpose, we turn now to positional and non-positional characteristics of state actors in the second image of regime analysis.

Positional Actor Characteristics and Foreign Policy

Positional characteristics of a state actor are not exactly what we usually mean by domestic sources of foreign policy. They are, however, clearly actor characteristics and should thus be seen as part of the second image of regime analysis (see n. 2 above). Moreover, positional characteristics may provide a starting-point for solving the puzzle of why the powerful United States failed so often in her attempts to initiate East–West regimes (five cases) and was successful in only three cases, whereas, for instance, the Federal Republic of Germany was not only almost as active but also much more successful than the United States (see Table 12.1). What does this mean?

First of all, it should be pointed out that it is impossible to draw any inferences from the observation that the Federal Republic most often initiated regime formation successfully in the cases under investigation. This observed 'salience' of the Federal Republic in attempts at regime initiation is an artefact resulting from the selection of cases, leading to a clearly disproportional amount of issue areas concerning questions relevant to Germany.[9] Rather, the puzzle concerns the ratio of successful to unsuccessful attempts of regime initiation: here, the Federal Republic clearly has a better record than the United States. It might be suspected that a selection bias, the disproportionately high number of East–West issue areas in question, causes this finding. Yet I see no convincing reason why this emphasis on East–West relations should systematically distort the results in the observed direction. And even if it were possible to demonstrate a systematic distortion as a result of the East–West focus, the findings would still be valid for this context.[10]

Why then has the United States a lower ratio of successful to unsuccessful attempts at regime initiation in the cases in question? To begin with, this observation suggests that power does not account for everything, to say the least. In fact, the US case is no exception. Using the simple power index employed in the project on East–West regimes,[11] it can be stated that small powers

---

[9] Moreover, inferences on the basis of a research design without variation on the side of the outcome to be explained, that is the so-called method of agreement, are not valid anyway (King, Verba, and Keohane 1991: 122–5).

[10] For a discussion of context-specific hypotheses see Ch. 11, sect. 3.2, above.

[11] See Ch. 11, n. 7, above.

displayed a regime-conducive foreign policy type much more often than great powers. Whereas small powers such as Sweden, Norway, Finland, and Austria in cases like Baltic Sea, LRTAP, and international status of Austria employed a foreign policy of the soft-faithfulness type when they played a prominent role in the issue area, great powers such as the USSR, USA, France, and Great Britain more often either attempted regime prevention or were not able to display a soft-faithfulness policy even when they wanted a regime to emerge. Apparently, the theory of hegemonic stability is turned upside-down. Why is this so?

To be sure, this result might be an artefact due to the unsophisticated selection of cases. It is conceivable that the sample neglects cases of unsuccessful attempts at regime initiation by less powerful states. Yet again, I see no systematic selection bias, since case studies in the project analysed successful and unsuccessful attempts at regime initiation in the same issue area over time and issue areas in which an international regime finally emerged as well as issue areas where a regime never came into existence. However, there is still the problem of 'non-decisions': less powerful states might forgo an attempt at regime inititation when they see no chance of success. While 'non-decisions' quite often cause selection problems which are difficult to control and thus not special to this case, it has to be repeated at this point that this chapter aims at reporting an exploratory data analysis and not a well-designed test of hypotheses.[12]

Putting aside this caveat, a closer look at power characteristics reveals that Norway's and Sweden's attempts in the early 1970s at initiating the formation of a regime regulating air pollution in Europe were the only two cases in which a soft-faithfulness type of foreign policy did not lead to regime formation. Of course, the inferior power of these two state actors compared to others in the issue area was one important reason for the failure (Schwarzer 1990*a*). That is to say, although power superiority does not necessarily lead to regime-conducive foreign policies, it can enhance the prospects of success of those policies when they are adopted.

[12] In-depth studies about interests and policies of less powerful states in the CSCE region appear to be one way of checking the problem of non-decisions. One has to examine whether or not less powerful states more often go for internal adaptation than powerful states when an issue area outcome is perceived as having changed for the worse (see sect. 2.2 above for an explication of 'internal adaptation').

In addition, no negative correlation between regime-conducive foreign policies and high power position can be observed if the power of the state actor is assessed only in terms of its labour productivity as the major indicator of economic power. Moreover, state actors with an economy displaying a high dependence on foreign trade (measured in per cent of exports of GNP) have a very high positive association with regime-conducive foreign policies. Therefore, it appears that a state having large amounts of 'traditional' power resources at its disposal more often relies on power politics and on unilateralism. In contrast, state actors with superior economic capabilities more often choose regime-conducive foreign policies. The finding can be stated as follows:

F II.1   A state actor with a competitive economy (in terms of labour productivity) and a high dependence on foreign trade (in terms of the share of exports in the GNP) which does not have abundant traditional power resources such as a strong military or a large population is most likely to pursue foreign policies of the regime-conducive type.

For this reason, the record of the United States, a state (for a long time) with an extremely competitive economy as well as a moderate dependence on foreign trade, but with a large internal market as well as enormous military power resources, is rather mixed. The record of power states with less competitive economies, such as the USSR, and also to some extent Great Britain and France after 1945, is clearly negative with respect to regime-conducive foreign policies, whereas the Scandinavian countries, Austria, and the Federal Republic of Germany display, on the average, more regime-conducive foreign policies. Yet these states are examples of what Richard Rosecrance (1986) calls 'trading states'. I conclude by formulating the following hypothesis regarding the relationship between actor properties and regime formation which can be tested in further studies: *The more trading states act in an issue area, the more likely is regime formation.*[13]

[13] According to Ludwig Dehio (1948), who has already introduced the distinction between trading and power states, modern world history has always been characterized by a confrontation between (at that time) a trading state such as, successively, Venice, the Netherlands, and Great Britain and (at that time) a power state (Spain, France, Germany). The implication of my argument is that trading states have always displayed more regime-conducive foreign policies than power states.

Regarding positional actor characteristics another finding deserves further consideration:

F II.2   State actors with a high institutional enmeshment in issue areas related to the one under consideration[14] significantly more often display regime-conducive foreign policies than institutionally unconstrained actors.

This finding supports the literature emphasizing the effects of international institutions on state behaviour. Thus, the corresponding hypothesis can be stated as follows: *The more states in the issue area in question already have a high number of institutional commitments, the more likely is regime formation.*

Put together, the findings reported so far clearly support the institutionalist theory of international politics against the neo-realist theory. States with a high dependence on international transactions are strongly enmeshed in international institutions and heavily use these institutions to initiate new regimes for regulating international transactions. Those states often display regime-conducive foreign policies and thus are relatively successful in their attempts at initiating regime formation. Although great powers might have a veto against regime formation, they neither initiate most processes of regime formation nor are they able to prevail automatically when they would like to see a regime emerge, because they often fail to behave in a way which is conducive to regime formation. This observation would thus seem to support Senator Fulbright's (1966) claim that power superiority leads to an arrogant and impertinent style of foreign policy which ends up being counterproductive.

Stable Non-Positional Characteristics and Foreign Policy

There are numerous possibilities for categorizing non-positional actor characteristics (East, Salmore, and Hermann 1978, Rosenau

---

[14] It was asked in the questionnaire to decide whether the institutional enmeshment of the state actor was high, low, or medium. A high enmeshment means that the state actor is part of a regime in a neighbouring issue area with the same actors *and* is part of a regime in a similar issue area with other actors. For example, the institutional enmeshment of the FRG in the issue area 'North Sea' is high, if Germany is part of a regime dealing with river pollution in Northern Europe and of the Baltic Sea regime. The institutional entanglement is assessed as medium if only one of these conditions holds, and as low if none of these condition holds.

1966). For the purpose of this chapter it suffices to distinguish between stable non-positional characteristics, which change with respect to one and the same state actor only slowly, and unstable non-positional characteristics, which change more often and more easily.

According to the more recent discussion in the field (Müller and Risse-Kappen 1990), the *internal strength* of the state, that is, the ability of central decision-makers to resist the desires, and to change the behaviour, of interest groups within the society is the most important stable non-positional characteristic of a state (Katzenstein 1978, Krasner 1978). There are, on the one hand, 'weak states' such as the United States or Great Britain with fragmented policy networks most often accompanied by a decentralized organization of societal interests. On the other hand, there are 'strong states' such as Japan and France with tightly integrated policy networks and mostly with more centralized, but state-influenced, forms of societal organization. While this field of research proved fruitful for explaining foreign economic policy, it has not led so far to commonly agreed-upon hypotheses about the effects of the internal strength of the state on international co-operation. Karns and Mingst (1991: 13) argue that more centralized decision-making—that is, in their case, parliamentary systems with strong political parties—is conducive to international co-operation. Similarly, Artis and Ostry (1986) contend that divisions within a government are often thought to hamper international co-operation. In contrast, Putnam and Henning (1989: 104–14) argue that the dispersion of national decision-making is a prerequisite for international co-operation, since it allows for transgovernmental coalitions which would otherwise be impossible.

In the light of the case studies in the project on East–West regimes a medium degree of state strength with a relatively high degree of centralization in the organization of societal interests is most likely to lead to regime-conducive foreign policies. This characteristic holds for states such as Austria, the Federal Republic of Germany, and Sweden. While strong states such as France (after 1958) and the USSR often failed to employ a regime-conducive foreign policy, the same is true for weak states such as the USA and France before 1958.[15] Strong states do not display

---

[15] The categorization of the socialist states as 'strong' might be called into question. However, the exclusion of the socialist states with respect to this variable

the regime-conducive foreign policy type because they lack the oppositional domestic factions which would have an interest in, and would be able to press for, a shift of foreign policy when the international conditions were favourable. For instance, the USSR did not respond to changes in the international environment in order to achieve mutual reductions in conventional forces in the early 1970s. In contrast, weak states seem to fail because they are unable to hold a course of action which is not ambiguous and clearly regime-conducive. France's behaviour during the negotiations about arms control in Western Europe during the 1950s is a case in point.

Another stable characteristic of state actors somewhat related to the issue of internal strength and even more strongly related to regime-conducive foreign policy is the extent of *social democratic influence* within a state. If the data of Manfred Schmidt (1982: 46) are utilized and a social democratic electorate of under 33.3 per cent is classified as small, of 33.3 to 50 per cent as medium, and of over 50 per cent as high, a very strong correlation shows: the higher the social democratic electorate in a state, the more likely it is that a regime-conducive foreign policy will be chosen.

The variable 'social democratic electorate' represents a set of related characteristics of which the share of public revenues in the GNP (welfare state) is the most important. This indicates that there is also a relationship between the internal strength of the state and the historical course of modernization of the society and economy (B. Moore 1966, Katzenstein 1984, 1985). Thus, it can be concluded that a cluster of closely connected non-positional properties consisting of three components accounts for regime-conducive foreign policies:

F II.3 A domestic structure with (i) a relatively high share of public revenues, (ii) a medium degree of state strength and a comparatively strong degree of centralization in the

does not decisively change the results. For an application of the concept 'internal strength of state' to socialist states see Comisso (1986). France before 1958 (the Fourth Republic) is categorized as weak, since permanently changing governments and their inability to carry out their own policies over opposition in Parliament were a permanent characteristic in this period. This feature of politics in the Fourth Republic explains to a large extent the failure of the French Government to assure 'satisfying' outcomes in the issue areas arms control in Western Europe and status of the Saar.

organization of societal interests, and (iii) a strong social
democratic electorate is most suitable to the regime-
conducive foreign policy type.[16]

Political systems displaying this cluster of domestic properties are
usually called 'corporatist'. In order to pursue a policy of allevi-
ating the domestic consequences of structural economic changes,
corporatist arrangements are increasingly dependent upon international norms and rules regulating competition on the world
market. Moreover, corporatism is a co-operative form of domestic
conflict management that might serve as a model of international
arrangements.[17] Therefore, the following hypothesis can be
formulated: *The more states in the issue area in question have a
corporatist domestic structure, the more likely is regime formation.*

Unstable Non-Positional Characteristics and Foreign Policy

So far my analysis of regime-conducive foreign policies has focused
on stable non-positional characteristics referring to domestic structure in the usual sense. Now I would like to focus on some
variables which change frequently over time within one state.
Whereas relationships between stable non-positional characteristics
and regime-conducive foreign policies tell us what kind of states
are most likely to choose a regime-conducive foreign policy, the
use of unstable non-positional characteristics aims at identifying
the conditions under which, and the point in time at which,
regime-conducive foreign policies are chosen. Whereas the analysis
of stable dispositions is an exercise in 'comparative statics', the
analysis of unstable dispositions focuses on 'change' in policies. I
am looking for domestic changes which have preceded the shift of
policy and, hence, can possibly account for it.

A new government in office is the most obvious example of how
a change in domestic politics may lead to a change of policy. In a
different context, Joe Hagan (1989) has done extensive research

---

[16] Of course, the variables underlying findings F II.1, F II.2, and F II.3 correlate
to a certain degree with each other. Thus, some of the correlations between the
independent and the dependent variable might be due to the correlations among
the independent variables. Which one of these independent variables is most
important can be decided, therefore, only if more sophisticated research designs
are employed (see sect. 4 below).

[17] This idea is further developed in Ch. 16, sect. 2.2, below.

on 'domestic political regime changes and foreign policy restructuring'. His suggestion to distinguish four types of *change in the
governing coalition* can be easily utilized for the purpose of this
study:

— type 1 indicates a change in the leadership body in terms of
its component factions or in terms of the rise or fall of a
single predominant leader;
— type 2 indicates a fundamental restructuring of a coalition
cabinet with entry or departure of at least one major
factional or party actor while other members continue in
office;
— type 3 indicates a replacement of the entire ruling party or
coalition by another party or coalition from within the
established political system;
— type 4 indicates a revolutionary transition in which a political
group is replaced by an 'anti-system' group that fundamentally
restructures the political system. (Hagan 1989: 144 f.)

In the questionnaire it was asked whether the states attempting to
initiate or prevent regime formation have experienced a change in
the governing coalition within the last five years and, if so, of
which type it was. In the light of our cases it seems that changes
of types 1 and 2 most often lead to the implementation of the
regime-conducive foreign policy type. In contrast, the absence of
any changes in the governing coalition within the last five years
before the attempt seems to be an obstacle to regime-conducive
foreign policies and, although Gorbachev appears to demonstrate
the opposite, changes of type 3 seem to make no systematic
difference.

However, the last part of this finding has to be considered very
cautiously. Changes in the governing coalition of type 3 have
occurred very rarely: besides the Gorbachev change, which of
course had a positive impact, changes of the governing coalition
in the Fourth Republic, which clearly had a negative impact, have
to be mentioned. The most striking feature of changes in the
governing coalition of the Fourth Republic, however, was their
frequency, so that no policy could be established with reliability.
I conclude tentatively that a change in the governing coalitions
(including type 3) precedes with some likelihood regime-conducive
foreign policies, whereas permanent changes and the absence of

any stability of the governing coalition is an obstacle to a regime-conducive foreign policy. In the absence of stability the policy loses predictability and the decision-makers lose the ability to make meaningful concessions that involve domestic costs. Such concessions are, however, part of the regime-conducive foreign policy type:

F II.4   A change in the governing coalition is more often followed by a change towards a more regime-conducive foreign policy than by a change towards a foreign policy type preventing regime formation.

Although this proposition is based on less significant correlations than the others reported so far, it indicates again support for the institutionalist interpretation of international politics. Considering the ubiquity of changes in governing coalitions, a general trend towards institutionalization of international politics would be the consequence. One important reason for this trend might be that regimes, once they are established, stabilize themselves by providing information as well as common expectations and by reducing transaction costs (Keohane 1984: 85–109), by strengthening those domestic groups that benefit from the international institutions (Rogowski 1989: 4–16), and by harmonizing the interest profiles of the participating actors (Zürn 1992: 133–5). The respective hypothesis can be stated as follows: *The more reformist changes that have taken place, short of revolutions, in the governing coalitions in the issue area in question, the more likely is the spread of international regimes (as a result of new regimes being formed and extant regimes being stabilized).*

Finally, even after changes in the governing coalition have taken place, sources of the continuity of a policy, whether regime-conducive or not, are abundant. Kjell Goldmann (1988: 26–69) put forward an entire inventory of so-called foreign-policy stabilizers. Of special interest are the effects of *bureaucratic routinization* of foreign policies. Accordingly, a foreign policy is highly routinized if (i) public commitments in its favour were given, (ii) it has been implemented for more than five years, and (iii) material resources were used to implement it.[18] Confronting the

---

[18] A policy was classified as very highly routinized when all three conditions were met, as highly routinized when two conditions were met, etc.

underlying hypothesis with the data, it can be shown that increased routinization of the established policy does indeed hamper change towards more regime-conducive foreign policy types.

In addition, analysing environmental policy, Volker von Prittwitz (1990) argues that the *technological and administrative capacity* to tackle pollution is a much better predictor for the rise of new policies than the objective ecological requirement to act. I found some support for this thesis in the sense that regime-conducive foreign policies, especially in environmental issue areas, occur more often when a new capacity for handling the problem internationally has been developed within the nation in question. Putting these two results together, the following final finding can be reported:

F II.5 A change towards a regime-conducive foreign policy type is likely (i) if the pre-established policy is not highly routinized (defined by commitments, age, used resources) and (ii) if new technological and institutional capacities to tackle the problem on the international level have become available.

This last cluster of findings establishes the fifth hypothesis about the domestic sources of regime formation: *The higher the (positive) ratio of domestic groups in the issue area in question likely to benefit from policy change to the domestic groups benefiting from the routinized status quo, the more likely it is that regime formation will take place.*

Table 12.4 recapitulates the hypotheses put forth in this section.

4. CONCLUSION

In section 2 of this chapter I argued that when attempting to explain regime formation in second image terms it is necessary to utilize an intermediary variable in order to link the subsystemic causes with the systemic outcome. For this purpose I suggested a model which contains 'foreign policy types' as such an intermediary variable.

In section 3, I reported some findings regarding the relationships indicated in this model which resulted from an exploratory data

TABLE 12.4. *Domestic Sources of Regime Formation*

1. The more trading states act in an issue area, the more likely is regime formation.

2. The more states in the issue area in question already have a high number of institutional commitments, the more likely is regime formation.

3. The more states in the issue area in question have a corporatist domestic structure, the more likely is regime formation.

4. The more reformist changes that have taken place, short of revolutions, in the governing coalitions in the issue area in question, the more likely is the spread of international regimes.

5. The higher the (positive) ratio of domestic groups in the issue area in question likely to benefit from policy change to the domestic groups benefiting from the routinized status quo, the more likely it is that regime formation will take place.

analysis on the basis of the case studies of the Tübingen project. The findings are as follows. First, a foreign policy type labelled as soft faithfulness appears to be regime-conducive and, hence, can bridge the gap between actor characteristics and regime formation. Second, the conditions under which such a regime-conducive foreign policy type can prevail depend upon (i) the competitiveness of the national economy and its degree of dependence on foreign trade, (ii) the degree of the state's enmeshment in international institutions, (iii) the existence of a corporatist domestic structure, (iv) a prior change in domestic power constellation, and (v) the the ratio of domestic groups benefiting from policy change to the domestic groups benefiting from the routinized status quo.

These findings are, mainly because of conceivable selection biases, by no means to be confused with results of a strict test of hypotheses. Yet they suggest hypotheses about the domestic sources of regime formation in need of stringent testing in subsequent studies (see Table 12.4). A strict test of these hypotheses might consist of a comparison of two carefully selected states which, despite being in a similar situation as regards interest and power constellation, choose different foreign policies in order to react to a dissatisfying outcome in an issue area. However, the findings of this study allow for the conclusion that the focus on the concept 'regime-conducive foreign policy type' and the subsequent study of the conditions under which policies of this type are implemented is by no means unwarranted, and deserves more consideration in regime analysis.

In addition, it might be worth looking for implications of the generated hypotheses which are testable independently of the concepts utilized in this chapter. I would like to mention two of them. First, if, for instance, states with few traditional power resources and with a high export dependence are more strongly disposed towards pursuing regime-conducive foreign policies and are, therefore, successful in initiating international institutions, then those states cannot be expected, as the 'realist theory of state action' (Mastanduno, Lake, and Ikenberry 1989) suggests, to respond to a dissatisfaction with the outcome in an issue area by internal adaptation more often than more powerful states. Rather, it should be expected that states with few traditional power resources and with an export orientation will often respond by utilizing international institutions. Thus, they can be expected to be on the top with respect to membership in international organizations. Furthermore, those states should be most often among the founders of international organizations.

Another implication that can be tested independently of the concepts used in this study concerns the external behaviour of states with corporatist domestic structures. According to my findings, these states more often display regime-conducive foreign policies than others. Transferring this finding to a comparison of regions, the 'regime density' in Scandinavia ought to be higher than in Mediterannean Europe, and the interactions between the highly developed neighbouring states Germany and the Netherlands should be more institutionalized than those between France and Spain. Moreover, the internationalization and liberalization in foreign investments and capital movements have created increased pressure for corporatist arrangements in the last decade (Scharpf 1987). The subsequent election of conservative governments in many developed countries has been accompanied by a weakening of corporatist structures. The correlations found in this study, which is based on many cases of regime formation from the late 1960s to the early 1980s, can therefore be expected to change when more recent cases of regime initiation and prevention are considered.

PART IV

Regime Consequences

13

Constructing Historical Counterfactuals to Assess the Consequences of International Regimes

The Global Debt Regime and the Course of the Debt Crisis of the 1980s

THOMAS J. BIERSTEKER

1. INTRODUCTION

Do regimes matter? Does the presence of an international regime in a particular issue area have significant effects independent of other causal explanations? How can we be sure it is regimes (and not something else) that produce these outcomes? Although international regimes have been identified in most issue areas, described in detail, and explained with great frequency in the theoretical literature in international relations for the last fifteen years, surprisingly little attention has been devoted to an examination of their consequences.

In the early 1980s, Stephen Krasner (1983*a*: 6) suggested that 'the independent effect of regimes is a central analytical issue'. However, the focus of the literature has remained on the issue of how and why regimes form, the ways they are maintained, and whether or not they are in decay. Only a handful of scholars of regimes (in particular, Charles Lipson and Peter Haas) have grappled directly with the independent effects of regimes, a point

This chapter was originally prepared as a paper for a conference on 'The Study of Regimes in International Relations—State of the Art and Perspectives', Tübingen, Germany, 14–18 July 1991. I am grateful to the conference organizers and participants for their comments on an earlier version of this chapter. I am especially appreciative of the insightful and constructive comments of Volker Rittberger, who initially challenged me to write on this topic.

underscored by Haggard and Simmons (1987: 492) in their review of the regimes literature.

Haggard and Simmons (1987: 513, 514) suggested both indirect and direct ways in which regimes might affect state behaviour. First, the presence of regimes can alter the environment within which states interact, increasing the incentives for their co-operation by lowering the transaction costs associated with bilateral contracting. Alternatively, regimes can alter the interests or preferences of key actors more directly, going as far as changing basic definitions of reality in some instances.[1]

Peter Haas (1989: 377, 380) has considered the direct effects of regimes with his focus on the ways in which regimes 'may serve as important vehicles for international learning that produce convergent state policies'. From his analysis of the Mediterranean Action Plan, Haas concluded that 'regimes may be transformative, leading to the empowerment of new groups of actors who can change state interests and practices'. If members of an epistemic community acquire and sustain control over a particular policy domain in a country, they may become an important constituency for a strengthening of the regime, as well as domestic constituents for compliance with it. Haas (1989: 401) also argues that members of this community are most likely to be consulted in a crisis in the issue area, have a decisive influence on the construction of national policies in the area, and contribute to a general policy convergence across different countries. This, in turn, may lead countries to negotiate more constructively internationally. Haas implicitly employs a counterfactual argument when he suggests that regimes can empower epistemic communities: that is, if there had been *no* regime, the communities might not have been so empowered.

Charles Lipson considered both the indirect and direct effects of regimes in his analysis of the global trade regime. He concluded that the trade regime has served as a catalyst for major US post-war trade legislation, created incentives for policy harmonization (both laws and practices) among trading countries, and expanded trade more generally (Lipson 1983: 262–7). To support his contention that the trade regime had a causal effect on the expansion of trade, Lipson (1983: 271) employs an explicit counterfactual argument:

---

[1] For further potential effects of international regimes see Ch. 2, sect. 4, above.

The connection between the Tokyo Round and trade volumes may seem weak, but it appears much stronger if we consider the most pertinent counterfactual: the regime's collapse . . . the Tokyo Round's success was an essential bulwark against a proliferation of new trade barriers. Those new barriers would probably have been quantitative and would have immediately limited trade.

Lipson's assessment of the significance of the trade-expanding effects of the international trade regime depends on assumptions he must make about the alternative trading system that would have emerged in the absence of the GATT system. In doing so, he has constructed a historical counterfactual alternatives argument. Constructing historical counterfactuals can be fraught with great difficulty and controversy, an area routinely avoided by the ordinarily cautious social scientist. However, as will be argued below, the evaluation of whether particular regimes matter to any significant degree virtually *always* requires counterfactual analysis of some kind, i.e. some explicit consideration of what would have happened if the regime had not existed.

Beginning with the assumption that it is better to proceed consciously and clearly with the analysis of historical counterfactuals than to make causal assertions based largely on implicit assumptions, faith, and/or conviction, this chapter will continue by considering the centrality of counterfactual analysis for the adjudication of competing causal claims in historical and social science research (sect. 2). Some general suggestions for the use of historical counterfactuals will be considered (sect. 3), and finally those suggestions will be applied to a preliminary evaluation of the consequences of the global debt regime that emerged during the 1980s (sect. 4).

2. THE CENTRALITY OF COUNTERFACTUAL ANALYSIS IN MAKING CAUSAL CLAIMS

Does A cause B? Does the presence of an international regime affect the course of a particular event or issue? Did the presence of the global debt regime affect the course of the debt crisis of the 1980s? To answer any of these particular questions about causation requires some form of counterfactual argument. Indeed, to make virtually any causal claim requires some form of counter-factual analysis:

> To distinguish causation from correlation we may point out that the former warrants the statement that if the cause had not occurred, then the effect would not have occurred, whereas no such counterfactual is implied by the latter. (Elster 1978: 175)

For example, what would have happened had there been no routine procedure for the adjudication of the competing claims of private commercial banks, sovereign governments, and inter-national financial institutions for developing country debt in the 1980s? If the absence of the global debt regime would have had no appreciable effect on the course of the debt crisis, then we can say with confidence that the regime made no difference. However, to make this claim (or its opposite) about the independent effects of regimes requires an assessment of counterfactual alternatives to the debt regime. Counterfactuals are often implicit in the analysis of particular events. Indeed, any time we begin to assert that something 'would' (or 'might') likely have had some effect, we are engaging in counterfactual analysis. As James Fearon (1991: 195) has recently reminded us, 'counterfactuals cannot be avoided in non-experimental hypothesis testing'.

In the most general sense, counterfactual analysis involves the creation of a case or situation for comparison where a presumed causal agent is removed, while at the same time holding every other relevant factor constant. Weber (1949*b*: 173) described the counterfactual as involving 'first the production of—let us say it calmly—"imaginative constructs" by the disregarding of one or more of those elements of "reality" which are actually present, and by the mental construction of a course of events which is altered through modification in one or more "conditions"'. Counterfactual arguments are common in the causal analysis of historical events (see sect. 2.1), the evaluation of different competing theoretical approaches (sect. 2.2), studies with a small sample (where N=1 or N is small) (sect. 2.3), and even in large-N statistical studies (sect. 2.4).

2.1. Historical Analysis

Historians concerned with the explanation of a particular historical event (where degrees of freedom are absent) frequently find themselves employing some form of counterfactual analysis. They often use counterfactuals implicitly in their effort to sort out competing arguments about the relative importance of different causes. As Weber (1949*b*: 180) suggests,

the assessment of the causal significance of an historical fact will begin with the posing of the following question: in the event of the exclusion of that fact from the complex of the factors which are taken into account as co-determinants, or in the event of its modification in a certain direction, could the course of events, in accordance with general empirical rules, have taken a direction in any way different in any features which would be *decisive* for our interest?

This mode of historical analysis has relevance for the evaluation of some of the effects of regimes. For example, when representatives of the three largest debtor countries (Brazil, Mexico, and Argentina) met to consider forming a cartel to co-ordinate their strategies in negotiations with their creditors in Cartagena in 1987, did the global debt regime of the 1980s have a causally significant effect on their deliberations? We know the outcome (the historical event), namely that the meeting did not produce an agreement to co-ordinate policy. To determine whether the debt regime influenced this particular outcome, we would have to be able to imagine a world without it.

In his essay on 'Objective Possibility and Adequate Causation in Historical Explanation' Max Weber (1949*b*: 185 f.) asserted that 'in order to penetrate to the real causal interrelationships, we construct unreal ones'. Weber argued that causal analysis proceeds logically, i.e. by isolation, generalization, and the construction of judgements of possibility, where judgements of possibility involve 'propositions regarding what "would" happen in the event of the exclusion or modification of certain conditions'.

In virtually any investigation of the relative significance of different causal explanations of an important historical event, scholars find themselves involved in the construction of arguments about the relative plausibility of different counterfactual statements. It is the only way they can determine the historical significance of different possible explanations. As Jon Elster (1978: 176) suggests, 'some historians have come to recognize, therefore, that they have been talking counterfactually all the time without recognizing it'.

2.2. Contending Theoretical Perspectives

Counterfactual analysis is also involved whenever one tries to evaluate a body of theoretical propositions associated with a particular research tradition, contrasting it with some alternative (or contending) theoretical perspective (Elster 1978). There are a great many illustrations of this in economics, economic history, and policy analysis. Consider, for example, the analysis of the consequences of foreign investment in developing countries. Many of the controversies about the consequences of foreign direct investment in developing countries (whether it facilitates an improvement in a country's balance-of-payments position, increases employment, or adversely influences consumption patterns) are based on implicit assumptions about the counterfactual alternatives to foreign investment (Biersteker 1981: 67 f.). Critics of foreign investment historically assumed that in the absence of foreign investment, 'locally owned firms could produce either the same quantity and quality of product or some alternative comparable product at roughly the same cost as multinational corporations' (Biersteker 1981: 93). Neo-classical economists, by contrast, tended to assume that local entrepreneurs were largely unable to undertake the productive activities of multinational corporations, and therefore adjusted their estimates of likely output accordingly.

Similar kinds of differences in counterfactual assumptions about alternatives pervade the analysis of international economic processes (the effects of foreign assistance, the benefits of international trade, the consequences of sovereign country borrowing, etc.). They are also central to the now classic economic history debates about the effects of railroads on nineteenth-century American economic development (Fogel 1964) and the economic consequences of slavery (Fogel and Engerman 1974). More recently, counterfactual alternatives arguments have figured prominently in the debate about the effects of structural adjustment policies in developing countries (Khan and Knight 1985, M. Goldstein 1986).

2.3. Small-Sample Studies

The need to employ some form of counterfactual analysis extends well beyond the historian or analyst of contending theoretical perspectives, however. A great many issues of central concern to political scientists and scholars of international relations involve explanation of a single event or a small number of events. This is especially true of international regimes. Although the regime idea has been criticized as being a slippery, imprecise concept (Strange 1983), we usually find ourselves talking about only one particular regime at a time (i.e. the post-war trade regime or the Bretton Woods monetary regime, etc.). Either the regime exists and has certain effects, or it does not. It is difficult to talk about a large sample of global trade or monetary regimes, unless we extend our analyses far back into history. This confronts the analyst of international regimes with the methodological problem of trying to make generalizations and causal assertions with only limited, zero, or possibly negative degrees of freedom.[2] As Fearon (1991: 172) suggests,

legitimate causal imputations cannot be made on the basis of negative degrees of freedom, so the analyst wishing to assess the relative weights of different causes has no choice but to add or create more cases: either a counterfactual case (or cases) that never actually existed or actual cases.

Adding more actual cases can be a difficult, and rather dubious, undertaking in the case of international regimes. Specific issues around which regimes might form in a general area might vary considerably, rendering their basic compatibility suspect. For example, ozone depletion and global warming are both environmental issues around which international regimes can be said to have formed recently. However, the actors, principles, and norms around which actor expectations converge vary considerably between them. The same can be said for service sector regimes in maritime shipping and international aviation. In the case of some regimes (say international shipping) one can go back in history to expand the sample of international shipping regimes (contrasting eighteenth-, nineteenth-, and twentieth-century regimes). However, the further back in time one goes to search for roughly comparable regimes, the more other basic factors change (i.e. principal actors and international norms). It is incumbent upon advocates of the essential comparability of regimes in a given

---

[2] Degrees of freedom equal the number of cases (usually one) minus the number of explanatory variables (again one, the regime) minus one.

issue area (e.g. environmental regimes) to demonstrate, rather than assume, their approximate equivalency.

Because of the small number of cases routinely involved in the analysis of international regimes (N=1) and the difficulty of adding more cases (especially when the comparability of different regimes becomes a limiting factor), it is difficult for the analyst of their effects to avoid making counterfactual arguments in some form. The same problem confronts scholars trying to explain the effects of a global hegemon, especially when there is arguably only one each century. When sample size is small, as it ordinarily is in the case of international regimes, either interrupted time series models or simulations can be used to evaluate causal assertions.

With interrupted time series models, the performance of some critical variable before and after the introduction of an assumed causal agent (the international regime) can be compared. With simulations, a formal model can be adjusted to test the effects of causal agents (international regimes) added or removed from different runs of the simulation. However, each of these approaches has certain deficiencies and/or biases of its own.

The applied literature on the effects of IMF stabilization programmes on a single country (where N=1) offers some instructive insights about the limitations of this methodological strategy. *Interrupted time series models* which compare performance before and after Fund intervention have been criticized for having a systematic bias against the Fund, since it is unrealistic to expect that the patterns observed prior to Fund intervention (the counterfactual alternative) could have been sustained for any period of time as a base point for comparison (Guitian 1981). Critics of interrupted time series approaches contend that it is important to take differences in pre-programme conditions into account, especially those that might matter for subsequent performance (M. Goldstein 1986: 45). Interrupted time series analysis routinely confronts questions about whether the programmes or policy reforms are initiated in the middle of some longer-term trend which may distort the results (Campbell 1973). They also have difficulty controlling for omitted variables. Because of these concerns about the potential for systematic bias from interrupted time series comparisons alone, most recent World Bank and IMF studies have gone beyond single case studies and employed some form of cross-country comparative analysis of programme performance (i.e. large-sample studies, see sect. 2.4).

Simulation models of optimal (or probable) alternative outcomes of IMF stabilization programmes are closely related to the construction of historical counterfactuals. However, while the formal and abstract character of simulations makes them generally more precise theoretically, the assumptions built into the models can easily be manipulated to produce outcomes either highly favourable (or highly critical) of the international financial institutions. Out of necessity, simulations tend to be highly aggregated, exceedingly abstract, and overly simple in structure (Khan and Knight 1985: 26; M. Goldstein 1986: 10 f.). Although they are amenable to counterfactual manipulation, their formal design is often driven by data availability.

While interrupted time series models and simulations facilitate analysis of the causal effects of small-sample phenomena such as international regimes, they are also subject to a variety of other methodological problems. For example, it is always difficult to control for broad changes in the global economic environment which may coincide with the introduction of an international regime. Moreover, in most instances, the consequences of a regime may take a long time before they can be clearly observed. Studies which focus exclusively on short-term effects may miss the beneficial medium- and long-term effects of international regimes. Finally, there are always problems isolating the effects of specific elements of a regime from the effects of the entire regime. Indeed, the interaction of different regime elements may produce different outcomes in different national contexts.

2.4. Large-Sample Studies

Behaviourally oriented scholars of international relations have tried to avoid some of the problems associated with small-sample, comparative case studies by engaging in large-N statistical studies using non-experimental data. However, in the effort to expand sample size, there is always the danger that the additional cases are not actually comparable, i.e. that they are not appropriately identical, an issue already considered in some detail above. Moreover, as Fearon has recently suggested, although they can avoid constructing historical counterfactuals, a counterfactual claim is nevertheless present even in large-sample, statistical studies.

The assumption of the statistical independence of different independent variables is not entirely unproblematic and entails implicit counterfactual assumptions about the lack of correlation between the explanatory variables and the error term (the *ceteris paribus* assumption). In large-N studies, support for one's hypothesis 'comes principally in the form of a frequency or magnitude of association across cases' (Fearon 1991: 175). Estimates of the effects of proposed causes will be biased unless the independent variables are uncorrelated with the contents of the error term (which contains the effects of unspecified, unmeasured causes). Therefore, one has to make the assumption that the explanatory variables and the error terms are uncorrelated. This is, in effect, a counterfactual proposition, namely that if you had altered the value of any variable, the contents of the error term would not vary systematically (Fearon 1991: 175).

The applied literature on the effects of IMF stabilization programmes once again offers some insights into the difficulty of making causal assertions with larger samples. In the case of cross-sectional comparison (with large-N samples), the performance of actors affected by (and actors excluded from the effects of) the assumed causal agent are compared (i.e. the performance of programme and non-programme countries is contrasted). However, countries with IMF programmes may differ systematically from those without them, rendering the definition of the control group generally suspect (Khan and Knight 1985: 18 f.). This may once again produce studies biased against the international financial institutions, since countries with Fund programmes are also likely to be those countries with the greatest economic difficulties. There is also a danger that the interdependence between programme countries and the control group of non-programme countries may cloud the comparison, especially if the non-programme countries begin to pursue some of the same policies in the absence of Fund advice (M. Goldstein 1986: 6 f.).

Thus, reliance on some form of counterfactual analysis is common in most historical and social science research (even large-sample studies). When it comes to an evaluation of the causal consequences of a phenomenon such as an international regime (where the number of reasonably comparable entities is small or zero) it is often impossible to avoid the construction of historical counterfactuals, either implicitly or explicitly. Indeed, there are some important issues that simply cannot be evaluated without this particular form of counterfactual analysis. As Fearon (1991: 179) suggests,

> where there are serious problems in identifying a sample, operationalizing and measuring variables, and conceiving of relevant controls, counterfactual argument about one or several cases may be more compelling than a statistical effort.

3. HISTORICAL COUNTERFACTUALS: SUGGESTIONS FOR THEIR CONSTRUCTION

Historical counterfactual analysis allows one to examine important questions that cannot be investigated with large-sample studies using conventional statistical methods. As Weber (1949*b*: 164) suggested, 'we must here question the view that questions which we cannot answer, or cannot answer with certainty, are on that account "idle" questions'. Despite their centrality (often implicitly) in causal analysis with small samples, relatively few scholars have dealt with the construction of historical counterfactuals explicitly.[3] The potential problems likely to develop from the use of historical counterfactuals are considerable. Accordingly, it is often relegated to the realm of science fiction and idle speculation. There is a widespread tendency to prefer to remain on 'firmer' ground, to assert that social scientists should focus on actual cases, derived from the 'real' world (Polsby 1982).

There are two principal problems associated with the construction of historical counterfactuals. First, there may be such an elaborate interdependence of different causal factors that it is

---

[3] Most of the principal exceptions in the social sciences have already been cited: Weber (1949*b*), Elster (1978), and Fearon (1991) in the theoretical realm, and in more applied work, Fogel (1964), Fogel and Engerman (1974), Khan and Knight (1985), M. Goldstein (1986), and Biersteker (1981). Alfred Stepan is also using explicit historical counterfactuals in a current project in which he examines how Latin American heads of state might have responded to challenges to democratic rule under parliamentary versus presidential systems of government.

impossible to separate them analytically and control for different explanations in an adequate manner. Second, given the infinite variety of counterfactual possibilities, how does one determine the plausibility of alternative explanations? Let us consider each in turn.

According to Jon Elster (1978: 179), J. S. Mill considered the construction of historical counterfactuals illegitimate because he assumed that all parts are 'interdependent to such a degree that no single part or subset of parts can be varied in the imagination, the other being held constant' (Elster 1978: 179). Elster views this as evidence of a pre-theoretic attitude and suggests that when one considers a topic such as the impact of free trade upon national prosperity, 'one has to use a theoretical framework with a finite number of specified variables, and it is not at all absurd to assume that two societies might have the same values for all but one of these variables'. Nevertheless, the problem articulated by Mill remains a vexing one for scholars who stress the organic inter-relationship between subjects and objects, parts and wholes, and resist the positivist inclination to separate phenomena into dependent and independent variables (Cox 1992). The problem of causal interdependence was also clearly evident in each of the examples presented above from the policy evaluation literature, where both interrupted time series models and simulations suffered from particular biases as a result.

Even more problematic, however, is the issue of how one determines the plausibility of different counterfactual constructions. Weber (1949*b*: 180) warned:

In fact, what 'would' have happened if a certain conditioning factor had been conceived of or modified in a certain way—this question, it will be asserted, is often *not* answerable definitely with any degree of probability by the use of general empirical rules even where the 'ideal' completeness of the source material exists.

In a footnote to this passage he added: 'The attempt to hypothesize in a positive way what "would" have happened can, if it is made, lead to grotesque results.'

Just how does one 'distinguish between the infinity of particular factors that would have precluded or reduced the likelihood of some interesting event had they *not* taken place' (Fearon 1991: 191) and avoid some 'grotesque' results? This is, in effect, a restatement of what has been termed the 'Cleopatra's nose problem': i.e. if Cleopatra's nose had been shorter, Mark Antony would not have fallen in love with her, and the entire course of subsequent western history would have been changed. Therefore, the length of Cleopatra's nose is a cause of subsequent events in western history. Alternatively, if A had not occurred, B would not have occurred; is A therefore a cause of B? It is one thing to assert the importance of some counterfactual alternative. It is quite another to demonstrate its plausibility. As Weber (1949*b*: 169) asked:

How in general is the attribution of a concrete effect to an individual 'cause' possible and realizable in principle in view of the fact that in truth an *infinity* of causal factors have conditioned the occurrence of the individual 'event' and that indeed absolutely all of those individual causal factors were indispensable for the occurrence of the effect in its concrete form?

Are all counterfactual assumptions equally justified? One can call for the construction of 'plausible' counterfactual alternatives arguments, but the difficulty of determining plausibility in an objective manner has led many to conclude that the use of historical counterfactuals is just too complex, subjective, and convoluted.

These problems are indeed daunting. However, given the small sample size involved in the analysis of international regimes (ordinarily N=1), it is difficult for the analyst interested in their causal consequences to avoid relying on the construction of historical counterfactual alternatives at some point, either explicitly or implicitly. Therefore, rather than throwing up our hands and dismissing the use of historical counterfactuals altogether, let us turn briefly to the methodological and philosophical literatures of the social sciences to consider some suggestions and general guidelines for their use.

First, *it is important that the counterfactual alternative(s) be stated explicitly.* Whenever one asserts that something has caused some consequence, one is engaging in an implied counterfactual statement. It suggests that if that something had *not* occurred, some other event (namely that something's consequence) would not have taken place. Similarly, efforts to determine or rank-order the causes of a particular historical event (as the principal cause) also ordinarily imply the use of a counterfactual. It is important that 'researchers who use counterfactual argument to support causal hypotheses should be methodologically aware of what they are doing and should make their counterfactual arguments as explicit and defensible as they can' (Fearon 1991: 170). This is especially important for analysts of small-N phenomena (such as regimes) who need counterfactual alternatives arguments to support their hypotheses. An explicit and careful statement of a counterfactual argument is preferable to an implied or unrealized one.

Second, *counterfactual alternatives arguments should be used with a clearly articulated theoretical framework*. As Elster (1978: 184) suggests, a theory is 'more than just an instrument that permits us to conclude from the hypothetical antecedent to the hypothetical consequent: it also serves as a filter for the acceptance or the rejection of the antecedent itself'. There is a double role for theory here, creating a paradox for the use of counterfactuals. The more deterministic the theory, the better grounded is the conclusion from antecedent to consequent, but the more vulnerable also is the legitimacy of the antecedent.

Thus for a successful counterfactual analysis, a delicate balance must be struck: the theory must be weak enough to admit the counterfactual assumption, and also strong enough to permit a clear-cut conclusion. (Elster 1978: 184)

Weber (1949*b*: 172) also has something to say about the importance of using historical counterfactuals with a clearly articulated theoretical framework. In considering the assertion that a particular battle allegedly 'decided' between two different possibilities, he suggests that 'without an appraisal of those "possibilities" and of the irreplaceable cultural values which, as it appears to our retrospective study, "depend" on that decision, a statement regarding its "significance" would be impossible'. He continues:

The 'knowledge' on which . . . a judgment of the 'significance' of the Battle of Marathon rests is . . . on the one hand, knowledge of certain 'facts' ('ontological' knowledge), 'belonging' to the 'historical situation' . . . and on the other . . . knowledge of certain known empirical rules, particularly those relating to the ways in which human beings are prone to react under given situations ('nomological knowledge'). (Weber 1949*b*: 174)

Thus, the analysis of the historical significance of a particular event cannot be understood without a theoretical framework that makes sense of the principal relationships among actors, or what Weber (1949*b*: 175) calls 'nomological empirical knowledge'.

Third, *the regularity and proximity of a causal relationship help us establish the plausibility of a counterfactual alternative, as well as distinguish between causes and background conditions of events.* There are an infinite number of factors that might have influenced a particular event (either precluded or reduced its likelihood had they not occurred). Are we then to conclude that they are all potential causes of that event? As Fearon (1991: 190) observes, social scientists often make arguments of the form: A is a cause of B, because 'had A not occurred, B might not have occurred'. However, in the example from the 1980s debt regime considered earlier (where a debtor cartel was *not* formed), one could conceivably argue that if oil prices had not risen precipitously in the 1970s, large-scale sovereign lending would never have taken place, the debt crisis might have been averted, and there would have been no meeting in Cartagena, and no failure to co-ordinate policy. Are we then to conclude that the OPEC oil price rise is itself a cause of the failure of the three countries to form a debtor cartel? One way to construct a plausible counterfactual is to search for regularity, where 'a cause is something that *produces* its effect whenever (or usually when) it occurs' (Fearon 1991: 191). In this sense, events like the oil price rise are not necessarily causes of the phenomenon being explained, even though they satisfy the logical condition, if ~A, then ~B. The other way is to insist on proximity of events, such that the causal attribution (and counterfactual alternative) are appropriately circumscribed in time and place to remain generally plausible. Indeed, this is one way of dealing with the 'Cleopatra's nose problem' in causal analysis.

Fourth, *ensure that the antecedents of your counterfactual alternative are legitimate.* That is, to be plausible, a counterfactual case has to have an antecedent that, with appropriate further premises (facts or empirical regularities), can produce its consequent. According to Elster (1978: 180), 'the nomological laws that we use in concluding from the antecedent to the consequent of a counterfactual statement must also be used in order to ensure that the antecedent itself is compatible with the elements that are *not* assumed to vary'. It is precisely for this reason that it is so important to have a specific theory that can circumscribe the set of legitimate counterfactual assumptions.[4]

It is important that, when constructing a historical counterfactual, the analyst should ensure that the core features of the counterfactual are consistent with the basic facts and general theories from which his causal inferences are derived. This is an important part of what constitutes a 'plausible' counterfactual alternatives argument. 'The fewer the changes from the actual world required by a counterfactual supposition, the easier it will be to draw and support causal inferences, and the more defensible they will be' (Fearon 1991: 193 f.). To make a defensible counterfactual for the case considered earlier, therefore, would require that if there had been no international debt regime, nothing else would have been different in a way that would significantly have influenced the eventual outcome.

Finally, to help ensure 'legitimacy', Elster has suggested that analysts using historical counterfactuals identify and articulate critical branching points in the history of a given phenomenon. In other words, a particular historical counterfactual scenario is relatively more plausible if there is a critical event or decision point during which several alternatives are considered, any of which might possibly have been decided upon. This helps to delimit the range of possible (or permissible) historical trajectories from that event or branching point, as well as to control for the infinite variety of possible changes in a phenomenon over time. Stated more formally, beginning with a theory T, an apparently plausible notion of relatively possible worlds could be the following:

A state s_t' is possible relatively to s_t if in the past history of s_t there is a state s_{t1} such that there is a permitted trajectory from s_{t1} to s_t'; that is, if there is some branching point from which the process may diverge to either s_t or s_t'. (Elster 1978: 190)

This implies, as did the previous discussion of proximity, that 'the further back we have to go in order to insert the possible state in the real history, the greater is the distance to that state'

---

[4] Fearon (1991: 193) contends that the real issue is one of 'cotenability' rather than legitimacy: 'A counterfactual assertion is judged true if (1) the counterfactual antecedent, when joined with appropriate theories and facts, implies the consequent; and (2) the counterfactual antecedent is "cotenable" with the facts or "initial conditions" used to draw the inference, meaning that if the antecedent had actually occurred, the initial conditions could also have occurred.'

(Elster 1978: 191). Thus, the range of time utilized to assess counterfactual alternatives can be critical for one's analysis (the greater the proximity, the greater the possibility). This leads Elster (1978: 218) to call for a 'genetic theory of counter-factuals', an idea that is broadly similar to the notion of path dependence.

4. THE USE OF HISTORICAL COUNTERFACTUALS TO ANALYSE THE EFFECTS OF THE GLOBAL DEBT REGIME OF THE 1980S

The international financial system was brought to the brink of collapse during the 1980s by the accumulation of developing-country debt. Many private commercial banks in the United States and Europe found themselves heavily overexposed from their sovereign lending to countries in Latin America, Africa, and East Asia. After the deep recession in 1981 and the sharp rise in global interest rates that accompanied it, a growing number of countries (beginning with Poland, Argentina, and Mexico) found them-selves unable to continue to make regular debt service payments on schedule. Mexico's severe balance-of-payments crunch in August of 1982 triggered the end of the period of petrodollar recycling by the transnational banks and the beginning of the debt crisis as we know it.

At the same time, the Mexican crisis also produced the broad outlines of a global debt regime that emerged to manage the problem for the rest of the decade. In the categories developed by Puchala and Hopkins (1983: 64 f.), it was a specific (not a diffuse) regime, one that involved a mix of formal and informal instru-ments (but tending increasingly toward the former), an evolu-tionary regime, with a clear distributive bias, one directed principally against the developing countries. In a highly informative descrip-tion of the Bretton Woods balance-of-payments regime (written just prior to the outbreak of the debt crisis), Benjamin Cohen (1983: 316) described the 1970s as a period in which a breakdown of the post-war Bretton Woods regime took place, 'a change of degree so profound that it appears to border on a transforma-tion of kind'. In retrospect, however, it now appears that the petrodollar recycling by the commercial banks during the 1970s was more of an interruption in the post-war balance-of-payments regime than an indication of its profound transformation.

Cohen (1983: 318) argues that countries confronting severe balance-of-payments disequilibria face basically two choices: they can either finance the disequilibrium (essentially postponing the costs), or adjust to it (bearing the costs immediately). Not surprisingly, the vast majority of countries prefer the former, postponing difficult decisions. The Bretton Woods financing regime was developed to ensure that countries would have an adequate supply of international liquidity to facilitate international trade and commercial transactions. Access to liquidity, however, was not intended to be unlimited: '. . . it has long been felt that, on principle, governments ought not to enjoy unlimited access to balance-of-payments financing' (Cohen 1983: 319). Although the term 'conditionality' does not appear in the original IMF Articles of Agreement, several critical policy decisions between 1948 and 1952 codified it as a defining principle of the regime (Cohen 1983: 321; Ruggie 1983b: 222 n. 90).

Cohen (1983: 323) summarized the post-war financing regime as based on the principle that 'nations should be assured of an adequate but not unlimited supply of supplementary financing for balance-of-payments purposes', norms of formally articulated rights and obligations accepted by each member of the Fund, rules of policy conditionality where access to higher tranche facilities was made subject to conditions embodied in Fund stabilization agreements, stand-by arrangements, letters of intent, and performance criteria, and decision-making procedures based on IMF staff decision routines, including administrative decision-making in the secretariat and voting (if necessary) in the Fund Executive Board.

The global debt regime that emerged in the 1980s is in many ways a re-establishment of many of these components that had fallen into disarray during the 1970s. The basic principle of the regime was re-established, and the principal formal institution of the regime (the IMF) restored to its original position of authority. The foundation upon which the 1980s global debt regime was based was the principle that debtor countries that pursued significant, market-oriented economic reform would be rewarded with some form of relief from their immediate debt burdens. At the outset, this meant balance-of-payments stabilization in exchange for debt rescheduling. After 1985 (under the Baker Plan), medium-term structural adjustment was required for fresh new money from commercial banks. In the Brady Plan, launched at the beginning of 1989, continued economic reform was to be rewarded with debt relief. In the different phases of the debt crisis, debtor countries pursuing economic reform were to be rewarded with rescheduling, new money, and/or relief.

The formally articulated rights and obligations of debtors and creditors (the norms of the regime) were essentially the same as those articulated in the Bretton Woods balance-of-payments regime. Access to new resources (whether from the IMF directly, or indirectly by way of requirements for its approval) was made contingent upon a serious and continued commitment to pursue market-oriented economic reforms. The rules of the global debt regime of the 1980s were also broadly similar to those established out of the Bretton Woods system. The IMF created several new facilities to deal with the 1980s debt problem (most notably the 'structural adjustment facility'), and it augmented some of its procedures (such as the introduction of enhanced surveillance, an increase in the frequency of Fund missions sent from Washington). However, the basic rules of the regime remained unchanged.

The IMF did not alter any of its basic decision-making procedures during the 1980s. However, creditor clubs such as the Paris Club (for the rescheduling of loans and credits extended by government and official creditors) and the London Club (for non-governmentally insured debts) were used with increasing frequency during the period. The creditor clubs developed decision-making procedures that ensured that no Paris Club rescheduling could begin without an IMF agreement in place, that developing-country debt would be treated on a case-by-case basis, and that the principle of burden sharing (where heavily indebted countries were expected to seek comparable relief from their different creditors, with the notable exception of the multilateral lending institutions) would be firmly established.

Did this regime matter? Did it influence either the environment within which states interacted, or did it alter the interests and the behaviour of key actors more directly? Did it have any significant effects independent of other causal explanations? In order to answer any of these questions, we need to consider counterfactual alternatives to the global debt regime (described above) that did emerge during the 1980s. Choosing from the infinite variety of possible alternatives confronts us squarely with one of the central problems customarily associated with the use of counterfactuals. Just how can we construct an alternative that allows us to control for the presence of the regime and is at the same time arguably 'plausible'?

In order to make this exercise more manageable, let us focus on the possible effects of the regime on two key aspects of the behaviour of the heavily indebted countries: first, the fact that they did not renounce their debt (and continued to make payments on their accumulated obligations), and second, the fact that they generally pursued sweeping market-oriented economic reforms. In the absence of the global debt regime of the 1980s, would debtor countries have defaulted on their obligations to commercial banks and multilateral lending institutions? Would they have embarked on such sweeping changes in their macroeconomic policy? How might we construct a plausible historical counterfactual case to evaluate this question?

In his analysis of Fogel and Engerman's classic study of the effects of slavery on the economy of the American South, Jon Elster (1978: 210) suggested four different ways to construct a plausible historical counterfactual which can be adapted to the question at hand:

1. We could take the actual 1990 world political economy, eliminate all features that stem directly from the 1980s debt regime, and assess the likelihood of default and continued economic reform.

2. We could take the actual 1990 world political economy, eliminate all features that stem directly (or indirectly, i.e. are mediated through other events and historical phenomena) from the 1980s debt regime, and assess the likelihood of default and continued economic reform.

3. We could go back in time to the latest branching point at which an alternative debt regime might have been established in the 1980s, develop an alternative 1990 world political economy, and assess the likelihood of default and continued economic reform.

4. We could go back in time to the latest branching point from which a development could have begun where the 1980s debt regime was never introduced (perhaps around 1950, when

the core principle of conditionality was first codified), develop an alternative world political economy for 1990, and assess the likelihood of default and continued economic reform in that environment.

This example clearly illustrates the complexity of engaging in explicit, historical counterfactual analysis. To begin with, it allows us to construct a control case, an alternative world where the 1980s global debt regime does not exist. This is important because since it is an international regime, with *global* reach, we cannot contrast the real experiences of countries located within and outside the regime to try to ascertain its effects. It also enables us to avoid some of the problems associated with an interrupted time series model that might attempt to consider the world political economy before and after 1982, but which would have difficulty controlling for all the other changes that took place between the 1970s and the 1980s. However, this historical counterfactual experiment also demonstrates some of the problems inherent in the use of the concept of regime. The imprecision (and breadth) of the regime idea is immediately apparent as soon as we try to imagine a world without it. There are so many interrelated components (the basic principles, the norms, the rules, and the myriad of decision-making procedures and institutions), that one faces difficult choices about which to exclude in the construction of the historical counterfactual alternative.

Of the four possible counterfactuals suggested above, the third offers the best promise for the construction of a plausible alternative. Unlike the first two, it employs branching points. The use of branching points enables one to reduce the infinite number of possibilities that might have developed, locates the counterfactual alternative in the prior course of history, and overcomes some of the problems of legitimacy (i.e. a basic consistency between the antecedent and its initial conditions). The third historical counterfactual also satisfies the condition of relative proximity. It is generally more plausible to imagine an alternative debt regime emerging from the early 1980s than the early 1950s (the fourth historical counterfactual), when the basic principles of limits on access to financial resources and the idea of conditionality were first established in practice.

The third historical counterfactual is also relatively plausible because the course of events at the time of the 1982 Mexican crisis was by no means certain. During the August weekend when the Mexican Finance Minister flew to Washington to appeal for emergency assistance, it took the critical intervention of the US Ambassador to Mexico to raise the issue on the policy agenda, along with the decisive action of the IMF Executive Director, and the imaginative forced lending scheme developed by Federal Reserve Chairman Paul Volcker to resolve the immediate crisis (Kraft 1984). It was a crisis in which a number of different, but plausible, scenarios were possible.

If we return to that critical, branching point in time (August 1982) and construct a world political economy in which there is no emergency financial package put together for Mexico, and no explicit link between an IMF agreement and continued access to commercial bank finance (the core elements of the 1980s global debt regime), it is possible to imagine that the probable course of the world political economy in the 1980s would have been *very* different. If we assume that the behavioural logic and theoretical relationships associated with the recent (1970s) global economic order would have remained the same (that is, the profit motive, intense bank competition, concern about potential losses from sovereign lending), we can reasonably speculate that Mexico almost certainly would have defaulted on its obligations, and the commercial banks would have red-lined the rest of Latin America (along with the rest of the developing world) even sooner than they did. This is an illustration of the importance of constructing a counterfactual alternative that is consistent with other probable developments, i.e. one that *could* have happened, given prior historical events and theoretical relationships.

Without the formative lesson provided by the Mexican rescue, the promise held out to all subsequent debtor countries (of rescheduling, new lending, or debt relief in exchange for substantial economic reforms) would have had significantly less meaning. The probability of other major defaults would have increased substantially, and the pace of the change in developing-country economic policy would probably have been far less significant. Although this historical counterfactual could be developed in much greater detail, one can nevertheless assert that the global debt regime of the 1980s had some effects, that it probably *did* matter.

5. CONCLUSIONS

The brief application considered in the previous section illustrates that the causal conclusions one can make about the effects of regimes using counterfactual analysis are highly dependent on the counterfactual alternatives constructed or deemed most plausible in any given area. It is relatively easy to speculate about what might have happened, constructing a counterfactual alternative that decisively 'proves' your causal assertion. This is what Lipson (1983: 271) did in the example cited previously, when he constructed a counterfactual alternative to the Tokyo Round of GATT negotiations (i.e. the regime's collapse and a 'proliferation of new trade barriers') that decisively proved his causal assertion about the importance of the trade regime. Ultimately more important, however, is the task of constructing and consciously defending the *plausibility* of the counterfactual alternative created.

Historical counterfactual alternatives must be articulated explicitly, in conjunction with a clearly identified theoretical framework. The use of proximate branching points limits the possible range of change to be considered, helps manage the problem of the infinity of possible alternatives, and ensures the basic legitimacy of the antecedents (i.e. that the counterfactual antecedent, taken in conjunction with appropriate theories and facts, implies the consequent, *and* that if the counterfactual antecedent could have taken place, so too could the initial conditions). Furthermore, as Haggard and Simmons (1987: 514) suggested, it is probably important to enter the realm of domestic politics at some point when establishing plausibility, in order to ensure that domestic-policy makers in the affected states were actually concerned with the issues articulated by the regime.[5]

The difficulty and subjectivity involved in using historical counterfactuals should not be minimized. However, given the centrality of counterfactual analysis for the making of causal claims with small samples (such as in the case of international

[5] For a study of 'regime effectiveness' focusing on domestic politics see Ch. 15 below.

regimes), it is better to try and articulate them consciously than to disguise (or ignore) them in vaguely formulated causal assertions. The explicit use of historical counterfactuals can also reveal the limitations of concepts such as international regimes. The effort to construct a world without the principles, norms, rules, and institutions typically associated with an international regime illuminates the ambiguity and imprecision of the regime concept. In the final analysis, some important issues involving the effects of international regimes simply cannot be addressed without the use of historical counterfactuals. Following Weber, speculating about what might have happened, therefore, is not always an 'idle' question.

14

Analysing Regime Consequences

Conceptual Outlines and Environmental Explorations

HELMUT BREITMEIER AND KLAUS DIETER WOLF

1. REGIME CONSEQUENCES: A NEGLECTED ISSUE OF REGIME ANALYSIS

Although the commitment to the 'regimes do matter' credo is an integral part of the corporate identity of the regime analysis community, amazingly few studies have focused on the question of regime consequences in a systematic fashion.[1] In this chapter we want to contribute to finding more systematic approaches that in the end may lead to generating theoretically sound hypotheses about regime consequences. In order to observe, describe, and measure systematically this dependent variable we will sketch a map of regime consequences (sect. 2), describing and evaluating such consequences according to the standard of a stable peace. As explanatory variables (sect. 3) we will concentrate on regime types, which are expected to account for variation in regime consequences. In an environmental case study (sect. 4) we want to illustrate the applicability of our categories of regime consequences.

The authors wish to thank Hannes Lacher, Martin List, Peter Mayer, Volker Rittberger, Frank Schimmelfennig, Gudrun Schwarzer, and Michael Zürn, whose critical ideas were very helpful for improving an earlier version of this chapter.

[1] Considering that regime analysis was launched in the mid-1970s, it took surprisingly long before the issue of regime consequences began to be (re)considered systematically, after having been raised as a general problem as early as 1983 by Krasner (1983b: 359–67). Important contributions have not been published at all (Zürn 1991 and Young 1991b) or only very recently (Nollkaemper 1992, Wettestad and Andresen 1991). Together with earlier suggestions (Efinger *et al.* 1990 or Kohler-Koch 1989a: 44–58) they provide the starting position for this paper.

Environmental regimes will also be employed in order to discuss the quality of the explanations based on regime types. The nature of section 4 remains explorative, but it may help to identify some fruitful directions for future research. Rather than searching for a fixed set of explanatory variables to be applied with equally satisfying results to the analysis of regime consequences in general, we suggest that regime properties or types (*a*) offer useful explanations for regime consequences only in specific issue areas and (*b*) need to be supplemented by 'exogenous' (Young 1991*b*) factors derived from the whole 'family' of explanations that have been developed in regime analysis so far.[2]

2. CONCEPTUALIZATION OF THE DEPENDENT VARIABLE: CRITERIA AND DIMENSIONS OF REGIME CONSEQUENCES

Who or what is affected by international regimes? As the realm of dependent variables to consider under this question is determined by our understanding of international regimes, we have (*a*) to specify our definition and (*b*) to state its implications for our typology of regime consequences. The notion that the principles, norms, rules, and procedures incorporated in an international regime do influence behaviour became part of the regime definition first introduced by Wolf and Zürn (1986: 204 f.) and elaborated further by the Tübingen research group (Rittberger and Zürn 1990).[3] Interpreting rule-consistent behaviour not as a regime consequence, but as that part of the definition of 'international regime' which guarantees that a regime is more than a piece of paper, our focus is directed from the question of the general relevance of international regimes ('do regimes make a difference at all?') to the more specific question of the kind of consequences that international regimes have. The criteria we offer for developing a typology to describe regime consequences are deliberately selective: for practical reasons, we doubt that it is advisable to pursue the course of Young (1991*b*), or Zürn (1991), whose much

---

[2] See the chapters in Part III of this volume.
[3] But see now the 'new consensus' definition of 'regime' as discussed in Ch. 1, sect. 3.1, and Ch. 2, sect. 3, above.

TABLE 14.1. *Dimensions and Criteria of Regime Consequences*

Dimensions	Criteria

Issue area	Problem solving:
	  just conflict regulation
	  sustainable conflict regulation

Context: domestic structure	Context change: democratization
Context: international system	Context change: civilization

more comprehensive typologies of regime consequences are of a basically *enumerative* nature.[4] Following the German tradition of regime analysis as part of peace and conflict studies,[5] we concentrate on distinct regime consequences which become relevant on the basis of certain normative premises. The criteria by which the categories used in our map (Table 14.1) were chosen are derived from certain value premises and correspond with different dimensions of regime consequences.

The three dimensions of regime consequences offered in Table 14.1 need no further explanation, as they are directly derived from levels of analysis familiar to International Relations (issue area, domestic structures, international system). However, the four evaluative criteria (1) just conflict regulation, (2) sustainable conflict regulation (to be subsumed under 'problem solving'), (3) domestic democratization, and (4) international civilization (to be subsumed under 'context change') are less self-evident. The common denominator is their relevance to a stable peace.

2.1. Problem Solving: Just and Sustainable Conflict Regulation by International Regimes?

The category of 'problem solving' refers to the question of how a problem is dealt with. Interested in the peacefulness of international

[4] The 'map of dependent variables' sketched by Zürn (1991: 25) chooses categories such as 'behaviour', 'capabilities', 'cognitions', 'values', 'interests', and 'constitution'. Young's (1991b: 23) enumeration of dimensions in which 'regime effectiveness' may be observed and measured contains criteria such as problem solving, goal attainment, constitution of a social practice, or domestic implementation of rules. That his definition of 'regime' differs from the one used in this study is reflected in the variable 'alteration of behavior'.

[5] See Ch. 1, sect. 3.2, above.

regimes, and given that the mere existence of a regime is almost synonymous with the renunciation of military force by regime members in dealing with the issues regulated by the regime (in this sense international regimes produce 'negative' peace almost by definition), our questions will have to focus on aspects of 'positive' peace. With reference to the issue area in which an international regime has been established, 'just' and 'sustainable' conflict regulation seem to be the most interesting categories for the identification and the measurement of the peacefulness of regime consequences, because these criteria may also decide upon the long-term success of 'negative-peace keeping'. We may measure 'justice' by the amount to which the procedures of conflict regulation and the value distribution within the issue area are regarded as fair by the participating actors. 'Sustainability' is achieved when the distribution of values is neither to the detriment of future generations nor insufficient with respect to the limits of the natural environment.

2.2. *Context Change: Civilization and Democratization as Regime Consequences?*

The kind of regime impact we subsume under 'context change' becomes apparent in spill-over effects that go beyond the issue area in which the regime is operating. The context of the regime may, according to the traditional levels of analysis in international relations, be divided into the systemic realm on the one hand, and the domestic realm on the other.

Systemic context change will show up in the structure of the overall relationships between members of a regime. Our main evaluative criterion here is the *civilizing* impact a regime may have on this relationship. For instance, regimes may 'civilize' relations among actors in the sense of fostering further co-operation by establishing epistemic communities and by contributing to confidence-building. They may have an effect on institution-building in neighbouring issue areas. Civilizing effects may also be achieved when regimes affect the distribution of capabilities among actors: regimes can make the use of traditional power resources more costly and thus devaluate their functionality *vis-à-vis* instruments of 'soft' power.

In the *domestic* realm, regimes may change actors' interests and preferences, or affect perceptions about other actors. In other words: regimes may support learning. Apart from this potential impact, our focus on 'stable peace' raises the question of whether international regimes can change the balance of domestic structures, i.e. the relationship between political systems and their respective domestic contexts. Can regimes lead to domestic changes in the sense of affecting *democratic* practices positively? Will, for instance, co-operative routines of conflict regulation within an international regime influence the way political systems interact with their domestic contexts? Or do international regimes contribute to a loss of democratic legitimacy by widening the distance between objects and subjects of decision-making?

3. WHAT DETERMINES REGIME CONSEQUENCES?

3.1. *International Regimes as Explanatory Variables: A General Discussion*

Having specified different manifestations of the dependent variable from the perspective of peace and conflict studies, we may now look at typologies for factors which operate as determinants of regime consequences. Even if we start from the premiss that regimes do have an impact (otherwise we would not have to study regime consequences), we have no evidence about the degree of importance to be attributed to international regimes as explanatory variables *vis-à-vis* other, 'exogenous' factors. There is no consensus as to whether regimes are 'underlying' or intervening factors.[6] Young (1991*b*: 16), for instance, treats them as 'endogenous' variables on the same level as his other two categories of potential sources of the 'effectiveness' of international regimes,

---

[6] Wettestad and Andresen (1991: 4) use 'problem types' as basic explanatory factors in the study of regime consequences. Their focus on the underlying variable 'problem complexity', which in their view allows one 'to delimit the 'room' for problem-solving capacity', of course, reduces the potential relevance of international regimes from the very beginning: regimes become mere 'supplementary' explanations. Although we certainly have to keep in mind the role of problem types for explaining the effectiveness of international co-operation, this approach cannot serve as a suitable starting-point for the study of *regime* consequences.

which he calls 'exogenous', and 'linkage variables'.[7] For the purpose of this chapter it seems, however, in a way 'natural' to build on the assumption of a major explanatory role of international regimes, and to regard other (such as 'exogenous') factors as secondary.

In a way similar to Young, Nollkaemper (1992: 51–61) differentiates between three approaches, which he labels 'structural', 'institutional', and 'internal'. While the structural approach concentrates on what Young calls 'exogenous' factors and ascribes a paramount role to systemic context structures, the institutional and the internal approaches explicitly emphasize the role of international institutions and their properties as determinants of state behaviour. Whereas the institutional approach is concerned with the more general question 'when and how institutions have an impact on state behaviour' (Nollkaemper 1992: 54), the internal approach is primarily interested in the importance of specific properties of rules as explanatory factors. Following Nollkaemper in this respect, we could therefore (1) conceptualize determinants of regime consequences by assigning certain effects to international regimes *in general*; we could, however, also (2) try to attribute *specific* consequences to particular *types* of regimes. Derived from an institutionalist understanding of regime consequences, regimes as such and specific regime properties are assumed to be basic explanatory factors, which will, however, have to be supplemented by additional 'exogenous' variables.

Some interesting hypotheses deal with the *general* impact of international regimes. As far as the criteria selected in Table 14.1 are concerned, we are interested in the following hypotheses: the communication provided by the regime may be assumed to

---

[7] Young's (1991*b*: 21) admittedly provisional typology is based on different schools of thought in international relations and comes to distinguish 'power factors, interest factors, and knowledge factors'. Trying to develop hypotheses according to this cluster the author is bound to lose himself in the maze of hegemonic stability theory, balance-of-power considerations, and other tracks. Being open to all kinds of social driving forces, Young's (1991*b*: 16, 20) 'exogenous' factors encompass 'an array of political, economic, and intellectual conditions that make up the environment in which an international regime operates'. This category, in particular, opens up a Pandora's box of all sorts of contextual determinants that may be held responsible for regime formation, structure, change, etc. as well. Theory-guided knowledge has so far not reached a point where more than an *ad hoc* introduction of such exogenous variables, whenever other explanations turn out to be insufficient, seems to be feasible.

lead to the exchange of information which may change actors' preferences (and thus affect problem solving), or even the balance of influence structures on the domestic level (and thus affect the degree of democratization). Based on their transnational networks non-governmental experts may increasingly free themselves from the control of their respective political systems. General regime consequences to be assumed on the systemic level include the supposed *civilizing effect* on international relations. They may also be observed when conflict regulation governed by the regime immunizes the issue area against deteriorating external conditions, a phenomenon which the Tübingen research team has drawn attention to and has called the 'resilience' (or 'robustness') of international regimes (Rittberger and Zürn 1990: 48 f.; Ch. 1, sect. 5, above).

3.2. Regime-Type Specific Consequences

Regime *types* seem to offer more precise hypotheses. Although there is a noticeable preoccupation with *regime typologies* to explain regime consequences, the literature about regime types is amazingly poor and selective about systematically relating regime structures or properties to regime consequences.[8] In addition, as regime typologies are usually tailored to studies covering specific issue areas, the fruitfulness of the various categories offered may not easily be demonstrated in studies focusing on one case or one type of cases (such as environmental regimes).

External/Internal Regimes

The distinction between external (or exclusive) and internal (or inclusive) regimes separates regimes which co-ordinate collective action among members in order to achieve relative gains *vis-à-vis* non-members from regimes which regulate the distribution of values among the members themselves (Keohane 1983: 167 f.; Zürn 1987: 39; Wolf and Zürn 1989: 38). The regimes that have been established by the Antarctic Treaty system may be regarded

---

[8] This is the case for Young's (1983, 1986) typology referring to the ways that regimes come about ('spontaneous', 'imposed', 'negotiated'), as well as for Ruggie's (1975) typological efforts, which seem to lead nowhere.

as exclusive (K. D. Wolf 1991): members aim at achieving relative gains *vis-à-vis* non-members. The same may be said for the CoCom regime (Wolf and Zürn 1989), which was established as an instrument of western industrialized nations to control the transfer of technology to Eastern Europe. In both cases no comprehensive membership is intended.[9] A major hypothesis based on this typology would be that external regimes will support an unequal distribution of resources between members and non-members in the issue area. This type of regime would therefore be detrimental to overall relationships among states by encouraging the pursuit of relative gains among actors. In section 4.2 this typology will be applied to environmental regimes.

Market-Oriented/State-Oriented/Internationalist Regimes

This typology of international regimes has been applied with some success in empirical studies dealing with regime consequences, particularly in global economic issue areas (K. D. Wolf 1981: 85; Krasner 1985: 6 f.; Zürn 1987: 40–5). State-oriented regimes are characterized by the fact that the implementation of norms and rules lies in the competence of the participating nation states, i.e. the regime structure does not prejudice national strategies for their implementation. The assumption following from this definition is that problem solving will largely depend on capacities and choices on the domestic level. The different impacts of the internationalist and market-oriented regime types have been studied with a focus on the just distribution of values on the issue area level. The main argument has been that internationalist regimes, which are characterized by the delegation of regulative and distributive authority to strong multilateral or supranational bodies, may be more effective with regard to distributional justice because these regimes have a machinery which is capable of implementing redistributional policies. Market-oriented (or liberal) regimes, in which the role of states is restricted to opening the

[9] The example of the non-proliferation regime (Müller 1989*b*) shows that discrimination may operate among the regime members themselves too. In this case the regime grants the status of nuclear powers only to some of its members. As the underlying intention is to attract a universal membership, we will not regard this as an external regime.

door for activities of non-state actors, are assumed to result in polarizing distributive effects.

These arguments have been brought forward in case studies mainly dealing with resource regimes in North–South relations. The study of market-oriented regimes among industrialized countries suggests, however, that this regime type may as well lead to a fair balance of interests (see Zürn 1987: 48), if the condition of a symmetrical interaction structure between actors is fulfilled. This observation invites the conclusion that the different distributional impacts attributed to regimes under this typology may not be generalized without further qualifications.

In order to make this typology fruitful for studying consequences of environmental regimes one should elaborate on whether hierarchical policy-making structures (as represented by internationalist as well as state-oriented regimes) are equivalent or even superior to non-hierarchical ones (such as market-oriented regimes) in terms of creating collective goods or avoiding collective bads.[10] Or, according to the capacity theorem put forward by Prittwitz (1990): can a type of regime that aims at encouraging companies to develop cleaner technology with market-oriented incentives be more successful than one which aims at a prohibition of dirty technology?

Internal and External Regime Compatibility

This distinction bears some resemblance with Nollkaemper's 'internal' and 'structural' approaches, external compatibility also resembling Young's (1991*b*: 16) category of 'linkage variables', which refers to the fit between a regime and its context. Under the criterion of internal compatibility consequences of international regimes may vary corresponding to the degree of consistency of the regimes' principles and norms. The respective hypothesis is that 'internal contradictions within the normative structure' (Nollkaemper 1992: 57) of an international regime will doom problem solving to failure. Incompatible goals may not be attained at the same time.

The second dimension of compatibility refers to the regime and its international and domestic contexts: as Nollkaemper (1992: 52)

---

[10] Scharpf (1991) recently dealt with this problematic in a brilliant article.

puts it, 'a rule must conform closely to the system's prevailing structure of power, interdependence and affinity relations'. This criterion of compatibility of the regime's constituents with the structuring features of the international system is also the subject of Young's category of 'linkage variables'.[11] A striking example for the relevance of explanations based on this typology is the more than likely failure of the UNCTAD commodity regime: according to our compatibility hypothesis this can be attributed to its failure to conform sufficiently to the prevailing liberal features of the international economic order.

Incompatibility may, however, not only exist between an international regime and certain features of the international system, but also between an international regime and the domestic structures of participating countries. How the philosophy of an international regime may exert pressure towards democratization on domestic political structures to adapt to international standards laid down in a regime can be studied by looking at the human rights agreements of the CSCE. This and similar examples[12] could give rise to the question under which circumstances the incompatibility between an international regime and certain domestic structures will not result in the failure of the international regime, but will lead to domestic reforms.

4. THE CONSEQUENCES OF ENVIRONMENTAL REGIMES: AN EXPLORATORY CASE STUDY

In this section the relevance of the analytical categories introduced so far is explored. We want to investigate their fruitfulness with recourse to international *environmental* regime-building. One might argue that, considering the overall situation of the environment, the analysis of the consequences of international environmental regimes is negligible. In our view, however, the degree of

---

[11] Compatibility is still relating to, but at the same time also transcending, the regime structure typology in the direction of 'exogenous variables'. This is why Young reserved a separate category ('linking variables') for them.
[12] Going even further, the economic breakdown of the Soviet and Eastern European systems could have been influenced by their incompatibility with the liberal international economic structures as incorporated in GATT—a conclusion that may be drawn if we follow Rosecrance (1986: 41).

differentiation within our typologies is particularly challenged by the disproportion between the efforts of regime-building for environmental protection and the ever more degenerating state of the environment in general. After all, there *are* regime consequences of a more subtle nature which may be identified within various environmental issue areas. Our empirical illustrations are the result of an evaluation of the regimes for the protection of the Baltic, the Mediterranean, the North Sea, and the stratospheric ozone layer, as well as the regime for the reduction of acid rain established under the ECE Convention on Long-Range Transboundary Air Pollution.

Our first focus lies on exemplifying how the categories and dimensions of regime consequences may serve to locate international environmental co-operation between success and failure in a more systematic fashion. In a first step (sect. 4.1) we seek to demonstrate the applicability of the criteria offered in Table 14.1. We do by no means claim to comprise all relevant consequences of environmental regimes. Instead, our intention is to describe and evaluate certain regime consequences on the basis of our four criteria (just conflict regulation, sustainable conflict regulation, democratization, and civilization). This concentration underlines the exploratory and anything but comprehensive character of our empirical illustrations. We want to demonstrate that the categories we have introduced bear some relevance and may help to identify interesting questions for future research. While hypotheses about the *general* impact of international regimes will also be discussed in section 4.1, the second part of our case study (sect. 4.2) will concentrate on discussing the explanatory power of hypotheses about *specific* consequences of the different regime *types* mentioned above.

4.1. Illustrating the Typology

Problem Solving: Just and Sustainable Conflict Regulation as Consequences of Environmental Regimes

Transboundary pollution is not only a kind of modern invasion, it also represents a special form of violence (Brock 1991: 408; Mayer-Tasch 1987: 112). The abatement of pollution may therefore help to reduce underlying causes of military conflict. But even if environmental co-operation is institutionalized in an international regime, 'ecological security' (Bächler 1990) may, however, be achieved only in the sense of a lasting 'negative' peace, unless environmental problem solving fulfils additional criteria, i.e. unless these regimes contribute to justice and sustainability in our understanding of 'positive' peace.

In the sense of a fair distribution of burdens and benefits, it is difficult enough to achieve ecological justice by national environmental legislation (R. Wolf 1991: 357), but even more so by international co-operation. An obstacle to justice results from the distribution of bargaining power involved in environmental problem solving: polluter states are often in the position to determine the conditions under which they are ready to commit themselves to reduce their own emissions. If the polluter states join the regime, environmental regimes can thus run the risk of reproducing the unequal distribution between victims and polluter states only on a lower emission level. If the major polluters do not join, there will be even more asymmetry. This happened with the ECE Convention on Long-Range Transboundary Air Pollution of 1979. While nearly all ECE members signed the convention, several main exporters of sulphur oxides later refused to join a protocol concerned with sulphur reduction (Schwarzer 1990*a*).

In most cases, the polluter states need not even bear the costs for the removal of former environmental deterioration. Actually, as Beck (1986) has pointed out, the environmental risk caused by a polluter is inversely proportional to the chances that he can be held responsible for it. The responsibility of certain polluter states for the deteriorating consequences of former transboundary pollution in other countries might be evident, but the liability and obligation of these polluter states for the removal of environmental damages is less developed. In practice, the victims of acid rain or of polluted seas have to bear the costs for an improvement of the environment themselves.

Injustice in the sense of an unjust allocation of goods within regimes arises as a problem in the context of North–South relations, in particular. Several environmental regimes foster a broad exchange of information, knowledge, and even technical assistance to countries without adequate capabilities at their disposal. These practices may be regarded as a starting-point for a more just design of environmental regimes, although their original function may be that of selective incentives (Olson 1965) to facilitate the entry of non-members into the regime. One striking positive example of environmental technology transfer is the establishment of a multilateral fund within the stratospheric ozone protection regime, supporting developing countries which were investing in the build-up of national CFC industries. Within the acid rain regime, however, demands for technology transfer measures aiming at the reduction of air pollution in Eastern Europe (Schwarzer 1990*a*: 42) have not been met. Neither does the Baltic Sea regime contain any provisions for financial or technology transfers (List 1991: 165).

Summing up, are environmental regimes characterized by a just distribution of burdens and benefits? Our category of just conflict regulation turned out to be applicable. It enabled us to grasp certain difficulties that seem to limit the realization of this normative claim of justice. Within a few environmental regimes, however, forms of a more just distribution of burdens and benefits could be developed.

With respect to *sustainability* we want to explore whether an environmental regime contributes to ecological problem solving in the long run, or whether it only transfers environmental burdens to future generations and therefore does not effectively lead to the preservation of the natural environment. Considering the type of problem to be dealt with in the regime, the following questions are important: are all relevant substances covered by the regime? do the reduction rates meet ecological criteria?

Within the wide range of environmental regimes, among those dealing with the protection of the marine environment several must be characterized as weak with respect to the sustainability of the measures agreed upon: one consequence of the Baltic Sea regime certainly was that the concentration of a few hazardous substances, such as DDT and PCBs, decreased in the 1980s. Furthermore, reception facilities for oily wastes and measures to improve the security of shipping may have contributed to prevent a further pollution of the marine environment (Strübel 1989: 263; List 1991: 163). However, the state of the Baltic marine environment continues to alarm. With regard to a number of newly detected contaminants (List 1991: 164; Kronfeld-Goharani and Wellmann 1991: 15 f.), the danger of hypertrophication, and the increase of pollution from land-based sources, it may even be a success of the regime that the status quo was preserved and no further deterioration occurred.

Considering regimes as dynamic institutions, evolving and changing over time (Gehring 1991), the sustainability of problem-solving efforts may increase. Environmental regimes often underlie a step-by-step approach, during the course of which they develop stronger problem-solving capabilities. The range of chemical substances incorporated into the reduction scenario of the regime may be widened, the time period within which reductions are to be achieved may be shortened. In the case of the stratospheric ozone protection regime, a first step toward environmental co-operation was taken under the Vienna Convention of 1985. But the convention did not 'identify any chemical as an ozone-depleting substance' (Benedick 1991: 45). Only in an annexe were different CFCs and other related chemicals listed as substances 'thought to have the potential to modify the chemical and physical properties of the ozone layer'. Under the Montreal Protocol of 1987 a high number of substances that were known as contributing to ozone depletion were not regulated. Most experts considered the reduction rates for the chemicals falling under the protocol too low and the time horizon for the implementation of the reduction scenario too long (Rowland 1988: 113). However, further drastic steps were taken, when in Helsinki 1989 and in London 1990 the contracting parties developed stricter reduction scenarios, which were strengthened once more in 1992. These observations suggest that a main consequence of environmental regimes lies in the initiation of a step-by-step process, gradually increasing problem-solving capabilities.

In evaluating the sustainability of a regime we also have to take into account whether potential future developments that might be detrimental to the state of the environment are anticipated in the construction of the regime. Factors such as population growth and ever-expanding industrialization as well as scientific discoveries may endanger the sustainability of present environmental regulations. None of the environmental regimes we have referred to meets all prerequisites of a sustainable conflict regulation in its present form. Several of them, however, contain institutional measures that guarantee some kind of adaptability to changing conditions. Review schedules, which may lead to a re-evaluation of scientific knowledge and measures taken, can be made out in the 1987 Montreal Protocol on Substances That Deplete the Ozone Layer. The contracting parties committed themselves to a periodical assessment of further control measures (Sand 1991: 277).

This short survey confirms that our category of sustainability is applicable: it seems to be crucial in assessing potential future effects of these regimes, although we have to admit that such an assessment requires additional knowledge and support from natural scientists. With regard to several dimensions of sustainability, we come to the conclusion that the sustainability of environmental regimes is improving under a long-term perspective. The question remains, however, if this improvement is far-reaching enough.

Context Change: Civilization and Democratization as Consequences of Environmental Regimes

Within the realm of context change we want to describe and evaluate regime consequences according to the normative criterion of civilization on the systemic level, and of democratization on the domestic level. As far as the systemic level is concerned, we will try to answer the following question: is the functionalist assumption, according to which regimes have a potential civilizing impact on international relations, supported by our case?

Our case study reveals that civilization does indeed take place, if we regard confidence-building and the emergence of epistemic communities as contributions to facilitating further co-operation. The establishment of institutions in neighbouring issue areas can be observed. The spread and increasing weight of these institutions have an impact on international relations by supporting soft power capabilities (Nye 1990) and strengthening the role of smaller countries as well as transnational NGOs.

Environmental regimes have fostered the establishment of epistemic communities (P. M. Haas 1989, 1990, and 1992*a*; Ch. 8 above). As the case of the Mediterranean Action Plan (Med Plan) demonstrates, regimes do not only mitigate conflicts, but may even lead to the emergence of new actors and thereby facilitate governmental learning (P. M. Haas 1989: 402). Transnational co-operation among scientists and ecologists was considerably intensified during the process of environmental regime-building in the North and Baltic Sea issue areas. Especially for the Baltic, these contacts turned out to be conducive to the development of a common definition of the environmental problem (List 1991: 196).

Confidence-building effects can be attributed to several environmental regimes. The littoral countries of the Baltic Sea were able to regulate environmental conflicts peacefully, in spite of the military tensions and systemic incompatibilities that existed between them (Efinger and Zürn 1989: 229; List 1991: 168). Once established, this regime became resistant to deteriorating effects caused by the overarching East–West conflict. The ECE Convention facilitated further co-operation between eastern and western countries to combat the causes of acid rain in Europe, when they agreed upon protocols not only for the reduction of sulphur dioxide but also for the stabilization of nitrogen oxide emissions (Chossudovsky 1988). Moreover, several countries committed themselves to further reduction measures outside the protocols.

To some extent environmental institution-building in a certain issue area served as an exemplary foil for institution-building in neighbouring issue areas. The Mediterranean Action Plan established under the leadership of UNEP serves as a model for the protection of the marine environment within the UNEP Regional Seas Programme (Strübel 1989: 267).

Environmental regimes have also strengthened the role of functional international organizations operating in the respective issue area. In fact, UNEP extended its role and functions in the field of international environmental policy, and could, as a consequence of successful efforts at regime-building, withstand criticism. Meanwhile this international environmental organization is involved in a great number of environmental regimes, playing not only the role of a catalyst, but also that of a lawyer for the natural environment in general.[13] The evolution of environmental regimes will raise the significance of international organizations in this issue area, and may even contribute to a general renaissance of international organizations.

Environmental institution-building has affected the international system in yet another way. Relying on soft power resources, small

---

[13] Other international organizations within and outside the UN system operate in a similar way (Kilian 1987).

countries have taken the initiative in regime creation because of their special vulnerability or of a specific domestic environmental concern. Scandinavian countries, in particular, have gained political prestige and credibility as environmental forerunners. But not only smaller nation states have gained political influence: the participation of NGOs in the formation and evolution of international regimes and the emergence of new actors, such as Greenpeace, in international policy-making processes contribute to qualifying the dominance of traditional power politics and the instruments that go with them.

This diffusion of actors and power resources on the systemic level is accompanied by changes in the balance of domestic structures. Non-governmental actors become more and more independent of their respective political systems in their transnational relations and become more influential *vis-à-vis* governments on the domestic level. In countries such as Germany and the United States, atmospheric and other natural scientists increasingly influence national attitudes towards global reductions of CFCs (Breitmeier 1992, Benedick 1991), based on their recognition by mass media and on their co-operation with international organizations.[14] It is doubtful, however, whether the empowerment of new groups is already a step towards more democracy. It may lead to a mere reign of experts (epistemic communities) emancipating themselves from any political control. The question therefore remains unsolved under which circumstances the establishment of international regimes may influence the balance of domestic structures in favour of democratization.

As result of the evaluation of regime consequences in the realm of context change, our analytical categories of civilization and democratization turned out to be fruitful. With respect to the category of *context change* we have already been able to provide some empirical evidence for hypotheses concerning the *general impact* of environmental regimes. Theory-building in the dimension of problem solving, however, has to take into account more specific, regime-type based hypotheses.

---

[14] A similar role was played by the epistemic community within the Med Plan, where the ecological epistemic community not only set the international agenda, but 'directed their own states toward support of international efforts and toward the introduction of strong pollution control measures at home' (P. M. Haas 1989: 84).

4.2. Regime-Type Specific Consequences of Environmental Regimes

The following exploration tries (*a*) to utilize our regime typologies for an analysis of regime consequences, and is (*b*) an attempt to test hypotheses concerning specific consequences of particular regime types.

Internal/External regimes

International environmental issues consist of problems where environmental damage can either be externalized or is indivisible (collective goods).[15] These types of environmental problems correspond with the creation of external and internal regime types, respectively. Pollution is *indivisible* with respect to global commons like the ozone layer or the global climate. Regional collective goods like the Mediterranean, the North Sea, and the Baltic are also representative of this type of problem. Since here the purpose of the regime is to protect the environment as a collective good and to prevent free-riding, all potential polluters have to be included in the regime. Building regimes for the protection of regional seas like the Baltic will therefore be characterized by an inherent logic for them to be internal regimes, aiming at comprehensive membership. Surprisingly, in our case study 'external' elements can be observed too. We may, however, not regard these regimes as external regimes (which we defined as exclusive regulations that aim at providing relative gains to regime members *vis-à-vis* non-members), because they do not aim at excluding others; on the contrary, such elements may serve as incentives for non-members to join a regime. For instance, the stratospheric ozone protection regime incorporates rules proscribing trade in CFCs and related products with non-members. As countries do not want

---

[15] For a more sophisticated typology of international environmental conflicts see Breitmeier and Zürn (1990). The authors differentiate the indivisible type into conflicts about global commons and conflicts about regional collective goods; different variants of externalization are the unilateral export of pollution and the export of pollution on the basis of an agreement between the exporting and the importing nation. A further type they take into account is called 'self-damaging with transboundary effects'.

to be excluded from this trade, this is a suitable incentive. The assumption according to which an unequal distribution of resources between members and non-members in the issue area will be a necessary consequence of an external regime, or of external elements within an inclusive regime, is not supported.

Conversely, when pollution costs are *divisible*, polluter states may seek to externalize environmental deterioration under the umbrella of international regimes. Within the range of our case study, there is no such evidence of external regimes. However, the question still remains whether regimes that are created to protect regional collective goods accept an externalization of costs into other regions, which are not participating in those regimes. For instance, it would be interesting (albeit difficult) to analyse whether regimes which were established to protect regional seas not only resulted in, but also aimed at, the export of hazardous waste into other regions.

Market-Oriented/State-Oriented/Internationalist Regimes

In contrast to market-oriented (liberal) regimes, which can be characterized by their non-hierarchical policy-making structures, internationalist and state-oriented regimes represent hierarchical policy-making structures. Are hierarchical policy-making structures equivalent or even superior to non-hierarchical ones with respect to the provision of collective goods? Since in the set of environmental regimes taken into account for this case study not all three types of regimes are represented, our remarks about their consequences for problem solving may but serve as a starting-point to reconsider the following assumptions.

Environmental regimes can be described as *state-oriented*: all the regimes we looked at do not prejudice national strategies for their implementation. In contrast to internationalist regimes, they are not equipped with a redistributive machinery. International organizations or other multilateral bodies are restricted to data-collecting and information-gathering activities. Their activities usually do not go beyond the management of technical assistance, monitoring, and scientific exchange or, as in the case of the stratospheric ozone protection regime, of a multilateral fund.

One main conclusion can be drawn from the fact that the state-oriented regime structure does not interfere with national strategies of implementation: the success of problem-solving measures is not determined by the structure of the regime, but depends to a much larger extent on domestic factors. According to Prittwitz's (1990) 'capacity theorem', a policy of incentives relying on self-regulation is preferable to purely prohibitive policies. Encouraging the competition between certain industries for the achievement of environmental goals is assumed to produce better and faster technical solutions. In Germany, for instance, the Federal Government not only tries to reach its national goals for a reduction of carbon dioxide by setting long-term goals: the Government has also established a running dialogue with relevant representatives of the energy sector, engineers, and natural scientists to develop common solutions for a structural change in this area. Although several industrial sectors are unwilling to follow such a policy, other industries expect that international environmental regimes may pay if they have the technical innovations at their disposal that are needed for implementation. One striking example is the positive attitude of the United States towards an early and extensive cut in CFCs, which obviously had to do with the fact that American industry had developed substitutes (Benedick 1991). Developing its technicological capacities may advance a country's export capabilities and, in the end, lead to an improvement of the environment. Structural changes in the domestic economy may therefore also have the effect of reinforcing the competition among transnational corporations for environmentally sound technologies.

Internal and External Regime Compatibility

Almost every environmental regime is characterized by *inconsistencies* on the level of its normative components, where ecological, economic, and other partial interests and goals are competing. We have assumed that such internal tensions might weaken the regime's contribution to problem solving. In the ECE Convention of 1979 the contracting parties declared their intention 'to protect man and his environment against air pollution' and to 'endeavour to limit and, as far as possible, gradually reduce and prevent air pollution' (Art. 2). Other formulations, like the intention to use 'the best available technology which is economically feasible' (Art. 6) indicate, however, substantive internal contradictions. But the evolutionary process of the regime in the 1980s overcame these internal contradictions. The result is a general trend towards the reduction of sulphur dioxide emissions, amounting to nearly 20 per cent in Europe since 1980 (Prittwitz 1989: 236; Wettestad and Andresen 1991: 75). As major reductions of sulphur dioxide and nitrogen oxides are still to be expected, the acid rain regime represents a more or less successful effort of environmental institution-building, compared to other environmental regimes. Other cases may, however, support our assumption concerning internal inconstistencies in the future: the prospective regime for the protection of the Alps also includes aims that are hardly compatible. It aims at the protection of the environment and at the expansion of the tourist industry at the same time.[16] These inconsistencies result from compromise formulas to overcome conflicting interests within the bargaining process, and may turn out to be a major hindrance to effective problem solving.

With respect to external regime compatibility, the hypothesis maintains that the structure of a regime must correspond to certain features of its context, i.e. the domestic and international context, if a regime is to contribute to problem solving effectively. On the one hand, provisions laid down in environmental regimes must not ask too much from the regime members: the dynamics of negotiating processes may result in agreements that cannot be met on closer inspection. On the other hand, our empirical findings show no basic contradictions between the regulations within the environmental regimes we looked at and the 'climate' of the international context. The stratospheric ozone protection regime contains certain provisions to restrict the trade of CFC-related products with non-members of the regime. However, these provisions do not challenge the prevailing practices of the capitalist world economy in any way, or the distribution of power in the international system. Trade barriers have frequently been agreed upon. As the problem-solving capacities of environmental regimes differ considerably, while they all meet the criterion of external compatibility, this does not seem to be a relevant factor. One might even go one step further: as external compatibility implies the absence of any contradiction to the prevailing philosophy of industrial modernization, 'compatible' environmental regimes

---

[16] The Winter Olympics in Albertville 1992 intending to promote further tourism in this region may serve as a striking example of the negative impact of such events. None the less, a number of cities in the Alps are considering applying for future meetings.

may in the long run be ineffective as devices of problem solving.

5. CONCLUSION

This exploratory approach to developing and illustrating categories of regime consequences and of factors determining such consequences leads to a number of conclusions. Our typology of selective categories for the description and evaluation of regime consequences, distinguishing problem solving and context change, proved to be analytically fruitful. For pragmatic reasons, we were not only obliged to concentrate on a small range of regime consequences, but were able to deal with only a limited number of regime types. While the *general* impact of international regimes, as far as our normative criteria are concerned, remains within the realm of context change, regime *types* have turned out relevant because of their respective impact on problem solving. However, the regime types discussed so far do not seem to be generally applicable to all kinds of issue areas, nor do they offer sufficient explanations in the environmental field under investigation in this chapter.

As a result of these observations future research could concentrate on the following two tracks. On the one hand, as the discussion of the different consequences of internal and external regimes has shown, links between certain regime properties and exogenous factors, such as problem types, need further investigation. This is also suggested by the rather limited results we could achieve by applying the category of state-oriented regimes, without taking into consideration domestic variables. The importance of the latter has been highlighted by this specific regime property, in particular. On the other hand, the still small number of regime typologies which allow for hypotheses about regime consequences should be enlarged, taking into account findings in case studies in other issue areas. Our expectation is that, rather than producing a small number of regime properties with great explanatory force, such case studies will suggest a variety of regime typologies shedding light on only very specific criteria of regime consequences.

15

The Internalization of Principles, Norms, and Rules by Governments

The Case of Security Regimes

HARALD MÜLLER

1. SECURITY REGIMES

The 'security regime' debate has suffered from the mistaken assumption that such regimes must cover the entire area of security. This assumption originated in the tendency of researchers to regard the Concert of Europe as a paradigm for security regimes (Jervis 1983, 1978). Yet, just as there is no 'regime for the global economy', but instead regimes in trade, finance, etc., it is the narrower sub-areas of security policy where we find co-operative institutions or regimes (Rittberger 1990*d*). Security regimes are systems of principles, norms, rules, and procedures regulating certain aspects of security relationships between states. A regime exists when all four elements can be identified and when the regime controls enough variables in a given issue area to affect (if obeyed) parties' behaviour by channelling or terminating unilateral self-help with regard to the regulated variables. Using these criteria we can currently identify four security regimes:

1. the strategic nuclear weapons regime (SALT I and II, ABM Treaty, parts of the INF Treaty and of the Outer Space Treaty, START) (Rice 1988);
2. the European military order (INF Treaty, Stockholm/Paris agreements on confidence-building, CFE Treaty, 2+4 Treaty, practices such as doctrine seminars and mutual visits of military personnel, the Crisis Control Centre, and the recent

mutual promises of unilateral reductions of short-range nuclear weapons);
3. the regime for the prevention of nuclear war (more than ten different agreements, aspects of the SALT Treaties and the recently adpoted practice of not keeping nuclear weapons in a high state of readiness) (Blechman 1988);
4. the nuclear non-proliferation regime (the NPT, the London Suppliers' Guidelines, the IAEA Statute, the safeguards rules in INFCIRC/66, the Tlatelolco and Rarotonga Treaties) (Müller 1989*b*).

2. THE PROBLEM OF REGIME EFFECTIVENESS

States' compliance with regime requirements is one important aspect of regime effectiveness. Realist theory maintains that co-operation is a matter of convenience and is quickly abandoned if unilateralism promises results which are superior from the perspective of national interest. States calculate not only expected gains against costs from international co-operation, but compare their net benefits against those of their partner-competitors. If the balance is negative they abstain from collaboration even if it promises a net gain (Grieco 1990).

Four other approaches assume that regimes do affect state behaviour:

1. The *neoliberal-utilitarian approach* assumes that states prefer higher certainty for the course of future competition and calculate their costs and benefits accordingly. Regarding choices on regime compliance, states review their cost-benefit analyses and the stability of co-operation, draw conclusions on its net present value, and adjust their behaviour accordingly (Keohane 1984, Zürn 1987).
2. *Pure institutionalism* maintains that states comply simply because the regime exists. Institutions assume a power of their own and socialize their members into compliant behaviour (Young 1989*a*). Moreover, because states suffer from an overload of information, they must create rules to avoid the need to review each case closely (Luhmann 1987). Regime norms and rules help states reduce the burden of

decision-making by creating incontestable rules of decision selection. State compliance is thus not dependent on repetitive cost-benefit analyses.

3. From the perspective of *theories of knowledge* regimes create a framework for states to 'learn'. States can 'test' their assumptions about the costs and the benefits of behaviour, and the adequacy of co-operation instruments. Thus they are able to improve regime structures, and they can gain experience about the character and behaviour of their partners (Nye 1989).[1]

4. *Complex institutional theory* sees regimes embedded ('nested') in general networks of norms and institutions. Compliance occurs because the normative systems of higher order work as frames of reference that reinforce compliance in specific regimes (Kratchowil and Ruggie 1986). Regimes are 'reflexive', referring in their substance to these higher-level systems from which they derive strength and stability.

This study reviews three cases of regime compliance. By tracking the process of decision-making, the influence of regime principles, norms, and rules on the way decision-makers frame state action is assessed. As a prerequisite for a case to be examined in this chapter, there had to be controversy on whether regime compliance was in the best interest of the state. Otherwise, compliance would pose no real test for regime effectiveness. It is for this reason that the regime on preventing nuclear war was exempted from the inquiry. It simply sailed too smoothly through the East–West conflict.[2]

3. CASE 1: THE UNITED STATES AND THE STRATEGIC DEFENSE INITIATIVE (SDI)

Since 1972, the Anti-Ballistic Missile (ABM) Treaty has been a cornerstone of the strategic nuclear arms regime. The ABM

---

[1] For the concept of learning see also Ch. 8, sect. 3, and Ch. 9, sect. 5, above.
[2] Space limitations prevent a comprehensive documentation of sources. For the cases, *The Arms Control Reporter*, *The National Journal*, *Arms Control Today*, *The Congressional Quarterly*, the bulletin of the Federal Government of Germany, *Nucleonics Week*, various newspapers, and the Soviet military writing section in *Strategic Review* have been systematically used.

Treaty rested on the assumption that vulnerability of the super-powers' homelands was a prerequisite for stability. It stipulated that both superpowers renounce a country-wide defence system and restrict themselves to two (later reduced to one) defence sites of 100 ABM launchers each. In the United States, the treaty and its underlying strategic 'philosophy' were contested from the beginning. The critics made three points:

1. In an age of strategic competition, placing the survival of the state in the hands of the main enemy was a flawed strategy.
2. The basic character of the USSR made the pursuit of arms control inadvisable. The Soviet Union was striving for world domination and its armament behaviour could be neither trusted nor controlled.

These two arguments challenged the rationale for security regimes: the complementation of self-help by 'islands' of co-operative security.

3. The Soviet efforts in strategic defences showed that its accession to the ABM Treaty was fraudulent (Iklé 1973).

This argument challenged a main tenet and function of security regimes: the assumption of reciprocity and the stabilization of expectations.

President Reagan's SDI speech was the consequence of increasing right-wing pressure. The reasoning was based on a unilateralist strategy, with no regard for the constraints emerging from existing security regimes. The President challenged the regime's principles of mutual vulnerability and strategic stability, and called for strategic defences as an alternative. His speech payed no attention to treaty obligations. Only at the end did he allege that his plan was compatible with the ABM Treaty. This was a late amendment to the core speech, inserted at the last moment by the State Department (Greve 1985). The follow-up studies to flesh out SDI, the reports of the Fletcher and Hoffman panels on the technical feasibility and strategic implications of anti-ballistic missile defences, followed the same line. The regime did not figure as a frame of reference for the proposed policy changes (Fletcher 1984, F. S. Hoffman 1983).

This 'regime denial' faced opposition from three sources. First, the State Department voiced its concern. It sought to preserve those regimes that it regarded as useful and in which it continued to place confidence. The second voice of opposition emerged from the arms control community, including those who had been involved in negotiating and implementing the ABM Treaty. The National Campaign to Save the ABM Treaty was launched in early summer 1984 and helped to influence considerably the perspective of the most important actor, Congress (Kubbig 1990). Initially, SDI sceptics in Congress questioned the President's vision, on grounds of technical feasibility and cost. Both aspects rested on a unilateral calculation of US interests. As an implication of these arguments, the development and deployment of SDI would be legitimate if the cost-efficiency relation changed, and if technological developments eliminated current obstacles. Yet, from 1984 on, Congress invested increasing attention in SDI's consequences for the strategic nuclear arms regime (Kubbig 1990). The third voice of opposition was that of the allies. They were concerned that a breakdown of the ABM Treaty amidst heightened East–West tensions would dispel all prospects of future arms control and lead to a dangerous deterioriation of security in Europe, put in doubt the validity of France's and Britain's deterrents, and undermine NATO's flexible response strategy (Müller 1987, Daalder 1988).

Under the weight of this triple attack, the Administration started an orderly retreat. At the end of 1984, it decided to abide by the ABM Treaty for four years, to postpone two SDI experiments because of their incompatibility with the treaty, and to design experiments for the coming period so that they would remain in treaty limits. Then the hardliners in the Administration shifted tactics. Increasing emphasis was laid on alleged Soviet violations of the ABM Treaty (US Department of Defense 1985). This marked a major concession. This argument suggested that the treaty as such was all right, but its utility undermined by Soviet non-compliance. Yet, by invoking the regime—and the principle of reciprocity as a justification for SDI—the Administration submitted itself to counter-arguments based on the substance of the regime. It never escaped from this trap. Opponents of the Administration could now point to the due regime procedure for pursuing complaints: to present its evidence to the Standing Consultative Commission (SCC), to seek clarification and corrective action. This procedure ran counter to the preferred strategy of the Pentagon, namely to scrap the ABM Treaty and to embark on a unilateral course. Consequently, from the restitution of strategic arms control talks in 1985 on, US negotiators attempted to convince their Soviet counterparts that amending the ABM Treaty was in their mutual interest. Simultaneously, US SCC commissioners tried to extract explications on all suspected treaty violations and demanded the destruction of the radar at Krasnoyarsk.

A second trap into which the Administration fell was its allegation that SDI had brought the Soviets back to the negotiation table. This argument justified exchanging SDI for Soviet concessions (Kubbig 1990). SDI proponents viewed this new course with the greatest concern. In order to make the present policy irreversible, they urged the earliest possible deployment of elements of a nation-wide defence, and the immediate scrapping of the ABM Treaty. Plans for an early deployment surfaced in 1986 but probably dated back to 1985. Early deployment would not await the ironing-out of US–Soviet divergences on compliance, or on amending the treaty. A new regime-related tool had to be created to justify the planned speeding-up of SDI activities. Consequently, a third wave of pro-SDI arguments was started in late 1985: the so-called 'broad interpretation' of the ABM Treaty. Until 1985 the treaty had been read by all Administrations as not permitting the testing and development, outside the laboratories, of ABM components based on new technology. The 'broad interpretation' (Garthoff 1987) held that the restrictions enumerated in the treaty only applied to those components explicitly mentioned; new technologies were not covered, and could be tested and developed. According to this position, the history of treaty negotiations was misrepresented, and its most far-fetched interpretation applied to the critical Article VIb and Agreed Statement D that dealt with forbidden component testing and exotic technologies. But even this reinterpretation was, in fact, a disorderly retreat by the Administration that led to defeat. The Administration used the treaty's substance to prove that what it planned to do was in agreement with the treaty's rules. This tactic implied that the rules were valid; if the Administration's interpretation could be proved wrong, SDI was illegal and, by right, had to be stopped.

The new interpretation faced an irresistible counter-attack. The allies made it clear that they preferred the traditional reading. Six former secretaries of defence joined forces with SALT/ABM negotiators to confirm that the 'narrow' interpretation was valid. The eminent defence expert Senator Nunn refuted the new interpretation and affirmed that the Senate had given its constitutional advice and consent on the basis of the 'narrow interpretation'. According to the Senator, a unilateral change of the meaning of the treaty amounted to a counter-constitutional *coup d'état*. Congress then adopted an amendment to the defence budget authorization. From fiscal year 1988 on, the Administration was obliged to forgo all activities that were at odds with treaty rules. Early deployment options and long-term space tests of exotic technologies were excluded. Secretary of State Shultz then developed a compromise: the new interpretation was valid, but Administration policy would comply with the narrow interpretation. Once the Administration had provoked the discussion about the meaning of the rules, it was held to these rules by the masters of the purse.

The hardliners returned to voicing complaints about Soviet compliance. Weinberger and Perle pressed for declaring the Krasnoyarsk radar a 'material breach of the ABM Treaty' and for abandoning the treaty on the ABM review in 1987. Eventually, Reagan agreed to the State Department's recommendation not to treat the radar as 'material breach'. While the debate on 'countermeasures' lingered on until 1989, such measures became impracticable, with the Soviets offering increasing concessions, and a Congress less and less willing to fund SDI at the levels desired by the Administration.

How did the strategic nuclear arms regime survive the assault? The regime was embedded in three institutional frames of reference: the strategic frame (deterrence), the political frame (arms control as part of security policy), and the constitutional frame (rights of the Senate). Thus, the regime was integrated into a 'reflexive' layer of systems. The attack on the regime provoked references to the higher systems. Each of these systems, in turn, had its interested constituency that rallied to the defence of its frame of reference: the allies and the conservative centrists (including the Joint Chiefs of Staff) for deterrence, the liberals and arms controllers for arms control, and those sensitive about executive infringements on Congressional rights. The coalition of these constituencies was too strong to be beaten by an Administration split internally.

The norms and rules of the treaty had helped to create a focus on which the various constituencies could converge. In the course of the dispute, rules that had not been understood in their full meaning for budgeting, research and development, and testing prescriptions were finally operationalized. Without the rules system of the ABM Treaty, it is highly unlikely that the Administration's plans would have encountered as determined and concentrated an opposition as they did.

4. CASE 2: THE SOVIETS AND KRASNOYARSK

Traditionally, Soviet defence policy was rooted in unilateral self-help. History and the manichaean Marxist-Leninist ideology, which imputed worst intentions to the enemy, made it inadvisable to keep Soviet security contingent on US goodwill. Thus, defence against strategic missiles was pursued from the 1950s as a necessary complement to offensive strategic nuclear strength. Strategic defence possessed a powerful lobby in the Air Defence Commmand (PVO), an independent command since 1948 (Garthoff 1990: 29–93).

The agreement on limiting ABMs as an integral part of a strategic nuclear arms control regime, at the outset of the SALT negotiations in 1969, engendered a shift in politico-strategic thinking. It caused protracted controversy in the Soviet security establishment and the political leadership. The Soviets had agreed that the build-up of ABM defences was a source of strategic instability and could lead to an acceleration of the arms race. Predictability of the future strategic relationship was contingent on the limitation of both offensive and defensive arms. This was a subject addressed frequently by civilian and military writers in the late 1960s and early 1970s. The Soviets did not embrace mutual vulnerability as a desired state of affairs. Yet, they agreed that an unlimited strategic offence–defence arms race was even worse. The strategic nuclear arms regime, and the ABM Treaty as its pivot, was thus incorporated into political and military strategy. This was documented by Soviet military writings, and by the seminal Tula speech of Brezhnev in 1977 in which he renounced military superiority. But not all military men were satisfied, and the PVO remained committed to expanding strategic defences (Garthoff 1984, 1990).

During the negotiations of the ABM Treaty, the Soviets had tried to protect air defences. They agreed only reluctantly to preclude the upgrading of air defence equipment to ABM missions, but repulsed all further attempts to curb the modernization and expansion of their air defence systems. Initially, the Soviet Union had indicated a willingness to accept a complete ABM ban and the prohibition of anti-tactical ballistic missile defences (ATBM). The United States, however, refused this step because of plans to upgrade the Patriot air defence missile to ATBM capabilities. When, in the 1980s, the USSR herself pursued such activities not proscribed under the treaty, the United States was concerned that the Soviet Union was preparing for a 'break-out' from the treaty and for the deployment of a nation-wide defence (Voas 1990). One problem was the overlap between early warning, space tracking, and ABM battle management radars. Early warning was indispensable for strategic stability, and space tracking was important for peaceful as well as military purposes. The treaty therefore permitted early-warning radars only at the periphery of national territories and facing outwards, thus preventing their use for battle management, and prohibited battle management radars except within a radius of 150 km of the one permitted ABM site, and allowed space tracking anywhere. But a technical definition of the different types of radars was not provided (Garthoff 1987).

In the early 1970s, the USSR decided to improve its early-warning system. The decision on procurement of a series of Pechora LPAR[3] was taken by the Defence Council. Initially, the necessity to deploy a Pechora at a site not permitted under the ABM Treaty was not obvious. But, in reviewing experiences with two radars located at the East Siberian periphery, the PVO concluded that radars in this region suffered from the unstable permafrost underground and could not be maintained because of the insufficient infrastructure. The Council thus decided to place the radar at Krasnoyarsk, close to the trans-Siberian railway. The military was aware that this plan was not in accordance with the

---

[3] 'LPAR' stands for 'large-phased array radar'. LPARs are the most advanced long-range sensing radars available for early warning against a ballistic missile attack.

ABM Treaty. The treaty was studied, and it was discovered that Agreed Statement F (dealing with space tracking) might provide a loophole. The decision was forced upwards through the hierarchy and was finally taken by Defence Minister Ustinov. Orders were issued to label the station a satellite-tracking device. On three occasions Soviet members of the SCC tried to prepare the ground for the inevitable controversy with the Americans. In 1978, they stated, with reference to another Pechora radar deployed 150 miles inland, that the radar was placed there for 'technical and practical reasons'. This distance from the border was then agreed to fall under the definition of periphery, but the Soviets had left a mark that pragmatic considerations affected their interpretation of the treaty. The Soviets repeated in October 1981 and in 1982 that the placement of radars had to take into account 'technical and practical considerations'.

Construction of the radar started in 1982. In 1983 the CIA identified on satellite pictures its parameters (size, form, angle, etc.) as those of the Pechora type. The radar faced north-east, guarding the approaches from the Bering Sea and the sea off Alaska, a US strategic submarine patrolling area. The United States raised the issue instantly at the next SCC meeting. Soviet commissioner Starodubov alleged that the radar was for tracking manned space objects. When construction was finished, the space-tracking function would be obvious. The United States requested a special SCC session on the radar, which the Soviets refused. It took a year before the Soviets came up with detailed technical and geographical data. By then, the space-tracking explanation had already been discarded by US research. The Krasnoyarsk radar faced towards the horizon—ideal for detecting approaching ballistic missiles, but at too low an angle for space tracking. The US debate turned to the question whether the radar was constructed for or at least capable of battle management. At the first SCC session in 1985, the USSR was asked to admit a violation of the treaty and to dismantle the radar or to render it incapable of performing battlefield missions (Voas 1986).

When the Soviet Defence Ministry had permitted the evasion of the treaty, it had counted on an irreversible US commitment to SALT, expecting that the Americans would tolerate the small manipulation of the regime's rules. When the Krasnoyarsk radar was discovered, however, the Soviet Union found itself in a fierce struggle to defend the regime against Reagan's SDI. The Soviet military were spelling out scrupulously the regime's rules. At the same time, they stuck stubbornly to the space-tracking pretext for Krasnoyarsk. This vulnerable flank also became exposed in the domestic Soviet discussion. The interpretation of the treaty terms was not in the purview of the military alone; it also fell into the authority of the Foreign Ministry to handle issues of treaty compliance. This made an inquiry into the issue inevitable. To fight SDI, the leadership had mobilized civilian scientists and scholars, who became involved immediately (a first major discussion was held in spring 1983 in the Academy of Sciences). Their newly prominent role gave them far more leeway. The involvement of academicians and instituteniks was yet another guarantee that critical questions would be asked about the space-tracking explanation.

In order to strengthen their position, the Soviets compiled counter-accusations of alleged US treaty violations, concerning especially the modernization of two early-warning radars, Thule in Greenland and Fylingdales in England, which allegedly violated the prohibition of early-warning radars stationed abroad. The United States responded that both radars were 'grandfathered' by the treaty, i.e. not affected by the treaty's constraints because they were already in existence when the ABM Treaty was signed. By using the strategy of counter-accusation, the Soviet Union ran into the same trap as had the US Administration on SDI: a breach of the treaty by one party justifies a violation by the other only after following due procedure. It can certainly not justify a counter-breach in advance. Nevertheless, counter-accusations remained the second line of defence in the next two years. Increasingly, it fell to the Foreign Ministry to respond to allegations of Soviet treaty violations. The last declaration under Gromyko was a statement by the Soviet embassy in Washington that the technical signature of the radar that could be picked up by national technical means of verification would demonstrate the innocent purpose of the device.

First signs of a crack in the Soviet position had appeared at the end of 1984. Then, it had been hinted (though unofficially) that the Soviets might be willing to trade Krasnoyarsk for Thule and Fylingdales. This demonstrated acceptance of the principle of mutual vulnerability. Then, in the spring of 1985, a Soviet source signalled in the SCC that Krasnoyarsk may have been built for military purposes, and that the USSR was in considerable trouble (Talbott 1988: 224). A sign of movement was first conveyed by Dobrynin, now director of the foreign relations department of the Politburo. Dobrinyn reaffirmed the space-tracking mission of Krasnoyarsk, but proposed that the peaceful objectives of the radar could be verified on site by US scientists. This was in obvious contrast to earlier statements that had constrained 'verification' to national technical means.

When Shevardnadze took over the Foreign Ministry in June 1985, his and Gorbachev's agenda deviated fundamentally from traditional Soviet policy. Both were convinced that the threat of nuclear war superseded differences built on Marxist-Leninist theory. Both regarded superpower armaments as vastly redundant, and both firmly believed that national security could only be achieved by promoting co-operative security. The strategic nuclear arms regime, with the ABM Treaty at its core, had to be maintained and expanded. Shevardnadze also realized quickly that the building of further security regimes depended crucially on the re-establishment of the reputation of the Soviet Union as a reliable partner. The Krasnoyarsk dispute undermined this effort (Garthoff 1990, Shevardnadze 1991: ch. 3). At this time, the Soviet Government must have been highly aware that the Krasnoyarsk dispute put long-term co-operative security and a good reputation in danger. Meanwhile, SDI not only threatened a US strategic breakthrough, it also jeopardized security co-operation. In the spring of 1985, twenty-three House Democrats had written to Gorbachev, warning against the consequences of Krasnoyarsk for arms control and the ABM Treaty. The pressure was renewed two years later when the House voted 418 : 0 to label the radar 'a blatant violation of the ABM Treaty'. The battle for the 'narrow' versus the 'wide' interpretation raged in Washington, further focusing attention on the ABM Treaty (Rivkin 1987: 493).

Shevardnadze became aware of the importance of the issue during his first days in office. An inquiry into the matter started almost immediately, and he ordered his ministry to become fully involved with the required expertise in arms control, in order to check the weight of the military. He created an office for arms control and disarmament which reported to him, staffed by arms control veterans. He enhanced the involvement of non-governmental experts by installing in the Foreign Office a Scientific Co-Ordination Committee, charged to integrate academic work into the arms control policy planning process (Shevardnadze 1991: ch. 3).

The Defence Ministry and the PVO fought a battle of retreat. First, they briefed the new authorities that the radar was for space tracking, that its signatures (i.e. the features that can be made out by means of satellites) could distinguish it from battle-management and early-warning radars, and that Thule and Fylingdales were a violation of the treaty. Hence, the new leadership was confident that the Soviet Union was acting in accordance with the ABM Treaty. However, to assuage US concerns, the Soviet Union began to resolve some of the other, minor, US complaints on Soviet compliance (Voas 1990). As to Krasnoyarsk, on the basis of PVO assurances, the leadership pursued two alternative proposals to the Americans in parallel. First, they offered on-site inspection. US visitors were allowed to check the distinct features of a space-tracking radar that PVO had assured would be discernible at the site. Second, the exchange of Krasnoyarsk for Thule and Fylingdales became an official proposal in June 1986. Both proposals were contested in the Soviet bureaucracy. Military spokespersons remained silent on the verification offer. And even in 1986, after the 'deal' offer had been officially made, some speakers declared the destruction of Krasnoyarsk out of the question for security reasons. On the other hand, after the November 1986 round of the SCC, rumours emerged that Soviet members had admitted Krasnoyarsk's illegality, but this remained unconfirmed for two years.

The United States reacted coolly: Krasnoyarsk was a violation of the treaty, while the US radars were not. Verifying peaceful purposes would be impossible because switching from space tracking to early warning involved merely an unverifiable exchange of software. Meanwhile, the Soviet Union had started another strategy: a proposal that both parties adhere to the treaty for fifteen years, at which time they would negotiate anew. At the Reykjavik summit, both sides agreed on a period of ten years, but disagreed on the follow-up: the Soviets wanted new negotiations on an ABM Treaty, while Reagan wanted freedom to deploy strategic defences.

In April 1988, the USSR admitted that the 'space-tracking radar' was 'in the wrong location' (a nonsensical statement: space-tracking radars had no local constraints; it was a veiled admission that Krasnoyarsk was for early warning). Shevardnadze was still convinced that the radar was for space tracking. But he understood that it was causing difficulties for some reason, and reaffirmed a readiness to exchange it for Thule and Fylingdales. Moreover, the USSR invited non-governmental US experts to the site. The visit confirmed that the radar was not capable of battle management, but left the US Government unconvinced that it could not be used for early warning.

Meanwhile, the Soviet leadership must have become very annoyed with the PVO. It became apparent by now that the argument of 'distinct space-tracking features' was a misfire and was used not only to fend off US accusations but to mislead the Soviet leadership. Speeding up the review became essential, since the United States was discussing declaring Krasnoyarsk a material breach of the treaty. In order to change the course, the resistance of the PVO and the Defence Ministry had to be broken. Then a young German amateur pilot landed on Red Square with a small aircraft, thereby discrediting the PVO at once. Gorbachev purged the top of the Defence Ministry and the PVO. Soon afterwards, the truth about Krasnoyarsk came to the fore, and Gorbachev announced a one-year moratorium (Rivkin 1987).

After the PVO purge, the Foreign Ministry had gained access to the files concerning the history of Krasnoyarsk and knew by now that the United States had reason for concern over treaty compliance. It was also revealed that a dispute was going on between the Defence Ministry, who argued for the completion of the radar, and arms control proponents, who preferred a dismantling. The Soviets gave up their request for the reciprocal destruction of Thule and Fylingdales in summer 1988—and requested in return only a promise to abide by the ABM Treaty's narrow interpretation. The Foreign Ministry's arms control and disarmament office had concluded that the American radars were not a problem equivalent to Krasnoyarsk.

Still, the internal debate was not over. The Soviet document for the summer 1988 SCC meeting insisted that Krasnoyarsk was for space tracking, and that Thule and Fylingdales were illegal. Defence Minister Yazov tried to persuade his new colleague

Carlucci to declare it a permitted ground-based 'sensor' analogous to space-based sensors permitted, according to the Pentagon line, under the ABM Treaty. In response, Reagan asked Gorbachev to resolve the Krasnoyarsk problem, but his letter neither called the radar a 'material breach' nor threatened countermeasures. Karpov, at that time the head of the Foreign Ministry's arms control department, at the SCC meeting again offered to dismantle the transmitter or to permit continuous on-site inspection. Of particular importance were proposals to replace current equipment with instruments that were unequivocally devoted to space missions. This was a very clear admission that the present equipment was not designed to perform these—peaceful—tasks. When the United States insisted on unconditional destruction of the radar, the Soviet leadership offered, in a sequence of proposals, face-saving ways out of the quandary and was prepared to give the United States the assurances needed: permanent verification, joint manning, handing over the site to the Academy of Sciences, and creation of an international space centre. Each proposal was meant to render the radar more unsuitable for military purposes than its predecessor.

At long last Shevardnadze realized that the radar had been built intentionally for military purposes and was an unequivocal breach of the treaty. On 22 September 1989, in a published speech to the Supreme Soviet, he stated that the Krasnoyarsk radar violated the treaty and undercut the efforts to save the strategic nuclear arms control regime, and that it would be dismantled completely and unconditionally. Military discontent flared up publicly afterwards. Yet the decision was made and dismantlement was in full swing in 1990.

5. CASE 3: THE WEST GERMANS AND NUCLEAR EXPORT CONTROLS

West Germany's attitude towards nuclear technology after the Second World War went through five phases, each defining a specific position towards the emerging, and later fully developed, non-proliferation regime (Kötter and Müller 1990).

In the first phase, the main rationale of West Germany was to regain its place among the western nations. Since constraints on the utilization of nuclear energy were an outgrowth of the occupation regime, recovering the right to nuclear research and industrial deployment assumed a highly symbolic value. When the country's admittance to the Western European Union and NATO was made conditional on its renouncing nuclear weapons, Adenauer bowed down in 1954. However, he maintained the opinion that this was a temporary setback (Schwarz 1989), in the narrowly circumscribed form that only production on German soil was excluded (a loophole which Franz Josef Strauß, Defence Minister, later tried to exploit when, in 1957, he concluded an abortive agreement with France and Italy to produce the bomb in France (Strauß 1989: 313–19)), and with the explicit declaration that this renouncement was valid *rebus sic stantibus*. Thus, during this first phase, the principle of non-proliferation was not accepted; West Germany submitted to it for utilitarian reasons. The policy debate was confined to close governmental circles, with the Office of the Chancellor, the Ministry for Atomic Energy (headed by Strauß), and later the Defence Ministry exerting leadership. After leading scientists pleaded for a nuclear-weapon-free Germany, they were quickly absorbed into the struggle for rebuilding civilian nuclear activities. In this endeavour, they supported governmental efforts to regain 'civilian nuclear sovereignty' (Radkau 1983, Eckert 1989). The setting up of EURATOM and its safeguards was greeted as a step forward: it put Germany on an equal level with its European partners, though it quickly appeared that France claimed a special position.

When the Non-Proliferation Treaty (NPT) was negotiated, West German politicians understood that equal rights with the nuclear-weapon states were not on the cards. Even the concept of a NATO multilateral force had fallen through, and the Nuclear Planning Group was the best the country could extract from a decade of discussions. The legally binding renunciation of nuclear weapons was still hard to swallow for the conservatives in the then ruling Grand Coalition (CDU/CSU together with SPD). Meanwhile, for the Social Democrats, the liberals, and a sizeable minority of the conservatives, the main perspective had shifted from politico-military to politico-economic issues. It was feared that IAEA safeguards under an NPT, combined with EURATOM measures, would disadvantage the German nuclear industry against its competitors from nuclear-weapon states. Consequently, West Germany insisted on the inclusion of Art. IV in the NPT that confirmed the 'inalienable right' of non-nuclear-weapon states to enjoy the benefits of nuclear energy. It also supported regular reviews of the treaty and a limited duration of twenty-five years.

A majority of the West German political class was now prepared to accept the principle of non-proliferation, but only if it was compromised by the principle of unimpeded civilian nuclear development. The majority of the conservatives still thought that consenting to 'second-class status' by acceding to the treaty was unacceptable. Again, the negotiations were conducted in narrow political circles. Industrial leaders became convinced that for uninterrupted fuel supply, with proper constraints on the intrusiveness of safeguards, it was advisable to accede to the NPT (Nerlich 1973, Häckel 1989: 73–5, 84–92).

In the third phase, the German nuclear industry conquered the world market. The general assumption was that the NPT had solved the proliferation problem, and that nuclear commerce could evolve without any additional barriers. Germany successfully tried to limit the authority of IAEA safeguards to minimum intrusiveness into industrial activities: over-reliance on material accountancy and limited access of IAEA inspectors to 'strategic points' in a nuclear factory were the consequences (Fischer and Szasz 1985).

With the NPT in place, West Germany took the offensive at the nuclear export front. Export policies were shaped by the letter, not necessarily the spirit of the treaty. The complex balance of the treaty's norms was interpreted in such a way as to give priority to civilian nuclear development and transfers—not to non-proliferation. Germany exported heavy-water technology, without safeguards, to India—because it did not concern 'special fissile material' addressed in Art. III, 2 of the NPT, collaborated with South Africa on jet-nozzle enrichment technology, exported a heavy-water reactor to Argentina, and agreed to transfer complete fuel cycle technology to non-NPT member Brazil (Müller 1989*a*). Germany, in collaboration with France, prevented the rule of 'full-scope safeguards' to be included in the London Guidelines by the group of suppliers; and Bonn delayed the conclusion of these guidelines long enough to grandfather its transfer of sensitive technology to Brazil.

But, for the first time, there were cracks in the united German front. First, the debate on NPT ratification in 1975, one of the rare examples of parliamentary involvement, demonstrated that the principle of non-proliferation and the norm of maintaining non-nuclear status now enjoyed the support of an overwhelming part of the polity. As early as 1974 the cabinet had cancelled the application for an official contract between the German company STEAG and South Africa on enrichment technology transfer. During the negotiations with Brazil, the Foreign Office prevailed in sharpening the safeguards and notification requirements. The Foreign Office also pressed the reluctant Ministries of Economics and of Research and Technology to accept the 'restraint' on the export of sensitive technology embedded in the London Guidelines. The Brazilian deal also stimulated for the first time some debate in the public on the obligations the NPT implied; yet the stronger part of the polity stuck to the pro-commercial position taken by the Schmidt Government in its dispute with the Carter Administration over measures for strengthening the regime at the expense of industrial interests (Kaiser 1978). However, the undertakings of the London Guidelines were quickly adopted by expanding the item lists attached to the export control legislation.

In the fourth period, from the early 1980s to 1988, the creation of a European Political Co-Operation (EPC) working party on non-proliferation enhanced Foreign Office involvement. The desk officers in the Foreign Office were now continually confronted with questions regarding the non-proliferation regime. The Foreign Office became increasingly concerned about the obvious weaknesses of the West German export control system. There was a protracted struggle between the Foreign Office and the Ministries of Economics and of Research and Technology over crucial export cases. Usually, the Foreign Office would oppose a licence, or request an inquiry, while the Ministry of Economics, with 'technical advice' from the Ministry of Research and Technology, would find arguments to grant the licence or to deny the Foreign Office the authority to get involved. In these inter-ministerial disputes, the Foreign Office pointed regularly to the obligations under the NPT and the London Guidelines. The other ministries countered that law and regulation were in accordance with these obligations, and that their own policy of letting the transfers in question go were covered by German law and regulation. While the meaning of the regime's rules was disputed, these rules served as the frame of reference for the dispute (Deutscher Bundestag 1990: 157–270).

Yet, for all the weaknesses of regime implementation at the operational level, the 1980s witnessed some important political steps. In 1985, during the third NPT review conference, West Germany was the major stumbling-block to an agreement on full-scope safeguards. But the conference called on NPT suppliers to make efforts to persuade their non-NPT customers to accept safeguards on all their nuclear activities (Fischer and Müller 1985). The West German Government took this recommendation seriously. Bonn denied Pakistan a bid for the power reactor tender. It requested that all nuclear material in Argentina must be under safeguards when new German nuclear supplies were to reach Argentina. Bonn also refused to permit the German company KWU to finish the Busheer reactors in Iran.

Meanwhile, nuclear power had begun to attract criticism, and had lost its image as being at the cutting edge of technology. The SPD, following the Greens, turned anti-nuclear once Helmut Schmidt had left the party's helm. And the SPD and the Greens were more ready to address issues of non-proliferation in Parliament once the conservative–liberal coalition had come to power.

In early 1988, the storm broke (Müller 1989*a*). Alarmed by (false) information from a journalist that weapons-grade material had been smuggled to Pakistan and Libya, the Bundestag set up a special committee to inquire about the case. The danger of a breach of regime rules had superseded ideological and/or domestic considerations for some of the actors involved. The deputies took great pains to investigate what the stipulations of the regime meant. They went into a detailed study of the files of the Ministry of Economics and the Foreign Office on nuclear exports. The President and desk officers of the export licensing agency (Bundesamt für Gewerbliche Wirtschaft) were questioned, and these hearings revealed understaffing and underequipment of the licensing agency.

Under the pressure of the investigation, the Government took action. The position of the Foreign Office in the licensing procedure was strengthened: it assumed a veto position over exports to 'suspect countries', and on all sensitive nuclear exports. The Government drafted stricter export regulations and law. Then the Rabta affair lent new momentum to the ongoing debate. A major revision of the export laws was concluded in 1990, and a second wave started shortly thereafter as a reaction to the Gulf War. This reform eliminated some cherished elements of German law and trade philosophy. Activities of German citizens abroad are now covered by criminal law if they work on the production of weapons of mass destruction; likewise, nuclear transit-trade transactions by German companies require a licence even when the traded goods do not touch German ground. Also, industry is far less protected against prosecution and its consequences: breaching the export control law is a crime. By contrast with previous regulations the new law no longer requires proof of a clear threat to peace, security, or German foreign policy interests. Courts are authorized to rule the confiscation of the sale value of illegal transfers (costs are not deductible, as in the past). This can easily ruin a company. Firms are obliged to nominate a foreign trade official who can be held personally responsible for illegal transactions; companies must report annually on their capability to transfer sensitive technology. The export licensing and custom offices are authorized to exchange their data on companies, licences, and commerce. In addition, more than thirty changes in export regulation, stiffening controls and constraints, were enacted in about twenty-four months. The export control sector was allotted more than 200 new positions. The Government turned to a full-scope safeguards policy shortly before the fourth NPT review conference in 1990 (Bundesministerium für Wirtschaft 1991).

At the end of the Gulf War, nuclear non-proliferation policy had been accepted as a priority of German foreign policy. Germany had been active in persuading Brazil and Argentina to set up a full-scope safeguards system, had lobbied South Africa and the Front Line States to accede to the NPT, had approached France with the same purpose, had pressed, within the European Community and the London Suppliers' Group, for the joint adoption of full-scope safeguards, had pressed North Korea to sign its due safeguards agreement with the IAEA, and had led a major European initiative on improving the safeguards system. In respect of this last phase, four points remain to be emphasized. First, abiding by the rules of the regime was seen as a matter of good versus evil in all political quarters; second, the public debate helped sharpen the awareness of the leadership; third, priorities were shifted from 'commerce over non-proliferation' to 'non-proliferation over commerce'; fourth, the Foreign Office had assumed the role of a determined regime defender.

6. WHY REGIMES MATTER

The Reagan Administration pursued a power-oriented strategy and used the standard of relative gains compared with the adversary. Yet this strategy did not prevail. In the winning counter-coalition, some calculated that a break-out from the ABM Treaty would give the Soviets short-term advantages that might turn out fatal if the promises of SDI were wrong. But the overwhelming majority were moved by the long-term prospects of arms control, and the obligations under the treaty. Neither consideration was a realist one.

In the Soviet case, the proposition that the Soviets just surrendered to the double pressure of SDI and their own economic crisis does not fit the timing of Soviet policy. When they were most concerned about the possible US gains from SDI (1983–6), they defended Krasnoyarsk, and worked on its completion. When the internal American debate had made SDI less alarming, the Soviets started to change their policy. After Reagan had chosen not to declare Krasnoyarsk a material violation, and after Congress confirmed its opposition to abandoning the treaty, the Soviets decided to dismantle the radar. The decision was taken before the full extent of the economic crisis became obvious, and before the Soviet empire in Eastern Europe was finally lost. The voices that argued the 'realist' way and warned against bowing to US demands lost. The realist approach does not help us to understand the change.

The German case is a counter-example to realism. Strong 'realist' arguments on the relative power and economic disadvantages *vis-à-vis* the nuclear-weapons states faded away between 1970 and 1990. They played no role in the great reform debate of 1988–92. It might be surmised that external pressure by the United States at a critical juncture of German history moved the Germans, yet this proposition is demonstrably wrong. First, the evolution started during the period between 1988 and 1989 when US pressure was minimal. Second, it gained steam before the Americans called the FRG to order on the Rabta affair, and before the fall of the Berlin Wall occurred. Third, after the unification process was finished, that is, after US support became less crucial, the Germans still continued with a new wave of export control reforms. And finally, the consideration of relative economic disadvantage was discarded during the reform discussion and revived only afterwards, as a necessity for persuading Germany's partners to apply the same standards.

The realist paradigm does not help us much in understanding our cases of regime compliance. First, it assumes a unified actor rationally calculating the national interest. In fact, security policy in all cases was chosen as the result of a controversial discourse. Highly contradictory definitions of national security were expounded by the parties. Realism is not very useful for analysing and predicting the course of these debates. Second, it is flawed empirically. In the debates, those most akin to the realist argument lost out. For these facts realism cannot account.

In the winning coalition defending the ABM Treaty in the United States, those who regarded the predictability of the strategic competition as a higher value than advantages from SDI were numerous. The risks of instability from an unregulated defence–offence relationship were repeatedly noted. The same applies to the Soviet debate. This assumption had persuaded the Soviets to negotiate the treaty in the first place. Sacrificing Krasnoyarsk, thus, was not done primarily to stop US technology, but to save a treaty that was seen as the backbone of an evolving strategic nuclear arms regime. Interest calculations played a relatively minor role in the German debate. It was assumed simply that the regime served global, and thereby German, security. Thus, the neoliberal-utilitarian thesis helps us to explain part, but not all of the US and Soviet decisions. However, it is not applicable to the German evolution.

Pure institutionalist theory assumes that working inside an institution exerts an overriding influence on states' behaviour. Norms and rules impose extraordinary pressures on actors in all cases. In the US–ABM case, the rules of the regime were used throughout the debate as the standard of measurement for permitted and prohibited behaviour. Despite great efforts by the

SDI proponents, they were not able to overcome the barrier the regime had created to their preferred projects. Opponents were able to mobilize around the ABM Treaty rules as 'system of reference', and also to rally opposition around the regime's norms against which SDI was basically directed. The power of regime rules was notable in budgetary discussions. Regime rules frame the choices for which defence funds can be allocated, and to surpass these limits requires extraordinary justification. Budgetary debates are no pure utilitarian discourses. The frame of this discourse is preformed by regime prescriptions. Most studies of Soviet behaviour confirm rule-compliant behaviour even where it contradicted initial development and deployment plans. The great achievement of the 1980s was the extension of compliance behaviour from the specific *rules* to the more general, but also more fundamental, *norms* of the regime. This was less visible in the Krasnoyarsk case, where the Soviet leadership had to correct a breach of rules. It was more visible in the numerous adjustments made concerning other US complaints cleared through the SCC where the Soviets, in order to demonstrate their regime-conforming behaviour, chose to respect the regime's norms even where the rules opened grey areas of interpretation. The German reforms are the clearest norm-directed behaviour. After the (false) allegation of an NPT breach was made, the German Parliament forced a review of the meaning of the regime norms. Government and Parliament adjusted German laws, regulations, and practices with a view to realizing the regime's norms even where the regime's rules were not clear-cut. We can conclude that regimes exert pressure on governments, even on those with reservations about the regime. Not only are regimes powerful behaviour-guides because it is so costly to construct alternatives: the sheer existence of a regime puts an 'extra' burden of proof on regime opponents because in discourses about proper behaviour of states and other regime actors, the regime structure serves automatically as frame of reference.

The US debate was partly a rerun of what took place in 1969–72. What was new was the certainty of SDI opponents that the Soviets were a reliable partner of arms control as far as unambiguously fixed rules were concerned. Co-operation within the regime context had made this learning possible. Apart from this fact, the US case is rather countering 'unlearning' through discourse than real learning. For the Soviets, the amount of learning was gigantic. Security co-operation with the United States had convinced a considerable part of the Soviet foreign policy élite and the security apparatus that their manichaean image of the world was wrong. The Soviet élite started understanding the interdependence of security policy. They now could interpret hostile steps by the United States as responses to Soviet actions. Arms control had helped to correct the Marxist-Leninist enemy image that had immobilized Soviet security policy. The learning process included insight into the failure of bullying through world politics, that reliance on military strength had resulted in the ruin of the economy, and the experience that arms control was an alternative way to realize security.

Learning was a factor in German export control reforms as well. West Germans learned that the fear of disadvantages from non-nuclear status did not come true. Then they learned that free-wheeling export, though not literally at odds with the NPT, did not serve the regime's goal. The termination of sensitive exports was the consequence. The shock caused by various scandals then motivated a new inquiry into the effectiveness of existing regulations. In the process political priorities were adjusted to the regime's norms; 'instrumental learning' helped to correct basic policy orientations. The modification of behaviour through experience is a basic feature of 'living in a regime'. Learning concerns whether the regime works or not, and whether one's efforts to comply with regime norms and rules are sufficient for the purpose. Most important, our cases reveal that being in a regime may force quite a fundamental review and overhaul of national policy priority and principles.

The cases reveal a powerful influence of four general-normative 'reflexive nesting complexes' on compliance:

1. The first complex consists of a hierarchical framework of norms: the necessity to avoid nuclear war, the necessity of security co-operation, arms control as the framework for such co-operation. This strand of argument was used by the arms control community in the SDI debate. The same frame of argument informed 'new thinking' and the debate on Krasnoyarsk, and is found in German Foreign Office and opposition deputy pronouncements on the need for export reform. Security regime compliance, hence, takes into account

the consequences that non-compliance might have for the broader framework of arms control, security co-operation, and peace.

2. The second complex is international law. The norm *pacta sunt servanda* puts a heavy burden on those who want to breach legally fixed regimes. It forced US proponents of SDI to look for loopholes in the substantive and procedural prescriptions of the regime rather than to scrap it unilaterally. It served Gorbachev and Shevardnadze to reduce the supervisory monopoly of the military over the compliance process. It was a main source of pressure for reform in Germany.

3. The third complex comprises status and prestige. In a regime context, these considerations concern reputation and responsibility. This factor was least visible in the US case, but it was of enormous importance for the Soviet Union. One goal of the new leadership was to improve the credibility of the USSR as a partner in security co-operation. Maintenance of reputation as a reliable partner was indispensable, and concessions in disputes of compliance were justified in this light (Shevardnadze 1991: ch. 3). Reputation was also crucial in the German case. It was feared that the damage done by the export scandals to the German image abroad could badly hurt the country's prestige at a critical juncture of its history. The imperative of 'new responsibility' of the united country provided even more pressure to repair the damage as quickly as possible.

4. The last 'nesting' frame of reference is domestic law. Treaty obligations are translated into domestic legislation. Those responsible for violations can thus be held responsible through legal procedures, and those desiring to breach regime rules violate laws of their land. The domestic law standard was strongly invoked in the debate on the German export control system. Even more significant was the double legal reflexivity of the American ABM debate. The treaty was the law of the land and had to be observed unless the law was changed. A unilateral change by the executive met a second law barrier, the Constitution. Because of the shared authority between Administration and Senate, unilaterally manipulating a treaty immediately becomes a constitutional matter. Changing the Constitution, however, is far higher a barrier than changing

a simple law. When rules are translated into domestic law, regimes gain strength from legal and constitutional reflexivity.[4]

7. THE DOMESTIC CONTEXT OF COMPLIANCE

The most relevant finding is that the politics of regime compliance involves a broad, controversial discourse. This point is important as the cases comprise three different political systems: a parliamentary democracy, a decentralized presidential democracy, and a one-party authoritarian regime. We can conclude that in most political systems—totalitarian dictatorships excluded—regime compliance will be developed through a political discourse, the boundaries and frames of which are preformed by the structure of the political system. The discourses in all cases put unilateralist self-help arguments against multilateralist, co-operative orientations. The discourses had two dimensions, an intellectual one (who is right? who is wrong?) and a power one (who is capable of forming the winning coalition?). The utilization of superior frames of reference and the invocation of the 'force of existing norms' helped decide the contests in favour of regime compliance.

There appears to be a regularity in that the more regime compliance issues become a matter of domestic discourse, the better the chances of compliance with regime rules. The danger of a breach of the ABM Treaty was most pressing while the US executive was engaged in internal discussion, and as long as operational compliance issues were handled by the Soviet Defence Ministry and the PVO. It was the involvement of additional actors that helped the regime prevail over the predilections of Soviet military and US unilateralists. Export control reform in Germany was successful when the Bundestag looked into the issue, and when the whole matter became an issue for public debate. The importance of a discourse for regime compliance provides one more argument for the hypothesis that democracies are best fitted for co-operative systems of international security (Doyle 1986).

Within such discourses, regime advocates are active throughout

---

[4] On the connection between international and domestic legal systems and compliance with regime rules see also Ch. 3, sects. 4.1 and 4.4, above.

the cases. They are those involved in regime-building and -maintenance. Foreign ministries/offices play a predominant role among regime advocates. The crucial importance of the dense collaboration on non-proliferation within the EPC for the 'regime enculturation' of German policy operators has been emphasized. The extragovernmental resistance in the United States against trespassing against the rules of the ABM Treaty united three former Secretaries of State, six former Secretaries of Defense, former negotiators of the ABM Treaty, and commissioners of the SCC. Within the Administration, negotiator Paul Nitze and SCC Commissioner Ellis were most inclined to follow prescribed procedures and to compromise in order to uphold the regime. The most fascinating case is the Soviet Union. As Shevardnadze notes, the Foreign Ministry was ripe for a substantial change in its policy when he took power. The long-standing experience of exchange with the West had convinced many Soviet officials of the flaws of the manichaean world-view. In the 'new thinking' policy many officials with years and decades of experience in arms control negotiations, instituteniks, and Pugwash scientists played an important role.

Domestic politics exerted an influence on the course of compliance policy in all cases. In the United States, the regime-neglectful policy of the Reagan Administration helped the democratic opposition to mount a counter-attack on an all too successful presidency with public opinion on its side. In the Soviet Union, Krasnoyarsk became a focus of the struggle of the new leadership over the forces of the *ancien régime*, and of the Foreign Ministry against the predominance of the military in the arms control area. In Germany, the slight majority in public opinion opposed to nuclear power helped to dissolve the prevailing, protective attitude of Government towards industry, and removed one main obstacle to export control reform. The effect was not unambiguous, however, since in the early and mid-1980s the opposition to nuclear power had initially hardened the same protective attitude.

Last but not least, dramatic political changes played a role by extricating policy from bureaucratic routine and complacency. For the United States, the revolution in Soviet behaviour helped regime defenders to prevail. For the Soviets, the double 'shock' of leadership succession and SDI challenge created the conditions wherein priority could be given to long-term co-operation. For

Germany, the scandal about the Transnuklear company (Müller 1989*a*), the Rabta affair, the unification, and the Gulf War created and kept the momentum for the reform process.

8. CONCLUSION

Our cases suggest that regimes have a strong influence on policy. States behave differently because of their regime membership. Regimes do not simply fall victim to relationalist recalculations of national interest. The advantages they confer make states hesitant to scrap them for short-term advantages. Norms and rules often prevail over unilateralist motivations. The reflexivity/nesting of regimes in normative frameworks of higher order adds to the persistence of regimes. Over time, states learn how to deal better with regime purposes, how to assess their partners' behaviour, and how to adjust their own priorities and their institutional and organizational framework.

PART V

Conclusion

16

Regime Theory

State of the Art and Perspectives

PETER MAYER, VOLKER RITTBERGER, AND MICHAEL ZÜRN

1. INTRODUCTION

The purpose of this chapter is twofold. In its first part (sect. 2) we seek to put regime analysis into the broader context of thinking about *social order*. Three issues are addressed: In section 2.1 we discuss the basic underlying concern of international regime analysis, i.e. the normative interest in exploring the ways through which *governance without government* can be achieved in order to avoid undesirable outcomes in international and transnational relations. In section 2.2 we seek to substantiate the validity of the notion 'governance without government' by offering a *comparative perspective on regimes and governance* across different levels of political and social organization (domestic and international), pointing out that non-hierarchical politics is not special to international relations but widespread even in societies with a hierarchical system of rule (government). Finally, in section 2.3 we describe the *contemporary international social order* as a heterogeneous composition of several coexisting components, one of which is international governance without government.

In the second part (sect. 3), the chapter aims at substantiating the claim that the frontiers of research have been moved forward by the contributions to this volume. Leaving aside conceptual issues, which in this volume are dealt with extensively by Keohane (Ch. 2, sect. 3) and Rittberger (Ch. 1, sect. 3.1), we focus on what we see as the *three main tasks of research on international regimes* and assess the achievements and shortcomings of the respective research efforts. The first task refers to the analysis of regime formation, persistence, and demise—an area in which regime analysis can point to many accomplishments but faces the challenge of moving beyond single-factor testing and of grappling with various ways of integrating hypotheses into more encompassing theories (sect. 3.1). The second main task of international regime analysis is to categorize and explain regime properties (sect. 3.2). Here, the assumption is that the analysis of international regimes falls short of its goal if it cannot account for the emergence of different types of regimes or for changes from one type of regime to another (change of regime or regime evolution). A first step, therefore, will have to be the construction of meaningful regime typologies. Such typologies may also be a prerequisite for dealing successfully with the third main task of international regime analysis, i.e. the study of regime consequences or effects (sect. 3.3). With respect to this task, regime analysis has yet to develop plausible hypotheses guiding systematic empirical research (but see Young 1992). Moreover, the conceptualization of what may be taken to be a consequence or effect of an international regime remains underdeveloped. Also, the methodological problems involved in studying regime consequences are far from being solved. Yet, the virgin nature of this segment of regime analysis holds the promise of rapid advance in the near future.

The chapter concludes by pointing to the further progress that could be achieved in this field of study by the development of a data base that would greatly enhance the chance of gaining reliable knowledge about social order in international politics (sect. 4).

2. SOCIAL ORDER IN INTERNATIONAL RELATIONS

2.1. Why Do We Need International Governance?

The basic underlying concerns of research on international regimes are captured by the titles of two eminent books in the International Relations literature: *Cooperation under Anarchy* (Oye 1986) and *Governance without Government* (Rosenau and Czempiel 1992). Regime theory is to explain the possibility, conditions, and consequences of international governance beyond anarchy and short of supranational government in a given issue area. *Governance*, with or without government, is distinguished from anarchy by the fact that states and other international actors recognize the existence of obligations and feel compelled, for whatever reason, to honour them by their behaviour. Governance both with and without government refers to purposive systems of rule or normative orders which have to be distinguished from regularities (natural orders) emerging from the unrestricted inter-actions of self-interested actors in a state of anarchy (balance of power, bipolar deterrence, etc.). In this sense, 'governance is order plus intentionality' (Rosenau 1992: 5), i.e. order as the result of several, at least partially co-ordinated, efforts of social engineering. In the case of governance without government obligations do not emanate from a hierarchical norm- and rule-setting process (government) but from voluntary agreements to play by a set of rules which are binding in the sense that they create convergent expectations and govern behaviour. Thus, *governance without government* is distinguished from government in that the compulsion exerted by the rules is not backed up by the threat or use of physical force (the state wielding the legal monopoly of violence); instead, it is the legitimacy of rules and their underlying norms which make international actors comply (Young 1979, Franck 1990). In other words, governance without government is based on non-hierarchical normative institutions involving a stabilized pattern of behaviour of a given number of actors in recurring situations. *Normative institutions* are based on a persistent and connected set of rules that defines behavioural roles, shapes activity and expectations, constrains the range of acceptable behaviour, and thus governs the relations among the participants (Keohane 1989*a*: 3; Young 1989*a*: 5). The specific object of regime analysis is voluntarily agreed-upon, *issue-area specific* normative institutions created by states and other inter-national actors, which are studied as the mainstay of establishing intentional social order by self-regulation in international relations.

Regime analysts implicitly or explicity consider non-hierarchical international institutions desirable. This *normative orientation of regime analysis* is founded on a relatively simple argument which consists of two components: (1) as a result of increasing exchange and transactions on the international level the need for political regulation 'beyond the nation state' has increased dramatically; (2)

the 'modern' response to an extended range of societal interactions, namely the formation of a kind of statehood, does not seem viable on the international level.

The Need for International Regulation

If social entities interact with each other on a steady basis the need for regulation of the interaction arises. Social regulation can be achieved by normative institutions. According to sociologists such as Emile Durkheim (1897) and Talcott Parsons (1949), the very fact of interaction presupposes convergent expectations based on some sort of common value orientation. Yet, the increased intensity of social interaction also fosters the convergence of value orientations, which, in turn, allows for further institutionalization of co-operation. Thus, the communicative process of value and interest formation has to be understood in order to account for the rise of normative institutions. This point of view—we might call it the *reflective approach* (Keohane 1988)—has been introduced into the analysis of international politics to explain intentional order among states by scholars standing in the tradition of Hugo Grotius (see Hurrell's Ch. 3 and Kratochwil's Ch. 4 above).

According to another point of view, interactions do not presuppose, yet create a demand for normative institutions, which are supposed to reduce the probability of undesirable outcomes. Jeremy Bentham and James S. Coleman (1990) are eminent representatives of this point of view, according to which the constellation of interests is most important for understanding social order. In International Relations we nowadays call this the *rationalistic approach* (see Ch. 2 as well as Ch. 6 above). For the purposes of our argument, it suffices to emphasize that both perspectives agree upon an enhanced need for, or an increased likelihood of, social regulation if the range and depth of interactions increase.

In fact, there is both an increased need for, and an increased likelihood of the creation of, normative institutions on the international level regulating the interactions among states and the transactions among individuals and collective actors across national borders. The interactions and transactions in the international arena have increased and resulted in a new quality of interdependence among international actors in a shrinking world.

The dramatically increased capital mobility and the high rate of foreign direct investment, especially in and among developed market economies, have led to improved exit options for business, which, in turn, significantly decrease the opportunities of governments to steer the economy towards desired outcomes such as stable growth, low inflation, and low unemployment rates. Even the physical security of citizens cannot be protected against external threats any longer by unilateral means alone, neither in the most powerful nation nor in an alliance of powerful nations. The global ecological dangers and the risks caused by the spread of weapons of mass destruction cannot be coped with by the means available to the Government of the United States or any other industrialized nations alone. Yet, not only has the capacity of the modern state to steer societal transactions by national means decreased, but the rising interdependence has also produced numerous problematic social situations in which the actors are partially in conflict with each other but could gain from co-operation.[1] If there are no international institutions allowing for co-operation among national states and other international actors, the likelihood of mutual defection and thus undesirable collective outcomes is high in this kind of situation.

The Problem of a World State

Increased interdependence among social actors as a result of extended exchange relations is one crucial element of the *civilizing process* described so persuasively by Norbert Elias (1939) with respect to the building of modern societies in Western Europe. The other, even more fundamental, component of the civilizing process is, according to Elias, the monopolization of the application of physical force leading to the formation of territorially defined states. Only later in this process did constitutionalism and democratization appear on the stage. During the civilizing process human beings learned to control their affects and subordinated themselves to, or internalized, norms and rules of social conduct. The result was a dramatic increase in symbolic and formalized patterns of conflict management and a decrease in violence among

---

[1] For an explication of the concept of problematic social situation see Raub and Voss (1986) and Zürn (1992: 153). See also Ch. 1, sect. 4.2, above.

the members of those civilized societies. Obviously, international relations would benefit from a civilizing process too.

According to Elias, the monopolization of the means of physical force which has accompanied the formation of modern territorial states reflects a general process towards power centralization in world history. Consequently, Elias (1939: 331 f.) expects a similar development to occur on the international level as well:

One can see the first outlines of a worldwide system of tensions composed by alliances and supra-state units of various kinds, the prelude of struggles embracing the whole globe, which are the precondition for a worldwide monopoly of force, for a single central political institution and, thus, for the pacification of the earth.

According to this vision, the parallel building of the modern states should find its replication in the building of a world state having the monopoly of physical force at its disposal and fostering the exchanges and interdependence of members of world society. The United Nations (in particular the Security Council) is of special importance in this vision, being often considered as the government of a world state *in statu nascendi*.

Yet, contemporary International Relations scholars agree upon little else but the *non-feasibility of a world state*. Accordingly, the international system is, and will be for the foreseeable future, characterized by a structure in which there is no central institution that sets, and guarantees compliance with, rules of conduct. In this sense, the central feature of international politics is still anarchy. Moreover, a world state does not even seem to be *desirable*. First, the formation of a world-wide monopoly of physical force would have to pass, as did the formation of nation states, through a period in which its establishment had to be supported by the use of force in order to disarm competing or resistant groups. Considering the potential of destruction stored in the weapons arsenals all over the world, this does not represent an especially attractive option; the very attempt to create a monopoly of physical force could result in the extinction of life on earth. Second, as Oran Young (1978: 196) argued some fifteen years ago, 'there are cases in which the percentage of the population destroyed in internal wars over specified time periods has exceeded the percentage destroyed over the same periods in international wars'. Indeed, after 1945 internal wars occurred more often than inter-state wars, and the number of internal war victims has also exceeded the number of inter-state war victims (Singer and Small 1982, Gantzel 1992). Both trends show that there is no hope of erasing war simply by creating a world state. Third, the breakdown of the Soviet Union and other socialist states in Eastern Europe has taught the lesson that, if anything, political hyper-centralization, which would be inescapable even in the case of a federal world state, is counterproductive in the long run and ultimately conducive to violence.

Does this account of the non-feasibility and undesirability of a world state exclude the prospect of a *civilized international society*? Elias (1985: 136) himself has, with some casual remarks, pointed to another path on which the goal of a civilized international society can be achieved: an increased moderation in dealing with social conflicts by all participants. However, this reference to the possibility of a civilized international society without a monopoly of physical force, to governance without government, challenges traditional notions confining political norm- and rule-setting to statehood. According to these traditional notions, politics and policy, understood as the authoritative allocation of values in the areas of welfare, security, and system of rule, require state action. A superior institution endorsed with the monopoly of physical force, Hobbes's Leviathan, is held necessary to make possible, and to enforce if required, co-operation and co-ordination among self-interested social actors. Protagonists of this point of view readily concede that numerous social relations are free of conflicts of interest or yield desirable outcomes as a result of the 'invisible hand' of free competition. They also agree that a wise government does not intervene in those situations since there is no obvious need for collective regulatory action, and any unnecessary intervention leads to bureaucratization which might diminish the societal performance in the long run. However, they insist that all interactions leading to collectively undesirable outcomes, e.g. the neglect of infrastructure, environmental protection, or basic sciences, ought to be regulated by state intervention. According to this point of view, collective regulatory action is doomed to failure in the absence of a monopoly of physical force to back it up.[2]

---

[2] Interestingly enough, most of the literature on the 'state' follows, at least implicitly, this traditional notion of politics. Both society-centred approaches to the analysis of domestic politics conceiving of the policy 'output' as a result of the

In contrast, according to regime analysts, normative institutions that effectively regulate social interactions do not need a central authority as a prerequisite. Governance without government as a result of non-hierarchical, voluntary self-organization is considered possible. By virtue of this conviction regime analysts separate themselves clearly from the point of view of realists. In order to substantiate the proposition that civilized international relations are possible without installing a world state,[3] we take a look at domestic politics. Here, we realize that the state-centred notion of norm- and rule-setting is not adequate, even when there is already a central governmental authority; rather, voluntary self-organization seems to be pervasive in a world of increased complexity, including the national and sub-national level.

2.2. Is Non-Hierarchical Politics Special to International Relations?

Regime theory (or, more generally, the theory of international institutions) conveys a notion of non-hierarchically ordered, yet non-anarchical international politics which is entirely compatible with a more differentiated understanding of political norm- and rule-setting in industrially developed societies. Here, too, politics is not necessarily tied to the activities of the state or to activities aiming at influencing state action. A wide variety of research exists showing that governance without government is widespread in industrially developed societies with a state and a modern bureaucracy. This research suggests that collective action, or solving problematic social situations, is possible among otherwise independent actors even if they are motivated by no more than

---

interplay among societal demands ('input') and approaches which emphasize the autonomy of the state, thus interpreting policies as a reflection of the interests of the state's various agents and bureaucracies, assume that norm- and rule-setting has, in any case, to be carried out by the state. For an overview see Skocpol (1985).

[3] Thomson (1992: 217) calls for caution in invoking terms like 'civilization', since the so-called moral progress in fields such as controlling terrorism and trade in drugs or arms have been, according to her study, mainly due to state interests. However, when referring to the civilizing process we neither talk about moral progress nor do we assume that this process is driven by societal demands. Rather, the civilizing process refers to an increasing internalization of norms which may take place in quite different ways.

the (intelligent) pursuit of self-interest. This would allow the general inference that, if politics by collective self-regulation is feasible without reliance on the state's ultimate law- and contract-enforcement monopoly on the level of an individual (national) society, this should be expected to happen even more so in a wider social setting, i.e. on the international level where a world state does not exist or, as in Western Europe, a supranational, federal state is at best emerging.

One of the most striking pieces of research in this connection is Elinor Ostrom's (1990) *Governing the Commons*, in which she demonstrates convincingly that users of common pool resources of various kinds and in a variety of settings are able and willing to deal successfully with collective action problems arising from their use of these resources. Users of common pool resources are able to set up non-hierarchical institutional arrangements in order to overcome the 'tragedy of the commons' (Hardin) without any support from the state. These 'local regimes' work in quite different cultural contexts: in Swiss mountain villages as well as in Japanese ones.

Another example is given in research by Volker Ronge (1979), who has shown that German commercial banks have engaged in what he calls 'quasi-politics'. Faced with a potential loss of confidence by the public in the security of their deposits and, thus, with the prospect of a falling propensity to save among low- and middle-income wage earners and pensioners they agreed among themselves on a mandatory deposit insurance scheme without awaiting state legislation and regulatory supervision. In fact, by collective self-regulation the banks managed to pre-empt intervention by the state. In showing that the commercial banks displayed a collectively regulated behaviour which was neither enforced by the state nor based on positive incentives provided by it, Ronge also took issue with the argument that there is a tendency towards increased state intervention in developed market economies for dealing with the problems created by the unregulated interactions in problematic social situations (Offe 1979).[4]

A third case in point is the tripartite bargaining processes dealing with macroeconomic goal-setting in industrially developed

---

[4] Similarly, C. H. Moore (1987), in an intriguing analysis, describes how, in the 1980s, banks in Lebanon completely regulated their interactions themselves when faced with the breakdown of the Lebanese state.

societies, in which business, labour, and government leaders participate as co-equals without the state exercising any prerogatives. This form of collective self-coordination for the purpose of achieving joint gains or avoiding joint losses and for managing distributive conflicts has been called 'liberal neo-corporatism' and has been observable as an institution in several industrially advanced countries for some time. While the state participates in this kind of institutional arrangement, it does not play the role of a superior decision-making unit in a hierarchical setting: rather it is one actor among equals. On the basis of their studies of liberal neo-corporatism Wolfgang Streeck and Philippe C. Schmitter (1985) argue that there are more *models of social order* than previously thought. Social order need not be the result of spontaneous solidarity (community), dispersed competition (market and anarchy), or hierarchical control (statehood); it can also result from, to use their term, 'organized concertation' (association):

At [the] core [of organized concertation] is a distinctive principle of interaction and allocation among a privileged set of actors. The key actors are organizations defined by their common purpose of defending and promoting functionally-defined interests, i.e. class, sectoral and professional associations. The central principle is that of concertation, or negotiation within and among a limited and fixed set of interest organizations that mutually recognize each other's status and entitlements and are capable of reaching and implementing relatively stable compromises (pacts) in the pursuit of their interests. A corporative-associative order is, therefore, based primarily on interaction within and between interdependent complex organizations. (Streeck and Schmitter 1985: 10)

The associative model of social order is an ideal type focusing exclusively on the interests of actors and disregarding the communitarian components. Yet in the real world associative and communitarian components of social order are hard to separate. In any case, these two models of social order add up to a third alternative to the old and well-known dichotomy between 'state' and 'market'. There is a way 'beyond market and state' (see also Lindblom 1977) which is increasingly acknowledged by analysts of domestic politics too. This underscores our proposition that political norm- and rule-setting is not tied to the state, that international relations are not necessarily anarchical if there is no hierarchically ordered policy-making system beyond the (nation) state, and that international politics instead takes place whenever states and/or other international actors engage in collective self-regulation to cope with conflictual or problematic collective situations. Moreover, the fact that these forms of self-regulation are pervasive in industrially developed societies casts doubts on the older institutionalist notion of 'world politics as a primitive political system' (Masters 1969): not only primitive, but also (post-)modern societies might choose orders that are based neither on market nor on state.

So far we have attempted to clarify the status and goals of regime analysis in the study of international relations by putting it into the context of theories about social order and by explicating the normative interest in international regimes. Moreover, by putting regime analysis into the context of the study of civilizing processes, it has become obvious that we regard international regimes as one important means of meeting the rapidly increasing demand for international regulation. Yet, obviously there are also other kinds of international order in contemporary international relations which cannot be overlooked.

2.3. What Kind of Order Exists in Contemporary International Politics?

Today's international politics cannot be analysed adequately if it is assumed that it must be structured through a single ordering principle. In fact, international politics today displays behaviour patterns which reflect the operation of competing ordering principles, including governance by collective self-regulation. Regime analysis strives to make the point that international relations cannot be reduced to a state of anarchy in the sense that the allocation of goods among states (and their societies) results from the intersection of their competitive self-help strategies which they pursue as relative-gains seekers (Grieco 1990).

Of course, there can be no doubt that for parts of the world the realist assessment of international relations as being in a *state of anarchy* still seems valid. The Cold War strategies of the United States and the USSR until the 1980s or the conflict processes in the Middle East, especially between Israel and its neighbours, but also among Arab states themselves as demonstrated by the Iraqi invasion of Kuwait, are telling evidence of this observation.

However, it would be an exaggeration if it were suggested that international politics could be said to be nothing but the sum total of individual or collective self-help strategies by which states seek to achieve relative gains (or to avoid or minimize relative losses). This realist assessment turns a blind eye on a wide variety of interaction patterns which cannot be reduced to competitive self-help strategies.

The image of competitive international politics produced by anarchy among sovereign states is most strongly challenged by the observation of instances of *hierarchically ordered supranational policy-making* (including implementation). Take the following two examples. The Security Council of the United Nations mandated collective sanctions against Iraq after its invasion of Kuwait and established monitoring and supervisory machinery; moreover, after Iraq's defeat the Security Council ordered the destruction of weapons, installations, etc. inside Iraq and had it carried out under its overall guidance. In this sense, the Security Council acted like a governmental body of an incipient world minimal state. A less spectacular case is the European Community, where hierarchical, supranational policy-making is quite common in several policy sectors. In the field of agricultural policy, for instance, policies are most often initiated in Brussels, while national governments are so strongly enmeshed in the 'joint decision trap' (Scharpf 1985) that they have no choice but to seek to influence the Community policies—there is no longer any exit option.

However, neither anarchy-induced competitive international politics nor hierarchically ordered international policy-making exhaust the reality of 'politics among nations'. An increasing part of international political interactions and processes has become the object of *international collective self-regulation*, i.e. the voluntary participation by states and other international actors in collective action to achieve joint gains or to avoid joint losses in conflictual or problematic social situations. Examples of this kind of collective self-regulation on the global level include the GATT-based international trade regime, the nuclear non-proliferation regime, or the regime for the protection of the stratospheric ozone layer. However, *international regimes* are only one manifestation, perhaps the most prominent, of collective self-regulation by states (and other international actors): it also comprises contractual arrangements short of a regime[5] as well as formal *international organizations* which facilitate collaboration short of generating compelling obligations, e.g. by the production and dissemination of information.[6]

To put it differently: the growth of institutions governing international political life has been quite remarkable. Taking the best-documented subset of international institutions—international governmental organizations (IGOs)—the count stands at about 300 (*Yearbook of International Organizations*, 1990/1). It goes almost without saying that this number comprises a wide variety of this species of international institution. If one looks at another subset, international treaties officially registered with the United Nations, the number of cases is in the thousands (*United Nations Treaty Series*). Our main concern here is with international regimes. Even though research on international regimes has generated a wealth of theoretical and empirical studies, it is as yet difficult to assess the quantity and quality of international regime formation that has actually taken place in the last few decades. There is no source for identifying existing international regimes comparable to the sources just cited for international organizations and international treaties.

Our reference to the literature on comparative politics (sect. 2.2) draws attention to yet another component of international order. Self-organization of corporate actors is not necessarily restricted to territorially defined organizations. All kinds of organizations with the purpose of defending or promoting func- tionally defined interests in the international realm are in principle able to implement relatively stable forms of co-operation in

[5] For an analysis of the relationship between international regimes, on the one hand, and various kinds of contracts, on the other, see Ch. 4, sect. 2, above.

[6] International regimes are a subset of international institutions, as are inter- national organizations. Both organizations and regimes are institutions in the sense defined above (sect. 2.1). Whereas international organizations represent 'purposive entities', international regimes are 'only' sets of norms and rules spelling out the range of admissible behaviour of different kinds of actors. The norms and rules of a regime pertain to particular sets of issues in international relations, i.e. they are issue-area specific. In contrast, international organizations can be issue-area specific (International Whaling Commission), related to several issue areas (UNESCO), or constitutional (United Nations). While issue-area specific organiza- tions often revise, and monitor the implementation of, regime rules, more broadly designed international organizations often serve as policy- or regime-making systems, as for example the CSCE with respect to confidence- and security-building measures and other issues.

P. Mayer, V. Rittberger, and M. Zürn

the pursuit of their interests. If international non-governmental organizations interacting in an issue area agree upon principles, norms, rules, and decision-making procedures in order to regulate their interactions, one can speak of *transnational regimes*. To be sure, this component of international order is still underdeveloped and under-researched. While one might, for instance, refer to the post-war arrangement of the seven big oil companies—the 'first oil regime' according to Frank (1985)—, it remains unclear whether 'cartels' ought to be considered regimes (a view strongly challenged by Virginia Haufler in Ch. 5 above). In short, while transnational regimes represent a segment of international order that may become more important in the near future, it is currently a minor component which nevertheless deserves more detailed study.

Regime analysis acknowledges that its field of inquiry does not cover the whole realm of today's international relations, even if we take into account both international and transnational regimes. It is limited, on the one hand, by those competitive interaction patterns which are described by the realist or neo-realist approaches in International Relations. On the other hand, regime analysis must give way to integration theory if, and to the extent that, co-operative interaction patterns move into a transformational mode leading to the creation of a new layer of political authority 'beyond the nation state'. Recognizing the practice of unregulated competition among states as well as the phenomenon of 'supranationalism', regime analysis seeks to avoid being tied down by the 'either/ or debate' in International Relations between 'anarchists' and 'governmentalists'. *Complex international governance*[7] might be an appropriate label for this peculiarity of contemporary international relations, in which different kinds of partial orders, varying in regional scope and function, coexist. As James Rosenau (1992: 13–14) has put it:

Global order is conceived here to be a single set of arrangements even though these are not causally linked into a single coherent array of

[7] The term 'complex governance' is borrowed from Hughes (1991), who has used it for the European Community. In any case, complex governance refers to a state of affairs in which there is no dominant principle of social order, but coexistence of several equally legitimate principles. On another occasion we used the term 'regulated anarchy' to describe the complex and ambiguous nature of present-day international relations (Rittberger and Zürn 1990: 53–5).

patterns. The organic whole that comprises the present or future global order is organic only in the sense that its diverse actors are all claimants upon the earthbound resources and all of them must cope with the same environmental conditions, noxious and polluted as these may be.

It is very unlikely that one kind of social order will dominate international relations in the near future and thus will reintroduce a state of affairs which can be described as organic or homogeneous. The coexistence of different partial orders each considered legitimate in its sphere may turn out to be a permanent feature of international politics. However, we suggest that the non-hierarchical normative institutions for dealing with conflicts or problematic social situations will gain in importance over time, whereas national governments as such will lose. The ensuing institutional complexity will enhance the demand for cognitive capacities of individuals and will put stress on democratic principles. Responses to this kind of pressure constitute an important field of inquiry for the social sciences in the future.

Summing up: non-hierarchical international institutions of the international and the transnational kind play, empirically as well as normatively, an important role in international politics. They are needed in order to meet the increasing demand for international governance and they frequently govern issue areas. With the existence and the rise of those institutions international relations are increasingly characterized by a complex blend of different kinds of social order. Moreover, the formula 'governance without government' might stand for a more desirable vision for a shrinking world than its major alternative: hierarchical norm- and rule-setting (and enforcement) on the international level. Thus, it appears worth while continuing research on the conditions and consequences of collective self-regulation and consolidating a research programme allowing for a cumulation of knowledge. The remainder of this chapter is devoted to discussing which more specific paths need to be explored in the future in order to approach this goal.

3. REGIME ANALYSIS: THE THREE MAIN TASKS

In the first part of this chapter an attempt has been made to locate the study of international regimes within the wider context of theories of social order, both international and domestic, and to assess the status of its object, international governance without supranational government, in present-day international relations. Against this background the second part of this chapter deals more specifically with the three main tasks of regime analysis as a theory-oriented endeavour: explaining the formation, persistence, and demise of international regimes (sect. 3.1); accounting for regime properties and their change (sect. 3.2); and, finally, determining regime consequences (or effects)[8] and explaining their variation (sect. 3.3). At present, none of these tasks seems close to accomplishment, although the still rapidly growing literature on international institutions and regimes is not short of seminal ideas, approaches, and theoretical conceptions. While a summary of this extensive body of research is beyond the scope of this chapter, the following sections seek to assess the achievements and shortcomings of regime analysis in the light of the contributions to this volume.

3.1. *Explaining Regime Formation, Persistence, and Demise*

While knowledge of the conditions under which regimes decline (i.e. do not persist) would also entail knowledge of the conditions under which regimes persist (i.e. do not decline) and vice versa, no such equivalence holds between explaining regime formation and explaining regime demise (and persistence, respectively). In fact, to demonstrate that, and why, international regimes can endure and evolve, although the circumstances that gave rise to them have disappeared, was a central theme of one of the most important contributions to regime theory so far, Robert Keohane's (1984) *After Hegemony*. Therefore, the first main task of regime analysis is actually twofold: investigating the determinants of regime formation as well as the determinants of regime persistence/demise. Nevertheless the two objects of study are very closely intertwined, at least in our thinking. This is also illustrated by Keohane's book, in which a theory put forward to account for regime formation—the theory of hegemonic stability—creates the puzzle that prompts the formulation of a theory of regime

---

[8] In this chapter the terms 'regime consequences' and 'regime effects' are used interchangeably.

persistence—the functional theory of regimes (Keohane 1984: 14). Unless it were natural to assume that the causes of regime formation are at least very similar to the causes of regime persistence the puzzle would not have arisen in the first place. It is this interrelationship of regime formation and regime persistence/ demise which justifies their discussion under one heading. Regime formation and regime persistence/demise have not been given equally extensive treatment in regime analysis. Emphases have varied both over time and across individual research agendas. In recent years studies of regime persistence and demise which were prominent in early regime analysis appear to have lost ground to studies of regime formation, which also seem to be more productive as far as the variety of hypotheses and theoretical approaches is concerned. However, the close relationship of the two subjects encourages and, to some extent, justifies transfers of ideas from one domain to the other (see Ch. 9 above), restricting the internal differentiation of the field.

A further complication arises from a certain ambiguity of the task itself. Students of regime formation may choose what could be labelled a *microscopic perspective* on their object, seeking to understand why international regimes emerge in some issue areas but not in others. Alternatively, they may adopt a *macroscopic perspective*, making the sum total of international regimes in the international system (or some subset of it) the dependent variable of their research. Such ambiguity is not peculiar to studies of regime formation and demise. Indeed, students of regime consequences face a similar choice, as they may either focus on accounting for the variation in effects of particular regimes or examine how the rise in international regimes has affected the structure of the international system or even the nature of international politics (see sect. 3.3 below). The special methodological problems associated with the macroscopic perspective, which almost precludes comparative designs, may explain why scholars have seldom engaged in this line of research (but see Young 1978). Besides, it can be assumed that a better insight into the conditions under which regime formation (or decline) is likely to occur in any given issue area is a prerequisite for reconstructing the forces driving the overall process of institutionalization in international politics. Therefore, initial emphasis on the microscopic perspective seems to be a matter of efficiency as well. Accordingly, most of the contributors to this volume, as far as they are concerned with issues of regime formation, tend towards taking this perspective. A notable exception is Keohane's sketch of a 'contractualist' theory of the rise in the number of international regimes in the post-war era (see Ch. 2, sect. 5.1). Examining the conditions of institution-building both on the supply and on the demand side he argues that, owing to the reduced concentration of power among western industrialized democracies, supply-side explanations cannot account for the proliferation of regimes since 1945. Emphasis must therefore be laid on changes on the demand side, in particular the growth of interdependence leading to a higher issue density (creating a demand for additional regimes) and the success of already existing institutions (creating a demand for the maintenance of regimes).

In the study of regime formation and persistence/demise, power-based (or *realist*) and interest-based (or *utilitarian*) approaches have for a long time clearly prevailed (Young 1989*b*). Indeed, various chapters in this volume suggest that the theoretical potential of these approaches has by no means been exhausted yet. Stephen Krasner (Ch. 7), for instance, breaks new ground for the *realist perspective* by applying it to the internationalization of human rights issues, presumably a 'home match' for liberal approaches. His central argument is that human rights regimes, which state principles and norms for the relationship between rulers and ruled, do not address political market failure problems and therefore cannot be adequately understood from the perspective of liberal co-operation theory (contractualism). Conversely, he argues, a realist perspective stressing power and the concern for relative gains can account, to a large extent, for both the content and the success of such institutions. Accordingly, in the four historical cases of human rights regimes he examines, success and failure were not a function of the regime's ability to reduce uncertainty and to supply information for its members but rather of the willingness of the most powerful states to enforce its principles and norms (which these states themselves had promoted).

Interest-based approaches in regime analysis and, more generally, in the study of international co-operation have repeatedly received inspiration from concepts and arguments originating in game theory (Axelrod 1984, Oye 1986). Discussing results from recent game-theoretical work, Andrew Kydd and Duncan Snidal (Ch. 6) suggest that regime analysis is likely to continue to benefit considerably from this branch of rational choice theory. New solution concepts such as 'trigger strategy', 'correlated equilibria', and 'cheap talk' may shed additional light on the way regimes facilitate co-operation among states and, thus, may enrich functionalist interpretations of regime formation and persistence. Yet, stemming from pure game theory and industrial organization theory, such concepts are by no means custom-designed for the needs of regime analysis and therefore should be applied to the analysis of international politics only with due care. Consequently, Kydd and Snidal stress the necessity for regime analysts not to lose sight of the substantive problems of international co-operation when making use of the insights gained in those theoretical contexts.

The dominance of the power-based and the interest-based approaches has always had its critics as well. The most fundamental opposition to these two analytical perspectives, which Keohane (1988) has subsumed under 'rationalistic theory', has come from the so-called 'cognitivists' (to use Haggard's and Simmons's (1987) term): scholars who criticize realists and utilitarians for not taking into account the pervasive ambiguity of reality and consequently emphasize factors such as perception, knowledge, and ideology. While critical adherents to rationalistic theory do not dismiss these objections altogether, they have pointed out that cognitivism, like other branches of 'reflective theory', has failed up to now to come up with a feasible alternative to the established research programmes in International Relations (in particular, neo-realism and neo-liberal institutionalism) (Keohane 1988: 392).

Christer Jönsson (Ch. 9) directly responds to this challenge by seeking to show that contemporary cognitive theory depicting man as an 'intuitive scientist', who uses various heuristic devices to make sense of the complex signals emanating from his environment, is capable of guiding empirical research on international co-operation and regimes. In particular, he demonstrates that the diverse branches of cognitive science offer numerous insights into human behaviour and thought from which concrete hypotheses pertaining to regime formation, persistence, and change can be derived. For example, the augmentation and discounting theorems of attribution theory may help to explain the success and the failure of strategies aiming at building up the minimum of mutual trust that is required for institutionalized co-operation among states to take place. Cognitive theory also suggests that mutual expectations of gains to be received from co-operation do not suffice to account for regime formation. Equally important is a common perception of the (collective action) problem, which is usually carried by a common metaphorical formula such as the famous 'common heritage of mankind', 'land for peace', or 'common security'. Moreover, such metaphors, to a considerable extent, prejudice the eventual solution of the common problem and, thus, the content of the regime.

To be sure, extending cognitivist arguments developed in psychology, linguistics, or anthropology to the study of international politics bears the risk that analogies are overdrawn. A case in point may be Jönsson's analogy between the institution of language and institutions such as international regimes (Ch. 9, sect. 4), where it is difficult to imagine that the grip regimes may have on the minds of those involved in them compares with the way our thinking is conditioned by language. However, in so far as the hypotheses thus derived are amenable to empirical testing (and are indeed tested), this risk need not unduly bother us. Presumably, the more acute problem will be with designing empirical studies helping us to decide whether the hypothesized relationship holds or not. Thus, difficult decisions will have to be taken when it comes to operationalizing concepts such as 'trust' or 'a common definition of the problem as reflected in a metaphorical formula'.

Jönsson probably is right to emphasize (as Keohane does for contractualism) the complementary role of cognitive theory. Notably, he even recognizes the priority (not the superiority) of rationalistic approaches, when he assents to Keohane's and Nye's (1977) proposal to begin with comparatively simple models (e.g. realist and utilitarian) and to add complexity (e.g. cognitive theory) as necessary. Indeed, observing this guideline can help achieve the desired synthesis of rationalistic and reflective approaches. On the other hand, it begs the important question of how such addition is to take place precisely. There is always the danger of ending up with a pseudo-synthesis, where cognitive factors (or other variables 'added') play the part of stopgaps to be invoked whenever other, prior explanations happen to fail. We return to this point later when discussing the contributions of Young and Osherenko as well as Efinger, Mayer, and Schwarzer to this volume.

A less fundamental if no less serious criticism of the prevailing line of analysis of international regimes has sometimes been voiced by adherents to the rationalistic research programme themselves: despite its roots in the interdependence literature, regime analysis has so far been overly state-centric, ignoring the impact of domestic politics on both the creation and the maintenance of international regimes. Focusing on regime formation and using the data of the Tübingen project on international regimes, Michael Zürn (Ch. 12) has made a start on exploring this virtually untouched territory. His central claim is that, to get hold of the domestic sources of regime formation, we must first establish the characteristics of a regime-conducive foreign policy. We then can go on to study the domestic variables affecting the probability that such a foreign policy will actually be pursued. Thus, it is assumed, links between domestic structures and processes, on the one hand, and institution-building at the international level, on the other, will come to light which otherwise would remain obscure. This strategy seems to be justified by success. First, it is possible to identify a particular type of foreign policy which seems to be associated with successfully initiating international regimes. This foreign policy type (labelled 'soft faithfulness') is characterized by a general orientation towards reciprocity attenuated by a tendency towards making concessions and a preference for economic and informational foreign policy instruments. Second, a number of domestic conditions or unit properties can be specified which apparently favour the choice of this type of foreign policy: a high degree of dependence on international trade, a high degree of enmeshment in international institutions, neo-corporatist domestic practices, shifts in the domestic power constellation, and a low level of foreign policy routinization. As far as these conditions are concerned, though, Zürn regards his study as an exercise in hypothesis generation rather than hypothesis testing.

Further studies confronting these (and other) hypotheses relating unit characteristics and foreign policy type with other cases would therefore seem to be a logical next step. Also, the somewhat surprising finding that an individual government or a small number of states acting as a group, through their foreign policy *actions*, are often able to induce a certain collective *interaction*, namely regime formation, certainly deserves further scrutiny. (Interestingly enough, it is not hegemons which normally display this ability —on the contrary.) In this connection, Jönsson's remarks on trust and 'conciliatory behaviour' (applying attribution theory to international politics) may shed additional light on the nature and the operation of regime-conducive foreign policies (see Ch. 9, sect. 3). Kydd and Snidal (Ch. 6, sect. 3.2) remind us that the focus on foreign policy types is not unrivalled as an attempt to overcome the state-centrism of regime analysis. Robert Putnam (1988) has proposed interpreting the actual bargaining processes from which regimes emerge as two-level games which governments simultaneously play with other governments and domestic actors such as parliaments or interest groups. This approach can be expected to yield insightful reconstructions of bargaining situations, which are beyond the reach of the foreign-policy type approach. On the other hand, the focus on foreign policy types has produced a number of hypotheses which have a considerable predictive value and do not charge the analyst with the notoriously intricate task of establishing preferences and win-sets (i.e. the sets of possible agreements on the international level which would be ratified on the domestic level) independently of the eventual choices of the players in the game.

Progress in the study of regime formation and persistence/demise does not depend only on the ingenious invention of new theories. It is equally important that these theories be subjected to strict empirical testing, and that this be done on the basis of a wide variety of cases rather than just one or two. Oran Young and Gail Osherenko (Ch. 10) as well as Manfred Efinger, Peter Mayer, and Gudrun Schwarzer (Ch. 11) report findings from two multi-case projects which were devoted to examining the empirical validity of various hypotheses purporting to explain the formation of international regimes. It is interesting to compare these two projects and their results. The Dartmouth-based project tested more hypotheses, whereas the Tübingen-based project relies on a larger sample of cases. In both projects, cases in which attempts at regime formation were successful are quite clearly in the majority (the ratio of regime to non-regime cases being somewhat more favourable, i.e. smaller, in the Tübingen-based project).

Both refrained from striving for something like a representative choice of cases. The Dartmouth-based project, with few exceptions, was concerned with issue areas geographically belonging to the Arctic region and substantively relating to natural resources and the environment. The Tübingen-based project focused, albeit not entirely, on co-operation and self-help in East–West issues in various policy areas (security, economy, environment, human rights). As a result only one case, long-range transboundary air pollution, was studied by both teams. Similarly, there is only a small overlap as regards the specific hypotheses tested.

In a way, therefore, the two projects may be considered complementary. Most of the hypotheses examined by the Dartmouth-based group pertain to the process of institutional bargaining, whereas those picked by the Tübingen-based team are more structural in nature, often relating to external conditions under which actual bargaining takes place. Many of these hypotheses, had they been studied by Young, Osherenko, and their colleagues, would probably have come under the so-called 'context factors' of the Dartmouth-based project. Thus, it is often difficult to compare the results of the two projects directly. However, as far as they are comparable, they seem to be fully compatible. Two common results are most striking. First, in both projects the power-based hypotheses, in particular the theory of hegemonic stability, did rather badly. Second, the most promising hypotheses in both projects are interest-based ones: the situation-structural hypothesis building on a typology of pay-off structures in the Tübingen project and the hypothesis stating the necessity of individual leadership for successful institutional bargaining in the Dartmouth-based project. These two hypotheses, of course, differ considerably, indicating that the notion of interest is rather broad, overly broad perhaps.

Another striking point of agreement between the two chapters is the call for efforts to overcome the stage of single-variable hypotheses and to engage in some sort of multivariate analysis of regime formation. Both teams of authors discuss various conceptions of multivariate explanations or theories which they hope may guide such efforts. Again there are notable similarities and parallels, although the informal character of these conceptions

makes a strict comparison difficult.[9] Young and Osherenko draw
attention to the occurrence of *substitution effects* in regime formation, i.e. the fact that successful institutional bargaining can
apparently follow any of a certain number of 'tracks' (Ch. 10, sect.
4.1). Obviously, this metaphor needs further interpretation. Thus,
Young and Osherenko leave it open whether they wish these
tracks to be understood as defining particular sequences of events
(or rather event types) one of which actors have to go through if
regime formation is to take place. However, they suggest that each
track is characterized by a particular critical variable (such as the
presence of a dominant power or the emergence of consensual
knowledge) on which the prospects for regime formation depend.
In this respect the concept of track seems very similar in function
to the concept of *context* as used in the chapter by Efinger, Mayer,
and Schwarzer (Ch. 11, sect. 3.2). These authors consider the
possibility that, in different contexts (defined as types of issue
area), different independent variables may adequately explain
regime formation, and that, correspondingly, hypotheses are to be
taken into account which hold only for a certain subset of the
universe of cases ('conditional hypotheses'). Moreover, they stress
the necessity of defining these contexts independently of the
variables that are hypothesized to be critical in them. Otherwise,
all kinds of delusive 'backwards explanations' of instances of
regime formation are invited: having ascertained the facts of our
case descriptively all we have to do is to look for a hypothesis that
happens to predict the actual outcome (regime formation or none)
and to conclude that the hypothesis is adequate to the context that
our case belongs to! Obviously, we do not end up with a proper
explanation that way. Young and Osherenko implicitly recognize
this point when they encourage inquiry into the conditions under
which the 'power track', the 'knowledge track', or the 'interest
track' are actually followed. A good example of an argument that
amounts to contextualizing a theory of regime formation is the one
put forward by Krasner (Ch. 7, sect. 1) that human rights issues,
because they are not instances of market failure, do not meet the

---

[9] The task is further complicated by the fact that Young and Osherenko have
preferred to express their ideas in the material mode, i.e. they talk about effects,
processes, causal chains, etc. *in the world*, whereas Efinger, Mayer, and Schwarzer
have chosen the formal mode, i.e. they refer to the constructing principles of
theories, i.e. linguistic representations of aspects of the world.

prerequisites for an application of liberal co-operation theory (functionalism). Thus, he implies that this theory is adequate for the context of market failure only, whereas another theory— presumably one of realist provenance—is needed to account for issue areas outside this context.

Another phenomenon, which is, according to Young and Osherenko, even more important, if also more difficult to account for in our theories, is the interaction of different variables. The examples provided by the authors suggest that such *interaction effects* can take basically two forms (Ch. 10, sect. 4.2). First, interacting variables can represent successive links in a causal chain: for instance, integrative bargaining, which is conducive to regime formation, may be possible only after actors' interests have been shaped in an appropriate way by an epistemic community. Second, factors may operate simultaneously giving rise to synergetic effects. Young's and Osherenko's example is the coincidence and fruitful interplay of structural and entrepreneurial leadership in the protection of the stratospheric ozone layer and reduction of long-range transboundary air pollution cases. The authors point out that the most crucial methodological problems involved in the study of interaction effects are the selection of the relevant variables and the assignment of appropriate weights to them. Again, a similar idea, albeit expressed in different language, can be found in the chapter by Efinger, Mayer, and Schwarzer in their discussion of *integrated theories* (Ch. 11, sect. 3.1). The characteristic feature of this type of theory is that predictions regarding the probability of regime formation are based on the values of more than one variable and that predictions can be derived for every possible combination of values (without any hierarchy holding among the integrated variables).[10] We suspect that integrated theories can be interpreted as formal expressions of the kind of phenomena Young and Osherenko have addressed as interaction effects. However, so far this is just a supposition which cannot be substantiated before a good deal of conceptual

[10] The second provision is introduced in order to distinguish integrated theories from another type of multivariate theory, which exploits the idea of context-dependent explanations as explained above. *Contextualized theories* consist of two components: (*a*) a context variable breaking down the universe of cases (issue areas) into discrete subsets (defined by the categories of the context variable) and (*b*) various explanatory variables or hypotheses, each one accounting for the cases of a particular subset (see Ch. 11, sect. 3.2, above).

clarification has taken place. It is clear that, by elaborating these methodological conceptions, the two teams have tried to draw attention to, and to some extent to frame, a problem rather than present a solution. Whatever the potential utility of these ideas it cannot materialize unless concrete empirical theories are constructed along these lines and prove able to withstand critical tests.

Efinger, Mayer, and Schwarzer make reference to a (partially) integrated theory, the situation-structural theory put forward by Zürn (1990, 1992), which has turned out to be a successful explanatory device for the cases of the Tübingen project. Peter Haas's (Ch. 8) theory of environmental 'regime patterns' can be regarded as another interesting example of an integrated theory. Regime patterns are types of regimes defined with respect to four features of regimes which are assumed to covary: the political process by which the regime is created and maintained; the regime's substance; compliance effects on leaders and laggards in environmental protection; and the institutional learning style. Haas distinguishes two basic patterns labelled 'follow-the-leader' and 'bargaining' and suggests that the variable selecting between these two patterns is the distribution of power: a high concentration of power leads to 'follow-the-leader' and a more diffuse distribution of power produces 'bargaining'. In addition, he introduces a second variable, presence of an epistemic community, which affects the basic patterns in predictable ways: if an epistemic community has formed in the issue area, 'follow-the-leader' is replaced by a pattern called 'modified follow-the-leader', and 'bargaining' is turned into a pattern named 'epistemically informed bargaining'; if no epistemic community has formed, the basic patterns remain unchanged. Thus, the theory meets the requirements of an integrated theory by including more than one variable and yielding a prediction for each of the four possible combinations of values.

Among the three main tasks of regime analysis the explanation of regime formation, persistence, and demise has presumably been attacked most vigorously and most systematically. Consequently, it is also the field that has produced the largest number of comparatively well-specified hypotheses (see Chs. 8–12). Still, it would be too bold to predict a theoretical breakthrough in the near future, at a time when efforts at multivariate theory-building are just beginning. Therefore, it looks as though the task of explaining regime formation, persistence, and demise will remain on the agenda of regime analysis for some time to come, even though the emphasis of research may shift to other, less advanced fields, where a higher marginal utility of research input can be expected. The importance and urgency of these other tasks notwithstanding (see the next two sections), scholars should keep looking into the causes of regime formation and persistence/demise, bearing in mind that a variety of plausible and, to some extent, empirically corroborated hypotheses is not a substitute for a well-tested, coherent theory. In the absence of such a theory, however, solid explanations of particular instances of regime formation, persistence, or demise are not possible.

3.2. Accounting for Regime Properties and Their Change

The second main task of regime analysis can be seen as a direct continuation of the first one. Students of international regimes do not only seek to understand why regimes are established in some issue areas and not in others, they are also interested in the factors that determine their specific properties (content, substance).[11] Questions arise such as: why do compliance mechanisms and monitoring provisions play such an important role in some regimes, while they are virtually absent in others? Or: under what circumstances are actors likely to invest an international institution with

---

[11] We use the terms 'content' and 'substance' interchangeably to refer to properties of the principles, norms, rules, and decision-making procedures of regimes. The term 'property' is more encompassing, covering also actor-related features of a regime such as its regional scope (bilateral, regional, global). Another property of regimes which cannot be reduced to regime content is *regime strength* or overall compliance with regime rules. Regime strength has so far received little systematic treatment in regime analysis. If we are right in assuming that regime analysis in future will put more stress on the study of regime consequences, the interest in regime strength and its measurement and explanation can be expected to rise as well. Presumably, variations in regime consequences, such as the extent to which the regime's stated goals are attained, are not entirely attributable to the degree of overall rule compliance. In order to assess the influence on goal attainment (regime effectiveness) as exerted by other factors, such as the content of the norms and rules of the regime, we therefore need to control for regime strength, which in turn presupposes a method of measuring strength (or overall compliance). Conversely, if the success of a regime to a large extent depends on its strength, the factors determining the degree of overall compliance with regime rules must be of central interest to students of regime effectiveness.

P. Mayer, V. Rittberger, and M. Zürn

the authority to assign property rights or to allocate resources? and when, in turn, are principles and norms which support rather than supplant market processes more likely to be established? During their life-cycles regimes not seldom undergo considerable *change* affecting their performance or distributional consequences. Accounting for change in the content of regimes, therefore, constitutes another integral part of this field of study.

In the literature on international regimes there have been occasional attempts to explain selected properties of a particular regime and also the modification of such properties over time (examples from the German International Relations community include K. D. Wolf 1991 and Schrogl forthcoming). Still, up to now systematic and concerted study of the determinants of regime content (comparable with the study of regime formation) has not taken place.[12] Consequently, explicit hypotheses with clearly specified domains are relatively scarce, although many of the ideas and observations scattered about in the literature might be turned into pertinent hypotheses quite easily. The most prominent hypothesis relating to regime properties is, of course, the theory of hegemonic stability, which is not simply a theory of regime formation, but also predicts, on condition of a high concentration of overall power, the emergence of *liberal* economic regimes.

A very general way of accounting for regime properties is explaining regime content in terms of the preferences of particular actors. A case in point is Krasner's proposition that human rights regimes reflect the preferences and values of the most powerful states (Ch. 7, sect. 7). This is a very simple hypothesis, but simplicity does not have to be to the detriment of a hypothesis. At any rate, however, some additional qualifications are needed to make it work. Not only must we be told how to identify, without circularity, 'the most powerful states' in a given issue area: instructions must also be given for how to deal with cases where the preferences of these states are not in harmony. (The history of East–West relations clearly shows that such cases are not a negligible quantity in human rights issues.) Provided with appropriate qualifications we may then go on to test the hypothesis and see how far we get.

---

[12] A good deal of research has been devoted to the determinants of 'regime change' in the special sense of change in regime strength or overall compliance with regime rules (Haggard and Simmons 1987: 496).

A notable aspect of such 'voluntaristic' hypotheses tracing back the concrete substance of a regime to the 'will' of certain key actors is that they do not specify a particular dimension on the part of the dependent variable (regime content) to be accounted for. Whatever trait of the regime we are interested in, it can be explained by the same variable: the preferences of the strong. As the examples of research questions at the beginning of this section illustrate, however, our interest in regime substance is not aroused by just any differences among regimes but by the variation in particular properties such as the allocation mode of the regime or the scope of its rules. Consequently, hypotheses have been advanced which, other than the one discussed above, specialize in particular dimensions of regime content. Inventing and testing hypotheses of this sort would be worth while, even if there were no evidence whatsoever suggesting that simple propositions of the type: 'The strongest actors determine the rules of the game' are sometimes misleading. The reason is that hypotheses tracing institutional features back to some actors' preferences, the precise nature of which is often concealed from the contemporary observer, have only a very moderate predictive value and thus are by no means optimal.

Examples of hypotheses seeking to account for differences in particular properties of regimes include Keohane's 'contractualist' explanation of the principles of institutional membership (open, conditionally open, restricted) in terms of the function the regime is to serve (co-ordination, collaboration, or cartelization) (Ch. 2, sect. 5.2). Another case in point is Friedrich Kratochwil's discussion of the circumstances and considerations governing actors' decisions in given situations to conclude a formal or informal, tacit or explicit, open or secret agreement (Ch. 4, sect. 3). Considerable predictive value can be ascribed to Peter Haas's theory of environmental regime patterns, some of whose implications refer to specific regime properties (Ch. 8, sect. 4). Thus, this theory states that the style of institutional learning that prevails in a regime as well as the scope and the stringency of its rules are dependent on the variables 'distribution of power', 'number of actors', and 'presence of an epistemic community'. For instance, it is predicted that in issue areas in which there is no epistemic community and power resources are concentrated, institutional learning in the light of new information will be 'simple', whereas in issue areas in which there is an epistemic community and the number of actors is small, learning will often be quite 'complex' in Joseph Nye's (1987) terms.

There are numerous 'institutional variables' (i.e. respects in which regimes can vary) that could be studied. Other examples besides the ones already mentioned include the geographic scope, the form of participation of members in the regime's decision-making procedures, the status of NGOs, the revenue base, the autonomy of the secretariat (if there is one), or the range of issues covered by the regime (E. B. Haas 1990: 64; Haggard and Simmons 1987: 496–8; Young 1991c). Depending on the categorization (range of variation) chosen, one or more *regime typologies* correspond to each of these variables. The task of accounting for regime properties then amounts to explaining the formation of a particular type of regime or the change of a regime from one type to another.

In principle, the list of institutional variables and thus regime typologies is open-ended. Which ones should we try to account for then? Perhaps the best criterion of selection is the explanatory leverage a regime typology gives us as regards the *consequences* of international regimes. Thus, if it can be demonstrated, or if there is at least a plausible hypothesis stating, that certain variations in regime consequences can be accounted for on the basis of a particular institutional variable, an explanation of this dimension of regime properties is desirable (to the extent that the respective type of regime consequence is considered worth studying). For example: the fact that liberal, state-oriented, and internationalist regimes are likely each to have clearly different distributional effects (see Ch. 14, sect. 3.2 above). would appear to be a good reason to study the factors determining which of the three allocation modes is institutionalized in a given issue area. Thus, this criterion of selection does not only link the study of regime properties to the study of regime consequences, it also implies that, in a sense, the latter is prior to the former: progress in the study of regime consequences is essential for providing the study of regime properties with a well-founded research agenda. The next section examines the conditions of and prospects for such progress.

3.3. Determining Regime Effects and Explaining Their Variation

'Do regimes matter?' Presumably the North American founders of regime analysis, who developed their ideas in an intellectual environment strongly influenced by Waltzian neo-realism, were more troubled by this sceptical question than their European colleagues (compare Ch. 3, sect. 2, and Ch. 2, sect. 4, above).[13] In the meantime, the evidence accumulated by various case studies on both sides of the Atlantic should have settled this issue (Lipson 1983, P. M. Haas 1989, Rittberger and Zürn 1990). Yet, if these studies have convincingly shown that regimes often do make a difference in one way or another they are no substitute for systematic research on the effects of international regimes, the forms they assume, and the conditions of their occurrence. Only recently do efforts to tackle these questions directly building on work begun by Krasner (1983b) in the early 1980s seem to have intensified again.

Various scholars (among them Hurrell and Keohane in this volume) have suggested that the impact of regimes is best demonstrated at the unit level of analysis with a focus on situations in which compliance with regime rules is inconvenient for governments. Harald Müller (Ch. 15) follows this maxim in his study of the politics of compliance with regime norms and rules in three security cases: the challenges to the ABM Treaty as part of the strategic nuclear weapons control regime stemming from the US Government's Strategic Defense Initiative and the Soviet Union's illegal setting up of an early-warning radar at Krasnoyarsk (considered separately by Müller, although he is sensitive to the cross-connections between these two cases); and the incompatibility of the West German nuclear export control policy with the non-proliferation regime. In each case the Government, influential parts of the Administration, or the military sought to implement measures, or already pursued a policy, which would have violated or actually violated central regime norms. And in each case the regime concerned proved to be a critical resource for those opposed to these measures or practices, helping them to get the upper hand in the subsequent controversy. In other words: not

---

[13] This is not to say that the question of whether regimes really make a difference has been addressed very often by regime analysts.

only did the apprehension that non-compliance was bound to endanger the regime (at least in the long run) mobilize the resistance of those who perceived the regime's maintenance to be in the national interest (obviously, in the eyes of policy-makers regimes make a difference!); Müller also shows that the regime itself, by virtue of its connection with both international and domestic law and the foreseeable effects of defection on the state's international reputation, produced important barriers to non-compliance, which could be utilized by its defenders.

Had there been no strategic nuclear weapons control regime (including the ABM Treaty), a debate in the United States on whether or not to abide by certain rules of the regime would not have been possible. Yet, a defence policy favouring strategic stability over the vague promise of future protection against nuclear missile attacks does not presuppose an international norm prescribing such a policy and thus might well have been possible in the absence of the regime. So how can we be sure that it is the existence of a strategic nuclear weapons control regime and not some other factor that caused the United States not to implement SDI in the way originally planned? How can we be sure that the regime made a difference and that the same policy would not have been chosen ultimately, even if the ABM Treaty had never been concluded? This uncertainty, which Müller seeks to eliminate by closely reviewing the decision processes and the arguments put forward in the domestic controversies over compliance or non-compliance, points to what is presumably a major reason why the empirical study of regime effects is underdeveloped as compared to the analysis of regime formation and persistence/demise: the methodological problems associated with determining the effects of international regimes are formidable.

Thomas Biersteker (Ch. 13) examines some of the most troublesome of them. He is sceptical of the feasibility of large-N studies as a means of uncovering the effects of international regimes, because he thinks that a sufficient comparability of the cases cannot be attained. Students of regime consequences therefore have to turn to individual regimes and seek to ascertain their effects. However, causal inference is not possible on the basis of a single case. There is no way out of this dilemma, Biersteker argues, but to resort to constructing historical counterfactuals, that is scenarios in which the regimes whose consequences we are interested in are absent. Comparing the counterfactual course of events with the real one we can then assess the aspects of reality which are caused by the regime rather than some other factor. However, many counterfactual scenarios can be constructed which all have in common that the regime in question does not exist in them. Which one is adequate? Addressing this problem Biersteker suggests various guidelines to be observed when embarking on counterfactual analysis: for example, using a clearly articulated theoretical framework; requiring that the alleged effect follow the respective cause regularly and be close to it in time; making sure that the counterfactual is 'legitimate' (i.e. its antecedent must be consistent with the facts that enter into the deduction of the consequent). These guidelines notwithstanding, imagining the world (or rather some aspect of it that is of interest to the analyst) as it would have been if the regime in question had not come into existence remains a very intricate task inviting much subjective input, particularly in the absence of precise theories of international politics. Therefore, Biersteker's thesis that counterfactual reasoning cannot be circumvented in the study of regime consequences may annoy regime analysts. All the more, it deserves their attention and critical discussion. One central issue in this discussion will certainly have to be whether Biersteker is right in dismissing comparative research designs (based on actual cases exclusively) for the study of regime consequences.

Another difficulty that the study of regime effects is confronted with and that complicates comparative research results from the myriad of conceivable regime consequences. All sorts of consequences of regimes have been identified or, at least, considered in the literature, ranging from change in actors' cognitions or beliefs (learning) to change in actors' capabilities, from goal-attainment (in varying degrees) to the fulfilment of evaluative criteria such as efficiency or distributive justice (again in varying degrees), etc. Discussions of (potential) regime effects can be found in the contributions to this volume by Rittberger (Ch. 1, sect. 5) and Keohane (Ch. 2, sect. 4) as well as Breitmeier and Wolf (Ch. 14, sect. 2). Just as there are numerous dimensions on which the contents of regimes vary (see sect. 3.2 above), there are many dimensions of regime consequences each of which constitutes a possible dependent variable for empirical research. Sufficient clarity about the most important of these variables

TABLE 16.1. *Dependent Variables for the Study of Regime Consequences*

Dimension	Unit of analysis		
	Government	Society/Domestic Politics	Issue Area
Behaviour	• implementation of regime rules • compliance with inconvenient commitments	• groups supporting regime rules • rule compliance by new governments	• problem solving • resilience against external changes
Capabilities	• resources at government's disposal	• domestic distribution of resources	• resources at disposal for the international endeavour
Cognitions	• cause–effect relationship regarding issues • intentions ascribed to other actors	• cause–effect relationship regarding issues • intentions ascribed to other actors	• cause–effect relationship regarding issues • mutual trust
Values and Interests	• preference ordering	• domestic interests	• situation structure
Constitution	• domestic political structure	• loyalities	• integration • civilizing process

therefore seems to be a prerequisite for systematic examination of the effects of international regimes. In order to help provide this prerequisite a 'map of dependent variables for the study of regime consequences' (Table 16.1), resulting from the cross-tabulation of five 'dimensions' and three 'units of analysis', has been presented (Zürn 1991: 25).

This table demonstrates how many different kinds of potential regime consequences there are.[14] This diversity suggests a practical need to define research priorities. Helmut Breitmeier and Klaus Dieter Wolf (Ch. 14, sect. 2) therefore propose a comparatively small set of dependent variables or 'criteria' based on the value premises of the peace research tradition, including two aspects of problem solving: justice and sustainability in conflict regulation, as well as two aspects of context change: democratization within states and civilization among states. Whether or not students of regime effects will be inspired in their research by this suggestion, in light of Table 16.1 and its many cells they are certainly well advised to make sure precisely which kinds of consequences they wish to examine and why.

For the time being, we assume that regimes *can* have significant consequences on all the dimensions and units specified in the table. The question then arises when they do and what exactly these consequences will be. Two issues have to be raised in this connection: the distinction between generic and specific effects, on the one hand, and the question of the appropriate independent variables, on the other. Breitmeier and Wolf distinguish between *effects that are common to all regimes* and *effects which occur only with certain types of regimes*. The assertion of generic effects of regimes is not unfamiliar to regime analysis. Thus, functionalist theories of regimes which explain the formation and persistence of regimes with reference to a particular set of—valued—effects (such as reduction of transactions costs and uncertainty), to the extent that they aspire to a general explanation of regimes, presuppose just this type of effect. While it is certainly not unreasonable to assume and study generic effects of regimes, in

---

[14] Note that one cell can contain more than one dependent variable: for instance, both the extent to which the regime solves the problem that gave rise to its creation and the degree of resilience of the regime against external changes are variables relating to the dimension 'behaviour' and the unit of analysis 'issue area'. Moreover, we assume that further variables could be added to most of the cells.

the long run more interesting insights can be expected from the study of regime-type specific effects. The regime-type specific hypotheses predicting such effects, of course, are the link which relates the study of regime effects to the study of regime properties that we have pointed to at the end of the preceding section. Examples of such hypotheses are presented, and confronted with the evidence gained from environmental regimes, in the chapter by Breitmeier and Wolf.

These authors also refer to an ongoing discussion of how to define the relationship of regimes as independent variables to other explanatory variables (Nollkaemper 1992). Krasner (1983*a*) suggested regarding regimes as intervening variables affecting the relationship between basic causal variables (in particular, power and interest) and related behaviour and outcomes. No such hierarchy among variables holds in Young's (1991*b*) distinction of 'endogenous variables' (properties of the regime), 'exogenous variables' (distribution of power, interests, shared knowledge), and 'linkage variables' (degree of fit between the regime's content and its environment), which, together, are supposed to account for various dimensions of 'regime effectiveness'. Finally, one could as well treat the regime itself as the primary causal agent, seeking to explain variation in regime consequences primarily in terms of varying regime properties. Indeed, the latter approach seems to be most adequate to the notion of effects *of the regime* (as opposed to those of other factors or a combination of factors including the regime). Conversely, 'regime effectiveness' in Young's sense seems to describe the change in some dependent variable (e.g. air pollution in a particular region) following regime formation, rather than the particular contribution to this change of the regime as such. Regarding the regime as such as the primary causal agent, however, does not require ignoring exogenous and linkage variables in Young's sense. Consider the following procedure: it seems safe to assume that regime effects do not depend only on regime content but on the strength of the regime (i.e. the degree of overall compliance with regime rules) as well. Obviously, when actors constantly disregard regime prescriptions, the regime cannot be expected to have a great impact, whereas significant consequences on a given variable such as goal attainment are at least possible in the case of a high degree of rule compliance. Consequently, we could, in a first step, try to evaluate general and regime-type specific hypotheses about regime effects controlling for regime strength, i.e. in the light of regime cases with roughly equal levels of overall rule compliance. In a second step, Young's exogenous and linkage variables could be used to explain levels of rule compliance. The procedure would seem to have two advantages. Relying primarily on endogenous factors in Young's sense it appears to be compatible with a conceptualization of the dependent variable as effects of the regime as such (and thus with the common notion of causality as a regular relationship between cause and effect). At the same time, a concrete starting-point for research (namely evaluating generic and regime-type specific hypotheses about regime consequences) is given, while other factors presumably bearing upon the consequences of regime formation do not have to be left aside but can be taken into account in a systematic fashion.

The issues discussed in this section reflect a stage in the evolution of the study of regime consequences, in which empirical research seems to be superseded by conceptual and methodological discussions. This fact may indicate what a long way regime analysts still have to go before a claim to solid knowledge about the effects of regimes can be made. Still, short cuts do not seem to be available in this case and without a thorough and conclusive discussion of these and other related issues (which, of course, could not be supplied within the limits of this chapter) our way is bound to become longer rather than shorter.

4. CONCLUSION: TOWARDS A DATA BASE OF INTERNATIONAL REGIMES

There are at least four good reasons to continue, individually and in collaborative efforts, to look into the formation, properties, and effects of international regimes. First, the study of international regimes is of practical relevance: regimes constitute an increasingly significant element of international order, and regimes are normatively appealing as the most important component of an envisioned world governance without a world state. Second, the study of international regimes is scholarly successful: regime analysis constitutes a research programme which has improved our understanding of international co-operation and international institutions. Third, important aspects of regimes are still heavily under-researched, in particular the content and the consequences of regimes. Fourth, strategies for further cumulation of knowledge are available: the integration of different hypotheses about regime formation and persistence/demise, the study of regime-conducive foreign policy and its roots in domestic politics, the application of cognitive theory to issues of regime creation, persistence, and change, the construction of regime typologies in order to make research on regime properties manageable, and the investigation of regime effects using conterfactual and comparative research designs have all been identified as promising paths.

All of the research tasks mentioned above need empirical grounding in a relatively high number of case studies. First, for understanding developments over time on the macroscopic level of the international system we need to determine the overall amount of institutionalization of co-operation in the international system and in subsets of it. While it would be pointless to create a 'Yearbook of International Regimes', a less formal and more theoretically informed source could be useful for assessing and analysing macroscopic changes in international institutions. Second, as to the question of how particular international regimes come into existence, persist, or decay, it is obvious that all strategies that promise to move the frontiers of this research forward need, for their implementation, a large amount of information: hypotheses about regime formation, persistence, and demise focusing on aspects of cognition and domestic politics refer to new units of observation for the independent variable(s), that is either decision-makers or states as actors. The number of these units by far exceeds that of power or interest constellations—the independent variables of realist and utilitarian approaches to the study of regime formation and persistence/demise. In other words, the testing of cognitivist and second image hypotheses requires considerable amounts of information which can hardly be gathered by individual researchers. Similarly, the strategies of contextualization and integration of hypotheses about regime formation both depend on the availability of a large number of case studies. The more restrictive the conditions of applicability of a hypothesis are or the more combinations of independent variables with different predictions regarding the dependent variable we want to put to a test, the more cases we need to obtain conclusive results. Third, the same is, of course, true when we want to account for different regime properties. Explaining typologically defined regime properties requires differentiation of our dependent variable (e.g. open, conditionally open, restricted, or no regime, instead of simply regime or no regime) as well as of our independent variables and thus requires focused comparison of more cases. Fourth, studying the effects which occur only with certain types of regimes creates the same problem. The strategy of differentiation can only yield results when the overall number of regimes under consideration is sufficiently large.

In short, further advances in empirically based and theoretically oriented research on international regimes would considerably benefit from a *data base* built up by interested researchers following widely agreed-upon guidelines. A first attempt at formulating such guidelines has already been made by participants in a 'Regime Theory Summit' at Dartmouth College in late 1991. Regime analysts will be asked to give certain kinds of information, by filling in a questionnaire, about the cases studied by them in exchange for the use of the data base. As many international regimes as possible will be 'coded' with respect to numerous categories along the dimensions 'regime type', 'exogenous factors (of regime formation and consequences)' and 'regime consequences'.[15]

Such a data base, incidentally, would supply regime analysts with information about the relative representation of different kinds of case studies in recent research. Currently, a large share of case studies, for instance, is devoted to environmental issues, while studies of international regimes in the North–South context presumably are under-represented. Thus, the data base might even help bring about a more efficient use of research capacity.

Yet, we want to emphasize that the projected data base should not be confused with the large-scale projects about the correlates of war which were in vogue during the 1960s and 1970s. First of all, the projected data base will not consume significant amounts of additional resources or require extensive fund-raising operations. Moreover, the information entering into the data base will retain its qualitative character. The data bank will not be built up

---

[15] See Young (1991c) for a summary of the discussions during the meeting. The participants are now in the process of developing different parts of the reporting form.

by graduate research assistants coding certain kinds of events, but will make available qualitative data on cases which are provided by the researchers who have themselves carried out in-depth studies of the respective cases. To put it differently, the projected data base is not meant to evolve into a 'COR' enterprise but is a comparatively modest attempt at drawing together already existing efforts and activating possible synergetic effects in the study of international regimes.

REFERENCES

Achen, C. H. (1989), 'When is a State with Bureaucratic Politics Representable as a Unitary Rational Actor?', paper presented at International Studies Association meetings, London.

Adams, A. M., and Emmerich, C. J. (1990), *A Nation Dedicated to Religious Liberty: The Constitutional Heritage of the Religion Clauses* (Philadelphia, Pa.).

Adelman, K. L. (1984), 'Arms Control without Agreements', *Foreign Affairs,* 63: 240–63.

Adler, E., and Haas, P. M. (1992), 'Conclusion: Epistemic Communities, World Order, and the Creation of a Reflective Research Program', *International Organization,* 46: 367–90.

Aggarwal, V. K. (1985), *Liberal Protectionism: The International Politics of Organized Textile Trade* (Berkeley, Calif.).

Albrecht, U. (1989) (ed.), *Technikkontrolle und Internationale Politik: Die internationale Steuerung von Technologietransfers und ihre Folgen* (Leviathan-Sonderheft 10; Opladen).

An-Na'im, A. A. (1987), 'Religious Minorities under Islamic Law and the Limits of Cultural Relativism', *Human Rights Quarterly,* 9: 1–18.

Argyris, C., and Schon, D. A. (1978), *Organizational Learning* (Reading, Mass.).

Artis, M., and Ostry, S. (1986), *International Economic Policy Coordination* (London).

Arzt, D. (1990), 'The Application of Human Rights Law in Islamic States', *Human Rights Quarterly,* 12: 202–30.

Ashley, R. K. (1981), 'Political Realism and Human Interests', *International Studies Quarterly,* 25: 204–36.

—— (1988), 'Untying the Sovereign State: A Double Reading of the Anarchy Problematique', *Millennium,* 17: 227–62.

Aubert, V. (1963), 'Competition and Dissensus: Two Types of Conflict and of Conflict Resolution', *Journal of Conflict Resolution,* 7: 26–42.

Aumann, R. J. (1974), 'Subjectivity and Correlation in Randomized Strategies', *Journal of Mathematical Economics,* 1: 67–96.

—— (1987), 'Correlated Equilibrium as an Expression of Bayesian Rationality', *Econometrica,* 55: 1–18.

Axelrod, R. M. (1984), *The Evolution of Cooperation* (New York).

—— and Keohane, R. O. (1986), 'Achieving Cooperation under Anarchy: Strategies and Institutions', in Oye (1986), 226–54.

Bächler, G. (1990), *Ökologische Sicherheit und Konflikt* (Arbeitspapiere der Schweizerischen Friedensstiftung 5; Bern).

Barbezat, D. (1989), 'Cooperation and Rivalry in the International Steel Cartel, 1926–32', *Journal of Economic History*, 49: 435–47.

Barry, B. (1989), *Theories of Justice* (London).

Bates, R. (1988), 'Contra Contractarianism', *Politics and Society*, 16: 387–401.

Baumol, W. J. (1971), *Environmental Protection, International Spillovers, and Trade* (Uppsala).

Beck, U. (1986), *Risikogesellschaft: Auf dem Weg in eine andere Moderne* (Frankfurt am Main).

Beitz, C. R. (1979), *Political Theory and International Relations* (Princeton, NJ).

Beller, E., Efinger, M., Marx, K., Mayer, P., and Zürn, M. (1990), *Die Tübinger Datenbank der Konflikte in den Ost-West-Beziehungen* (Tübinger Arbeitspapiere zur internationalen Politik und Friedensforschung 13; Tübingen).

Beller, E. A. (1970), 'The Thirty Years War', in *The New Cambridge Modern History*, iv: *The Decline of Spain and the Thirty Years War 1609–48/59* (Cambridge), 306–59.

Benedick, R. E. (1991), *Ozone Diplomacy: New Directions in Safeguarding the Planet* (Cambridge, Mass.).

Bethell, L. (1970), *The Abolition of the Brazilian Slave Trade: Britain, Brazil and the Slave Trade Question, 1807–1869* (Cambridge).

Biersteker, T. J. (1981), *Distortion or Development? Contending Perspectives on the Multinational Corporation* (Cambridge, Mass.).

Birnie, P. (1992), 'The Scope, Limits, and Theoretical Basis of International Legal Regulation', in Hurrell and Kingsbury (1992), 51–84.

Black, C. E., Falk, R. A., Knorr, K., and Young, O. R. (1968), *Neutralization and World Politics* (Princeton, NJ).

Blechman, B. M. (1988), *Efforts to Reduce the Risk of Accidental or Inadvertent War*, in George, Farley, and Dallin (1988), 466–81.

Boczek, B. A. (1986), 'The Concept of Regime and the Protection and Preservation of the Marine Environment', *Ocean Yearbook*, 6: 288–95.

Boehmer-Christiansen, S. (1984), 'Marine Pollution Control in Europe', *Marine Policy*, 8: 44–55.

Boulding, K. (1978), *Stable Peace* (Austin, Tex.).

Bozeman, A. B. (1960), *Politics and Culture in International History* (Princeton, NJ).

Breitmeier, H. (1992), *Ozonschicht und Klima auf der globalen Agenda* (Tübinger Arbeitspapiere zur internationalen Politik und Friedensforschung 17; Tübingen).

—— and Zürn, M. (1990), 'Gewalt oder Kooperation: Zur Austragungs-
form internationaler Umweltkonflikte', *antimilitarismus information*,
20/12: 14–23.

Breslauer, G. W., and Tetlock, P. E. (1991) (eds.), *Learning in U.S. and
Soviet Foreign Policy* (Boulder, Colo.).

Brickman, R., Jasanoff, S., and Ilgen, T. (1985), *Controlling Chemicals:
The Politics of Regulation in Europe and the United States* (Ithaca, NY).

Brock, L. (1991), 'Peace through Parks: The Environment on the Peace
Research Agenda', *Journal of Peace Research*, 28: 407–23.

Brzoska, M. (1991), 'Warum gibt es so wenige Atomwaffenstaaten?
Zum Erklärungswert verschiedener theoretischer Ansätze', *Politische
Vierteljahresschrift*, 32: 34–55.

Buchanan, J. M. (1975), *The Limits of Liberty: Between Anarchy and
Leviathan* (Chicago, Ill.).

Bull, H. (1966), 'The Grotian Conception of International Society', in
Butterfield and Wight (1966), 51–73.

—— (1977), *The Anarchical Society: A Study of Order in World Politics*
(London).

—— (1981), 'Hobbes and the International Anarchy', *Social Research*,
48: 717–38.

—— (1983), 'Justice in International Relations', unpub. manuscript, the
Hagey Lectures, University of Waterloo, Oct. 1983.

—— and Watson, A. (1984) (eds.), *The Expansion of International
Society* (Oxford).

—— Kingsbury, B. W., and Roberts, A. (1990) (eds.), *Hugo Grotius and
International Relations* (Oxford).

Bundesministerium für Wirtschaft (1991), *Dokumentation zur Reform der
Exportpolitik* (Bonn).

Butterfield, H., and Wight, M. (1966) (eds.), *Diplomatic Investigations*
(London).

Caldwell, D. (1981), *American–Soviet Relations: From 1947 to the Nixon–
Kissinger Grand Design* (Westport, Conn.).

Caldwell, L. K. (1990), *International Environmental Policy: Emergence
and Dimensions*[2] (Durham).

Campbell, D. T. (1973), 'Reforms as Experiments', in J. Caporaso and
L. Roos (eds.), *Quasi-Experimental Approaches: Testing Theory and
Evaluating Policy* (Evanston, Ill.), 187–225.

Carlsnaes, W. (1986), *Ideology and Foreign Policy: Problems of Comparative Conceptualization* (Oxford).

Carr, E. H. (1981), *The Twenty Years' Crisis, 1919–1939*[2] (London).

Carroll, J. E. (1988) (ed.), *International Environmental Diplomacy*
(Cambridge).

Cassese, A. (1988), *International Law in a Divided World* (Oxford).

Chilton, P. A. (1989), 'What Do We Mean by "Security"?', Center for International Security and Arms Control, unpub. paper, Stanford University.

Chopra, J., and Weiss, T. G. (1992), 'Sovereignty is no Longer Sacrosanct: Codifying Humanitarian Intervention', *Ethics and International Affairs,* 6: 95–117.

Chossudovsky, E. M. (1988), *East–West Diplomacy for Environment in the United Nations: The High-Level Meeting within the Framework of ECE on the Protection of the Environment* (New York).

Choucri, N. (1993) (ed.), *Global Accord: Environmental Challenges and International Responses* (Cambridge, Mass.).

Clark, G., and Sohn, L. B. (1958), *World Peace through World Law* (Cambridge, Mass.).

Claude, I. L., Jr. (1955), *National Minorities: An International Problem* (Cambridge, Mass.).

Coase, R. H. (1937), 'The Nature of the Firm', *Economica,* 4: 386–405.

Cobbah, J. A. M. (1987), 'African Values and the Human Rights Debate: An African Perspective', *Human Rights Quarterly,* 9: 309–31.

Cohen, B. J. (1983), 'Balance-of-payments Financing: Evolution of a Regime,' in Krasner (1983c), 315–36.

Cohen, R. (1981), *International Politics: The Rules of the Game* (London).

Coleman, J. S. (1990), *Foundations of Social Theory* (Cambridge, Mass.).

Comisso, E., (1986), 'Introduction: State Structures, Political Processes, and Collective Choice in CMEA States', *International Organization,* 40: 195–238.

Cooper, J. C. (1947), *The Right to Fly* (New York).

Cooper, R. N. (1989), 'International Cooperation in Public Health as a Prologue to Macroeconomic Cooperation', in Cooper *et al.* (1989), 178–254.

—— Eichengreen, B., Henning, C. R., Holtham, G., and Putnam, R. D. (1989), *Can Nations Agree? Issues in International Economic Cooperation* (Washington, DC).

Coplin, W. D. (1966), *The Functions of International Law: An Introduction to the Role of International Law in the Contemporary World* (Chicago, Ill.).

Cox, R. W. (1983), 'Gramsci, Hegemony, and International Relations: An Essay in Method', *Millennium,* 12: 162–75.

—— (1986), 'Social Forces, States, and World Orders: Beyond International Relations Theory', in Keohane (1986b), 204–54.

—— (1987), *Production, Power, and World Order* (New York).

—— (1992), 'Towards a Post-Hegemonic Conceptualization of World Order: Reflections on the Relevancy of Ibn Khaldun', in Rosenau and Czempiel (1992), 132–59.

Crane, B. B. (1993), 'International Population Institutions: Adaptation to a Changing World Order', in Haas, Keohane, and Levy (1993), 351–93.

Czempiel, E.-O. (1981), *Internationale Politik: Ein Konfliktmodell* (Paderborn).

—— (1986*a*), *Friedensstrategien: Systemwandel durch Internationale Organisationen, Demokratisierung und Wirtschaft* (Paderborn).

—— (1986*b*), 'Der Stand der Wissenschaft von den Internationalen Beziehungen und der Friedensforschung in der Bundesrepublik Deutschland', in K. v. Beyme (ed.), *Politikwissenschaft in der Bundesrepublik* (PVS-Sonderheft 17; Opladen), 250–63.

—— (1989), 'Internationalizing Politics: Some Answers to the Question of Who Does What to Whom', in E.-O. Czempiel and J. Rosenau (eds.), *Global Changes and Theoretical Challenges: Approaches to World Politics for the 1990s* (Lexington, Mass.), 117–34.

—— (1991), *Weltpolitik im Umbruch: Das internationale System nach dem Ende des Ost-West-Konflikts* (Munich).

Daalder, I. H. (1988), *NATO Strategy and Ballistic Missile Defence* (Adelphi Papers 233; London).

D'Amato, A. (1971), *The Concept of Custom in International Law* (Ithaca, NY).

Dasgupta, P. (1990), 'Trust as a Commodity', in Gambetta (1990*c*), 49–72.

Dehio, L. (1948), *Gleichgewicht oder Hegemonie: Betrachtungen über ein Grundproblem der neueren Staatengeschichte* (Krefeld).

Dessler, D. (1991), 'Beyond Correlations: Toward a Causal Theory of War', *International Studies Quarterly*, 35: 337–55.

Deutsch, K. W., Burrell, S. A., Kann, R. A., Lee, M., Jr., Lichterman, M., Lindgren, R. E., Loewenheim, F. L., and Wagenen, R. W. V. (1957), *Political Community and the North Atlantic Area: International Organization in the Light of Historical Experience* (Princeton, NJ).

Deutscher Bundestag (1990), *Beschlußempfehlung und Bericht des 2. Untersuchungsausschusses* (Drucksache 11/7800; Bonn).

Donelan, M. (1990), *Elements of International Political Theory* (Oxford).

Donnelly, J. (1981), 'Recent Trends in U.N. Human Rights Activity: Description and Polemic', *International Organization*, 35: 633–55.

—— (1986), 'International Human Rights: A Regime Analysis', *International Organization*, 40: 599–642.

Douglas, M. (1987), *How Institutions Think* (London).

Downs, G. W., and Rocke, D. M. (1990), *Tacit Bargaining, Arms Races and Arms Control* (Ann Arbor, Mich.).

Doyle, M. W. (1986), 'Liberalism and World Politics', *American Political Science Review*, 80: 1151–69.

Dunn, J. (1990), 'Trust and Political Agency', in Gambetta (1990c), 73–93.

Durkheim, E. (1897), *Suicide: A Study in Sociology,* trans. J. A. Spaulding and G. Simpson, ed. G. Simpson (Glencoe, Ill., 1963).

East, M. A., Salmore, S. A., and Hermann, C. F. (1978) (eds.), *Why Nations Act: Theoretical Perspectives for Comparative Foreign Policy Studies* (Beverly Hills, Calif.).

Eatwell, J., Milgate, M., and Newman, P. (1987) (eds.), *The New Palgrave: A Dictionary of Economics* (New York).

Eckert, M. (1989), 'Die Anfänge der Atompolitik in der Bundesrepublik Deutschland', *Vierteljahreshefte für Zeitgeschichte,* 26: 116–43.

Eckstein, H. (1975), 'Case Study and Theory in Political Science', in F. L. Greenstein and N. W. Polsby (eds.), *Handbook of Political Science,* vii (Reading, Mass.), 79–137.

Eden, L. (1991), *Bringing the Firm Back In: Multinationals in IPE* (The Centre for International Trade and Investment Policy Studies Discussion Paper 1991–01; Ottawa).

Edmead, F. (1982), 'Changes in Perception During the Course of Conflict', in Jönsson (1982), 158–77.

Edwards, S. (1989), 'Structural Adjustment Policies in Highly Indebted Countries', in J. D. Sachs (ed.), *Developing Country Debt and Economic Performance: The International Financial System,* i (Chicago, Ill.), 159–207.

Efinger, M. (1990), 'Preventing War in Europe through Confidence- and Security-Building Measures?', in Rittberger (1990d), 117–50.

—— (1991a), *Vertrauen ist gut, Kontrolle ist besser: Entstehungsbedingungen effektiver Verifikationsvereinbarungen im Politikfeld Sicherheit* (Baden-Baden).

—— (1991b), 'Rüstungsbegrenzung in Westeuropa', unpub. paper, University of Tübingen.

—— and Rittberger, V. (1992), 'The CSBM Regime in and for Europe: Confidence Building and Peaceful Conflict Management', in M. C. Pugh (ed.), *European Security—Towards 2000* (Manchester), 104–23.

—— and Zürn, M. (1989), 'Umweltschutz und Ost-West-Konfliktformation: Zur Bedeutung problem- und situationsstruktureller Faktoren für die Entstehung internationaler Regime', in Moltmann and Senghaas-Knobloch (1989), 224–42.

—— —— (1990), 'Explaining Conflict Management in East–West Relations: A Quantitative Test of Problem-Structural Typologies', in Rittberger (1990d), 64–89.

—— Rittberger, V., and Zürn, M. (1988), *Internationale Regime in den Ost-West-Beziehungen: Ein Beitrag zur Erforschung der friedlichen Behandlung internationaler Konflikte* (Frankfurt am Main).

—— —— Wolf, K. D., and Zürn, M. (1990), 'Internationale Regime und internationale Politik', in Rittberger (1990c), 263–85.

Elias, N. (1939), *Power and Civility: The Civilizing Process,* ii, trans. E. Jephcott with some notes and revisions by the author (New York, 1982).

—— (1985), *Humana Conditio: Beobachtungen zur Entwicklung der Menschheit am 40. Jahrestag eines Kriegsendes (8. Mai 1985)* (Frankfurt am Main).

Elster, J. (1978), *Logic and Society: Contradictions and Possible Worlds* (Chichester).

—— (1985), *Making Sense of Marx* (Cambridge).

Evans, P. B., Jacobson, H., and Putnam, R. D. (in progress) (eds.), *International and Domestic Explanations of World Politics.*

—— Rueschemeyer, D., and Skocpol, T. (1985) (eds.), *Bringing the State Back In* (Cambridge).

Falk, R. A. (1981), *Human Rights and State Sovereignty* (New York).

—— Kratochwil, F., and Mendlovitz, S. H. (1985) (eds.), *International Law: A Contemporary Perspective* (Boulder, Colo.).

Farrell, J. (1987), 'Cheap Talk, Coordination, and Entry', *Rand Journal of Economics,* 18: 34–9.

—— and Gibbons, R. (1989), 'Cheap Talk Can Matter in Bargaining', *Journal of Economic Theory,* 48: 221–37.

Faupel, K. (1984), 'Internationale Regime als Gegenstände für sozialwissenschaftliche Forschung', *Jahrbuch der Universität Salzburg 1981–1983,* 94–105.

Fearon, J. (1990), 'Deterrence and the Spiral Model: The Role of Costly Signals in Crisis Bargaining', paper presented at 1990 American Political Science Association meetings, San Francisco.

—— (1991), 'Counterfactuals and Hypothesis Testing in Political Science', *World Politics,* 43: 169–95.

Fellner, W. (1949), *Competition among the Few* (New York).

Ferejohn, J. (1991a), 'Rationality and Interpretation: Parliamentary Elections in Early Stuart England', in Monroe (1991), 279–305.

—— (1991b), 'The Second Image Revised: Foreign Policy and Domestic Political Institutions in Early Stuart England', unpub. paper, Stanford University.

Fischer, D. A. V., and Müller, H. (1985), *Nonproliferation beyond the 1985 Review* (CEPS Papers 26; Brussels).

—— and Szasz, P. (1985), *Safeguarding the Atom: A Critical Appraisal* (London).

Fletcher, J. D. (1984), *Strategic Defense Initiative* (Defensive Technology Study; Washington, DC).

Flora, P., Alber, J., Eichenberg, R., Kohl, J., Kraus, F., Pfennig, W., and Seebohm, K. (1983), *State, Economy, and Society in Western Europe 1815–1975* (Frankfurt am Main).

Fogel, R. W. (1964), *Railroads and American Economic Growth* (Baltimore, Md.).

—— and Engerman, S. (1974), *Time on the Cross* (Boston, Mass.).

Forges, F. (1986), 'An Approach to Communication Equilibria', *Econometrica*, 54: 1375–85.

Forsythe, D. (1983), *Human Rights and World Politics* (Lincoln, Nebr.).

Franck, T. M. (1990), *The Power of Legitimacy among Nations* (New York).

Frank, L. P. (1985), 'The First Oil Regime', *World Politics*, 37: 568–98.

Fudenberg, D., and Maskin, E. (1986), 'The Folk Theorem in Repeated Games with Discounting or with Incomplete Information', *Econometrica*, 54: 533–54.

Fulbright, J. W. (1966), *The Arrogance of Power* (New York).

Gagliardo, J. (1980), *Reich and Nation: The Holy Roman Empire as Idea and Reality, 1763–1806* (Bloomington, Ind.).

Galtung, J. (1969), 'Violence, Peace, and Peace Research', *Journal of Peace Research*, 7: 167–91.

Gambetta, D. (1990a), 'Can We Trust Trust?', in Gambetta (1990c), 213–37.

—— (1990b), 'Foreword', in Gambetta (1990c), ix–xii.

—— (1990c) (ed.), *Trust: Making and Breaking Cooperative Relations* (Oxford).

Gantzel, K. J. (1992) (ed.), *Die Kriege nach dem zweiten Weltkrieg bis 1990: Daten und Tendenzen* (Münster).

Garthoff, R. L. (1984), 'BMD and East–West Relations', in A. B. Carter and D. N. Schwartz (eds.), *Ballistic Missile Defense* (Washington, DC), 275–339.

—— (1987), *Policy Versus the Law: The Reinterpretation of the ABM Treaty* (Washington, DC).

—— (1989), *Reflections on the Cuban Missile Crisis* (Washington, DC).

—— (1990), *Deterrence and the Revolution in Soviet Military Doctrine* (Washington, DC).

Gauthier, D. (1986), *Morals by Agreement* (Oxford).

Gehring, T. (1991), 'International Environmental Regimes: Dynamic Sectoral Legal Systems', *Yearbook of International Environmental Law*, i (London), 35–56.

George, A. L. (1979), 'Case Studies and Theory Development: The Method of Structured, Focused Comparison', in P. G. Lauren (ed.), *Diplomacy: New Approaches in History, Theory, and Policy* (New York), 43–68.

—— (1988), 'Strategies for Facilitating Cooperation', in George, Farley, and Dallin (1988), 692–711.

—— and Keohane, R. O. (1980), 'The Concept of National Interests', in George, *Presidential Decisionmaking in Foreign Policy: The Effective Use of Information and Advice* (Boulder, Colo.), 217–37.

—— and McKeown, T. J. (1985), 'Case Studies and Theories of Organizational Decision Making', in L. S. Sproull and P. D. Larkey (eds.), *Advances in Information Processing in Organizations,* ii (Greenwich, Conn.), 21–58.

—— Farley, P. J., and Dallin, A. (1988) (eds.), *U.S.–Soviet Security Cooperation: Achievements, Failures, Lessons* (New York).

Gilpin, R. (1981), *War and Change in World Politics* (Cambridge).

Goldmann, K. (1988), *Change and Stability in Foreign Policy: The Problems and Possibilities of Détente* (New York).

Goldstein, J. (1986), 'The Political Economy of Trade: Institutions of Protection', *American Political Science Review,* 80: 161–84.

Goldstein, M. (1986), *The Global Effects of Fund-Supported Adjustment Programs* (IMF Occasional Paper 42; Washington, DC).

Good, D. (1990), 'Individuals, Interpersonal Relations, and Trust', in Gambetta (1990*c*), 31–48.

Gourevitch, P. (1986), *Politics in Hard Times: Comparative Responses to International Economic Crises* (Ithaca, NY).

Gowa, J. (1988), 'Public Goods and Political Institutions: Trade and Monetary Policy Processes in the United States', *International Organization,* 42: 15–32.

—— (1989), 'Rational Hegemons, Excludable Goods, and Small Groups: An Epitaph for Hegemonic Stability Theory?', *World Politics,* 41: 307–24.

Greve, F. (1985), 'Out of the Blue: How "Star Wars" was Proposed', *Philadelphia Inquirer,* 17 Nov., 1 and 5.

Grieco, J. M. (1988), 'Anarchy and the Limits of Cooperation: A Realist Critique of the Newest Liberal Institutionalism', *International Organization,* 42: 485–507.

—— (1990), *Cooperation Among Nations: Europe, America, and Non-Tariff Barriers to Trade* (Ithaca, NY).

Gross, L. (1979), 'Some International Law Aspects of the Freedom of Information and the Right to Communicate', in K. Nordenstreng and H. I. Schiller (eds.), *National Sovereignty and International Communication* (Norwood, NJ), 195–216.

Guitian, M. (1981), *Fund Conditionality: Evolution of Principles and Practices* (Washington, DC).

Haas, E. B. (1964), *Beyond the Nation-State: Functionalism and International Organization* (Stanford, Calif.).

—— (1975), 'Is There a Hole in the "Whole"?', *International Organization,* 29: 827–76.

Haas, E. B. (1980), 'Why Collaborate? Issue Linkage and International Regimes', *World Politics*, 32: 357–405.

—— (1990), *When Knowledge is Power: Three Models of Change in International Organizations* (Berkeley, Calif.).

Haas, P. M. (1989), 'Do Regimes Matter? Epistemic Communities and Mediterranean Pollution Control', *International Organization*, 43: 377–403.

—— (1990), *Saving the Mediterranean: The Politics of International Environmental Cooperation* (New York).

—— (1992*a*), 'Banning Chlorofluorocarbons: Epistemic Community Efforts to Protect Stratospheric Ozone', *International Organization*, 46: 187–224.

—— (1992*b*), 'Introduction: Epistemic Communities and International Policy Coordination', *International Organization*, 46: 1–35.

—— (1992*c*) (ed.), *Knowledge, Power and International Policy Coordination* (Special Issue of *International Organization*, 46/1).

—— (1993) (with J. Sundgren), 'Evolving International Environmental Law: Changing Practices of National Sovereignty', in Choucri (1993), 401–29.

—— Keohane, R. O., and Levy, M. (1990), 'International Environmental Institutions', unpub. paper.

—— —— —— (1993) (eds.), *Institutions for the Earth: Sources of Effective International Environmental Protection* (Cambridge, Mass.).

Häckel, E. (1989), *Die Bundesrepublik Deutschland und der Atomwaffensperrvertrag: Rückblick und Ausblick* (Bonn).

Haftendorn, H. (1989), 'Außenpolitische Prioritäten und Handlungsspielraum: Ein Paradigma zur Analyse der Außenpolitik der Bundesrepublik Deutschland', *Politische Vierteljahresschrift*, 30: 32–49.

Hagan, J. D. (1989), 'Domestic Political Regime Changes and Foreign Policy Restructuring in Western Europe: A Conceptual Framework and Initial Empirical Analysis', *Cooperation and Conflict*, 24: 141–62.

Haggard, S. (1985), 'The Politics of Adjustment: Lessons from the IMF's Extended Fund Facility', *International Organization*, 39: 505–34.

—— and Simmons, B. A. (1987), 'Theories of International Regimes', *International Organization*, 41: 491–517.

Haile, H. G. (1980), *Luther: An Experiment in Biography* (Princeton, NJ).

Halliday, F. (1983), *The Making of the Second Cold War* (London).

Hanson, D. W. (1984), 'Thomas Hobbes's "Highway to Peace"', *International Organization*, 38: 329–54.

Harsanyi, J. (1977), *Rational Behaviour and Bargaining Equilibrium in Games and Social Situations* (Cambridge).

Hart, H. L. A. (1961), *The Concept of Law* (Oxford).

Hartigan, K. (1992), 'Matching Humanitarian Norms with Cold, Hard Interests: The Making of Refugee Policies in Mexico and Honduras, 1980–89', *International Organization*, 46: 709–30.

Hartwich, H.-H. (1989) (ed.), *Macht und Ohnmacht politischer Institutionen* (Opladen).

Haufler, V. A. (1991), 'Risk and Reaction: State and Market in the International Risks Insurance Regime', Ph.D. dissertation, Cornell University.

Hays, S. P. (1968), *Conservation and the Gospel of Efficiency* (Cambridge, Mass.).

Heclo, H. (1974), *Modern Social Politics in Britain and Sweden* (New Haven, Conn.).

Henkin, L. (1979), *How Nations Behave: Law and Foreign Policy*[2] (New York).

Hermann, C. F., Kegley, C. W., Jr., and Rosenau, J. N. (1987) (eds.), *New Directions in the Study of Foreign Policy* (Boston, Mass.).

Herzog, D. (1989), *Happy Slaves: A Critique of Consent Theory* (Chicago, Ill.).

Hildebrand, D. K., Laing, J. D., and Rosenthal, H. (1977), *Prediction Analysis of Cross Classifications* (New York).

Hirschman, A. O. (1970), *Exit, Voice, and Loyalty: Responses to Decline in Firms, Organizations, and States* (Cambridge, Mass.).

Hobbes, T. (1651), *Leviathan*, ed. C. B. Macpherson (Harmondsworth, Middlesex, 1968).

Hoberg, G. (forthcoming), 'Governing the Environment: Comparing Policies in Canada and the United States', in K. Banting and R. Simeon (eds.), *Canada and the United States in a Changing World*, ii.

Hoffman, F. S. (1983), 'Ballistic Missile Defenses and US National Security', Summary Report Prepared for the Future Security Strategy Study (Washington, DC).

Hoffman, M. (1989), 'Critical Theory and the Inter-Paradigm Debate', in H. C. Dyer and L. Mangasarian (eds.), *The Study of International Relations* (London), 60–86.

Hoffmann, S. (1965), 'Rousseau on War and Peace', in Hoffmann, *The State of War* (London), 54–87.

—— (1984), 'The Problem of Intervention', in H. Bull (ed.), *Intervention in World Politics* (Oxford), 7–28.

Holsti, K. J. (1985), *The Dividing Discipline: Hegemony and Diversity in International Theory* (Boston, Mass.).

Hughes, B. B. (1991), 'Delivering the Goods: European Integration and the Evolution of Complex Governance', paper prepared for the annual meeting of the American Political Science Association (Washington, DC).

Hurrell, A. J. (1990), 'Kant and the Kantian Paradigm in International Relations', *Review of International Studies,* 16: 183–205.

—— and Kingsbury, B. W. (1992) (eds.), *The International Politics of the Environment* (Oxford).

Hüttig, C. (1989), 'Regime in den internationalen Beziehungen: Zur Fruchtbarkeit des Regime-Ansatzes in der Analyse internationaler Politik', in Hartwich (1989), 405–9.

—— (1990), 'Die Analyse internationaler Regime: Forschungsprogramm-matische "Sackgasse" oder Aufbruch zu neuen Ufern einer Theorie der Internationalen Beziehungen?', *Neue politische Literatur,* 35: 32–49.

Iida, K. (1992), 'The Second Image under Uncertainty: A Game-Theoretic Analysis', unpub. manuscript, Princeton University.

Iklé, F. C. (1973), 'Can Nuclear Deterrence Last Out the Century?', *Foreign Affairs,* 51: 267–81.

Imber, M. (1989), *The USA, ILO, UNESCO, and IAEA: Politicization and Withdrawal in the Specialized Agencies* (New York).

Jackson, R. (1987), 'Quasi-States, Dual Regimes, and Neo-Classical International Theory: International Jurisprudence and the Third World', *International Organization,* 41: 519–49.

Jacobson, H. K. (1984), *Networks of Interdependence: International Organizations and the Global Political System* (New York).

Jervis, R. (1970), *The Logic of Images in International Relations* (Princeton, NJ).

—— (1976), *Perception and Misperception in International Politics* (Princeton, NJ).

—— (1978), 'Cooperation under the Security Dilemma', *World Politics,* 30: 167–214.

—— (1983), 'Security Regimes', in Krasner (1983c), 173–94.

—— (1985), 'Perceiving and Coping with Threat', in R. Jervis, R. N. Lebow, and J. G. Stein (eds.), *Psychology and Deterrence* (Baltimore, Md.), 13–33.

—— (1988), 'Realism, Game Theory, and Cooperation', *World Politics,* 40: 317–49.

Johansson, S. R. (1991), '"Implicit" Policy and Fertility during Development', *Population and Development Review,* 17: 377–414.

Johnson, J. D. (1991), 'Rational Choice as a Reconstructive Theory', in Monroe (1991), 113–42.

Jones, D. V. (1991), *Code of Peace: Ethics and Security in the World of the Warlord States* (Chicago, Ill.).

Jones, E. E., and Davis, K. E. (1965), 'From Acts to Dispositions: The Attribution Process in Person Perception', in L. Berkowitz (ed.), *Advances in Experimental Social Psychology,* ii (New York), 219–66.

Jönsson, C. (1982) (ed.), *Cognitive Dynamics and International Politics* (London).
—— (1987), *International Aviation and the Politics of Regime Change* (London).
—— (1990), *Communication in International Bargaining* (London).
Junne, G. (1972), *Spieltheorie in der internationalen Politik: Die beschränkte Rationalität strategischen Denkens* (Düsseldorf).
—— (1990), 'Theorien über Konflikte und Kooperation zwischen kapitalistischen Industrieländern', in Rittberger (1990c), 353–71.
—— (1992), 'Beyond Regime Theory', *Acta Politica*, 27: 9–28.
Kaiser, K. (1978), 'Auf der Suche nach einer neuen Welt-Nuklearordnung: Zum Hintergrund deutsch-amerikanischer Divergenzen', *Europa-Archiv*, 33: 153–72.
Kamen, H. (1967), *The Rise of Toleration* (New York).
Kapstein, E. B. (1989), 'International Coordination of Banking Regulations', *International Organization*, 43: 323–47.
Karns, M. P., and Mingst, K. A. (1990) (eds.), *The United States and Multilateral Institutions: Patterns of Changing Instrumentality and Influence* (Boston, Mass.).
—— —— (1991), 'Domestic Sources of International Cooperation: A Conceptual Framework', paper prepared for the annual meeting of the International Studies Association, Vancouver, 20–23 March 1991.
Katzenstein, P. J. (1978) (ed.), *Between Power and Plenty: Foreign Economic Policies of Advanced Industrial States* (Madison, Wis.).
—— (1984), *Corporatism and Change* (Ithaca, NY).
—— (1985), *Small States in World Markets: Industrial Policy in Europe* (Ithaca, NY).
Keal, P. (1984), *Unspoken Rules and Super-Power Dominance* (London).
Keeley, J. F. (1990), 'Toward a Foucauldian Analysis of International Regimes', *International Organization*, 44: 83–105.
Kelley, H. H. (1971), 'Attribution in Social Interaction', in E. E. Jones, D. E. Kanouse, H. H. Kelley, R. E. Nisbett, S. Valins, and B. Weiner (eds.), *Attribution: Perceiving the Causes of Behavior* (Morristown, NJ), 1–26.
Kennedy, R. (1971), *Thirteen Days: A Memoir of the Cuban Missile Crisis* (New York).
Keohane, R. O. (1980), 'The Theory of Hegemonic Stability and Changes in International Economic Regimes, 1967–1977', in O. R. Holsti, R. Siverson, and A. L. George (eds.), *Change in the International System* (Boulder, Colo.), 131–62.
—— (1983), 'The Demand for International Regimes', in Krasner (1983c), 141–71.

Keohane, R. O. (1984), *After Hegemony: Cooperation and Discord in the World Political Economy* (Princeton, NJ).

—— (1986a), 'Reciprocity in International Relations', *International Organization,* 40: 1–27, reprinted with minor changes in Keohane (1989b).

—— (1986b) (ed.), *Neorealism and Its Critics* (New York).

—— (1988), 'International Institutions: Two Approaches', *International Studies Quarterly,* 32: 379–96, reprinted in Keohane (1989b).

—— (1989a), 'Neoliberal Institutionalism: A Perspective on World Politics', in Keohane (1989b), 1–20.

—— (1989b), *International Institutions and State Power: Essays in International Relations Theory* (Boulder, Colo.).

—— (1990), 'Multilateralism: An Agenda for Research', *International Journal,* 45: 731–64.

—— and Hoffmann, S. (1991) (eds.), *The New European Community: Decisionmaking and Institutional Change* (Boulder, Colo.).

—— and Nye, J. S., Jr. (1977), *Power and Interdependence: World Politics in Transition* (Boston, Mass.).

Khan, M. S., and Knight, M. D. (1985), *Fund Supported Adjustment Programs and Economic Growth* (IMF Occasional Paper 41; Washington, DC).

Kilian, M. (1987), *Umweltschutz durch Internationale Organisationen* (Berlin).

Kimble, G. (1968), 'Learning: Introduction', in D. L. Sills (ed.), *International Encyclopedia of the Social Sciences,* ix (New York), 114–26.

Kindleberger, C. P. (1981), 'Dominance and Leadership in the International Economy: Exploitation, Public Goods, and Free Rides', *International Studies Quarterly,* 25: 242–54.

King, G., Verba, S., and Keohane, R. O. (1991), 'Scientific Inference in Qualitative Research', draft manuscript Department of Government, Harvard University, Cambridge, Mass.

Kiss, A. C. (1983) (ed.), *Selected Multilateral Treaties in the Field of the Environment* (Nairobi).

—— and Shelton, D. (1991), *International Environmental Law* (Ardsley-on-Hudson, NY).

Kohler-Koch, B. (1989a), 'Zur Empirie und Theorie internationaler Regime', in Kohler-Koch (1989b), 17–85.

—— (1989b) (ed.), *Regime in den internationalen Beziehungen* (Baden-Baden).

Koskenniemi, M. (1989), *From Apology to Utopia: The Structure of International Legal Argument* (Helsinki).

Kötter, W., and Müller, H. (1990), *Germany and the Bomb: Nuclear*

Policies in the Two German States, and the United Germany's Non-proliferation Commitments (Peace Research Institute Frankfurt PRIF Reports 14; Frankfurt am Main).

Kraft, J. (1984), *The Mexican Rescue* (New York).

Krasner, S. D. (1976), 'State Power and the Structure of International Trade', *World Politics*, 28: 317–47.

—— (1978), *Defending the National Interest: Raw Materials and U.S. Foreign Policy* (Princeton, NJ).

—— (1983*a*), 'Structural Causes and Regime Consequences: Regimes as Intervening Variables', in Krasner (1983*c*), 1–21.

—— (1983*b*), 'Regimes and the Limits of Realism: Regimes as Autonomous Variables', in Krasner (1983*c*), 355–68.

—— (1983*c*) (ed.), *International Regimes* (Ithaca, NY).

—— (1985), *Structural Conflict: The Third World Against Global Liberalism* (Berkeley, Calif.).

—— (1988), 'Sovereignty: An Institutional Perspective', *Comparative Political Studies*, 21: 66–94.

—— (1991), 'Global Communications and National Power: Life on the Pareto Frontier', *World Politics*, 43: 336–66.

Kratochwil, F. (1985), 'The Role of Domestic Courts as Agencies of the International Legal Order', in Falk, Kratochwil, and Mendlovitz (1985), 236–63.

—— (1986), 'Of Systems, Boundaries, and Territoriality: An Inquiry into the Formation of the State System', *World Politics*, 49: 27–52.

—— (1989), *Rules, Norms, and Decisions: On the Conditions of Practical and Legal Reasoning in International Relations and Domestic Affairs* (Cambridge).

—— and Ruggie, J. G. (1986), 'International Organization: A State of the Art on an Art of the State', *International Organization*, 40: 753–75.

Krebs, D. (1990), 'Corporate Culture', in J. E. Alt and K. A. Shepsle (eds.), *Perspectives on Positive Political Economy* (Cambridge), 90–143.

Krehbiel, K. (1988), 'Spatial Models of Legislative Choice', *Legislative Studies Quarterly*, 13: 259–319.

Kremenyuk, V. A. (1991) (ed.), *International Negotiation* (San Francisco, Calif.).

Kriesberg, L. (1982), *Social Conflicts*[2] (Englewood Cliffs, NJ).

Kronfeld-Goharani, U., and Wellmann, C. (1991), *Saubere Ostsee—ein Ziel für Konversion: Vorschlag zur Gründung einer Bundesanstalt für Ostseeschutz und -überwachung (BfO)* (Projektverbund Friedenswissenschaften Kiel, PFK-Texte 9; Kiel).

Kubbig, B. W. (1990), 'Die SDI-Debatte in der Reagan-Administration und im Kongreß ab 1983', in Kubbig (ed.), *Die militärische Eroberung des Weltraums*, i (Frankfurt am Main), 94–167.

Lake, D. (1988), *Power, Protection, and Free Trade: International Sources of U.S. Commercial Strategy, 1887–1939* (Ithaca, NY).

Lakoff, G. (1987), *Women, Fire, and Dangerous Things: What Categories Reveal About the Mind* (Chicago, Ill.).

—— and Johnson, M. (1980), *Metaphors We Live By* (Chicago, Ill.).

Larson, D. W. (1987), 'Crisis Prevention and the Austrian State Treaty', *International Organization*, 41: 27–60.

—— (1988), 'The Psychology of Reciprocity in International Relations', *Negotiation Journal*, 4: 281–301.

Lewellyn, K. (1931), 'What Price Contract: An Essay in Perspective', *Yale Law Journal*, 40: 704–51.

Lewis, B. (1992), 'Muslims, Christians, and Jews: The Dream of Coexistence', *New York Review of Books*, 34/6: 48–52.

Lewis, P. (1992), 'Fixing World Crises Isn't Just a Job for Diplomats', *The New York Times*, 5 Apr., p. 4.

Lindberg, L. N., and Scheingold, S. A. (1970), *Europe's Would-Be Polity: Patterns of Change in the European Community* (Englewood Cliffs, NJ).

Lindblom, C. E. (1977), *Politics and Markets: The World's Political-Economic Systems* (New York).

Lipson, C. (1983), 'The Transformation of Trade: The Sources and Effects of Regime Change', in Krasner (1983*c*), 233–71.

—— (1986), 'Bankers' Dilemmas: Private Cooperation in Rescheduling Sovereign Debts', in Oye (1986), 200–25.

—— (1991), 'Why are Some International Agreements Informal?', *International Organization*, 45: 495–538.

List, M. (1990*a*), 'Cleaning up the Baltic: A Case Study in East–West Environmental Cooperation', in Rittberger (1990*d*), 90–116.

—— (1990*b*), 'Wissenschaftlich-technische Beziehungen zwischen West und Ost: Eine Untersuchung unter dem Aspekt der Verregelung von Konfliktaustrag', unpub. paper, University of Tübingen.

—— (1991), *Umweltschutz in zwei Meeren: Vergleich der internationalen Zusammenarbeit zum Schutz der Meeresumwelt in Nord- und Ostsee* (Munich).

—— (1992), 'Rechtsstaatlichkeit in (West)Europa: Eine regimeanalytische Betrachtung', *Politische Vierteljahresschrift*, 33: 622–42.

—— and Rittberger, V. (1992), 'Regime Theory and the Management of the International Environment', in Hurrell and Kingsbury (1992), 85–109.

Lorenz, E. H. (1990), 'Neither Friends nor Strangers: Informal Networks of Subcontracting in French Industry', in Gambetta (1990*c*), 194–210.

Lowenthal, A. F. (1991) (ed.), *Exporting Democracy: The United States and Latin America* (Baltimore, Md.).

Luhmann, N. (1987), *Soziale Systeme: Grundriß einer allgemeinen Theorie* (Frankfurt am Main).

Lundqvist, L. J. (1980), *The Hare and the Tortoise: Clean Air Policies in the United States and Sweden* (Ann Arbor, Mich.).

Macartney, A. C. (1934), *National States and National Minorities* (London).

McGinnis, M. D., and Williams, J. T. (1991), 'Configurations of Cooperation: Correlated Equilibria in Coordination and Iterated Prisoner's Dilemma', unpub. manuscript, Indiana University.

—— —— (1992a), 'Policy Uncertainty in Two-Level Games: Examples of Correlated Equilibria', unpub. manuscript, Indiana University.

—— —— (1992b), 'A Model of Domestic Coalitions and International Rivalry', unpub. manuscript, Indiana University.

Machiavelli, N. (1532), *The Prince and The Discourses*, trans. L. Ricci (New York, 1950).

Maddox, R. L. (1987), *Separation of Church and States: Guarantor of Religious Freedom* (New York).

Mansbach, R. W., and Vasquez, J. A. (1981), *In Search of Theory: A New Paradigm for Global Politics* (New York).

Marden, P. G., Hodgson, D. G., and McCoy, T. L. (1982), *Population in the Global Arena* (New York).

Martin, L. L. (1992), 'Interests, Power, and Multilateralism', *International Organization,* 46: 765–92.

Mastanduno, M., Lake, D. A., and Ikenberry, J. G. (1989), 'Toward a Realist Theory of State Action', *International Studies Quarterly,* 33: 361–87.

Masters, R. D. (1969), 'World Politics as a Primitive Political System', in J. N. Rosenau (ed.), *International Politics and Foreign Policy: A Reader in Research and Theory* (New York), 104–18.

Matthews, S. A., and Postlewaite, A. (1989), 'Pre-Play Communication in Two-Person Sealed-Bid Double Auctions', *Journal of Economic Theory,* 48: 238–63.

Maturana, H. R., and Varela, F. (1980), *Autopoiesis and Cognition: The Realization of the Living* (Dordrecht).

Mayer-Tasch, P. C. (1987), *Die verseuchte Landkarte: Das grenzen-lose Versagen der internationalen Umweltpolitik* (Munich).

Mearsheimer, J. J. (1990), 'Back to the Future: Instability in Europe after the Cold War', *International Security,* 15: 5–56.

Mendler, M. (1990), 'Working Conditions of Foreign Journalists in East-West Relations: Regulating a Conflict about Values without Regime', in Rittberger (1990d), 216–49.

Miller, E. F. (1979), 'Metaphor and Political Knowledge', *American Political Science Review,* 73: 155–70.

Mintzberg, H., and Waters, J. A. (1985), 'Of Strategies, Deliberate and Emergent', *Strategic Management Journal*, 6: 257–72.

Mo, J. (1990), 'International Bargaining and Domestic Political Competition', unpub. manuscript, Stanford University.

Modelski, G. (1990), 'Is World Politics Evolutionary Learning?', *International Organization*, 44: 1–24.

Moltmann, B., and Senghaas-Knobloch, E. (1989) (eds.), *Konflikte in der Weltgesellschaft und Friedensstrategien* (Baden-Baden).

Monroe, K. (1991) (ed.), *The Economic Approach to Politics: A Critical Reassessment of the Theory of Rational Action* (New York).

Moore, B., Jr. (1966), *Social Origins of Dictatorship and Democracy* (Boston, Mass.).

Moore, C. H. (1987), 'Prisoner's Financial Dilemma: A Consociational Future for Lebanon?', *American Poltical Science Review*, 81: 201–18.

Moravcsik, A. M. (1989), 'Disciplining Trade Finance: The OECD Export Credit Arrangement', *International Organization*, 43: 173–205.

—— (1991), 'Integrating International and Domestic Politics: A Theoretical Introduction', draft manuscript, to appear in P. B. Evans, H. Jacobson, and R. D. Putnam (eds.), *International and Domestic Explanations of World Politics* (in progress).

Morrow, J. D. (1992), 'Modelling International Regimes: Coordination Versus Communication', unpub. manuscript, Hoover Institution.

Mosse, G. L. (1970), 'Changes in Religious Thought', in *The New Cambridge Modern History*, iv. *The Decline of Spain and the Thirty Years War 1609–48/59* (Cambridge), 169–201.

Müller, H. (1987), *Strategic Defences: The End of Alliance Strategy?* (CEPS Papers 32; Brussels).

—— (1989a), *After the Scandals: German Nonproliferation Policy,* (Peace Research Institute Frankfurt, PRIF Reports 9; Frankfurt am Main).

—— (1989b), 'Regimeanalyse und Sicherheitspolitik: Das Beispiel Nonproliferation', in Kohler-Koch (1989b), 277–313.

—— (1993), *Die Chance der Kooperation: Regime in den internationalen Beziehungen* (Darmstadt).

—— and Risse-Kappen, T. (1990), 'Internationale Umwelt, gesellschaftliches Umfeld und außenpolitischer Prozeß in liberaldemokratischen Industrienationen', in Rittberger (1990c), 375–400.

—— and Rode, R. (1984), 'How to Talk about Interdependence and Keep Ignoring it: Parochial World Politics', *Bulletin of Peace Proposals,* 15: 79–91.

Nadelman, E. A. (1990), 'Global Prohibition Regimes: The Evolution of Norms in International Society', *International Organization*, 44: 479–526.

Nalebuff, B. (1991), 'Rational Deterrence in an Imperfect World', *World Politics*, 43: 313–35.

Nardin, T. (1983), *Law, Morality, and the Relations of States* (Princeton, NJ).

Nau, H. R. (1990), *The Myth of America's Decline* (New York).

Nerlich, U. (1973), *Der NV-Vertrag in der Politik der Bundesrepublik Deutschland: Zur Struktur eines außenpolitischen Prioritätenkonflikts* (Ebenhausen).

Nollkaemper, A. (1992), 'On the Effectiveness of International Rules', *Acta Politica*, 27: 49–70.

Nye, J. S., Jr. (1971), *Peace in Parts: Integration and Conflict in Regional Organization* (Boston, Mass.).

—— (1987), 'Nuclear Learning and U.S.–Soviet Security Regimes', *International Organization*, 41: 371–402.

—— (1989), 'Nuclear Learning and the Evolution of US-Soviet Security Competition', in G. T. Allison and W. L. Ury (eds.), *Windows of Opportunity* (Cambridge), 131–62.

—— (1990), *Bound to Lead: The Changing Nature of American Power* (New York).

Odell, J. (1990), 'Understanding International Trade Policies: An Emerging Synthesis', *World Politics*, 43: 139–67.

Offe, C. (1979), '"Unregierbarkeit": Zur Renaissance konservativer Krisentheorien', in J. Habermas (ed.), *Stichworte zur "Geistigen Situation der Zeit"*, i. *Nation und Republik* (Frankfurt am Main), 294–318.

Olson, M. (1965), *The Logic of Collective Action: Public Goods and the Theory of Groups* (Cambridge, Mass.).

Onuf, N. G. (1989), *World of Our Making: Rules and Rule in Social Theory and International Relations* (Columbia, SC).

Osgood, C. E. (1962), *An Alternative to War or Surrender* (Urbana, Ill.).

Ostrom, E. (1990), *Governing the Commons: The Evolution of Institutions for Collective Action* (Cambridge).

Oye, K. A. (1986) (ed.), *Cooperation under Anarchy* (Princeton, NJ).

Parry, C. (1969) (ed.), *The Consolidated Treaty Series*, i. *1648–1649* (Dobbs Ferry, NY).

Parsons, T. (1949), *The Structure of Social Action* (Glencoe, Ill.).

Patchen, M. (1987), 'Strategies for Eliciting Cooperation from an Adversary: Laboratory and International Findings', *Journal of Conflict Resolution*, 31: 164–85.

Polsby, N. (1982) (ed.), *What If? Essays in Social Science Fiction* (Lexington, Mass.).

Porter, G., and Brown, J. W. (1991), *Global Environmental Politics* (Boulder, Colo.).

Powell, R. (1990), *Nuclear Deterrence Theory: The Search for Credibility* (Cambridge).

Prittwitz, V. v. (1984), *Umweltaußenpolitik: Grenzüberschreitende Luftverschmutzung in Europa* (Frankfurt am Main).

—— (1989), 'Internationale Umweltregime: Ein Fallvergleich', in Kohler-Koch (1989*b*), 225–45.

—— (1990), *Das Katastrophenparadox: Elemente einer Theorie der Umweltpolitik* (Opladen).

Pruitt, D. G. (1981), *Negotiation Behavior* (New York).

Puchala, D. J., and Hopkins, R. F. (1983), 'International Regimes: Lessons from Inductive Analysis', in Krasner (1983*c*), 61–91.

Putnam, R. D. (1988), 'Diplomacy and Domestic Politics: The Logic of Two-Level Games', *International Organization*, 42: 427–60.

—— and Henning, C. R. (1989), 'The Bonn Summit of 1978: A Case Study in Coordination', in Cooper *et al.* (1989), 12–140.

Radkau, J. (1983), *Aufstieg und Krise der deutschen Atomwirtschaft 1945– 1979: Verdrängte Alternativen in der Kerntechnik und der Ursprung der nuklearen Kontroverse* (Reinbek).

Rasmusen, E. (1989), *Games and Information: An Introduction to Game Theory* (Oxford).

Raub, W., and Voss, T. (1986), 'Conditions for Cooperation in Problematic Social Situations', in A. Diekmann and P. Mitter (eds.), *Paradoxical Effects of Social Behavior: Essays in Honor of Anatol Rapoport* (Heidelberg), 85–103.

Ray, J. L. (1989), 'The Abolition of Slavery and the End of International War', *International Organization*, 43: 405–39.

Rice, C. (1988), 'SALT and the Search for a Security Regime', in George, Farley, and Dallin (1988), 293–306.

Rittberger, V. (1990*a*), 'International Regimes in the CSCE Region: From Anarchy to Governance and Stable Peace', *Österreichische Zeitschrift für Politikwissenschaft*, 19: 349–64.

—— (1990*b*), 'Editor's Introduction', in Rittberger (1990*d*), 1–8.

—— (1990*c*) (ed.), *Theorien der Internationalen Beziehungen: Bestandsaufnahme und Forschungsperspektiven* (PVS-Sonderheft 21; Opladen).

—— (1990*d*) (ed.), *International Regimes in East-West Politics* (London).

—— and Zürn, M. (1990), 'Towards Regulated Anarchy in East–West Relations: Causes and Consequences of East–West Regimes', in Rittberger (1990*d*), 9–63.

—— —— (1991*a*), 'Regime Theory: Findings from the Study of "East– West Regimes"', *Cooperation and Conflict*, 26: 165–83.

—— —— (1991*b*), 'Transformation der Konflikte in den Ost-West-Beziehungen: Versuch einer institutionalistischen Bestandsaufnahme', *Politische Vierteljahresschrift*, 32: 399–424. (English translation in *Law and State*, 45 (1992), 7–36.)

—— Efinger, M., and Mendler, M. (1990), 'Toward an East–West

Security Regime: The Case of Confidence- and Security-Building Measures', *Journal of Peace Research*, 27: 55–74.

Rivkin, D. B., Jr. (1987), 'The Soviet Approach to Nuclear Arms Control', *Survival*, 19: 483–511.

Rogowski, R. (1989), *Commerce and Coalitions: How Trade Affects Domestic Political Alignments* (Princeton, NJ).

Ronge, V. (1979), *Bankpolitik im Spätkapitalismus: Politische Selbstverwaltung des Kapitals?* (Starnberger Studien 3; Frankfurt am Main).

Ropers, N., and Schlotter, P. (1990), *Regime Analysis and the CSCE Process* (Peace Research Institute Frankfurt, PRIF Reports 13; Frankfurt am Main).

Rose, R. (1991), 'What is Lesson-Drawing?', *Journal of Public Policy*, 11: 3–30.

Rosecrance, R. (1986), *The Rise of the Trading State: Commerce and Conquest in the Modern World* (New York).

Rosenau, J. N. (1966), 'Pre-Theories and Theories of Foreign Policy,' in B. R. Farrell (ed.), *Approaches to Comparative and International Politics* (Evanston, Ill.), 27–92.

—— (1986), 'Before Cooperation: Hegemons, Regimes, and Habit-Driven Actors in World Politics', *International Organization*, 40: 849–94.

—— (1992), 'Governance, Order, and Change in World Politics', in Rosenau and Czempiel (1992), 1–29.

—— and Czempiel, E.-O. (1992) (eds.), *Governance without Government: Order and Change in World Politics* (Cambridge).

Ross, L. (1977), 'The Intuitive Psychologist and His Shortcomings: Distortions in the Attribution Process', in L. Berkowitz (ed.), *Advances in Experimental Social Psychology*, x (New York), 173–220.

Rousseau, J.-J. (1762), *The Social Contract*, anon. trans. 1767, ed. L. G. Crocker (New York, 1973).

—— (1782), 'Judgement on Saint Pierre's Project for Perpetual Peace', trans. C. E. Vaughan, in M. G. Forsyth, H. M. A. Keens-Soper, and P. Savigear (eds.), *The Theory of International Relations: Selected Texts from Gentili to Treitschke* (London, 1970), 157–66.

Rowland, S. F. (1988), 'Chlorofluorocarbons, Stratospheric Ozone, and the Antarctic "Ozone Hole"', *Environmental Conservation*, 15: 101–15.

Rubinstein, A. (1982), 'Perfect Equilibrium in a Bargaining Model', *Econometrica*, 50: 97–109.

—— (1989), 'The Electronic Mail Game: Strategic Behavior under "Almost Common Knowledge"', *The American Economic Review*, 79: 385–91.

Ruggie, J. G. (1972), 'Collective Goods and Future International Collaboration', *American Political Science Review*, 66: 874–93.

Ruggie, J. G. (1975), 'International Responses to Technology: Concepts and Trends', in J. G. Ruggie and E. B. Haas (eds.), *International Responses to Technology* (Madison, Wis.), 557–83.

—— (1983*a*), 'Continuity and Transformation in the World Polity: Toward a Neo-Realist Synthesis', *World Politics*, 35: 261–85.

—— (1983*b*), 'International Regimes, Transactions, and Change: Embedded Liberalism in the Postwar Economic Order', in Krasner (1983*c*), 195–231.

—— (1991*a*), 'Embedded Liberalism Revisited: Institutions and Progress in International Economic Relations', in B. Crawford and E. Adler (eds.), *Progress in International Relations* (New York), 201–34.

—— (1991*b*), 'The Meanings of Multilateralism', unpub. paper.

Rummel-Bulska, I., and Osafo, S. (1991) (eds.), *Selected Multilateral Treaties in the Field of the Environment*, ii (Cambridge).

Russett, B. M. (1967), *International Regions and the International System* (Chicago, Ill.).

Sadik, N. (1991), 'World Population Continues to Rise', *The Futurist*, 25 (Mar./Apr.), 9–14.

Saetevik, S. (1988), *Environmental Cooperation between the North Sea States* (London).

Sagoff, M. (1992), 'The Governance of Enclosed and Coastal Seas: Does Jurisdiction Make a Difference?', paper presented at the annual conference of the American Association for the Advancement of Science, Chicago, Feb. 1992.

Salmore, S. A., Hermann, M. H., Hermann, C. F., and Salmore, B. G. (1978), 'Conclusion: Toward Integrating the Perspectives', in East, Salmore, and Hermann (1978), 191–209.

Sand, P. H. (1991), 'International Cooperation: The Environmental Experience', in J. T. Mathews (ed.), *Preserving the Global Environment: The Challenge of Shared Leadership* (New York), 236–79.

Schachter, O. (1982), 'General Course in Public International Law', *Recueil des Cours*, 5: 1–395.

Scharpf, F. W. (1985), 'Die Politikverflechtungs-Falle: Europäische Integration und deutscher Föderalismus im Vergleich', *Politische Vierteljahresschrift*, 26: 323–56.

—— (1987), *Sozialdemokratische Krisenpolitik in Europa* (Frankfurt am Main).

—— (1991), 'Die Handlungsfähigkeit des Staates am Ende des zwanzigsten Jahrhunderts', *Politische Vierteljahresschrift*, 32: 621–34.

Schelling, T. C. (1960*a*), *The Strategy of Conflict* (Cambridge, Mass.).

—— (1960*b*), 'Reciprocal Measures for Arms Stabilization', *Daedalus*, 89: 892–914.

—— (1966), *Arms and Influence* (New Haven, Conn.).

—— (1978), *Micromotives and Macrobehavior* (New York).

—— (1985), 'What Went Wrong with Arms Control?', *Foreign Affairs,* 64: 219–33.

Schmidt, M. G. (1982), *Wohlfahrtsstaatliche Politik unter bürgerlichen und sozialdemokratischen Regierungen: Ein internationaler Vergleich* (Frankfurt am Main).

Schön, D. A. (1979), 'Generative Metaphor: A Perspective on Problem-Setting in Social Policy', in A. Ortony (ed.), *Metaphor and Thought* (Cambridge), 254–83.

Schrogl, K.-U. (1990), *Die Begrenzung konventioneller Rüstung in Europa: Ein regimeanalytisches Konfliktmodell* (Tübinger Arbeitspapiere zur internationalen Politik und Friedensforschung 14; Tübingen).

—— (1993), *Zivile Satellitennutzung in internationaler Kooperation* (Cologne).

Schwarz, H.-P. (1989), 'Adenauer und die Kernwaffen', *Vierteljahreshefte für Zeitgeschichte,* 37: 567–94.

Schwarzenberger, G., and Brown, E. D. (1966), *A Manual of International Law* (London).

Schwarzer, G. (1990*a*), *Weiträumige grenzüberschreitende Luftverschmutzung: Konfliktanalyse eines internationalen Umweltproblems* (Tübinger Arbeitspapiere zur internationalen Politik und Friedensforschung 15; Tübingen).

—— (1990*b*), 'The Berlin Regime', in Rittberger (1990*d*), 189–215.

—— (1992*a*), 'Der Saarkonflikt', unpub. manuscript, University of Tübingen.

—— (1992*b*), 'Das internationale Regime zur Erhaltung der Unabhängigkeit Österreichs', unpub. manuscript, University of Tübingen.

Sebenius, J. K. (1983), 'Negotiation Arithmetic: Adding and Subtracting Issues and Parties', *International Organization,* 37: 281–316.

—— (1984), *Negotiating the Law of the Sea* (Cambridge, Mass.).

Senghaas, D. (1971), *Kritische Friedensforschung* (Frankfurt am Main).

—— (1988), *Konfliktformationen im internationalen System* (Frankfurt am Main).

—— (1990), 'Frieden in einem Europa demokratischer Rechtsstaaten', *Aus Politik und Zeitgeschichte,* B 4–5: 31–9.

Sharp, A. (1979), 'Britain and the Protection of Minorities at the Paris Peace Conference, 1919', in A. C. Hepburn (ed.), *Minorities in History* (New York), 170–88.

Shevardnadze, E. (1991), *The Future Belongs to Freedom* (New York).

Shoup, P. S. (1981), *The East European and Soviet Data Handbook* (New York).

Simon, J. (1990), *Population Matters: People, Resources, Environment, and Immigration* (New Brunswick, NJ).

Singer, J. D., and Small, M. (1982), *Resort to Arms: International and Civil Wars 1816–1980* (Beverly Hills, Calif.).

Skocpol, T. (1985), 'Bringing the State Back in: Strategies of Analysis in Current Research', in Evans, Rueschemeyer, and Skocpol (1985), 3–37.

Smith, R. K. (1987), 'Explaining the Non-Proliferation Regime: Anomalies for Contemporary International Relations Theory', *International Organization,* 41: 253–82.

Snidal, D. (1979), 'Public Goods, Property Rights, and Political Organizations', *International Studies Quarterly,* 23: 532–66.

—— (1985), 'The Limits of Hegemonic Stability Theory', *International Organization,* 39: 579–614.

—— (1991), 'International Cooperation among Relative Gain Maximizers', *International Studies Quarterly,* 35: 387–402.

Snyder, G. H., and Diesing, P. (1977), *Conflict among Nations: Bargaining, Decision Making and System Structure in International Crisis* (Princeton, NJ).

Stein, A. A. (1983), 'Coordination and Collaboration: Regimes in an Anarchic World', in Krasner (1983c), 115–40.

Stopford, J. M., and Strange, S. (1991) (with J. S. Henley), *Rival States, Rival Firms: Competition for World Market Shares* (Cambridge).

Strange, S. (1983), '*Cave! Hic Dragones*: A Critique of Regime Analysis', in Krasner (1983c), 337–54.

—— (1988), *States and Markets: An Introduction to International Political Economy* (New York).

Strauß, F. J. (1989), *Die Erinnerungen* (Berlin).

Streeck, W., and Schmitter, P. C. (1985), 'Community, Market, State— and Association? The Prospective Contribution of Interest Governance to Social Order', in Streeck and Schmitter (eds.), *Private Interest Government: Beyond Market and State* (Beverly Hills, Calif.), 1–29.

Strübel, M. (1989), 'Umweltregime in Europa', in Kohler-Koch (1989b), 247–73.

Sutton, B. A., and Zacher, M. W. (1988), 'Mutual Advantage, Imposition, and Regime Formation: Evolution of International Shipping Regulations', paper delivered to the 14th World Congress of the International Political Science Association, Washington, DC, 28 Aug.–1 Sept. 1988.

Sylos-Labini, P. (1987), 'Oligopoly', in Eatwell, Milgate, and Newman (1987), iii. 701–4.

Talbott, S. (1988), *The Master of the Game: Paul Nitze and the Nuclear Peace* (New York).

Tan, T. C.-C., and Werlang, S. R. da C. (1988), 'The Bayesian Foundations of Solution Concepts of Games', *Journal of Economic Theory,* 45: 370–91.

Thacher, P. S. (no date), *Global Security and Risk Management,* a publication of the World Federation of United Nations Associations (Geneva).

Thomas, D. (1991), 'Social Movements and International Institutions: A Preliminary Framework', paper presented at the American Political Science Association Annual Convention, Washington, DC.

Thompson, M., Ellis, R., and Wildavsky, A. (1990), *Cultural Theory* (Boulder, Colo.).

Thomson, J. E. (1992), 'Explaining the Regulation of Transnational Practices: A State-Building Approach', in Rosenau and Czempiel (1992), 195–218.

Tilly, C. (1990), *Coercion, Capital, and European States, AD 990–1990* (Cambridge, Mass.).

Tismaneanu, V. (1992), *Reinventing Politics: Eastern Europe from Stalin to Havel* (New York).

Ullmann-Margalit, E. (1977), *The Emergence of Norms* (Oxford).

Underdal, A. (1982), 'Causes of Negotiation Failure', *European Journal of Political Research,* 11: 183–95.

US Department of Defense (1985), *Soviet Strategic Defense Programs* (Washington, DC).

Vasquez, J. A. (1987), 'Foreign Policy, Learning and War', in Hermann, Kegley, and Rosenau (1987), 366–81.

Vattel, E. de (1758), *The Law of Nations,* trans. and ed. J. Chitty (New York, 1983).

Vincent, R. J. (1986), *Human Rights and International Relations* (Cambridge).

Voas, J. (1986), 'The Arms-Control Compliance Debate', *Survival,* 18, 8–32.

—— (1990), *Soviet Attitudes towards Ballistic Missile Defence and the ABM Treaty* (Adelphi Papers 255: London).

Walker, R. B. J. (1987), 'Realism, Change, and International Political Theory', *International Studies Quarterly,* 31: 65–86.

Waltz, K. N. (1959), *Man, the State, and War: A Theoretical Analysis* (New York).

—— (1979), *Theory of International Politics* (Reading, Mass.).

Warner, E. (1945), 'The Chicago Air Conference: Accomplishments and Unfinished Business', in US Department of State, *Blueprint for World Civilization: The Chicago International Conference of 1944 as Viewed by Four Members of the United States Delegation in Recent Magazine Articles* (Washington, DC), 24–33.

Wassmund, H. (1982), *Grundzüge der Weltpolitik: Daten und Tendenzen von 1945 bis zur Gegenwart* (Munich).

Weber, M. (1949a): '"Objectivity" in Social Science and Social Policy', in Weber (1949c), 49–112.

Weber, M. (1949*b*): 'Objective Possibility and Adequate Causation in Historical Explanation', in Weber (1949*c*), 164–88.

—— (1949*c*), *The Methodology of the Social Sciences*, trans. and ed. E. A. Shils and H. A. Finch (New York).

Wettestad, J., and Andresen, S. (1991), *The Effectiveness of International Resource Cooperation: Some Preliminary Findings* (Lysaker).

Weiss, L. (1987), 'Cartel', in Eatwell, Milgate, and Newman (1987), i. 372–4.

Wheatcroft, S. (1964), *Air Transport Policy* (London).

Wight, M. (1966), 'Western Values in International Relations', in Butterfield and Wight (1966), 89–131.

Wijkman, P. M. (1982), 'Managing the Global Commons', *International Organization*, 36: 511–36.

Wildavsky, A. (1987), 'Choosing Preferences by Constructing Institutions: A Cultural Theory of Preference Formation', *American Political Science Review*, 81: 3–21.

—— (1989), 'A Cultural Theory of Leadership', in B. D. Jones (ed.), *Leadership and Politics* (Lawrence, Kan.), 87–113.

Williams, B. (1990), 'Formal Structures and Social Reality', in Gambetta (1990*c*), 3–13.

Williams, H. (1992), 'Banking on the Future', *Nature Conservancy*, 42 (May/June), 23–7.

Williamson, O. E. (1975), *Markets and Hierarchies* (New York).

Winham, G. R. (1977), 'Negotiation as a Management Process', *World Politics*, 30: 87–114.

Wolf, K. D. (1981), *Die Dritte Seerechtskonferenz der Vereinten Nationen* (Baden-Baden).

—— (1991), *Internationale Regime zur Verteilung globaler Ressourcen: Eine vergleichende Analyse der Grundlagen ihrer Entstehung am Beispiel der Regelung des Zugangs zur wirtschaftlichen Nutzung des Meeresbodens, des geostationären Orbits, der Antarktis und zu Wissenschaft und Technologie* (Baden-Baden).

—— and Zürn, M. (1986), '"International Regimes" und Theorien der Internationalen Politik', *Politische Vierteljahresschrift*, 27: 201–21.

—— —— (1989), 'Regeln für oder wider den Markt: Internationale Regime als Mittel der Analyse von internationalen Technologietransfers', in Albrecht (1989), 30–75.

Wolf, R. (1991), 'Im Fiaker der Moderne: Von den Schwierigkeiten ökologischer Gerechtigkeit', *Kritische Justiz*, 24: 351–62.

Wood, G. (1991), 'Novel History', *New York Review of Books*, 27 June.

World Commission on Environment and Development (1987), *Our Common Future* (New York).

Young, O. R. (1968), *The Politics of Force* (Princeton, NJ).

—— (1975) (ed.), *Bargaining: Formal Theories of Negotiation* (Urbana, Ill.).

—— (1978), 'On the Performance of the International Polity', *British Journal of International Studies,* 4: 191–208.

—— (1979), *Compliance and Public Authority: A Theory with International Applications* (Baltimore, Md.).

—— (1980), 'International Regimes: Problems of Concept Formation', *World Politics,* 32, 331–56.

—— (1983), 'Regime Dynamics: The Rise and Fall of International Regimes', in Krasner (1983*c*), 93–113.

—— (1986), 'International Regimes: Toward a New Theory of Institutions', *World Politics,* 39, 104–22.

—— (1989*a*), *International Cooperation: Building Regimes for Natural Resources and the Environment* (Ithaca, NY).

—— (1989*b*), 'The Politics of International Regime Formation: Managing Natural Resources and the Environment', *International Organization,* 43: 349–75.

—— (1991*a*), 'Political Leadership and Regime Formation: On the Development of Institutions in International Society', *International Organization,* 45: 281–308.

—— (1991*b*), 'On the Effectiveness of International Regimes: Defining Concepts and Identifying Variables', working paper prepared for use by the Dartmouth-based Research Team Studying the Effectiveness of International Regimes, May 1991 (Draft).

—— (1991*c*), 'Workshop Report: Regimes Summit', Minary Center, Dartmouth College, 23–24 Nov. 1991, unpub. manuscript.

—— (1992), 'The Effectiveness of International Institutions: Hard Cases and Critical Variables', in Rosenau and Czempiel (1992), 160–94.

—— (1993), 'Negotiating an International Climate Regime: The Institutional Bargaining for Environmental Governance', in Choucri (1993), 431–52.

—— and Osherenko, G. (1993) (eds.), *Polar Politics: Creating International Environmental Regimes* (Ithaca, NY).

Zacher, M. W. (1987), 'Trade Gaps, Analytical Gaps: Regime Analysis and International Commodity Trade Regulation', *International Organization,* 41: 173–202.

—— (1990), 'Toward a Theory of International Regimes: Explorations into the Basis of Mutual Interests', *Journal of International Affairs,* 44: 1–19.

Zartman, I. W., and Berman, M. R. (1982), *The Practical Negotiator* (New Haven, Conn.).

Zoller, E. (1984), *Peacetime Unilateral Remedies* (Dobbs Ferry, NY).

Zürn, M. (1987), *Gerechte internationale Regime: Bedingungen und Restriktionen der Entstehung nicht-hegemonialer internationaler Regime untersucht am Beispiel der Weltkommunikationsordnung* (Frankfurt am Main).

—— (1989), 'Das CoCom-Regime: Zum Erklärungswert rationalistischer Theorien', in Kohler-Koch (1989*b*), 105–49.

—— (1990), 'Intra-German Trade: An Early East–West Regime', in Rittberger (1990*d*), 151–88.

—— (1991), 'Consequences of Regime Definitions and Definitions of Regime Consequences: Proposals for a Data Bank on International Regimes', working paper prepared for the Regimes Summit at Dartmouth College, Denver, Oct. 1991 (Draft).

—— (1992), *Interessen und Institutionen in der internationalen Politik: Grundlegung und Anwendungen des situationsstrukturellen Ansatzes* (Opladen).

CONTRIBUTORS

Thomas J. Biersteker is Henry R. Luce Professor of International Relations at Brown University. He received his Ph.D. from the Massachusetts Institute of Technology. He is the author of *Distortion or Development? Contending Perspectives on the Multinational Corporation* (1981) and *Multinationals, the State and Control of the Nigerian Economy* (1987). His most recent book is an edited collection of teaching cases on international financial negotiations, entitled *Dealing with Debt: International Financial Negotiations and Adjustment Bargaining* (forthcoming).

Helmut Breitmeier is a doctoral candidate at the Center for International Relations/Peace and Conflict Studies, University of Tübingen. He has taught International Relations at the University of Stuttgart. His dissertation deals with international environmental politics.

Manfred Efinger is Controller at the University of Koblenz-Landau. He was a research associate at the Center for International Relations/Peace and Conflict Studies, University of Tübingen, until 1991, and earned his Dr. rer. soc. from the same university. He is the author of *Vertrauen ist gut, Kontrolle ist besser: Entstehungsbedingungen effektiver Verifikationsregelungen* (1991), and has published extensively on verification and arms control issues in journals such as *Österreichische Militärzeitschrift, Journal of Peace Research*, and *Aussenpolitik*.

Peter M. Haas is an Associate Professor of Political Science at the University of Massachusetts at Amherst. He earned his Ph.D. in political science from the Massachusetts Institute of Technology. He is the author of *Saving the Mediterranean: The Politics of International Environmental Cooperation* (1990), the editor of a special issue of *International Organization* on 'Knowlege, Power and International Policy Coordination' (1992), and co-editor of *Institutions for the Earth: Sources of Effective International Environmental Protection* (1993).

Virginia Haufler received her Ph.D. from Cornell University. She is an Assistant Professor in the Department of Government and

Politics at the University of Maryland in College Park. Currently, she is completing a book manuscript on international regimes in political risks insurance. Her other work addresses issues of sovereignty and institution-building in the areas of environmental management and defence-industrial restructuring in Eastern Europe.

Andrew Hurrell is University Lecturer in International Relations at Oxford University and a Fellow of Nuffield College. He has a D.Phil. in International Relations from Oxford University and taught previously at the Johns Hopkins School of Advanced International Studies in Bologna. He has written on the theory of international relations and the international relations of Latin America, including (as co-editor and contributor) *Latin America in Perspective* (1990), *The International Politics of the Environment* (1992), and *The Quest for Autonomy: Brazil in the International System* (forthcoming).

Christer Jönsson received his Ph.D. at the University of Lund, where he is Professor of Political Science. He has been visiting professor at Stanford University and Kyung Hee University, Seoul. He is the author of *Soviet Bargaining Behavior* (1979), *Superpower: Comparing American and Soviet Foreign Policy* (1984), *International Aviation and the Politics of Regime Change* (1987), and *Communication in International Bargaining* (1990).

Robert O. Keohane is Stanfield Professor of International Peace at the Center for International Affairs, Harvard University. He reveived his Ph.D. from Harvard. He is the author of *After Hegemony: Cooperation and Discord in the World Political Economy* (1984) and of *International Institutions and State Power: Essays in International Relations Theory* (1989). He is co-author of *Power and Interdependence: World Politics in Transition* (1977, 2nd edn. 1988) and co-editor of *The New European Community: Decision-Making and Institutional Change* (1991), *Institutions for the Earth: Sources of Effective International Environmental Protection* (forthcoming), and *After the Cold War: International Institutions and State Strategies in Europe, 1989–1991* (1993).

Stephen D. Krasner is Graham H. Stuart Professor of International Relations at Stanford University. He received his Ph.D. from Harvard University. He is editor of *International Regimes* (1983). His most recent studies include *Asymmetries in Japanese–American*

Trade (1987) and *Structural Conflict: The Third World against Global Liberalism* (1985).

Friedrich Kratochwil is Lawrence B. Simon Professor in the Department of Political Science at the University of Pennsylvania. He received his Ph.D. in International Politics from Princeton University. He is the author of *International Order and Foreign Policy* (1978) and, most recently, of *Rules, Norms and Decisions: On the Conditions of Legal and Practical Reasoning in International Relations and Domestic Affairs* (1989). In addition, he co-edited *International Law: A Contemporary Perspective* (1985) and *The Organization of International Politics* (1993).

Andrew Kydd is Coordinator of the Program on International Politics, Economics, and Security (PIPES) at the University of Chicago. His interests include the application of both game theory and empirical methods to international relations. His dissertation, which he is at present completing, develops an incomplete information model of the security dilemma, focusing on the intentions of states.

Peter Mayer is research associate at the Center for International Relations/Peace and Conflict Studies, University of Tübingen. He is preparing a doctoral dissertation dealing with normative aspects of international regimes.

Harald Müller received his Dr. phil. from the Johann-Wolfgang-Goethe University Frankfurt. He is Director of International Programs at the Peace Research Institute Frankfurt (PRIF). In 1984–6 he served as Senior Fellow for security studies at the Centre for European Policy Studies, Brussels. He is the author of *Die Chance der Kooperation: Regime in den internationalen Beziehungen* (1993), the co-editor of *European Non-Proliferation Policy: Prospects and Problems* (1987), and the editor of *How Western European Nuclear Policy is Made: Deciding on the Atom* (1991).

Gail Osherenko is a Senior Fellow of the Institute of Arctic Studies at Dartmouth College, Hanover. A natural resources lawyer, she is a graduate of the University of California, Davis, School of Law. She co-authored *The Age of the Arctic: Hot Conflicts and Cold Realities* (1989) and co-edited *Polar Politics: Creating International*

Environmental Regimes (1993). She is currently studying alternative arrangements for the protection of the environment and indigenous cultures of western Siberia.

Volker Rittberger is Director of the Center for International Relations/Peace and Conflict Studies, University of Tübingen, and most recently he held the Theodor-Heuss-Professorship at the Graduate Faculty of Political and Social Science, New School for Social Research, New York. He earned his Ph.D. in International Relations from Stanford University. From 1978 on he has been Fellow of the United Nations Institute for Training and Research (UNITAR). He is the author of *Evolution and International Organization: Toward a New Level of Sociopolitical Integration* (1973), and co-author of *Internationale Regime in den Ost-West-Beziehungen* (1988). He edited *International Regimes in East–West Politics* (1990) and *Theorien der internationalen Beziehungen* (1990).

Gudrun Schwarzer has been a member of the Tübingen project on international regimes. She has written about environmental international politics from a conflict point of view. At the moment she is about to finish her dissertation dealing with the peaceful regulation of territorial conflicts.

Duncan Snidal is Associate Professor of Political Science and Public Policy, and Director of the Program on International Politics, Economics, and Security (PIPES) at the University of Chicago. He has recently published articles in the *American Political Science Review* and *International Studies Quarterly* that demonstrate the possibility of co-operation even when states seek relative gains. Snidal is currently working on a project exploring the relationship between patterns of interdependence and military and economic conflict.

Klaus Dieter Wolf is Professor of Political Science at the University of Darmstadt. He earned his Dr. rer. soc. from the University of Tübingen. For many years, he was an Assistant Professor and research associate at the Center for International Relations/Peace and Conflict Studies, University of Tübingen. He is the author of *Die Dritte Seerechtskonferenz der Vereinten Nationen: Beiträge zur Reform der internationalen Ordnung und Entwicklungstendenzen im Nord-Süd-Verhältnis* (1981) and of *Internationale Regime zur*

Verteilung globaler Ressourcen (1991). He is currently preparing a volume entitled *Internationale Verrechtlichung*.

Oran R. Young is Research Professor of Government, Adjunct Professor of Environmental Studies, Director of the Institute of Arctic Studies, and Senior Fellow of the Dickey Endowment for International Understanding at Dartmouth College. He earned his Ph.D. from Yale. His scientific work encompasses both basic research on collective choice and social institutions and applied research on issues relating to the Arctic and international environmental concerns. Among his recent books are *International Cooperation: Building Regimes for Natural Resources and the Environment* (1989) and *Arctic Politics: Conflict and Cooperation in the Circumpolar North (forthcoming)*.

Michael Zürn is Assistant Professor at the Center for International Relations/Peace and Conflict Studies, University of Tübingen. He has received his Dr. rer. soc. from the University of Tübingen. Most recently, he has been Thyssen Fellow at the Center for International Affairs, Harvard University. He is the author of *Gerechte internationale Regime* (1987) and *Interessen und Institutionen in der internationalen Politik* (1992). He (co-)authored articles that have been published in journals such as *Politische Vierteljahresschrift*, *Leviathan*, and *Cooperation and Conflict*.

INDEX

ABM Treaty, *see* strategic nuclear
  weapons regime
Achen, C. H. 128–30
actor (state) characteristics:
  non-positional 290, 303–9
  positional 289–90, 300–3
air pollution:
  regime for the reduction of long-
    range transboundary 226, 227,
    259, 350
Arctic haze:
  reduction of: as an issue area 226
arms control in Western Europe:
  as an issue area 257–8
Austrian State Treaty 208, 255–6
authority 81
aviation regime 214, 219–20
Axelrod, R. M. 61–2, 84, 183, 295–6

Baltic Sea regime 259, 351–2
bargaining 205
  institutional 184–7
  integrative: and regime
    formation 234
  tacit 119–20
Berlin regime 256–7
Bull, H. 50–1, 55, 63–4
bureaucratic politics:
  and the unitary rational actor
    assumption 127–30

Carr, E. H. 52
cartelization:
  as regime purpose 39–40
cartels 101–2
chicken Fig. 6.2
civilizing process 395–7
Clemenceau, G. 159
cognitive theory:
  and rationality 203, 221–2
  see also knowledge
cognitivist approach in the study of
    regimes 409–10
  see also knowledge
Cohen, B. J. 331–2
collaboration:

as regime purpose 40–1
compliance mechanisms:
  availability of: and regime
    formation 233–4
compliance with international norms:
  democracy as furthering 386
  domestic politics and states'
    386–8
  and explicitness 86
  and the legal structure of the
    international system 58–61
  legitimacy as basis for 393
  a shared sense of justice as explaining
    states' 65–6
  theoretical accounts of states' 362–3,
    381–6
conflict:
  about absolutely assessed goods 14
  consensual and dissensual 14
  about means 14
  about relatively assessed goods 14
  types of 14
  about values 14
constitutionalism in Western Europe:
  regime for the protection and
    promotion of 258
consultation:
  as regime purpose 41
contextualized theories 274–7, 414
contracts:
  types of 75–9
contractualism:
  and functionalism 36 n. 6
  and regime formation 34–8
  and regime properties 38–44
conventional forces in Europe:
  reduction of: as an issue area 258
conventions 29
co-operation:
  and concerns for relative gains and
    losses 58–9, 139–40
  defined 23, 84–5
  and historical analogies
    (lessons) 211–12
  information, beliefs, and 115–17
  and international law 58–61, 66–7

466 *Index*

co-operation (*cont.*)
  liberal theory of 139–42, 166–7; *see also* functional regime theory
  and morality 65–9
  and political culture 212
  in prisoner's dilemma situations 86
  rationalist (functionalist) explanation of 54–69; *see also* game theory
  role of formulas and metaphors in the initiation of 209–13
  and a sense of community 61–5
  strategies for achieving and maintaining 117–18, 207–8, 295–9
  and trust 205–9
co-ordination games (problems) 86, 120–2, 265 n. 16
  and distributional conflict 17
corporatism:
  and foreign policy 304–6
counterfactual arguments 32
  and the assessment of regime consequences 318–23, 422–3
  and causal claims 317–25
  constructing plausible 325–31
crises:
  exogenous shocks or: and regime formation 234–5
CSBM regime 258–9
cultural differences:
  as a problem for regime creation 212
customary law 89–90

debt regime 331–6
decision-making procedures 87–8
dilemma games 17, 265 n. 16
domestic change:
  and foreign policy 306–8
domestic law:
  as a general-normative complex stabilizing regimes 385–6
Douglas, M. 213–15
Downs, G. W. 118–20

economic position:
  and foreign policy 302
Elias, N. 395–7
Elster, J. 318–31
environmental regimes 170–3
  impact of 348–60
  and the (in)divisibility of environmental damage 356–7
epistemic communities 179–80, 187–90, 200–1, 215

as a civilizing force 342
and regime formation 237
as 'thought collectives' (Fleck) 214–15
equity:
  and regime formation 232–3
European Community 42

Faupel, K. 3–4
Fearon, J. 318–30
Fleck, L. 215
foreign policy:
  defined 288–9
  domestic sources of regime-conducive 299–309
  interests 289–90
  models of 290–1
  regime-conducive: types 285, 295–9
  strategies 295–6
  styles 296–7
  types of 295–9
functional regime theory 80, 83
  and contractualism 36 n. 6
  and international law 51–7
  and regime formation 36 n. 7
  weaknesses of 57–71
  see also contractualism; co-operation: liberal theory of

Gambetta, D. 205–6
game theory:
  and institutions 119–20
  use of: in explaining international regimes 112–15, 134–5
GATT 39–40, 316–17
Gilpin, R. 180
Goldmann, K. 308–9
Grieco, J. M. 180
GRIT 208
Grotian tradition in international relations theory 50–1
  see also international society tradition
Grotius, H. 62

Haas, E. B. 204, 218–19
Haas, P. M. 316
Hagan, J. D. 306–7
Haggard, S. 27
hegemonic stability theory 13, 55, 95, 181, 229, 300–1
Hildebrand, D. K. 267–8
Hobbes, T. 51, 145